HARVARD ECONOMIC STUDIES

Volume 150

The studies in this series are published under
the direction of the Department of Economics
of Harvard University. The department does
not assume responsibility for the views expressed.

Competition in the Open Economy

A MODEL APPLIED TO CANADA

Richard E. Caves
Michael E. Porter
A. Michael Spence
with
John T. Scott

HARVARD UNIVERSITY PRESS

Cambridge, Massachusetts, and London, England   1980

Library of Congress Cataloging in Publication Data

Caves, Richard E
    Competition in the open economy.

    (Harvard economic studies ; 150)
    Bibliography: p.
    Includes index.
    1.   Industrial organization—Canada. 2. Competition,
International. I. Porter, Michael E., 1947–   joint
author. II. Spence, Andrew Michael, joint author.
III. Title. IV. Series.
HD70.C2C38   338.8′0971   79–23908
ISBN 0–674–15425–8

Preface

An act of authorship is an act of salesmanship. We wrote this book because we wish to "sell" two propositions to readers interested in the empirical analysis of industrial markets. One is substantive, the other methodological. Our substantive concern is to convert the standard paradigm of industrial organization from one that implicitly assumes a market that is large and largely closed to international, influences to one that recognizes the burgeoning links between national markets forged by international trade, the multinational company, and international transactions in technology (and other intangible assets). Our procedural goal is to show that statistical research in industrial organization can be successfully weaned from its dependence on single-equation methods of estimation—a dependence ill suited for the testing of models that proclaim that many things are determined simultaneously in a unified market bargain (or equilibrium).

The need for a full internationalization of the field of industrial organization grows more apparent every day. International trade among the industrial countries has, since World War II, steadily risen at a faster rate than their national incomes, so that every day more transactions are international transactions. A large amount of trade in manufactures is intraindustry trade, in which countries sell each other more or less the same lines of goods. More and more large firms are becoming multinational, and multinational companies based in different nations crisscross national boundaries on the way to found new subsidiaries. An international market in proprietary technology (patents, trademarks, production know-how) has burgeoned. All these forces throw firms based in different national markets into increased competition with one another. The few investigations of international

v

competition with U.S. manufacturing industries have regularly found evidence of its influence. Yet the influence has been only partly ingested—either theoretically or empirically—into research on industrial organization in the United States. And it has made even less headway in other countries, despite the fact that the United States remains the *least* open to trade of any of the Western industrial economies.

The Canadian economy—in particular, its manufacturing sector—provides an attractive site for testing the hypothesized influences of smallness and openness on the organization and performance of industries. Although openness is always a matter of degree, Canada's degree is decidedly above that of the United States. The share of the typical industrial market held by imports is more than twice as large; the share of domestic sales accounted for by foreign-based multinational companies is many times larger. Canada is also distinguished by the small size of its markets, roughly one-tenth that of the United States. These structural traits, coupled with a high degree of general similarity to the United States in laws and institutions, make Canada an attractive subject.

With that said, however, we admit that we chose Canada as the locus for our investigation not from cool reflection on the alternatives but rather through seizing an opportunity offered by the Royal Commission on Corporate Concentration. The commission was given a broad charge to examine many questions of industrial organization in Canada and the behavior of the large corporation in the Canadian economy. R. B. Bryce, the former chairman of the commission, proved receptive to our proposal to assemble a massive (by the standards of industrial organization) data base for the testing of a number of hypotheses. That data base was put together in late 1975 and 1976. In the summer of 1976, working under a tight deadline, we completed a series of statistical studies that examined a number of questions that vitally interested the commission. These studies were published in 1977 as one of a series of volumes of studies issued by the commission. We are grateful to the commission for financial support during that phase of the project and to its research director, Donald N. Thompson, for assisting with the assembly of the data base and execution of the project.

With our study in the hands of the Royal Commission, we were left in happy possession of the assembled data base but with a sense of postpartum depression over the necessary patchiness of the topics we had covered for the commission and the informality with which we had handled the simultaneity in the model. With time out for various other commitments, we then began work on the present volume. We sought to solve both the statistical problems associated with simultaneous estimation of a model using this data base and the substantive problem of building a system of relations from the available data that could claim to achieve the complete coverage of the principal constituents of the industrial organization paradigm that seemed necessary to a logically complete model. This phase of the research was generously supported by the General Electric Foundation, and we are deeply indebted to them for their aid in this project and for their general support of a lively and ongoing program of research in industrial organization at Harvard University.

The resulting volume is addressed to professional economists and others interested in industrial organization, but we have tried to present it in a way that serves the needs of a wide variety of users. Part I of the volume contains a substantive chapter outlining the theoretical foundations of the study and a methodological one explaining our estimation procedures. These are required reading for understanding the chapters in part II. Part II presents our model of industrial organization in Canada. We recognize that not all readers will have equal interest in the details of all parts of the model. Therefore these chapters can be read independently of one another, and each ends with a full summary that can be grasped independently of the chapter itself.

In part III we shift from a simultaneous model based on industry-level data to a series of studies that utilize data for a sample of large companies. Here we principally explore questions raised in part II that could not be readily answered by sticking to the industry as the unit of observation. But in part III we also pursue bigger game, because our industry-company data base lets us investigate two questions that we feel have been inadequately treated in industrial organization research overall—not just in Canada. One of these is the structural determinants of a company's choice of its long-run business strategy and the consequence of that choice for market performance. The other is the theoretical and empirical effect of the structural traits of industrial companies on their access to the capital market.

The book concludes with a reflection on the implications of our findings for industrial policy. Although the last chapter is somewhat specific to Canada, we stress that our study utilizes Canada as a convenient laboratory for studying industrial organization in a small, open economy. The book assumes of the reader no institutional knowledge of Canada, or even any necessary interest in the Canadian economy per se. More or less the same policy findings should apply to any small, open economy.

The authors have worked together throughout the project, discovering once again that the old adage about the virtues of multiple heads applies nowhere better than to complex projects of empirical research. We should, however, indicate the division of labor among us, while recognizing that no author's areas of primary responsibility have escaped detailed and careful inputs from the others. Richard Caves supervised the construction of the data base, undertook the general coordination of the project, and took principal responsibility for drafting chapters 3, 4, 8, 11, and 14. Michael Porter took charge of chapters 5, 6, and 7. A. Michael Spence developed the research methodology set forth in chapter 2 and contributed chapter 10. Three chapters are strictly joint products: chapter 9 is the work of Caves and Porter, chapters 1 and 12 of Caves, Porter, and Spence. John Scott prepared chapter 13 and contributed a great deal to the original work of developing the data base.

Besides acknowledging our debts to the Royal Commission on Corporate Concentration and the General Electric Foundation, we wish to thank a number of others who aided our work. Bronwyn Hall assisted with the organization of the data base and the transformation of statistical inputs from many sources into usable form. Additional programming was done by Mary Hyde. Kurt D. Brown and Thomas A. Barthold executed most of the large volume of computations and undertook various other chores of research assistance. James Linfield helped extensively with the collection and calculation of variables taken from published sources. F. M. Scherer provided comments on the entire manuscript, and many other helpful comments were received from persons associated with the Royal Commission on Corporate Concentration and from seminar audiences at several universities. Finally, we are grateful to Michael Aronson of the Harvard University Press for his sympathetic help in moving the manuscript toward publication.

Contents

PART ONE
RESEARCH DESIGN AND METHODS

1   Industrial Organization in a Small, Open Economy   3
2   Research Design and Statistical Methodology   21

PART TWO
A MODEL OF CANADIAN INDUSTRIES

3   Seller Concentration and Its Components   41
4   International Trade, Multinational Companies, and Market Structure   67
5   Comparative Structure of Retailing   93
6   Advertising Expenditures   123
7   Research and Development Spending   165
8   Diversification   195
9   Profits, Wages, and Market Power   223
10   Technical Efficiency   257

PART THREE
LARGE COMPANIES IN THEIR MARKET CONTEXT

11   Corporate Size and Its Bases   277
12   Corporate Strategy, Market Structure, and Performance   297
13   Corporate Finance and Market Structure   325

PART FOUR
CONCLUSIONS FOR POLICY

14   Industrial Policy in a Small, Open Economy   363

Appendixes

A.   Data Base: Definitions and Sources   389
B.   Advertising: Canadian and Comparative U.S. Data   418

References   426
Index   439

PART ONE

Research Design and Methods

1 Industrial Organization in a Small, Open Economy

This study has two objectives: to develop an integrated set of hypotheses about industrial organization and performance pertaining to markets that are small, geographically dispersed, and strongly exposed to the pushes and pulls of conditions in world markets and to test these hypotheses by methods more appropriate to this simultaneous-cum-recursive system than those usually employed in the field of industrial organization. The Canadian economy is the setting for the empirical investigation.

1.1 The Structure-Conduct-Performance Paradigm

The starting point for the analytical framework employed in this study is the structure-conduct-performance paradigm that originated in the work of Joe S. Bain.[1] This paradigm has evolved from a line of oligopoly theory that can be traced from E. H. Chamberlin and finds its major statement in William Fellner's *Competition among the Few*.[2] Chamberlin and Fellner accepted the proposition that there is no unique equilibrium in markets with few sellers. To predict outcomes in these markets, Chamberlin proposed, we should set our compasses on the equilibrium reached when rival sellers fully recognize their mutual interdependence (with perfect information and no transactions costs) and allocate resources as a monopolist would. Incomplete collusive arrangements among oligopolists generally induce outputs greater (and profits lower) than this reference-point solution. The problem for further development of oligopoly theory, then, was to

1. See Bain (1968), Bain (1972, chaps. 1, 3, 6, 12, 14), and Scherer (1970, chap. 1).
2. See Chamberlin (1962, chap. 3), and Fellner (1949).

3

identify the sources of incompleteness of collusive arrangements and to predict their consequences for output and other variables. Fellner expanded this framework with a full analysis of the behavioral factors determining the ability of oligopolists to reach a joint maximizing bargain. Much more theoretical work has been built on these foundations, including game-theoretic approaches to interdependent behavior and analyses of the enforceability of collusive agreements.

Chamberlin and Fellner focused on the ability of established oligopolists to sustain joint maximizing bargains and neglected the effect on the bargain of potential competition from new firms and other competitive forces outside the group of incumbent sellers. Bain and others filled this gap with the theory of entry barriers, which identifies structural or contrived deterrents to entry into the group of established sellers and their effect on market equilibria. The theory of entry barriers has undergone much additional development, but theoretical research has otherwise tended to concentrate on precise analyses of interdependent behavior rather than on the consequences of other structural constraints on the market decision makers. Empirical researchers have therefore devised their own informal extensions of the Chamberlin-Fellner framework. The resulting hypotheses expose further traits of the bargaining parties that affect the market outcome (for example, Newman, 1978) or demonstrate how the organization of the buyers' side of the market affects the interdependent bargain struck by the sellers (for example, Porter, 1976b).

While this body of theory contains many determinate models developed under restrictive sets of assumptions,[3] there is still no determinate general model of oligopoly. What has evolved, to guide empirical research, is a taxonomy of interacting forces that shape the oligopolistic bargain. The taxonomy encompasses the possibility of no bargain —that because the market environment is hostile to the recognition of interdependence among sellers or to the sustained distortion of a competitive outcome once interdependence is recognized, pure or monopolistic competition prevails. Rather than hold out for a determinate model of oligopoly rich enough to capture the complex deterrents to a competitive outcome, Bain proposed that we organize this taxonomy of forces and proceed with the work of studying oligopoly. The resulting structure-conduct-performance paradigm (henceforth SCP) develops the taxonomy in terms of a set of measurable concepts that can be used to express testable propositions about industrial competition.

3. For example, Gaskins (1971) and Osborne (1976).

While putting work clothes on the Chamberlin-Fellner variety of oligopoly theory, the SCP framework also shifted its emphasis. Fellner's analysis concentrates on the cognitive and motivational properties of the agents at the bargaining table. The SCP paradigm steps back to the structural environment that determines the opportunity set of each bargaining party. It concentrates on what determines the cards held by each bargainer rather than the skill and aggression with which he plays them. It can also encompass entry barriers, powerful buyers, and other aspects of market structure outside the narrowly defined bargain among incumbent sellers.

The SCP paradigm rests first on the definitions of its three central concepts. The elements of market structure are environmental forces that systematically determine the opportunity set for each party to the market bargain. The elements of market conduct are the policies of the bargaining parties (going sellers, buyers, and potential entrants) toward market variables that are determined or affected by the market bargain. The elements of market performance are dimensions of the resulting allocation of resources that are significant for economic welfare.[4] Our view of this paradigm, as it has evolved from Bain's work through many users, can be set forth in the following three general functional relationships:

$$S_{it} = S(S^*_{it}, C_{it-1}), \tag{1.1}$$

$$C_{it} = C(S_{it}, S^*_{it}, C_{it-1}), \tag{1.2}$$

$$P_{it} = P(C_{it}, C_{it-1}). \tag{1.3}$$

That is, the typical element of market structure viewed at time t (S_{it}) depends on a subset of other elements of market structure (S^*_{it}) that are truly exogenous to the system as well as on the past values of a subset of elements of market conduct (C_{it-1}). The elements of market structure prominently identified by Bain and others have included seller and buyer concentration, product differentiation, entry barriers, international competition, the size of the fixed component in short-run costs, and the rate of growth of demand. An exogenous element of market structure (S^*_{it}) might be scale economies in production (a component of entry barriers). An endogenous element might be seller concentration, dependent on scale economies, other components of entry barriers, and perhaps past market conduct.

In equation 1.2 the typical element of market conduct (C_{it}) is deter-

4. Although the causal forces run from structure to performance, the intellectual motivation of the system runs from the elements of performance that we deem important back to the behavioral and structural elements that the theory of markets designates as their determinants.

mined by the current state of all elements of market structure as well as the legacy of all elements of market conduct as they have been established in the past. Important aspects of conduct include the determination of production capacity, short-run price or output, advertising and related sales promotion, other nonprice dimensions of the product such as the quality and variety offered, and conduct intended directly to coerce or persuade other market participants. The elements of conduct are simultaneously determined. Each rival selects its policies as a package, with the objective of maximizing the present value of fixed assets (tangible and intangible) that it has acquired; this selection process is identified in the business literature with the formation of corporate strategy. The strategic choices of competing firms are then reconciled in the market by rivalrous processes that set the values of key market parameters. This process of determination depends in a general way on behavior learned in the past, but particular elements of conduct such as pricing may depend on other classes of decisions such as production capacity made in the past.

In equation 1.3 the typical element of market performance (P_{it}) is an indicator of the normative quality of the resource allocation that results from current and past market behavior. The elements of performance are jointly determined when the market bargain is struck. Allocative efficiency, one key dimension of performance, depends on the degree to which conduct patterns set competitive shadow prices on all components of the market bargain. We allow for a lag because some malfunctions of performance (such as excess capacity) may be the legacy of past decisions.

Formally, this system is recursively dependent on present and past values of the exogenous elements of market structure (S^*_i), and the reduced-form version of equation 1.3 could be written $P_{it} = P'(S^*_{it}, S^*_{it-1})$. Most statistical research in industrial organization has employed something deceptively similar—estimating equations in the form $P_{it} = f(S_{it}, S^*_{it})$. This procedure is flawed, because the variables on the right-hand side include both exogenous and endogenous elements of structure. We believe it vital to recognize that the SCP system is laced with simultaneity. Profit rates and advertising outlays may determine each other. Seller concentration may affect profits, wages paid to labor, and technical efficiency (these three elements are simultaneously determined), but concentration in turn is affected by scale economies and product differentiation. Concentration may affect advertising, which changes the attained state of product differentiation, which in turn affects concentration. By neglecting these relations, many studies have employed an estimating equation not properly "reduced" from an explicit account of the full system and hence not correctly specified.[5] More subtly, this procedure has diverted attention from important features in the unexamined structural relations, such as the distinction between product differentiation (as an attained state of market structure) and the market conduct (such as advertising) that firms undertake in order to achieve it.

This simultaneous-cum-recursive character of the SCP system prompts one of the compelling concerns of this study—to examine simultaneously the fullest practicable version of the relations in this system. Hence we seek to estimate a model encompassing all the major variables that have been measured and studied in industrial organization and to use statistical procedures appropriate to the task. We hope thereby to identify the variables that are endogenous in the larger system and to determine which of their structural determinants are truly exogenous. An incidental and procedural objective is to assess the efficiency gains in the research process from assembling data to test a number of hypotheses at the same time and using the results from one part of the model to improve the specifications of other parts.

In specifying the model, we shall be concerned with the influence of smallness and openness on industrial structure and performance. Apart from the issues of constructing a system of relations, we shall argue that these fundamental structural traits demand that particular functions in the model be specified differently from those appearing in studies of the United States (or studies that have ignored the roles of smallness and openness, whether dealing with the United States or not). While the SCP paradigm tells us how to model the industrial organization of any particular country, the models set up for application to different countries may vary substantially in their details.

This methodological premise is not manifestly ideal and therefore needs some defense and discussion. It is best to explain much with little: one wishes to explain market performance with a small, simple model that works equally well for any country. Indeed, industrial organization appears to have enjoyed some success with this approach. Khalilzadeh-Shirazi (1976) found that he could not reject the hypothesis that price-cost margins in a matched sample of British and American industries are explained by the same regression model, and Jones, Laudadio, and Percy (1977) have less formally applied the same model

5. Statistically, the unacknowledged simultaneities in the system can produce biased coefficients and test statistics when this procedure is followed. Economically, the standard statistical procedure can lead to the incorrect rejection or acceptance of hypotheses, especially in mistaking a partial structural relation in the system for a reduced form.

to Canada and the United States without noticing major differences between the respective statistical fits.

But do we maximize our understanding by showing that the same simple model fits several countries equally well (or equally badly)? Should the same model explain profits in two countries' consumer-good manufacturing sectors when their household income levels—and hence their retail distribution systems—vary greatly? If these differences are not represented in the model, it must be formally incomplete. Should the same model (omitting explicit account of multinational companies) apply equally well to a country that is a major home base of multinational companies and to one that hosts large numbers of their subsidiaries? Our provisional view is that the universal model—always a desideratum—cannot be nailed down until we know how to attain a model of industrial organization that is reasonably complete for all major classes of market economies. We thus view our exercise as showing how the standard models of industrial organization, implicitly developed for application to a large and closed economy, must be respecified and estimated in order to make the model suitable for national markets in which these conditions do not hold.

1.2   International Linkages, Structure, and Performance

Although a respectable handful of empirical studies has now accumulated to confirm the influence of international market linkages on market performance,[6] the international links among markets have been ingested only incompletely into the SCP paradigm. To a large part this has occurred because insufficient attention has been given to the underlying theory of equilibrium in imperfectly competitive markets subject to international influences—import competition, export opportunities, multinational companies, and international trade in proprietary intangible assets. The neglect surely results from the focus of so much research on the United States, for which international linkages can be ignored with some (though debatable) impunity. But most countries are relatively small and open, including besides Canada some whose industrial organization has been subject to a great deal of research—Great Britain, Japan, Australia, Sweden.

The standard models of markets determine the allocative and technical efficiency of markets (whether output levels are appropriate and

6. Studies of the United States and the United Kingdom include Esposito and Esposito (1971), Khalilzadeh-Shirazi (1974), Pagoulatos and Sorenson (1976a), and Pugel (1978).

costs minimized), but their predictions are altered when the market is small (relative to the scale of the efficient production unit) and exposed to some international competition. Some of what follows has been developed formally by other economists. Other propositions have been implicit in the literature on industrial organization in Canada and other small countries, but their assumptions and implications need to be more clearly developed.[7] What we shall present is therefore more synthesis than original derivation, and our aim is to develop strategic empirical hypotheses rather than to display formal rigor.

Open Markets with Homogeneous Products

The theoretical implications of international market linkages turn heavily on whether we assume product differentiation to be present. First we take up the conditions for equilibrium in an open-economy market in which sellers offer an undifferentiated product. To insure that the individual seller does not face his own downward-sloping demand curve, we also assume away transport costs within the national market even though they are assumed to affect international trade. The national demand curve DD facing the industry is truncated by the presence of the world market in the way shown in figure 1.1. If, as we assume, national production and consumption are both small relative to world production, the demand curve facing domestic producers becomes perfectly elastic at a price PM equal to the world price plus transport costs (from the relevant foreign producing locations) plus the tariff on imports; if domestic production costs exceed this price, the whole market is taken by imports. Likewise, the demand curve of domestic sellers becomes infinitely elastic at a price PX equal to the world price (net of foreign tariffs) less transport costs to the relevant foreign markets minus any national export taxes (plus any export subsidies).[8]

If the industry consists of a large number of purely competitive sellers, then domestic price, output, and the net trade position are determined by the intersection between this domestic demand curve, as truncated by world-market prices, and the industry's supply curve.

7. Some of these models and hypotheses have appeared in previous studies of Canadian industrial organization, notably Rosenbluth (1957), Fullerton and Hampson (1957), Eastman and Stykolt (1960, 1967), English (1964), Stykolt (1969, chap. 7), and Bloch (1974).

8. The industry's cost curve is, of course, shifted upward by any tariffs on its inputs; thus exporting industries often suffer from negative effective protection.

COMPETITION IN THE OPEN ECONOMY

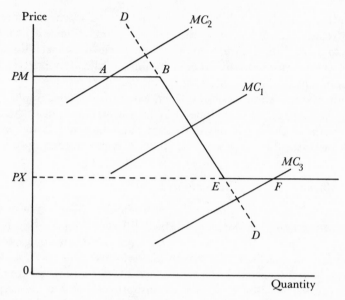

Figure 1.1   An industry's comparative advantage and competitive position.

In this competitive industry the scales of domestic plants, profit rates, and the technical efficiency of the domestic producers are unaffected by the industry's net position in international trade. Whether domestic sellers compete with imports, sell some exports on the world market, or are sheltered from trade flows by tariffs and transport costs, they still operate at minimum cost and earn normal profits. (This condition is consistent with the upward-sloping supply curves shown in figure 1.1, which can be thought of as reflecting general-equilibrium shifts in the structure of the economy's factor prices as a single industry changes the scale of its demand for factors of production.)

If scale economies are substantial in relation to the domestic market, so that sellers are few and pure competition cannot prevail, the outcome is more complicated. We first consider the case in which scale economies are so pronounced relative to the national market that there is room for only one efficient domestic producer. In figure 1.1 we superimpose several possible marginal-cost curves for the assumed domestic monopolist on the discontinuous demand curve (solid line). These marginal-cost curves reflect alternative degrees of comparative advantage that this industry might possess. If the monopolist's marginal cost curve is MC_1, cutting the domestic demand curve in its "sheltered" segment, the monopolist's profit-maximizing price may lie between PM and PX, or it may be constrained by PM. Either way, no imports should occur, because the monopolist maximizes profits by supplying the whole domestic market. But the excess profits earned by the monopolist depend on the relation between his long-run marginal costs and the import price (as well as the elasticity of domestic demand). If the monopolist's marginal cost is MC_2, the monopolist's price is locked at PM, imports AB flow in, and no excess profits appear. These propositions also apply to an oligopolistic group to a degree depending on its ability to collude. If MC_1 describes their combined costs, the import price PM may provide a convenient focal point for collusion, as Canadian writers have often suggested. Collusion would be fruitless, however, if MC_2 prevails. The model implies that the height of the Canadian tariff would be unrelated to the profits earned by a competitive industry,[9] but a higher tariff could increase the profits earned by a domestic monopoly or oligopolistic group that recognizes its mutual interdependence. A bit paradoxically, this increase occurs not in the MC_2 situation, with some imports flowing in both before and after the tariff increase, but when the industry's situation is that of MC_1 after (if not before) the tariff rise. That is, for excess profits to accrue, an increase in a tariff must raise PM enough to place its intersection with the industry demand curve above that demand curve's intersection with MC. The profits of monopolistic or collusive oligopolistic sellers may increase with the industry's comparative advantage; if the operative marginal cost curve is MC_1, potential profits increase as MC_1's intersection with DD nears PX.

In the case of marginal costs MC_3, a competitive industry would export EF. Concentrated sellers with marginal costs MC_3, if they sell abroad at the world price and cannot set a different price on the domestic market, are in effect locked into a purely competitive equilibrium (no monopoly profits) and also export EF. In the situation of MC_3 profits could increase with the industry's seller concentration only under certain sets of specified circumstances.

First, if the sellers can segregate the home market from the domestic market, they generally profit from charging a higher price at home and "dumping" abroad. Other things equal, discriminating monopoly is more profitable than simple monopoly. Dumping is facilitated by tariffs and transport-cost barriers to the reimport of goods sold cheaply abroad and by the exporting industry's control of distribution chan-

9. Profits here must be distinguished from rents that could accrue to an industry with rising long-run marginal costs.

nels for its output (to prevent access by domestic customers to supplies assigned to the export market). Dumping requires effective collusion, so elevating the price to domestic customers and maintaining the segregation of the domestic and foreign markets are joint problems of collusion for concentrated sellers.

Second, a concentrated industry with aggregate marginal costs of MC_3 might forego exporting if it cannot both export and segregate the domestic market. This choice, if it must be made, depends on the relative size of the potential monopoly profits from selling exclusively in the domestic market and the potential producers' surplus from expanding output to sell a much enlarged quantity on the world market.

Third, the industry's average cost may diminish over a substantial range of outputs, so that scale economies are important relative to the size of the national market. In this case export opportunities can increase profits even without price discrimination, because the expansion of output is associated with a reduction of average costs.[10] The achievement of scale economies through the export of homogeneous products implies a monopolistic market structure or a high level of seller concentration. For that reason concentration in exporting industries might be associated with high profit rates, although the profits would be producers' surplus rather than monopoly rents (unless dumping is also taking place).

Most of this analysis has assumed that scale economies, while not necessarily trivial, do not extend to and beyond the scale of the national market. If they do, the small size of the national market clearly constrains production scales and raises unit costs for domestic producers except for those able to gain access to export markets. Commentators on industrial policy in small countries often seem obsessed, however, with the idea that small market size constrains the scale economies attained by domestic firms even when they do not imply a condition of natural monopoly. If products are differentiated, firm size and market size may be related even if there is room for several firms large enough to exhaust the available economies of scale. If the product is homogeneous, however, can market size be related to the sizes attained by production units? The Sylos-Bain model synthesized by Modigliani (1958) explains how such a relation could arise. Consider first an industry whose cost level (at efficient scales of production) lies between PM and PX in figure 1.1. Given the elasticity of demand

10. See Frenkel (1971) for a theoretical demonstration.

in the national market, Modigliani showed that the smaller the market (measured in minimum-efficient-scale production units), the greater the chance that an entrant's most profitable scale will be less than the smallest scale that minimizes unit costs. Suboptimal firms would tend to expand to efficient scale over time if they remain viable, but that goal may be frustrated by technology that precludes incremental expansion of an established unit.[11]

If the industry can attain minimum long-run average costs below the export price PX, the national market's size should lose its influence on the sizes of production units, whether or not concentrated sellers can segregate domestic and export markets. If potential entrants, like going firms, can achieve minimum costs that are below the world price at efficient scales of production, then it never pays to enter at a suboptimal scale.

For the industry that competes with imports, the case is more complicated. If the domestic producer's minimum average costs are just equal to PM, the determinants of the scale of producing units are like those for an exporter. Market size has no effect on plant size. The situation is less clear, though, if we bend the logic of the model to allow industries facing actual import competition to have minimum average costs between PM and PX while collusively setting a price equal to PM. The potential entrant then considers that his entry may not just displace imports but also fracture the going oligopolistic consensus on price PM and drive the domestic price to a lower level. This conjecture implies that the entrant perceives the residual demand curve to be downward sloping and raises the possibility that his profit-maximizing scale may be less than the minimum efficient scale of production. Hence for producers of homogeneous goods there is no unqualified prediction about the relation between the amount of import competition and the actual (relative to efficient) sizes of production units.

The preceding paragraph neglected the distinction between scale economies to the plant and to the multiplant firm. The distinction matters for industries that cannot export and for industries in which market size is small relative to the efficient-scale firm, even if there is room for at least a moderate number of efficient-scale plants. This situation favors the appearance of multinational enterprises, if the economies of multiplant operations are not negated by a national boundary separating the plants under common ownership.[12]

11. Also see Scherer's (1973) analysis of market size in relation to transport costs—an influence so far omitted from our discussion.

12. This was pointed out by Eastman and Stykolt (1967, chap. 4).

Open Markets with Differentiated Goods

Small market size and openness to trade, when incorporated into theoretical models of seller competition, yield predictions about monopolistic distortions of the market and the achievement of efficient scales in production. Now in the case of differentiated products, such that each seller perceives a downward-sloping demand curve (the quantity demanded may depend recognizably on the prices charged by other sellers), industries can no longer be theoretically distinguished as either import-competing, trade-sheltered, or exporting. Some domestic producers in a given industry perceive little sensitivity of their demands to import prices while the sales of others are sensitive; some make significant export sales while others find exporting unprofitable. Members of an industry who make substantial sales abroad may also face significant import competition—a phenomenon called intraindustry trade.[13] Although the position of an industry's typical member firm in relation to import competition and export opportunities still depends on the relation between its cost curve and world prices, the concept of a single world price (PM and PX in figure 1.1) no longer applies. Instead of the conceptually clean indicators of an industry's trade status supplied by the alternative MC curves, one must use ad hoc continuous indicators of trade exposure. For producers of a differentiated good, the industry's net trade exposure or comparative advantage (exports minus imports as a percentage of their sum) and gross trade exposure (exports plus imports as a percentage of production) are independent pragmatic indicators of the extent and character of its contact with the world market.

This theoretical analysis of the consequences of seller concentration, trade exposure, and market size tends to hold with differentiated products, except that the loss of a clear classification of industries by foreign-trade status creates a band of indeterminacy around the conclusions derived. But differentiation adds important new functional relations, notably between company size and market size. In an industry sheltered from trade the profit-maximizing scales of some enterprises may be smaller than the scale that minimizes unit costs of production. The lower the buyers' elasticities of substitution between brands, the less elastic the demand curve facing the individual producer, and the less the number of viable enterprises declines when

13. Intraindustry trade was noticed as an empirical phenomenon without a very clear explanation in microeconomic terms; see Balassa (1966), Grubel (1967), Gray (1976, chap. 11). There is some empirical evidence that differentiated-product industries exhibit more extensive intraindustry trade (Grubel and Lloyd, 1975, p. 37).

the market's size shrinks. Correspondingly, company size may change in proportion to market size; to put the same condition another way, the elasticity of company size with respect to the size of the national market may approach unity.[14] This is more likely if buyers' elasticities of substitution between brands are low and the cost disadvantages of suboptimal-scale production not too great.

When the national market can be supplied partly by imports, we must recognize the forces that determine how production of a product's brands or varieties is allocated among countries. The relation between the size of the national market and the size of the typical national producer now depends on the mechanism that determines which brands are produced domestically and which are supplied from abroad. Suppose that every variety of a good is produced subject to the same production function and at identical costs in each country but that the proportions of buyers choosing the different varieties or brands vary substantially (when each brand is priced at its average cost). Under the assumption that transportation and distribution costs are on the average significantly less within national markets than for goods shipped between them, only the more popular varieties of a differentiated good tend to be produced in small national markets, with specialized varieties in small demand produced only in the large national markets and exported to smaller nations. Thus substantial exposure to import competition should increase the average size of outputs of varieties of a given product in a small country—and also the sizes of its firms, if each produces one variety. Higher tariffs, on the other hand, reduce the average scale of production while increasing the number of varieties, because the production of varieties in smaller demand becomes feasible behind the tariff wall. This conclusion runs counter to the usual intuitive proposition that a tariff, by enlarging the market for domestic producers, fosters the achievement of economies of scale.

Now we remove the assumption of identical costs in all countries and allow the domestic industry's cost position to improve relative to those of its foreign rivals. Varieties of the product in smaller demand can be produced domestically in competition with relatively more costly imports. Such an improvement in comparative advantage need not reduce average output scales, however, once we take into account the role of exports. Sellers of a differentiated product who can export profitably face not only a larger market, other things being equal, but

14. In cross-industry studies, with samples including both differentiated and undifferentiated goods, this elasticity commonly takes a value near 0.5 for both Canada and the United States. See Saving (1961) and Gorecki (1976, chap. 4).

also one that is likely to be more price-elastic than the domestic one. (A condition implying this difference is that more varieties must be available on the world market than are sold domestically.) Thus any shift in underlying conditions (such as a reduction in unit costs of domestic production) that increases exports also tends to increase the average scale of production, even though of the less popular varieties of the good. Hence comparative advantage itself does not have a clear relation to the average scale of domestic outputs, because an improvement in comparative advantage in general both induces domestic production of less popular varieties and allows larger outputs of them as it creates export opportunities. On the other hand, average output scale tends to increase with exposure to trade—whether import competition or export opportunities are involved.

The small country with a comparative advantage turns out some product varieties less popular than those it would make if its industry served only a sheltered domestic market But how do its output scales compare with those observed in a large exporting country? The small country's set of produced varieties might still differ, for two reasons. First, between producers supplying differentiated varieties to the world market, the one in the larger country still enjoys the advantage of access to more customers who can be served (by assumption) at no transportation costs within his national boundaries. This fact always gives a virtual advantage to producing the least popular varieties within the largest national markets and tilts producers in the small exporting country toward varieties that are less unpopular (the more popular a variety, the more likely is each country to produce its own supply). Second, Dreze (1960) argued that the popularity of a variety itself depends on whether a large country produces and consumes it, because the large country's culture weighs more heavily in the international dissemination of taste and amounts to free advertising for the differentiated goods emanating from its factories. On this argument, the popularity of product varieties exported by a small country is influenced by its exports of them, rather than the other way around (as we have been assuming).

So far, we have supposed that differentiated varieties differ in their popularity in the marketplace, but all share the same cost curve. Now we reverse the assumptions and suppose that all varieties command equal shares of any market when they are priced at the same multiple of minimum long-run average cost but that cost curves differ in the output scale necessary to attain minimum average cost (although not in the minimum cost level attained). A small country that has a comparative disadvantage and cannot export would tend to produce the varieties with small minimum efficient scales (MES) of production and with small cost disadvantages when produced at suboptimal scales. Varieties with the opposite characteristics would be imported. If varieties produced with large MESs and great disadvantages in small-scale production use more capital-intensive techniques, then the small nation's industry would carry on more labor-intensive production than its foreign competitors.[15] In this case a tariff would make feasible the domestic production of larger-scale and more capital-intensive varieties (rather than varieties in smaller demand, as in the case in which varieties differ in the scale of market demand). An improvement in the industry's cost position relative to foreign rivals would unambiguously increase its average scale of production and capital intensity—even before we take account of the role of exports. (The added products with larger MES values would not necessarily be produced at efficient scales.)

If varieties differ in their production functions and MESs, any country with cost conditions that allow it to export should produce large-scale varieties for the export market. A country's size influences its ability to export because what matters for the potential domestic producer is total demand—export plus domestic. If cost conditions differ between countries and favor the small country, exports of large-scale varieties are still inhibited by the small domestic market. The varieties with the largest MESs are still not found among the small country's outputs. Improvements in a small country's comparative advantage unambiguously increase the MES of the typical variety produced, although not necessarily the actual average output. Any change that increases exposure to trade (reduces the margin between PM and PX) has ambiguous effects on the MES of the typical variety.

Our exploration of openness and smallness in markets with differentiated goods has so far assumed a Chamberlinean equilibrium without rival sellers' recognizing their mutual dependence. The implications of oligopoly in a model with differentiated goods do not appear to differ greatly from those emerging from models with homogeneous goods, with one exception. That exception pertains to the case (MC_1, in figure 1.1) in which no trade would occur if the domestic industry were competitively organized. An oligopolistic equilibrium is possible with all rivals producing at inefficiently small scales. The effective elasticity of demand perceived by the potential price cutter determines

15. Fullerton and Hampson (1957, p. 81) analyze this effect.

the likelihood of a breakdown of oligopolistic consensus—which if it occurs leads to larger scales, lower prices, and lower unit costs. The effective elasticity is presumed lower when the product is differentiated, an outcome with sustained inefficient-scale facilities is more likely in a differentiated oligopoly than in one producing a homogeneous product. A tariff increase that raises the delivered price of imports, and thus the focal point for colluding domestic oligopolists, is more likely to create or preserve inefficient-scale capacity in differentiated than in homogeneous goods (Stykolt, 1969, chap. 7).

Multinational Companies

Models of industrial organization in an open economy need to take full account of the multinational company, because the prevalence of foreign subsidiaries is often a conspicuous feature of its market structure. In recognition of the substantial net imports of foreign direct investment that characterize small economies such as Canada's, we shall couch our analysis in terms of multinationals based outside the national economy under study. We shall also limit our analysis in another way. Foreign investment is a form of geographic diversification for the firm, and its transnational activities can be related to the parent's base operation as a horizontal extension of its basic business, as vertical integration, or as product-market diversification. We deal only with the first of these: the subsidiary produces the same good as its parent. The others are not needed for specifying our model.

Product differentiation is a condition that predictably favors the development of multinational companies (Caves, 1971). The enterprise that successfully vends a differentiated product in the United States or in another major industrial country acquires intangible assets and skills that can profitably be exploited by selling in other national markets as well. These markets could be served either by exports or through local production by a subsidiary. Organizing a subsidiary tends to have advantages, however, for making the fullest use of the enterprise's intangible assets in the foreign market, because of contractual problems in trading intangibles between firms at arm's length. The multinational company's choice between exporting to a country and establishing a subsidiary is affected by the market's size: the smaller the country, the more likely is the foreign producer to opt for exporting from its efficient-scale facilities abroad. Conversely, the small country's tariff tilts the choice toward the establishment of a subsidiary. The foreign subsidiary can be commercially feasible at a smaller scale of production than its domestically controlled rival because its skill at product differentiation presents it, in effect, with a less elastic demand curve over the relevant range of prices. Thus the presence of foreign subsidiaries tends to produce or amplify a negative relation between the height of tariffs and the average scale of production in protected manufacturing industries. Such a relation was predicted on certain restrictive assumptions about the character of product differentiation, but without the presence of multinational companies.

Students of the multinational presence in Canada have hypothesized that tariff-induced foreign investment by U.S. firms turns Canadian industries into "miniature replicas" of the counterpart industry in the United States.[16] The assumptions needed for this result are worth developing for their relevance to the specification of our model. First, each multinational company must possess some bundle of intangible goodwill assets that allow it to claim a similar market share in any market that it enters. That is, the structure of buyers' preferences must be similar from country to country, and the multinationals' competence at appealing to those preferences must transfer freely across national boundaries even if separate production facilities are maintained for each market served. Second, not too much influence can be wielded by scale-economy effects that filter out the less popular varieties and those subject to large-scale production from the small country's output set, because these discourage domestic production by multinational companies as well as by domestic producers. Otherwise, unfavorable cost conditions would exclude the potential multinational companies with the weaker goodwill assets, leaving the replication truncated to some subset of the larger firms in the U.S. market.[17]

The problems of economic performance invoked by the replica model are the same as for any other differentiated oligopoly in a small market, but the model raises interesting behavioral questions: Does seller concentration in Canada and the United States grow more similar as multinational companies become more prevalent in the industry? Do the multinational companies' goodwill assets travel across the

16. See Eastman and Stykolt (1960, 1967), English (1964).
17. Horst (1972b) finds that within U.S. industries size is the only trait of companies that significantly predicts which are multinational. That conclusion is consistent with "truncated replication." He also finds, though, that U.S. companies often start out toward full multinational status with a subsidiary in Canada; if replication operates anywhere, it is presumably across the Canada-U.S. border, where information and transaction costs are minimal.

Canadian borders as specific spillovers of their sales-promotion outlays in the United States?

These theoretical analyses were designed to show how the presence of international competition and a small national market affect market structure and performance—the variables that are central to industrial organization. The analysis has aimed only at providing the apparatus needed to specify the equations to be estimated in the chapters that follow. We have not attempted a complete survey of the linkages between international transactions and industrial organization; such a survey would also include international vertical integration and diversification through the multinational company—essentially the same as domestic vertical integration and diversification. We have omitted consideration of the international market for proprietary knowledge, distinctive because of the unique character of the assets transmitted and the incidence of market failures due to impacted information and contractual incompleteness.

2 Research Design and Statistical Methodology

This chapter describes the theoretical and statistical underpinnings of the substantive chapters that follow. The goal of the study is to apply a simultaneous-equation model of market structure and performance to a sample of Canadian manufacturing industries. This chapter sketches the structure of that system and explains and justifies the statistical procedures used to deal with the pervasive interrelations among the variables and the problems presented by the data base.

2.1 The System of Equations

The small size and openness of the Canadian economy complicates rather than simplifies the application of standard theoretical models of markets by drawing more variables into the system of industrial organization and creating complex theoretical interdependencies among them. Our model therefore includes numerous endogenous variables, listed in the second column of table 2.1. The model also includes some variables that are not usually counted among the chief endogenous concerns of industrial organization. For instance, it includes the proportion of output exported among the variables determined within the system; it also considers the statistical proxies often used for purely technical aspects of scale economies to be endogenous when computed from a Canadian industry's size distribution of plants —itself affected by market size and international influences.

How large to make the system is necessarily a matter of judgment; although current theory flags some variables as necessary inclusions, it does not provide an exhaustive list. Therefore the decision represents a balancing of marginal benefits and costs—even if the budget con-

Table 2.1 Endogenous variables included in the model of structure and performance of Canadian manufacturing industries.

Concept	Dimensions measured	Chapter
Concentration	Four-firm seller concentration	3
"Apparent" scale economies	Minimum efficient scale	3
	Cost disadvantage ratio	3
Trade exposure	Imports' share of domestic disappearance[1]	4
	Exports' share of production	4
Multinational competition	Foreign subsidiaries' share of sales	4
Advertising	Advertising as a percentage of sales	6
Research and development	Outlays as a percentage of sales	7
Diversification	Outbound	8
	Inbound	8
Union organization	Workers covered by collective bargaining	9
Allocative efficiency	Measures of profitability[2]	9
	Wage rates	9
Technical efficiency	Productivity	10
	Actual-MES plant scale	10

1. Domestic disappearance is defined to be domestic production plus imports minus exports.

2. The measures used are discussed in chapter 9.

straint of available research funds were not imposed. Broadly speaking, our system includes all the industry-level variables previously subject to serious investigation in industrial organization, either because they indicate normatively important dimensions of resource allocation or because the theory of markets identifies them as important structural determinants of those performance dimensions. This list is then augmented according to the dictates of the theory of competition in the open economy. At the extensive margin it is difficult to weigh possible errors of omission; there are additional candidates, but no body of literature exists to suggest how easily they could be explained or how much they might contribute to the model. We do not explain buyer concentration within the formal structure of the model because the appropriate data could be constructed only with a massive effort. We try to mitigate this omission by looking independently at the distributive sector; retail sectors are analyzed statistically but could not be matched to the manufacturing industries used in the balance of the study. We omit the financial or organizational structures of firms as endogenous variables at the industry level, although we do examine them separately for a population of large companies. We could not explain the strategic-group structures of Canadian industries for lack of data, although we do investigate what determines strategic choice for a sample of large companies. Of course, many other aspects of market structure and behavior continue to defy empirical measurement.

Although many economists working in industrial organization have recognized that much research traditionally carried out in a single-equation context should really employ a simultaneous model, little progress has so far been made to achieve that goal. Some studies have employed two-stage or three-stage least squares to estimate simultaneous relationships for particular variables. Comanor and Wilson (1974, chap. 7) were concerned with advertising and profits, Strickland and Weiss (1976) with concentration, advertising, and profits. Saunders's (1978) model turns on the determinants of technical efficiency. There have been at least two attempts to construct comprehensive models of the system of relations that relate market structure and performance, but these are relatively small in scale. Pugel's (1978) five-equation model for the United States concentrates on international influences, and Gupta (1977) presents a six-equation model for Canada. There may well be other work that has not come to our attention. We hope to show that a relatively large model is not only logically appropriate for testing the chief hypotheses of industrial organization, particularly in an open economy, but also feasible and that it indeed enjoys scale economies because of the low marginal cost of testing additional hypotheses and specifications.

2.2 The Data Base

The master data base prepared for this project contains observations on approximately 150 structure and performance variables for 123 Canadian manufacturing industries. The industries in the sample consisted of the entire population enumerated in the Canadian standard industrial classification in the late 1960s, except those of a miscellaneous character that were not economically meaningful. The industries include both consumer- and producer-good industries, the former representing a somewhat greater fraction of the total. That data base is described fully in appendix A. In addition to industry variables, the data base includes data on strategy, financial structure, and performance of 125 large manufacturing companies. These large companies are matched to the manufacturing industries in which they are active. A mnemonic and a brief description for the variables from the data base are provided in the text when they are used. A fuller description that includes the source of the variable is found in appendix A.

A sample of 84 manufacturing industries were defined comparably in the Canadian and in the U.S. standard industrial classifications in use during the latter 1960s, in particular the 1967 U.S. and 1968 Canadian censuses of manufacturing. These 84 industries are a subset of the 123 industries in the master data base. The industries are aggregated to the three-digit level of the Canadian classification; in the U.S. classification they may be anything from single four-digit industries to aggregates of three-digit industries. A sample of U.S. industries comparable to Canadian industries is of considerable importance for our research design.

Although the data provide a rich picture of the Canadian industry and its counterpart in the United States, two problems in the design of the research methodology require explicit treatment. First, the data do not represent an ideal or complete description of an industry. The modeling must therefore take into account that some basic structural characteristics of demand and of technology are not measured directly. Variables are inevitably missing from the model, and their absence has implications for the interpretation of the structural relationships estimated. Second, observations are missing. Depending on the variable, the number of industries for which the variable is not available ranges from zero to as many as twenty-five. (Caves et al., 1977, appendix A, table 4.3 gives a summary of the data availability.) The missing data not only penalize degrees of freedom but also create statistical problems that have implications for both the estimating techniques and our methods for reporting results. They are particularly a problem for estimation techniques that are designed to deal with simultaneous-equation problems.

2.3 Derivation of the Form of the Model

An industry's structure and performance can be described by a vector of characteristics z. These characteristics divide into two groups—endogenous variables, including structural traits and measures of performance denoted by y, and exogenous characteristics denoted by x. Together the variables describe the industry: $z = (y,x)$. In principle, the theory of industrial structure and performance provides a set of relationships f that determine the endogenous variables given the exogenous ones. We can write this system

$$f(y,x,\alpha) = 0, \qquad (2.1)$$

where α is a set of parameters defining the magnitudes of the relationships among the variables. Theory does not tell us the magnitudes of the parameters α; they require estimation. For example, theory suggests that rates of return are positively related to industry concentration, but it does not tell us the magnitude of the effect.

There may be a certain irreducible amount of noise in the cause-and-effect relationships that would prevent the analyst from passing without error from an industry's characteristics x to its structure and performance y. If that is the case, then the fundamental underlying relationships become

$$f(y,x,\alpha,w) = 0,$$

where w is a vector of random variables with a distribution that requires estimation.

If the model embodied in the relationships f is correct, then the parameters α determine relationships among variables that hold across industries. What distinguishes one industry from the next is the vector of exogenous structural characteristics x. In practice, we do not observe all the relevant attributes x. To take a familiar example, the cross elasticities of demand among substitute products are usually inaccessible. Similarly, the parameters in the cost functions cannot be measured directly with currently available data. As a result, the relationships among observable x's and the endogenous variables y may appear to vary from one industry to the next.

If one could observe all the y's and x's for a sample of industries, then one could estimate the parameters α. However, as Edward S. Mason and other pioneers in industrial organization noted, the number of relevant industry characteristics may well exceed the number of industries. Thus with complete data on industry characteristics, one might face the problem of too few degrees of freedom. In practice, many of the relevant endogenous and exogenous characteristics cannot be measured. Thus we cannot estimate the underlying theoretical model; we can only estimate one that is adapted to the available data. This problem is sometimes ignored in industrial organization; equations explaining individual variables are often developed without considering their relationship to the larger system.

To understand the relationship between the underlying model and the estimated model, we can divide the endogenous and exogenous variables into two groups, those that are observed and those that are not. We shall use the superscript o if they are observed and u if they are unobserved. Thus

$$y = (y^o, y^u) \quad \text{and} \quad x = (x^o, x^u).$$

We can solve the system 2.1 to eliminate the unobserved endogenous variables. The result is a new set of relationships

$$g(y^o, x^o, x^u, \alpha, w) = 0. \tag{2.2}$$

This system is a partial reduced form of 2.1 and is close to the system that can be estimated. The equations in this system do not consist directly of the structural equations that theory either does or might provide; rather, the estimating equations are structural equations that have been partially solved to eliminate unobserved endogenous variables. The influences of some of the x's on the y^o's and the influences of some of the y^o's on the other y^o's may therefore be indirect. That is, they may occur through the mediating influence of the unobserved y^u's. It is useful to bear this in mind in assessing the plausibility of the specifications of estimating equations.

Another consequence of using a partial reduced form for estimation is evident in the functional form of the relationships. The system 2.2 has usually been linearized in its parameters. The original variables in 2.1 may, in the process, have been subjected to nonlinear transformations. Let us assume that the transformations have been carried out. The linearized version of 2.2 is then

$$Ay^o + Bx^o + Cx^u = w. \tag{2.3}$$

Here the parameters α are subsumed in the matrices of coefficients A, B, and C in the new linearized version of the model. Equation 2.3 can be thought of as a first-order, or linear, approximation of the system of equations 2.2. Once again, in specifying the partial reduced-form system, one must take care to interpret functional forms with this transformation process in mind.

The second issue in estimating the system 2.2 is that the variables x^u are not observed. They therefore represent disturbances from a statistical point of view. Let $v = -Cx^u$, where v are disturbances that result from unobserved variables.

The partial reduced-form equations can then be written

$$Ay^o + Bx^o = v + w, \tag{2.4}$$

where v is now an error. This system of relations is the one that can be estimated. There is clearly a potential problem with the errors in the equations: there is little a priori justification for assuming that v and x^o are uncorrelated, because x^u and x^o may be correlated. But for statistical purposes it is necessary to proceed on the assumption that x^o and v are not correlated. The only real solution to this problem is to measure the x^u variables. In lieu of that the estimated coefficients will be biased and may sometimes capture the influences of the unmeasured attributes. These potential biases can be acknowledged in interpreting estimated coefficients, and where such a problem may be present, we have tried to draw attention to it.

The errors in the model, $v + w$, consist in part of linear combinations of unobserved exogenous variables. Since $v = -Cx^u$, the variance-covariance matrix of v will be CHC^T where H is the variance-covariance matrix of x^u. There is no a priori reason to expect that either H or CHC^T is a diagonal matrix. Therefore the errors are almost certainly correlated across equations even if the errors w are not. The importance of this fact is in its implications for estimating techniques. Although some industrial organization theory suggests that the structural equations may be prerecursive (that is, the matrix of structural coefficients A has zeros above the diagonal), ordinary least-squares estimates are still biased unless the errors in the equations are uncorrelated.[1] We have therefore included two-stage, least-squares estimates of the relationships in the model, not only because of the simultaneity of the determination of the endogenous variables, but also because of the correlation among the errors in the equations.

To summarize, the equations that are estimated are a quasi-reduced form of the "true" structural system. The errors include the effects of unmeasured exogenous characteristics as well as pure noise. A resulting danger is that the errors are correlated with measured exogenous variables. In addition, the errors are almost certainly correlated across equations in the structural system. Thus while the direction of causality may run from structure to performance, consistent estimates still require simultaneous-equation techniques.

The remarks thus far apply to cross-industry research designs in general. The problems of unobserved exogenous and endogenous variables are not unique to Canada or to open economies. They are a factor in all cross-industry studies known to us, including those that recognize and deal with the simultaneity problem.

1. Prerecursive means that the matrix of structural coefficients A has no nonzero entries above the diagonal. As a result, the interdependencies among endogenous variables are one way. If y_1 influences y_2, then y_2 does not influence y_1.

2.4 Estimation Techniques

Before complicating the problem with open-economy issues, let us consider how one would estimate the system 2.4. The estimation problem is a simultaneous-equation problem. Because the errors in the equations are likely to be correlated, and because the feedback effects of performance on structure are of uncertain magnitude, so that one cannot be confident that the system is prerecursive, the application of ordinary least squares may yield biased coefficients.

There are several well-known techniques for avoiding these biases. We have used instrumental variables, sometimes called two-stage least squares (TSLS). This technique involves regressing the endogenous variables separately on all the exogenous variables. Then the predicted values from those reduced-form regressions are used in lieu of the actual values, wherever an endogenous variable appears on the right-hand side of another equation. We chose this technique for the practical consideration that it kept estimation costs within the feasible set.

Two other familiar estimators are limited- and full-information maximum likelihood (LIML and FIML, respectively). LIML, like instrumental variables, is a single-equation technique. FIML uses information more efficiently than either TSLS or LIML. It takes into account the correlations among errors and the identifying structure in the matrix of structural coefficients. But it is costly and known to give badly biased estimates if the system is misspecified. That is, if coefficients are inappropriately set equal to zero, then the remainder may be poorly estimated.

Another well-known technique is three-stage least squares. This technique uses the errors from the TSLS estimates to construct an estimate of the variance-covariance matrix of the errors across equations. One then does generalized least squares on the system as specified for the TSLS estimates.

In practice, because the sample of industries, 84 in our case, is not huge by statistical standards, we estimate an equation using both ordinary least squares and two-stage least squares. This is done both to check the difference between TSLS and OLS estimates and to provide a comparison with the OLS estimates that are commonly reported in the literature. Moreover, because the two-stage estimates are only consistent, in small samples they may be inaccurate estimates. The OLS estimates, when they are close to the TSLS estimates, are also a check on the latter. We have found that the divergences between OLS and TSLS are generally not large in our system of equations. But there are some notable and economically important exceptions in which an apparently significant OLS estimate is rendered insignificant in TSLS and vice versa.

Our estimates are essentially OLS and TSLS. However, gaps in the data complicated the estimation problem and forced us to fill in missing data before applying these estimation techniques.

2.5 The Use of Matched Canadian and U.S. Industries

This study uses matched industries in Canada and the United States, for several reasons. The U.S. data can be used to measure or approximate basic industry characteristics that are not measurable in the Canadian context. Because the U.S. economy is larger, certain statistics pertaining to the U.S. industry are better proxies for underlying structural conditions than are the comparable statistics for the Canadian industry. For example, we usually measure the minimum efficient plant scale (MES) by the ratio to industry shipments of the average U.S. plant among the largest plants accounting for 50 percent of U.S. industry employment in the industry. A comparable figure calculated from Canadian data might be poorly correlated with a technology-based estimate because the small scale of the Canadian market constrains the size of Canadian plants. The U.S. ratio is therefore more appropriate for most purposes. Similar remarks hold for the cost disadvantage ratio, a measure of the cost disadvantage of small plants introduced by Caves, Khalilzadeh-Shirazi, and Porter (1975). The cost disadvantage ratio (CDR) is the value added per worker in plants below MES divided by the value added per worker in plants above MES.

Other benefits to having the U.S. data are associated with problems of estimation. Because the U.S. and Canadian economies are similar in many respects, a complete theoretical model of industrial performance could apply to both economies. There would be differences in industry characteristics, of course, but these would result in principle from measurable differences in underlying structure.[2] Among the structural differences are the size or scale of the market, the regulatory environment (antitrust), tariffs, other aspects of trade policy, and population density. If we accept the hypothesis that the model applies to markets in both countries, then the estimated structural equations 2.4 would apply to both countries. However, it would be incorrect simply to pool the Canadian and U.S. samples where we face the pragmatic problem of incomplete measurement of industry character-

2. An interesting study of differences in Canadian and U.S. industry using discriminant analysis can be found in Oksanen and Williams (1978).

COMPETITION IN THE OPEN ECONOMY

istics. The errors associated with the matched pair of industries, being traceable in part to common unobserved structural characteristics, would be positively correlated, in violation of a basic premise of all standard regression models—that the errors are uncorrelated with the predetermined, right-hand-side variables.

The U.S. data can be used to improve our estimates in another way. Consider the structure of errors in the model. Let y^o denote observed endogenous variables and x^o denote observed exogenous variables. Let (y_{ci}^o, x_{ci}^o) be the vector of observations for the ith industry in Canada and (y_{ui}^o, x_{ui}^o) to be the vector for the matched industry in the United States. Let v_{ci} and v_{ui} be the errors in the model for the ith industry in Canada and the United States, respectively. It seems reasonable to suppose that these errors consist of (1) factors that are specific to the country (like scale) but common to industries within the country, and (2) factors that are specific to the industry but common to the matched pair, (3) random noise. In addition, if we assume that some further industry-specific variance is associated with the Canadian industry because of the openness of the Canadian economy, then the errors in the model can be written

$$v_{ui} = k_u + w_i \tag{2.5}$$

and

$$v_{ci} = k_c + w_i + u_i. \tag{2.6}$$

The terms k_c and k_u are constants that differ across countries, the w_i are industry-specific variances, and the u_i are the industry-specific variances for the Canadian industry. The error components w_i and u_i have zero means and are uncorrelated by assumption. It is the component w_i that captures common, unobserved industry characteristics.

Given these assumptions, we can write the estimating version of the model for the two countries as

$$Ay_{ui} + Bx_{ui} - k_u = w_i, \qquad i = 1, \ldots, 84, \tag{2.7a}$$

$$Ay_{ci} + Bx_{ci} - k_c = w_i + u_i. \tag{2.7b}$$

Here the correlation between errors in pairs of industries is highly visible. The $\text{cov}(w_i, w_i + u_i)$ is equal to the $\text{var}(w_i)$. By taking differences, one can eliminate the correlation. Thus we could replace 2.7b by

$$A(y_{ci} - y_{ui}) + B(x_{ci} - x_{ui}) - (k_c - k_u) = u_i. \tag{2.8}$$

Equation 2.8 can be used for estimating purposes in two ways. It can be used in conjunction with 2.7a to estimate the model. Then the pooled sample would consist of the U.S. data (y_{ui}, x_{ui}) and the differences $(y_{ci} - y_{ui}, x_{ci} - x_{ui})$. The constants vary across the two countries; this can be handled easily with dummy variables. Such a model would have the problem of heteroscedasticity, resulting from the different variance-covariance structures of the w_i and the u_i. Because our resources were limited, we did not pursue this estimating procedure although it remains an interesting direction for future research.

There is another use for equation 2.8. The nonzero correlation between x^o and v may pose statistical problems, but the correlation between x^o and u is likely to be less severe because u captures extraneous factors that distinguish the Canadian industry and not the full collection of unobserved exogenous industry characteristics x^u. Equation 2.8 can thus be used as an alternative to 2.7b for estimation purposes when a correlation between exogenous variables and the error is suspected, because of unobserved exogenous variables. Largely because of limited resources, we have focused on 2.7b and used 2.8 as an alternative specification, where the data permitted it, to check for problems of correlation between errors and exogenous variables.

This argument is purely formal. The substantive theory leading to the specification of the equations has been left to the following chapters. There is some cost in terms of exposition in proceeding in this way. The endogenous variables are jointly determined by the interaction of several structural relationships. Nevertheless, because the structural system is a partial reduced form, in the sense described earlier, and because of the complexity of the factors influencing each variable, the single-equation approach to specification seemed expositionally superior.

2.6 Missing Observations and Estimation

Because we have tried to collect data on a reasonably comprehensive group of industry characteristics, in some cases we lacked observations of important variables for a subset of the industries. We shall refer to missing observations as NAs (not available). NAs occur for a variety of reasons. Often the figure cannot be reported by government statistical agencies without disclosing confidential, firm-specific information. Some data are published, for this or other reasons, only for sectors more aggregated than our 84-industry sample or on a different classification scheme. In other cases, a statistic from a distribution of plants within an industry could not be computed because of lack of dispersion in the distribution.

The set of industries that have NAs changes from variable to variable. Moreover, the collection of industries with a complete vector of observations over all the variables in our data base is five or fewer. We therefore do not have the option of throwing out those industries for which the vector of observations is incomplete. Some variables were observed for all industries, however, and their presence has proved useful in dealing with the problem.

If it were sufficient to use only OLS estimation, and if the locations of the NAs were randomly related to or uncorrelated with the vector (y, x), then one could estimate each equation using the set of industries for which observations are complete on every included variable. Some information would be lost but no biases introduced. Unfortunately, neither of these hypothetical conditions holds. The NAs are not random with respect to the underlying data. For example, the fraction of assets in the Canadian industry owned by foreign companies is more likely to be missing when the number is low. Because the NAs are nonrandom, following the procedure just described would bias the subsample used on an equation including foreign subsidiaries' market share toward industries with high foreign ownership.

The easiest way to obtain crude evidence that the NAs are not random is to select a variable, to construct a dummy that is zero if the observation is available for that variable and one if it is not, and then regress the dummy on a set of variables to which the observations are complete. Table 2.2 reports the results for a few important variables for which observations are missing. The F-statistics for the regressions are significant for foreign ownership and close to significant for exports and imports. Many of the t-statistics are also significant. This evidence, although not definitive, does suggest that the simple assumption of random NAs will not do and that a more careful treatment is called for.

The nonrandomness of the NAs with respect to the industry characteristics causes several problems. First, throwing out industries for which the variables in a particular equation are not all observed may introduce biases. Second, since two-stage least squares uses all the exogenous variables to predict the endogenous ones, one would have to eliminate industries with an NA for any exogenous variable, not just the ones that are included in the equation. Thus the NAs create particularly difficult problems for the simultaneous-equation estimates.

If however, the NAs were random, we could form consistent estimates of the variance-covariance matrix of all the variables, simply by taking the sample variances and covariances in a pairwise way. That is, if the two variables x and y have missing observations, but these are random, then the sample variances and covariances are con-

Table 2.2 Determinants of Missing Observations.

Dependent variable dummy[2]	Independent variables[1]								$\bar{R}^2$	F-ratio	Degrees of freedom
	C868	LAB2C	CONO	CNPR	GSI	NPW67	VPW67	REG			
FSE	−0.0057 (−2.516)	−0.0044 (−2.81)	−0.093 (−0.6252)	−0.0102 (−0.089)	3.062 (2.667)	0.7273 (2.177)	−0.034 (−2.897)	−0.065 (−0.5645)	0.3367	4.759	75
Imports and exports	−0.0012 (−0.8384)	−0.0022 (−2.183)	−0.045 (−0.4771)	0.075 (1.019)	−0.5439 (−0.7372)	−0.444 (−2.069)	0.0065 (0.8695)	0.0218 (0.2946)	0.1572	1.749	75
EFT	0.0006 (0.384)	0.0013 (1.167)	0.0046 (0.043)	−0.0244 (−0.2924)	0.4327 (0.5155)	0.2454 (1.004)	0.0064 (0.7439)	0.0586 (0.694)	0.0525	0.520	75

1. The variables are as follows: C868 is the eight-firm concentration ratio in the Canadian industry. LAB2C is the ratio of number of employees to total assets in Canada. CONO is a dummy with the value one if the industry is a convenience good industry, zero otherwise. CNPR is a dummy with the value one if it is a consumer good, zero otherwise. GSI is the coefficient on time in a regression of the log of shipments on time. NPW67 is the ratio of nonproduction workers to total employees. VPW67 is the value added per worker. REG is a dummy with the value one if the industry is regional, zero otherwise. FSE is the fraction of shipments from establishments belonging to enterprises that are 50 percent or more foreign controlled. EFT is the effective rate of protection for the Canadian industry.

2. The dependent variable has the value one if the underlying variable is observed and the value zero when none is available. Imports and exports are missing for the same industries.

COMPETITION IN THE OPEN ECONOMY

sistent estimates of the underlying variances and covariances. The estimated variance-covariance matrix could then be used to generate both OLS and TSLS estimates, provided that it is positive definite.[3]

Since the NAs are believed to be nonrandom, the underlying problem is to find a consistent estimate of the variance-covariance matrix of the variables in the model. To do that, one must pay attention to the probability model that accounts for the missing observations.

Since the NAs are not random with respect to the vector (y, x), it is necessary to specify the probability model that jointly generates $(y, x) = z$ and the missing observations. The model is described briefly here and in more detail in Hausman and Spence (1977). We deal with a single variable at a time in order to keep the complexity manageable. Let the variable containing NAs be q, and let s be a vector of variables for which the observations are complete. The vector s includes a constant. Let d be a variable that has the value 1 if the observation on q is observed and 0 otherwise. There are two critical assumptions.

1. The distribution of q conditional on s is normal with the density $f(q; \beta s, \sigma)$ where βs is the mean and σ is the variance of the distribution.
2. The conditional probability that $d = 0$ given (q, s) is given by $N(\alpha q + Rs)$ where $N(\cdot)$ is a unit normal cumulative distribution; α and R are parameters.

Let $\delta = (a, R, \beta, \sigma)$, the vector of parameters in the model. The joint distribution of (d, q) conditional on s is as follows. If $d = 1$, the probability density is

$$(1 - N(\alpha q + Rs))f(q - \beta s, \sigma) = M_0(q, s, \delta).$$

If $d = 0$, the probability is

$$N(\alpha q + Rs) f(q - \beta s, \sigma).$$

3. With missing observations, the estimated variance-covariance matrix is not necessarily positive semidefinite. If $Z_t = (Z_{1t}, \ldots, Z_{nt})$ is the vector of variables for industry, t, and Γ_i, $i = 1, \ldots, n$, is the set of industries for which the variable i is not missing, and $N(\Gamma)$ is the number of elements in the set Γ, then elements of the estimated variance-covariance matrix are

$$V_{ij} = \frac{\Sigma t \varepsilon \Gamma_i \cap \Gamma_j (Z_{it} - Z_i)(Z_{jt} - Z_j)}{N(\Gamma_i \eta \Gamma_j)}.$$

The matrix $V = (V_{ij})$ is not necessarily positive definite because it is not the product of a data matrix with itself. If there were no NAs, the estimated variance-covariance matrix would be $V = \frac{1}{T} \sum_{t=1}^{T} Z_t Z'_t$, and that is positive semidefinite.

However, when $d = 0$, we do not observe q. Integrating q out, we have the conditional density for $d = 0$ given s. It is

$$\int N(\alpha q + Rs)f(q - \beta s, \sigma)dq = M_1(s, \delta).$$

Let Γ be the set of industries for which $d = 0$ and let $\bar{\Gamma}$ be its complement. The likelihood function for the sample of observations that we have is

$$L = \underset{i \in \bar{\Gamma}}{\overset{\pi}{}} M_1(s_i, \delta) \underset{i \in \Gamma}{\overset{\pi}{}} M_0(q_i, s_i, \delta).$$

The procedure then is to maximize L with respect to δ. This procedure generates estimates of the parameters (β, σ) of the underlying conditional distribution $f(q - \beta s, \sigma)$ and of the parameters (d, R) of the process that generates NAs. The estimate of β is used to generate the conditional mean of q, given s, for each industry for which there is an NA. The missing observation is replaced by the conditional mean. This completes the data base by replacing NAs with unbiased estimates of the missing value.

The procedure can be simplified if $\alpha = 0$. In that case the likelihood function can be written

$$L = \left[\underset{i \in \Gamma}{\overset{\pi}{}} N(Rs_i + k) \underset{i \in \bar{\Gamma}}{\overset{\pi}{}} (1 - N(Rs_i + k)) \right] \cdot$$
$$\left[\underset{i \in \bar{\Gamma}}{\overset{\pi}{}} f(q_i - \beta s_i, \sigma) \underset{i \in \Gamma}{\overset{\pi}{}} \int f(q - \beta s_i)dq \right]$$

The function is separable in R and (β, σ). Therefore when $\alpha = 0$ the conditional mean of q given s can be estimated directly by a regression of q on s for the subset of industries for which q is observed. Note that this can be done even when the NAs are not random with respect to the data. That $\alpha = 0$ does not mean that $R = 0$. But when $\alpha = 0$, the regression of q on s is the maximum likelihood estimate of in the conditional distribution of q given s.

In our sample the maximum likelihood procedure ran into difficulty because of suspected nonnormality in the data combined with the relatively small size of the sample. Although we suspected that the value of the variable itself was in some cases influential in determining whether it was observed, the size of the sample prevented us from estimating α through maximum likelihood. We were therefore forced to set $\alpha = 0$ and to let the vector s capture that part of the probability of an NA that may be attributable to the value of the variable itself. With α set equal to zero, the missing observations could be filled in

COMPETITION IN THE OPEN ECONOMY

with predicted values from a regression of y on s. That is what we did for the industry data base. We hope that the vector s does capture most of the nonrandomness in the pattern of NAs. Unfortunately, the maximum likelihood estimates with α not constrained to be zero could not be calculated to confirm this. The problem remains an open one.

2.7 Estimating Techniques

In the subsequent chapters, where hypotheses are framed and the results of regressions reported, we report three sets of estimated coefficients, for two reasons. First, the comparative results may be of interest to researchers in the field. Second, in justifying any of the approaches, we have been forced to make some strong assumptions with which others may disagree. On the whole, it seems best to have the menu of options laid out.

For each specification of each equation, the three regressions that are reported are referred to by the letters A, B, and C. They are as follows.

A. An ordinary least-squares regression using only industries for which there is a vector of complete observations for the variables in the equation. The number of degrees of freedom is reported in each case.
B. An ordinary least-squares regression using the full sample. Missing observations are replaced by the estimates described in section 2.4, with the assumption that $\alpha = 0$. Therefore the missing observations are replaced by the predicted values in a regression of the relevant variable on a subset of the complete variables.
C. A two-stage least-squares equation using the same completed data base as in B.

Because missing observations are replaced by their conditional means, the sample moment matrix understates the variances and covariances of the variables. This understatement does not affect the consistency of the two-stage estimates, but in the regressions B and C, which use filled-in samples, the standard errors of the estimated coefficients are biased downward. To deal rigorously with this problem, one would have to generate consistent estimates of the variances and covariances, conditional on the NAs. This would require a multiple-variable maximum likelihood estimation procedure that is well beyond our computational resources.

2.8 Summary

Several points are worth stressing. The model of industry structure and performance has 15 endogenous variables and 15 structural equations that determine these variables. Because of our inability to observe certain variables, including some that are endogenous, the structural equations that are used for estimating have the unobserved endogenous variables "solved out." They are, in this sense, a partial reduced form. There are also unobserved exogenous variables. These form a component of the errors in the estimating equations and create the possibility that the errors and the predetermined variables are correlated. For the same reason, the errors in the equations of the model may be correlated. As a result, simultaneous-equation estimating techniques are required to obtain consistent estimates of structure coefficients. We have used two-stage least-squares, a single-equation simultaneous-equation estimator.

U.S. data are used to measure certain industry attributes such as minimum efficient scale. They are also used in the form of differences with the Canadian variables, as a partial control for the correlation of errors and predetermined variables. Missing from the data are observations that are not randomly related to the underlying values of the variable itself or other variables. These gaps are unavoidable. We have filled in the missing observations using regressions of the variables in question on other variables for which a complete set of observations is available. This is necessary in order to apply two-stage least squares.

For each structural equation we report three regressions: (A) an OLS regression with industries eliminated if any variable in the regression equation has an NA, (B) an OLS regression with the full matrix of actual and filled-in data, and (C) a two-stage least-squares regression using the full, filled-in data matrix. Each structural equation whose form is developed and defended in later chapters deals with one of the structural variables or with a closely related group of them.

PART TWO

A Model of Canadian Industries

3 Seller Concentration and Its Components

Concentration is a good starting point for our model because of its central role in theoretical models of markets. Previous studies of concentration's determinants suggest that it depends on technology (minimum efficient scale of production), the size of the market, and other structural forces that regulate the effect of these two key variables. The explanatory strength of this approach is most easily seen in studies that make international comparisons. The influence of technology is revealed by the tendency of a given industry to claim about the same rank by seller concentration, no matter in what country we observe it. Pryor (1972) showed that concentration in industry x in the United States is a good predictor of concentration in industry x in another industrial country. Rosenbluth (1957, pp. 89–93) reported a correlation of 0.71 between concentration levels in Canada and the United States, although he was inclined to emphasize the looseness rather than the tightness of the relation. The effect of the market's size appears in the strong negative relation between concentration and the size of the national market. We seek to improve on previous studies in two principal ways—to consider more fully the influence of international market linkages and to use more appropriately variables that can be linked to concentration by an identity relation.

3.1 Concentration: Components and Determinants

A serious deficiency of most studies of concentration's determinants[1] is that they include among the independent variables both truly independent behavioral variables and variables describing other dimen-

1. For a survey of this literature see Ornstein et al. (1973).

41

sions of the number and size distribution of the industry's firms. This is poor practice for two reasons. Variables in the second group are related to concentration through an identity, which disposes the regression analysis to indicate a significant relation. Such a relation tells nothing about the direction of causation, even though it may be useful to relate concentration through an identity to other parameters of the number and size distribution of firms in order to find what those parameters contribute to the variance of concentration from industry to industry. We also object to the usual practice because behavioral variables that influence concentration may do so through these other parameters of an industry's number and size distribution of firms. If so, the regression runs into multicollinearity and a double counting of the behavioral influences on concentration.

To avoid these problems, we approach the determinants of concentration through a series of steps. First, we develop an identity relation that shows how concentration is associated with underlying parameters of the number and size distribution of firms and examine the correlations among the components of the identity. Then we employ regression analysis to test hypotheses about the behavioral determinants of concentration. Finally, we measure the association between these behavioral variables and the underlying characteristics of the size distribution of firms, in order to identify the channels through which the behavioral variables shape the level of seller concentration.

Identities involving seller concentration can be written in various ways. We define S as sales, NP as number of plants, N as number of companies, and add the number 4 after a symbol to indicate that it pertains to the largest four companies (otherwise, to the whole industry). Rosenbluth employed an identity that, written in terms of the four-firm concentration ratio, would be

$$\frac{S4}{S} = \frac{S4/4}{S/N} \cdot \frac{4}{N}.$$

That is, concentration is decomposed into the relative size of the largest companies and the proportion they make up of the total number of companies. We expand that identity in order to encompass the amount of multiplant operation in the industry:

$$\frac{S4}{S} = \frac{S4/NP4}{S/NP} \cdot \frac{NP4/4}{NP/N} \cdot \frac{4}{N}.$$

The relative size of the largest companies has now been decomposed into the relative size of the largest companies' plants, the relative extent of the largest companies' multiplant operation, and the largest companies' proportion of the total number of companies.

In our data base the three terms of the right-hand side of this identity are designated PLSZ, PLCN, and NENT; the first two are defined exactly as in the identity, while NENT is simply the number of companies in the industry. The concentration measure is four-firm seller concentration in 1968 (C468).[2] The correlations among these variables are

	C468	PLSZ	PLCN	NENT
C468	1.0000	−0.5242	−0.2815	−0.5516
PLSZ		1.0000	0.0346	0.5725
PLCN			1.0000	0.5638
NENT				1.0000

High concentration is strongly associated with few companies in the industry, as Rosenbluth (1957, chap. 2) found in his analysis of data for 1948. Contrary to our expectations, however, the largest firms in concentrated industries exhibit relatively less multiplant development than their counterparts in less concentrated industries, and the plants of large and small firms in concentrated industries are more similar in size than in unconcentrated industries. With the number of companies held constant, the first-order partial correlation between C468 and PLCN becomes positive but is very small (0.043), and the first-order partial correlation between C468 and PLSZ remains negative (−0.305). The greater uniformity of plant sizes in the more concentrated industries may reflect the presence in these sectors of large minimum efficient scales and severe diseconomies of small scale, which shrink the number of establishments (and companies) that can occupy the market and at the same time reduce their size inequality.[3]

2. The analyses described in this chapter were performed on both four-firm and eight-firm concentration ratios, giving essentially identical results.

3. This correlation analysis of levels of concentration in 1968 can be compared to Khemani's (1978) study of changes over 1948–1972. He found that the proportional change in the number of plants per multiplant firm contributed positively significantly to the growth of concentration, as did the change in an index of the concentration of plant sizes (in national industries, although not in regional ones). Our cross section at a point in time brings out variations in minimum efficient scale, it appears, much more strongly than Khemani's analysis of changes over time. He concurs with our result in finding that changes in concentration were negatively related to changes in the number of companies (even with the growth of shipments controlled).

3.2 Behavioral Influences on Concentration

We obtain the simplest determinate model of concentration if we assume that a single optimal size of firm exists for each industry (the optimum may depend on relative input prices) and that the sellers face a well-defined market demand curve. If entry is not restricted and competition prevails, the four-firm concentration ratio becomes $4/n$ when n is the number of optimal-size firms that can be fitted into the market of competitive equilibrium.[4]

This simple reference model can be modified to take account of other influences. The operative size of the market depends on the industry's comparative advantage in international trade, as well as on the geographic size of the country and the regional distribution of demand (in the case of products with significant transportation costs). Entry barriers are important, especially if (as most evidence suggests) optimal firm size spans a substantial range rather than taking a single value. If entry barriers stem from forces other than scale economies in production, going firms may attain sizes larger than warranted by scale economies in production. These impediments could include absolute-cost entry barriers, especially those due to high capital costs, and barriers associated with product differentiation (scale economies in sales promotion or high absolute initial costs of establishing a new brand). As Eastman and Stykolt (1967, chap. 1) pointed out, the effect of product differentiation on concentration is ambiguous. If it raises entry barriers, it could raise concentration. On the other hand, Chamberlin (1962) demonstrated that it makes production viable at a scale smaller than that required to minimize unit costs of production and thus enlarges the potential number of sellers. The latter effect of differentiation must surely be part of the explanation for one of the most puzzling results to come from the international comparative study of market structures: the sizes of plants and companies seem to vary sensitively with the size of the national market in ways that cannot be explained by differences in input prices or scale economies.[5] Variations in market size could hardly have such a strong effect if an industry's demand were not often fragmented by differentiation.

We shall employ two strategies for testing the behavioral determinants of concentration. One is simply to regress a measure of concentration in Canadian manufacturing industries on variables indicated

4. The influence of market size has often been measured in statistical studies by the number of firms of efficient size that can fit into the market. See Eastman and Stykolt (1967) and Pashigian (1969).

5. See Bain (1966), Pryor (1972), and Scherer et al. (1975, chap. 3).

by the preceding analysis. The other is to employ as a dependent variable the difference between concentration in Canada and in the same industry in another country—with the United States serving as the reference country. The latter procedure lets concentration in the U.S. industry serve as a summary of the hard-to-observe technological influences on concentration. This shortcut cannot be relied on totally, however, because the U.S. concentration ratio also reflects all the behavioral influences operating in the U.S. market, which will be collinear in varying degrees with those at work in Canada.

As statistical determinants of seller concentration, we first consider minimum efficient scale and market size. We do not have direct (engineering) estimates of minimum efficient size, so we employ statistical proxies for the missing technical information. The unit cost curve for the plant or firm in an industry can be described by two parameters, the smallest output at which average total unit costs reach a minimum (minimum efficient scale, MES) and the extent to which costs are elevated at an output that is some arbitrary fraction of MES. Both parameters need to be taken into account, because a cost curve with a large MES could have no major influence on concentration if the diseconomies of small scale are trivial. Previous research (Caves, Khalilzadeh-Shirazi, and Porter, 1975) has supported the use of two proxies for these parameters.

> MES Shipments per establishment by the largest establishments accounting for (approximately) half of industry employment, divided by total industry shipments, expressed as a percentage of industry shipments.
>
> CDR Value added per worker in the smaller establishments accounting for half of employment in the industry divided by value added per worker in the larger plants accounting for the balance.

MES is not thought to measure minimum efficient scale directly but to be correlated with it, and this presumption is supported by the statistical evidence. CDR is but the roughest indicator of diseconomies of small scale and reflects many other influences as well, but from past studies it seems to contain some relevant information.[6]

So far, we have not mentioned the data source for estimating MES

6. For evidence on the correlation between MES and engineering estimates of scale economies, see Weiss (1976). Weiss points out that an alternative measure of MES using the median plant size rather than the average of the top half exhibits a somewhat higher correlation; unfortunately, that result appeared only after the variable defined in the latter way was installed in our data base. CDR is explained more fully in Caves, Khalilzadeh-Shirazi, and Porter (1975).

and *CDR*. In the case of *CDR* the case for using U.S. data rather than Canadian is compelling. The small size of the Canadian economy and the possibility that substantial proportions of capacity in some industries are of inefficiently small scale argue convincingly that *CDR* measured from U.S. data (*CDRU*) is more likely to contain information about the true cost curve. The case of *MES* is slightly less clear, because differences between U.S. and Canadian factor prices and industries' output mixes could cause relevant information to be contained in the variable measured from Canadian data (*MESC*) that is lost when it is measured from U.S. data (*MESU*). Therefore both were employed. They gave similar results in the regression analysis, but *MESC* proved somewhat more significant statistically; therefore results using *MESC* are reported.

Because of the weakness of *CDR* as a statistical proxy, we used *CDRU* not as a continuous variable but to "switch on" *MESC* in those industries for which the cost disadvantage of small establishments seems particularly great. That is, *MES* provides a floor for the number of efficient establishments only when the cost disadvantage of smaller establishments is substantial, that is, when *CDR* is appreciably less than unity. Previous empirical research has placed the threshold value of *CDR* in the range of 0.8 to 0.9. The variable we use is

> *MUS9* *MESC* for industries in which *CDRU* is less than 0.9, zero otherwise.

Although some studies have combined minimum efficient scale and market size into a single variable, we have chosen to examine them separately, because the actual scale of establishments and firms is not independent of market size. The measurement of market size is complicated by the presence of both international trade and regional fragmentation, which can make the operative market respectively larger or smaller than Canada itself. We were influenced by evidence summarized in chapter 4, suggesting that imports behave characteristically as if they were differentiated from competing Canadian production, or as if they were imperfect substitutes for Canadian goods. Therefore we measure market size by domestic production and not domestic consumption. There remains, though, the question whether the influence of market size (production) should be the same when a substantial export market exists as when producers are more strictly confined to Canadian sales. Demand in the export market should be more elastic for producers as a group, and perhaps for them individually, and so market size may be less of a constraint on firm size. We allow the relation of concentration to market size to take a different slope in industries with substantial export markets.

Given that size is to be measured from production, what variable is most appropriate? The seemingly obvious answer is value of shipments. However, the room made available for an industry's production apparatus should bear on plant and company sizes in terms of how much total value added the market can accommodate and not how large a flow-through of purchased inputs results. Furthermore, because changes in production technique as scale expands seem associated with process technologies and indivisible equipment, the market that makes room for a large labor force need not have the same effect on unit size and hence concentration as the market that makes room for a large capital stock. Hence we used the following three variables:

ECA67   Total employment in the Canadian industry.
XECA   Total employment in those industries for which more than 10 percent of output is exported.
LAB2C   Total number of employees divided by total assets.

We expect a negative coefficient for ECA67, a positive and partly offsetting one for XECA. This pattern would imply that expansion of activity for the domestic market reduces concentration but that the concentration-reducing effect of larger outputs is smaller when more of the output is exported.[7] LAB2C, an inverse measure of capital intensity, should take a negative sign. Its inclusion would not be necessary if we thought that MESC and CDRU contained all relevant information on scale economies.[8] A positive influence of the capital-labor ratio on concentration in the United States is reported by Ornstein et al. (1973).

The effect of regional fragmentation of markets within Canada is taken into account by

REG   Dummy variable that equals one if the industry is judged to be regional, zero otherwise.

Unless national firms have plants in each region, concentration measured at the national level should be lower in regional industries, be-

___

7. A corollary of this reasoning is that expansion of the export market tends to enlarge the sizes of plants and companies proportionally more than expansion of the domestic market. This is supported in chapter 8 and in Khemani's (1978) finding that plant sizes grew more during 1948–1972 in export industries than in those insulated from international trade.

8. See Haldi and Whitcomb (1967).

cause company sizes are likely to be constrained by the smaller sizes of the regional markets. The statistical influence of REG on concentration should be negative.

Concentration might be higher than warranted by scale economies and market size if entry barriers are present. Two sources of barriers can be considered—absolute capital costs and product differentiation. The standard procedure for measuring capital-cost barriers is by the estimated capital cost of a plant of minimum efficient scale. Thus our variable is

$$CAPC = MABC \cdot ATS$$

where $MABC$ is the value of output of the estimated MES plant (the numerator of $MESC$) and ATS is the industry's average assets-to-sales ratio. The variable should be positively related to concentration.

The treatment of product-differentiation barriers is more problematical because the hypotheses are complex. Product differentiation is not directly measurable except in crude and judgmental ways. Advertising outlays are undertaken by producers in order to differentiate their products. But advertising is not a good indicator of structural differentiability of a product; nor do we expect advertising to increase concentration in general, although it can in selected sectors that are marked by substantial scale economies in sales promotion. The most practicable approach is to designate the convenience-good industries in the consumer-good sector as the set with the highest structural differentiation barriers. Convenience goods are bought frequently by consumers in relatively small quantities; they are distributed through retail outlets that provide little information to the consumer, who therefore depends mainly on national advertising to inform his choice (Porter, 1976b). Scale economies may prevail in national advertising, a matter of controversy, and allow high advertising outlays to augment capital-cost entry barriers.[9] Therefore we include the variable

$ADIC$ Advertising-to-sales ratio for those industries classified as convenience-good industries. In terms of variables described in the data base (appendix A), $ADIC = ADI \cdot CONO$.

Product differentiation has an ambiguous influence on concentration because it can also increase the viability of companies too small to achieve minimum efficient scale. If so, the constraining influence of

9. This influence is not registered in the variable $CAPC$ because advertising outlays are treated as current costs on firms' books, so that the capitalized goodwill asset does not appear in the assets-to-sales ratio. Rosenbluth (1957, p. 50) found some evidence of advertising's effect.

minimum efficient scale should be weaker in industries with differentiated products. Using advertising as the best available indicator of product differentiation, we allowed the regression coefficient of *MUS9* to take a different value in industries with higher-than-average values of the industry's ratio of advertising to sales. This is done by including

ADMUS MUS9 when advertising-to-sales ratio (*ADI*) is greater than 1.5 percent, zero otherwise.

The coefficient of *ADMUS* should be negative, partially offsetting the expected positive coefficient of *MUS9*.

A regression analysis of the determinants of the four-firm concentration ratio in Canada (*C468*) is provided in table 3.1. Variables endogenous in our model are those constructed from *ADI* and *EXP*. The equations are estimated by methods A, B, and C, explained in chapter 2. In the two-stage least-squares regression (C), all coefficients carry the expected signs and are statistically significant at 5 percent or better (one-tailed tests). In the two ordinary least-squares estimations, A and B, the level of significance is somewhat more variable, but the pattern of signs is the same and the values of most coefficients remain fairly stable. The influence of advertising (*ADIC*) is significant only in the two-stage least-squares equation. Because advertising is an endogenous variable in the system of industrial organization, this result is hardly surprising.[10] We accept our hypotheses about the nonlinear influence on concentration of scale economies (weaker for differentiated products) and Canadian market size (weaker in exporting industries). One puzzle, though, is provided by the coefficient of *ADMUS*, which is larger absolutely than that of *MUS9*, though not big enough to make the net coefficient of *MUS9* negative in high-advertising industries.

Difference between Canadian and U.S. Concentration

We can verify and extend these conclusions by relating concentration in the Canadian industry to concentration in its U.S. counterpart. In the 85 matched industries for which U.S. concentration ratios are available, the relation between the two is quite close. The correlation coefficients are 0.75 for both the four-firm and eight-firm concentration ratios. When the Canadian four-firm ratio is regressed on its U.S. counterpart, the slope coefficient is not significantly different from unity for the four-firm ratio. The mean Canadian concentration ratio

10. Strickland and Weiss (1976) report a similar though less dramatic effect of shifting from OLS to TSLS estimation.

Table 3.1 Determinants of seller concentration (*C468*).

Independent variable	Estimation method		
	A	B	C
ADIC	25.6	7.82	314[b]
	(0.27)	(0.09)	(2.13)
ADMUS	−122[c]	−97.2[c]	−272[b]
	(−1.40)	(−1.35)	(−1.94)
XECA[1]	0.021	0.36[c]	0.104[b]
	(0.71)	(1.47)	(1.86)
MUS9	165[a]	135[a]	151[b]
	(2.70)	(3.34)	(2.18)
LAB2C	−0.152[b]	−0.172[a]	−0.117[b]
	(−2.27)	(−2.96)	(−1.67)
ECA67[1]	−0.084[a]	−0.87[a]	−0.140[a]
	(−3.15)	(−3.85)	(−3.22)
REG	−7.38[c]	−10.2[b]	−9.86[b]
	(−1.46)	(−2.18)	(−1.80)
CAPC	0.274[a]	0.228[a]	0.193[b]
	(3.60)	(3.49)	(2.37)
Constant	66.1	71.2[a]	70.4[a]
	(n.a.)	(13.3)	(11.2)
$\overline{R}^2$	0.434	0.486	−
F	7.42	10.8	3.30
D.f.	59	75	75

Note: n.a. = not available. Levels of statistical significance (one-tailed test) are a = 1 percent, b = 5 percent, c = 10 percent. Variables listed above the horizontal line contain components that are endogenous in our model.

1. We have multiplied this variable by 0.01 in order to scale it conveniently.

is 43 percent higher (53.8 percent versus 37.8 percent). For the eight-firm ratios the regression coefficient is significantly less than unity, because the eight-firm ratio for the more concentrated Canadian industries is constrained by the ceiling of 100 percent. Although Canadian and U.S. concentration ratios are similar, we proceed in the hope that the difference between them, *C468* − *US467*, varies among industries and thus sheds further light on our hypotheses.

One hypothesis underlying table 3.1 is that technologically given cost curves interacting with the size of the effective market provide the

Table 3.2 Determinants of difference between seller concentration in matched Canadian and U.S. industries.

Independent variable	Estimation method		
	A	B	C
MKSZ[1]	−0.048[b]	−0.034[a]	−0.041[a]
	(−2.23)	(−3.70)	(−3.38)
MSU9	−31.2	−51.1	−75.7
	(−0.67)	(−0.64)	(−0.75)
LAB167	−1.61[b]	−1.59[b]	−1.66[b]
	(−1.73)	(−2.07)	(−2.14)
REG	−1.19	−0.728	−1.099
	(−0.25)	(−0.18)	(−0.27)
EFT	−25.9[b]	−16.4[b]	−18.2[b]
	(−2.19)	(−1.83)	(−2.00)
Constant	50.8[a]	46.2[a]	48.8[a]
	(4.29)	(4.87)	(5.03)
$\overline{R}^2$	0.102	0.190	—
F	2.31	3.67	1.00
D.f.	53	78	78

Note: Levels of statistical significance (one-tailed test) are a = 1 percent, b = 5 percent, c = 10 percent. The independent variable listed above the horizontal line contains components that are endogenous in our model.

1. We have divided this variable by 100 in order to scale it conveniently.

core explanation of concentration. If indeed the cost curves are technical data, $MUS9$ should not be a significant explanation of the difference in concentration, although the size of the Canadian market should. To test this proposition in its purest form, we employ in table 3.2 a scale-economies variable $MSU9$ based on $MESU$ rather than $MESC$ (to remove any influence of Canadian conditions) and a market-size variable that approximates domestic disappearance in Canada. The size variable is

$$MKSZ = ECA67(1 + IMP - EXP)$$

where $ECA67$ is total employment in the Canadian industry in 1976 and IMP and EXP are respectively imports and exports as a percentage of domestic shipments. We expect the difference in concentration to be negatively related to $MKSZ$ but unrelated to $MSU9$.

The difference in concentration should be affected not by the Canadian capital-labor ratio but by a differential of the Canadian from the American ratio. That is provided inversely by

LAB167   Payroll as a percentage of value added in Canada divided by payroll as a percentage of value added in the U.S. counterpart industry.

The higher the elasticity of substitution of labor for capital, as an industry shifts from an environment of U.S. to Canadian factor prices, the lower should be the Canadian concentration ratio relatively to the U.S. ratio. Thus the coefficient of LAB167 should be negative.

Two other variables are included in the equations reported in table 3.2 to depict Canadian conditions that might influence differential concentration. REG is used to establish whether the geographic dispersion of the Canadian economy makes for a stronger influence of regional fragmentation than in the United States. That is, we expect industries classified as regional in Canada to be classified as regional in the United States as well. If the geographic density of economic activity in Canada is thinner than in the United States, the constraints of the local market might reduce the extent to which Canadian concentration is greater than that in the United States, when both are measured at the national level. The hypothesis implies a negative coefficient for REG. The other variable we include is

EFT   Effective rate of tariff protection for the Canadian industry.

Tariffs might have their effect simply by enlarging the proportion of the Canadian market available to domestic sellers, thus increasing the number of viable Canadian sellers and reducing the level of concentration. By reducing the intensity of international competition, tariffs may either increase the viability of relatively small and inefficient producers or make room for more producers who are efficient under Canadian cost conditions. Either way, concentration should be lessened. Unfortunately, we cannot distinguish statistically between these two interpretations, both of which predict a negative sign for EFT. We do not subtract the U.S. tariff from EFT, implicitly assuming that it does not significantly affect concentration in the large U.S. economy.

The equations presented in table 3.2 confirm the roles of minimum efficient scale and market size as we have analyzed them. With concentration in the United States controlled, MSU9 has no significant influence on concentration in Canada and indeed takes a negative sign. MKSZ is highly significant, though with a coefficient somewhat smaller than that of *ECA67* in table 3.1. Tariffs (*EFT*) and the ability to substitute labor for capital at Canadian factor prices both reduce concentration. The coefficient of *REG* is negative, as we expected, but not significant, so we conclude that regionality affects national seller concentration similarly in Canada and the United States.

Our data on concentration in Canada and the United States permit a test of another traditional hypothesis about market structures in Canada—the influence of the multinational company. The analysis summarized in chapter 1 predicts that in import-competing, tariff-ridden Canadian industries subject to product differentiation, multinational companies enter and claim shares similar to those they manage in their home markets. The Canadian industry, the analysis concludes, is then likely to be a miniature replica of the same industry in the United States, with the same companies present, holding similar shares and producing at scales that are likely to be inefficiently small. The model implies the high correlation already noted between Canadian and U.S. concentration.

Foreign investment varies greatly in its prominence from one industry to another, suggesting a method of testing this model statistically. Suppose that we divide the industries in our sample into halves according to whether the share of shipments accounted for by foreign-controlled companies (*FSE* in the data base) is above or below its median value. The industries characterized by low foreign investment would be ones structurally unsuited to foreign investment and not likely to be much affected by the presence of foreign companies or by the shares they can command in U.S. markets. Specifically, we can derive the following hypotheses.

1. Foreign investment tends to occur in industries with high entry barriers (because the same structural traits cause both), and multinational companies may make a significant contribution to the net supply of potential entrants into barrier-protected industries. If so, concentration in Canada should be lower (relative to its U.S. value) in industries with high foreign investment. We accept this hypothesis if the regression coefficient of *C468* on *US467* is lower in industries with high foreign investment. If so, we conclude that foreign investment mitigates high concentration in Canadian industries which (judged by concentration in their U.S. counterparts) would otherwise be more highly concentrated. We regress *C468* on *US467* and also on

FUS4 Equals *US467* in industries where the fraction of shipments accounted for by foreign-controlled firms exceeds 0.45, zero otherwise.

The hypothesis implies that the coefficient of *FUS4* should be negative. We include *LAB167* and *MKSZ* in the equation (on the basis of table 3.2) and derive the following TSLS estimation (method C):

$$C468 = 29.6 + 1.72\ US467 - 0.485\ FUS4 - 0.36\ MKSZ - 1.81\ LAB167.$$
$$(2.50)\ (4.82) \qquad (-1.82) \qquad (-3.32) \qquad (-2.14) \qquad (3.1)$$

The equation has 79 degrees of freedom and its *F*-ratio is 15.1. The negative coefficient of *FUS4* confirms our hypothesis at the 5 percent confidence level.

2. In industries congenial to foreign investment, seller concentration in Canada should be more similar to concentration in the United States. Statistically, *US467* should be a better predictor of *C468* in industries with high foreign investment than in industries where foreign investment is low. To test this conjecture, we reran the equation 3.1 but replaced *US467* with the following variable:

> *NFUS4*   Equals *US467* in industries where the fraction of shipments accounted for by foreign-controlled firms is less than 0.45, zero otherwise.

The equation run with *FUS4* and *NFUS4* is of course identical to equation 3.1 except in the coefficients and *t*-statistics of these two variables. The *t*-statistic of *FUS4* is almost exactly twice that of *NFUS4*, and its beta coefficient (contribution to explained variance) is more than twice as large. The hypothesis is confirmed.

Thus we conclude that the miniature replica model of market structures in Canada is supported by our data.

Determinants of Components of Concentration

Concentration can usefully be factored into its components, relative size of the largest companies' plants (*PLSZ*), relative multiplant development of the largest companies (*PLCN*), and number of enterprises (*NENT*). In table 3.3 we regress each of these variables on the same set of independent variables shown in table 3.1, in order to investigate the channels by which the behavioral variables influence concentration. For each dependent variable the A and C estimations are shown; the B equation in each case is quite similar to the A equation. Market size (*ECA67*) has a powerful positive influence on the number of companies; the beta coefficient for *ECA67* in the A equation for *NENT* is 0.92. This influence is strong enough to offset the positive influence of market size on relative plant size and plant concentration. A bigger market increases the leading firms' relative size,

Table 3.3 Determinants of components of seller concentration: relative plant size (PLSZ), relative plant concentration (PLCN), and number of enterprises (NENT).

Dependent variable		Constant	ADIC	ADMUS	XECA	MUS9	LAB2C	ECA67	REG	CAPC	$\bar{R}^2$	F/D.f.
						Independent variables						
PLSZ	A	3.28	−0.855	−8.65	−0.014[c]	−7.67	0.025[c]	0.015[b]	−0.541	−0.013	0.039	1.33
		(n.a.)	(0.03)	(−0.33)	(−1.51)	(−0.44)	(1.32)	(1.97)	(−0.37)	(−0.57)		56
	C	2.41	−24.7	24.6	−0.022[c]	−6.72	0.206	0.026[a]	−0.451	−0.015	—	0.07
		(1.59)	(−0.69)	(0.72)	(−1.64)	(−0.40)	(1.21)	(2.50)	(−0.34)	(−0.76)		75
PLCN	A	1.98	3.65	−5.68	−0.010[a]	−8.16	−0.008	0.017[a]	1.05[b]	−0.017[b]	0.349	5.30
		(n.a.)	(0.33)	(−0.52)	(−2.75)	(−1.11)	(−0.95)	(5.26)	(1.70)	(−1.73)		56
	C	1.74	3.24	−8.30	−0.018[a]	−4.20	−0.008	0.019[a]	0.997[b]	−0.003	—	4.01
		(2.62)	(0.21)	(−0.56)	(−2.97)	(−0.57)	(−1.15)	(4.04)	(1.68)	(−0.40)		75
NENT	A	−54.4	−250	−132	−2.10[a]	−1309[c]	1.36[c]	2.59[a]	22.9	−1.25	0.453	7.62
		(n.a.)	(−0.18)	(−0.09)	(−4.39)	(−1.43)	(1.36)	(6.50)	(0.29)	(−1.04)		56
	C	−64.9	−499	1777	−1.73[a]	−1122	1.34[c]	2.17[a]	37.3	−0.836	—	12.8
		(−0.81)	(−0.26)	(0.99)	(−2.42)	(−1.27)	(1.49)	(3.89)	(0.53)	(−0.80)		75

Note: n.a. = not available. Levels of statistical significance (one-tailed tests) are a = 1 percent, b = 5 percent, c = 10 percent. The three independent variables listed to the left of the space contain components that are endogenous in our model.

but it increases the number of firms proportionally more. The effect of substantial exports is to offset the impact of national market size on each component of concentration; in the export industries there is no net relation between Canadian market size and any of the components. The effect of regionality (REG) on concentration is also shown to be the result of opposed forces. Relative multiplant development (PLCN) is greater in regional industries, presumably because national firms operate plants in each region while the smaller enterprises are confined to single regions.[11] But regionality also increases the number of companies and reduces the relative size of the largest firms, and these influences on balance make regionality a negative influence on concentration measured at the national level. As we would expect, large minimum scale (MUS9) increases concentration mainly by lowering the number of companies, but it also reduces the relative plant size and plant concentration of the largest firms. Smaller firms must have relatively large plants to survive. The same pattern holds for capital-cost barriers to entry (CAPC) and capital intensity (measured inversely by LAB2C).

The influences on concentration discussed so far run predictably through the channels of plant sizes and numbers of firms. There remain for consideration the only two behavioral variables that should not necessarily affect concentration through these channels of the production apparatus. ADMUS and ADIC embody the effects of product differentiation on concentration—respectively, making suboptimal plants feasible and creating entry barriers. Neither is directly related to scale in production, and so their significant effects on concentration (table 3.1) might be without corresponding effects on the components of concentration analyzed in table 3.3. That indeed turns out to be the case. Thus table 3.3 indicates that some behavioral forces influence concentration through the physical organization of production while others affect the shares of the leading firms independent of this physical appartus.

3.3 Scale Economies, Plant Sizes, and Efficiencies

The variables CDRC and MESC were originally proposed to capture purely technological variables, yet we know that these statistical proxies can also reflect market influences (such as product differenti-

11. Rosenbluth (1957, p. 69) noted that multiplant development occurs only in some regional industries—those for which advertising (and presumably the national scale economies to sales promotion) is important.

ation); in particular that the small size and openness of Canadian markets can affect the size distribution of plants and thereby the values of these measures. So we now make them endogenous variables and inquire whether these nontechnological influences can be isolated statistically.

Cost Disadvantage Ratio

CDRC is particularly suspect as a measure of exogenous technology. In a purely competitive market with no transportation costs, suboptimally scaled plants would not survive to be measured—as the statistic requires. Their presence depends on circumstances that cause suboptimally scaled plants to be built and to survive in the face of competitive pressures. The effect of these circumstances is multiplied by the small size of the national market which, at the limit, may leave little or no room for production units of efficient scale. But while small market size disposes units toward inefficiently small size, the presence of international trade promotes efficient scales. Whether an industry is an exporter and price taker on the world market or faces competing imports and takes their delivered price as given, producers' optimizing decisions should not lead them to choose inefficiently small plant scales. Some evidence suggests that the influence of openness is potent. Rosenbluth (1957) noted that the average size of companies differs little between Canadian and U.S. industries, so that the most conspicuous structural difference lies in the number of companies. This conclusion is surprising, given one's casual impression that the largest companies in U.S. industries seem much larger than Canada's industry leaders. The variance of company sizes in Canada must be substantially less than in the United States, with smaller absolute numbers of very large enterprises but also proportionally fewer small ones.[12] Correspondingly, the correlation analysis of section 3.1 showed that interindustry variation of concentration in Canada is strongly associated with the number of companies in the industry but inversely related to the inequality of plant sizes. This suggests that in concentrated Canadian industries scale economies tend to have crowded the market participants out to similar and relatively efficient scales of operation. If so, CDR calculated from Canadian data will offer little of its intended information about the cost curve. The correlation be-

12. This finding was reported by Rosenbluth (1957, pp. 82–85) and confirmed for Canadian plants (companies were not investigated) by the Economic Council of Canada (1967, p. 153).

tween *CDRU* and *CDRC* is, as expected, quite low, 0.146 (significant only at the 13 percent level). An appropriate *CDR* measure should be negatively correlated with concentration, and indeed a negative though small correlation appears between *CDRU* and *US467*, -0.066. The correlation between *CDRC* and *C468*, however, is $+0.054$. Our statistical analysis of *CDRC* therefore turns on two questions: Does it contain *some* evidence about technical diseconomies of small scale? What other forces influence the relation between plant size and labor productivity in Canadian industries?

Several variables in our data base should indicate the technical bases for diseconomies of small scale and thus permit an answer to the first question. One is a measure of the capital intensity of production in the U.S. counterpart industry:

> *KLU* Assets per employee, U.S. counterpart industry (inverse of *LAB2U,* described in the data base).

KLU should be negatively related to *CDRC* if small-scale establishments are at a relatively greater disadvantage in capital-intensive industries. This technological hypothesis is suggested by direct evidence on scale economies in particular pieces of capital equipment and in capital-intensive processing industries.[13] U.S. data are preferred to Canadian because the Canadian figures may be affected by other independent variables in this analysis. We also use a variable to indicate the weight of fixed costs other than in capital equipment—the relative importance of nonproduction workers in the labor force (*NPW*, nonproduction workers as a fraction of total employees). An analysis of Canadian productivity by West (1971) found that fixed costs could be identified with an industry's requirements for nonproduction workers. *NPW* should be negatively related to *CDRC*.

The small size of the Canadian market should interact with the structural bases for diseconomies of small scale in determining *CDRC*. If minimum efficient scale is small enough that most Canadian sellers attain minimum long-run average costs, the smaller ones should exhibit no systematic disadvantage. On the other hand, if MES is large enough that most Canadian producers suffer at least some diseconomies of small scale, the smaller ones should be at the greater disadvantage. Therefore the proxy for MES calculated from U.S. data, *MESU,* should be negatively related to *CDRC*.

We include several variables that should indicate the economic viability of small establishments. A firm operating at a technologically

13. See, for example, Haldi and Whitcomb (1967).

suboptimal scale can be viable (and perhaps economically efficient as well) if it can command higher unit revenues to cover its higher-than-average minimum costs. Product differentiation is a classic factor making small-scale operations viable. Lacking a measure of the intrinsic differentiation of a product we use a behavioral one,

ADI Ratio of advertising outlay, to total sales.

The viability of small sellers is increased if the market is regionally fragmented, so that the small producer can efficiently serve a small pocket of demand. Our dummy variable designated a regional industry in Canada is REG. Finally, tariff protection for an industry with a heterogeneous output makes viable producers of a smaller scale than could otherwise survive in the Canadian market, and so high effective rates of protection (EFT) should increase the thickness of the value-added slice that small sellers can achieve. ADI, REG, and EFT should all be positively related to $CDRC$.

In table 3.4 the signs of all variables are as predicted except for KLU, which is positive and even significant in the A equation. The reason is that KLU and NPW are highly correlated; capital and non-production workers appear to be complementary inputs. The zero-order correlation between $CDRC$ and KLU is negative, -0.052, though low. The influence of ADI is more apparent in the TSLS equation, the influence of EFT and REG less strong. EFT is really an endogenous variable, related to market structure through the political mechanisms that determine industries' different tariff rates (Caves, 1976). Advertising, on the other hand, reflects fundamental and independent characteristics of the product and its use, although ADI is associated with other variables through complex chains of causation. The result is particularly interesting because $CDRU$ exhibits a strong negative correlation with ADI, -0.289, and therefore is probably negatively correlated with the U.S. advertising-to-sales ratio (not included in our data base). Because of the small size of the Canadian market and the presence of many multinational companies as actual and potential market entrants, nationwide sales promotion through advertising media subject to scale economies is probably less important for putting small firms and potential entrants at a disadvantage than in the United States.

Following the procedure used in section 3.2 we can check the conclusions of table 3.4 by examining the difference between Canadian and U.S. values of an industry's cost disadvantage ratio:

$$CDRDIF = CDRC - CDRU.$$

COMPETITION IN THE OPEN ECONOMY

Table 3.4 Determinants of cost disadvantage ratio (*CDRC*).

Independent variables	Estimation method		
	A	B	C
ADI	1.08	1.66[b]	2.39[b]
	(1.04)	(1.80)	(1.89)
KLU	4.14[b]	0.680	1.83
	(2.39)	(0.72)	(1.27)
NPW67	−0.276[c]	−0.363[a]	−0.443[a]
	(−1.60)	(−2.41)	(−2.72)
MESU	−2.54[b]	−1.72[b]	−2.02[b]
	(−2.24)	(−1.96)	(−2.22)
REG	0.122[b]	0.055	0.059
	(1.92)	(1.14)	(1.19)
EFT	0.695[a]	0.160[c]	0.163[c]
	(3.78)	(1.54)	(1.51)
Constant	0.775	1.006	0.997
	(n.a.)	(15.6)	(14.4)
$\overline{R}^2$	0.409	0.191	—
F	4.96	3.03	2.10
D.f.	43	77	77

Note: n.a. = not available. Levels of statistical significance (one-tailed test) are a = 1 percent, b = 5 percent, and c = 10 percent. The variable listed above the horizontal line is endogenous in our model.

We find no theoretical basis for expressing this relation as a difference rather than a ratio, but the choice turns out to make no difference to the statistical results. Of the variables included in table 3.4 we take over advertising (*ADI*), tariffs (*EFT*), and the regional dummy (*REG*) as influences that might depend on their distinctive Canadian values. Capital intensity and nonproduction workers should affect *CDR* in both countries, and each of these variables should be expressed as a Canadian-U.S. differential. For capital intensity we used the inverse proxy *LAB167* (payroll as a fraction of value added, Canada divided by United States). For nonproduction workers we take

$$NPWDIF = NPW67 - NPWUS.$$

The resulting TSLS equation is

$$CDRDIF = 0.191 - 0.23\,LAB167 - 1.02\,NPWDIF$$
$$(1.00)\ (-1.37)\qquad\qquad (-2.16)$$
$$+\ 6.74\,ADI + 0.010\,REG + 0.132\,EFT\,.$$
$$(3.16)\qquad\quad (0.15)\qquad\quad (0.96)$$

The coefficients of the capital-intensity, nonproduction-worker, and advertising variables are all correctly signed and significant ($LAB167$ only at 10 percent), although the F-ratio for the equation is only 0.206 (78 degrees of freedom). Both REG and EFT are insignificant; the influence of regionality is similar in both the Canadian and U.S. economies, and Canadian tariffs are probably correlated with those in the United States. Alternatively, these undifferenced variables may have picked up something in the error term of the equation.

Minimum Efficient Scale

Like the cost disadvantage ratio ($CDRC$), our proxy for minimum efficient plant size in Canada ($MESC$) was developed in order to provide information about the technical forces determining the structure and performance of Canadian industries. $MESC$ is defined as the market share occupied by the average-size plant among the largest plants accounting for half of Canadian net output. Its construction rests on the hypothesis that the larger plants in an industry have typically exhausted the available economies of scale, so that their mean size should be correlated (across industries) with the output at which plant economies of scale are approximately exhausted. Weiss (1976) and others have found this variable to be quite highly correlated with direct measures of minimum efficient scale, in U.S. industries for which the latter are available. For reasons already considered this correlation might be much weaker in Canada, and our calculated $MESC$ may (like $CDRC$) reflect behavioral forces. Gorecki (1976b, chap. 4) found evidence of some behavioral relations between another statistical proxy for MES and several market-structure traits of Canadian industries.

The quest for determinants of $MESC$ is closely related to that for $CDRC$. The variable is taken from the actual size distribution of plants, which should reflect the influence of both unobserved technical MES and environmental forces shaping the actual number and size distribution of plants. Capital intensity (KLU) is included for the same reason that it was for determining $CDRC$ and should be positively related to $MESC$. The influence of REG should be negative. Effective tariff protection (EFT) is also included, although its sign is now in doubt. It may increase the feasibility of small companies (as was indicated in the analysis of $CDRC$), but it also enlarges the market available to domestic suppliers and could increase the size of the larger establishments.

Product differentiation again should be taken into account, but the appropriate variable is somewhat different from the advertising-to-sales ratio (ADI) used with $CDRC$. Advertising can create a barrier to entry into some industries and thereby enlarge the viable size of the market's initial tenants, so its effect on $MESC$ is uncertain. Therefore we revert to the proportion of an industry's sales going to final consumption ($CONS$) as a weak indicator of its structural potential for product differentiation. The presence of international trade relaxes the constraint of differentiation on company size, both by allowing specialized tastes to be served by imports and by letting successful domestic producers expand by exporting. Hence we use an interaction variable that weights the industry's consumer-good status by the degree to which the Canadian market is closed from trade:

$$CONFT = CONS(1 - IMP - EXP),$$

where IMP and EXP are respectively imports and exports as a percentage of domestic shipments. This variable should be negatively related to $MESC$.

In section 3.2 we noted the copious evidence that sizes of plants and companies are influenced by the size of the market they serve. Various studies have formulated this relation as an elasticity, with its estimated value around 0.5.[14] So far as $MESC$ reflects the actual mean size of plant expressed as a percentage of market size, $MESC$ should be negatively related to market size if this elasticity is less than unity. Market size is measured here in terms of employment, $ECA67$.

Finally, we consider the influence of foreign investment. Foreign-controlled plants in Canada are on the average larger than domestic-controlled ones. Hence the proportion of an industry's sales made by foreign-controlled enterprises (FSE) should have a positive influence on the industry's average plant size and thereby on the average size of the larger plants ($MESC$). Behind this arithmetical implication may lie some behavioral influences: multinational companies may use more scale-oriented techniques, or their nonproduction skills and

14. See Gorecki (1976b, p. 43).

assets may give them potential access to large market shares that are then conveniently claimed by building large plant facilities. A positive relation between *FSE* and *MESC* can thus be given diverse interpretations.

Table 3.5 presents regressions of *MESC* on the variables just described. As with *CDRC*, an appreciable proportion of the variance can be explained, and most of the variables prove significant. *KLU* is unexpectedly negative in equation A although it becomes positive (though not significant) in B and C. *REG, CONFT,* and *ECA67* are signed as expected and marginally significant, and *FSE* is positive and highly significant. *EFT* is negatively related to *MESC* but insignificant if we apply a two-tailed test.

Table 3.5 Determinants of estimated minimum efficient scale (*MESC*).

Independent variables	Estimation method		
	A	B	C
CONFT	−0.050c	−0.022b	−0.036b
	(−1.52)	(−1.71)	(−1.80)
FSE	0.077b	0.094a	0.107a
	(2.35)	(5.32)	(3.59)
KLU	−0.810	0.172	0.369
	(−1.22)	(0.78)	(0.99)
REG	−0.35b	−0.026b	−0.019c
	(−1.81)	(−2.31)	(−1.64)
EFT	−0.088c	−0.042b	−0.035c
	(−1.52)	(−1.71)	(−1.35)
ECA67	−0.000	−0.000c	−0.000c
	(−1.25)	(−1.48)	(−1.31)
Constant	0.101	0.049a	0.037b
	(n.a.)	(3.28)	(2.06)
$\overline{R}^2$	0.285	0.410	—
F	3.46	10.6	2.57
D.f.	31	77	77

Note: n.a. = not available. Levels of statistical significance (one-tailed test) are a = 1 percent, b = 5 percent, and c = 10 percent. The independent variables listed above the horizontal line contain components that are endogenous in our model.

The results for both *FSE* and *EFT* are somewhat disquieting. Does tariff protection reduce the size of the larger plants in Canada, or have Canadian tariff makers simply chosen to give protection to small-business industries? Does *FSE* really have such a potent positive influence, or does foreign investment occur in industries in which sellers tend to be concentrated and therefore to operate plants that are large relative to the market? To resolve these equations we replaced *MESC* as a dependent variable with the ratio of MES estimated from Canadian data relative to its value estimated from U.S. data:

$$MESR = MESC/MESU.$$

Two changes were made in the independent variables listed in table 3.5. The absolute size of the Canadian industry was replaced by its size (measured in employment) relative to the U.S. industry:

$$EMR = ECA67/EUS.$$

And *KLU* was replaced by *LAB167*, the measure of relative labor intensity of Canadian production. The following TSLS equation was estimated:

$$MESR = -17.6 + 0.149\,LAB167 - 6.60\,REG + 15.8\,EFT$$
$$(0.07) \qquad\quad (-0.63) \qquad\quad (0.76)$$
$$+ 12.6\,CONFT + 2.68\,EMR - 15.5\,FSE.$$
$$(0.68) \qquad\quad (1.58) \qquad (-0.71)$$

The overall equation is quite insignificant, and the signs of *FSE* and *LAB167* are reversed in the corresponding equation B. Thus most of the statistical influences identified as operating on *MESC* do not appear to be specific to Canada, with the sole exception of relative market size. In particular, foreign investment, product differentiation, and regionality all lose the influence that they exerted on *MESC* by itself.

3.4 Summary

Our analysis of the determinants of seller concentration confirms the influence of market size and minimum efficient scale, noted in previous studies for Canada and other countries. It goes beyond previous studies in elaborating the influence of entry barriers other than scale economies (advertising and absolute capital costs), which let established firms grow beyond minimum efficient scale. We show that dis-

economies of small scale are important for precluding the survival of
sub-MES units, though their influence is weaker where product differentiation is present. We also find that the negative influence on concentration of the size of Canada's national market is weaker for industries that sell significantly in export markets. We establish the role of
international factor-price differences as an influence on concentration
by showing that Canadian concentration is lower (relative to the
counterpart industry in the United States) where labor is extensively
substituted for capital at Canadian factor prices.

Several hypotheses about the influence of foreign competition in
Canada were tested and confirmed. Tariffs lower the level of seller
concentration in Canada (we cannot tell at this stage whether the
additional firms accommodated are of efficient scale). We show that
foreign investment provides a supply of entrants in industries with
high entry barriers and makes their concentration levels lower than
otherwise. And we test and confirm the miniature-replica hypothesis
that concentration in a Canadian industry is more similar to its U.S.
counterpart in industries with heavy foreign investment.

Concentration can usefully be related by an identity to other
parameters of the number and size distribution of units in an industry, such as the number of companies, the relative size of the largest
companies' plants, and the relative degree of multiplant operation by
the largest companies. These variables cannot be treated as determinants of concentration, but they reveal evidence about the channels
through which behavioral forces influence seller concentration. We
found quite definite patterns; for example, although larger market
size enlarges the differential plant size and multiplant operation of
the largest companies, it raises the total number of companies even
more strongly and on balance lowers concentration. The only behavioral influences on concentration that do not affect these identity
components are the ones involving product differentiation, whose
influence does not operate through the size distribution of plants.

Our analysis yields much information about the relation between
scale economies and concentration in the small, open Canadian economy. If scale economies in production were of modest importance for
explaining concentration (as most research suggests for the United
States), we would expect concentration to be positively correlated with
the relative plant size and multiplant operations of the largest companies. In Canada, however, both variables are negatively correlated
with concentration, suggesting that plant scale economies in concentrated Canadian industries impel most viable competitors to attain

COMPETITION IN THE OPEN ECONOMY

minimum efficient scale.[15] We find further statistical support for this conclusion in our analysis of the determinants of the cost disadvantage ratio, a statistical proxy for the production-cost disadvantage of plants smaller than minimum efficient scale. The variable contains some information about technical diseconomies of small-scale production (for example, the disadvantages of small plants rise with the importance of nonproduction workers, who in part carry on overhead functions). But it is also affected by market structure and policy variables. Tariffs improve the viability of small-scale enterprises and thus reduce their apparent cost disadvantage, a finding that suggests that the negative relation between tariffs and concentration does not imply that the extra firms operating behind the tariff wall attain efficient scale. The adverse effect of tariffs on scale and efficiency is also revealed by the negative effect of tariff protection on the average sizes of the larger plants in Canadian industries.

15. This evidence is consistent with Khemani's (1978) finding that the growth of Canadian markets 1948–1972 was apparently accompanied by increased efficiency in the scale of production (for example, smaller variance of sizes of firms outside the top four).

4 International Trade, Multinational Companies, and Market Structure

The analysis of chapter 3 confirmed our a priori expectations that the international-trade position of Canada's industries and the prevalence of foreign direct investment have important influences on seller concentration. Therefore we consider the relation between international variables and other elements of market structure.

4.1 International Trade and Market Structure

International economists treat the exposure of a country's industries to import competition and the scale of their export business as determined by the economy's factor endowment and general "climatic" forces, not by variables familiar in industrial organization.[1] We disagree, for two reasons. First, the behavior of sellers (conditioned by the market's structure) may influence the volume of trade. A monopolized export industry may practice price discrimination against the domestic market and thereby export more than a competitive industry would; or an import-competing monopolist facing an uncertain price of imports may rationally set a price that increases the average volume of goods imported.[2] The volume of trade thus depends on market structure, for these and other reasons. Second, the technological properties of Canadian industries that determine their comparative advantage in international trade also influence their market structures. If Canada is richer in capital than most countries, and capital-intensive industries typically have large minimum efficient scales of produc-

1. Among the exceptions are Hufbauer (1970), Baumann (1976), and Carlsson and Ohlsson (1976).
2. Both propositions are demonstrated theoretically by White (1974).

tion, then the export industries should display high seller concentration in the Canadian market and large sizes of plant and enterprise. Because we need to include exports and imports as exogenous variables in other equations, this fact calls for making them endogenous in our model in order to avoid correlation between these variables and error terms in other equations.

The dependent variables to be explained are imports as a fraction of domestic disappearance (*IMPD*) and exports as a fraction of domestic shipments (*EXP*).[3] Each variable has been used in a number of previous studies (as well as our own) to indicate trade exposure as a determinant of an industry's market performance. Each is readily measured and easy to interpret. Neither, however, lies very close to the theoretical concept appropriate to describe the integration of a national industry with the world market. More appropriate would be the parameters describing the world's excess supply function for competing imports and its excess demand function for the nation's exportables. Econometric research in international economics has made little headway estimating these parameters for finely disaggregated industries, and we shall not attempt the task here. We shall assume that high values of imports as a fraction of domestic disappearance and exports as a fraction of shipments are good indicators of elastic excess-demand or excess-supply functions at competitive prices.

Our quest for the determinants of *IMPD* and *EXP* covers both the variables indicated by the theory of international trade and those suggested by the field of industrial organization. Baumann's (1976) analysis of Canada's bilateral trade with the United States found some scope for explanations drawn from both the neoclassical factor-proportions (Heckscher-Ohlin) theory of international trade and the so-called neotechnology approach that concentrates on factors such as scale economies, transfer of technology, and certain elements of market structure. Specifically, Baumann found the net export position of a Canadian industry negatively related to the skill content of its labor force and positively related to its utilization of primary materials. Among the neotechnology factors, he found imports positively related to a product's newness in international trade and to a structural indicator of product differentiation; neotechnology factors apparently have little to do with Canada's exports, though Baumann confirmed that exports are slanted away from consumer goods.

3. The imports variable in our data base is not *IMPD* but *IMP*, imports as a fraction of domestic shipments. *IMPD* can be secured by calculating $IMP/(1 + IMP - EXP)$.

Imports and Domestic Production

Our investigation of trade determinants concentrates on variables that are strategic in industrial organization and appear elsewhere in our system of relations. Baumann found that Canada was a net importer (from the United States, at least) of newly developed goods. These goods presumably have a high innovation content, and it is desirable to confirm the predicted importance of research and development for Canada's import-competing industries. The appropriate variable—the depreciated current stock of proprietary technical knowledge—is unobservable. As a reasonable substitute, we take a current-flow measure of R&D input for Canada's major trading partner.

RDIU   Research and development outlays as a percentage of sales in the U.S. counterpart industry.

This variable has been found to be strongly associated with the export participation of U.S. industries.[4]

Although research should be positively associated with imports, another major outlay on intangible assets—advertising—should be negatively associated. In some types of industries advertising can prove to be a substantial barrier to entry by new domestic competitors. It also impedes entry by imports, the seller of which must incur the fixed costs of creating a goodwill asset in the national marketplace. Furthermore, the analysis of multinational companies (Caves, 1974) raises a presumption that the firm skilled in the differentiation and promotion of a product will choose to serve a foreign market by means of local production instead of exports. In various ways local production aids the quest for maximum rents to the firm's intangible goodwill asset. If advertised goods tend to be produced locally rather than traded, we also know that goods that are structurally heterogeneous but not subject to advertising are especially prominent in international trade.[5] Advertising, which is applied most heavily to goods that are relatively simple and homogeneous, is thus a negative predictor of the sorts of physically heterogeneous goods that many countries' buyers can acquire only through trade. Therefore we expect a negative relation between IMPD and

ADI   Advertising outlays expressed as a percentage of sales.

4. See Gruber, Mehta, and Vernon (1967) and Hufbauer (1970).
5. Caves and Khalilzadeh-Shirazi (1977) find evidence that for the United States trade is important for these heterogeneous goods and unimportant for heavily advertised goods. Baumann (1976) reports a positive relation between Hufbauer's proxy for structural differentiation and Canada's imports from the United States.

The negative relation is expected both because heavy advertising designates goods disposed toward local production and because its absence may signify intrinsically heterogeneous goods that enter extensively into trade.

Another factor that should expand imports is the prevalence of scale economies in a good's production. The theoretical effect of scale economies is to impel some country to specialize in a good's production and others not to produce it, a proposition that implies an increased variance among sectors for *IMPD* but no regression relationship. Because Canada's market is smaller than those of its leading trading partners, however, such goods should be produced elsewhere, and we therefore expect a positive relation. Scale economies should be measured from the production technology of a country larger than Canada in which they are more fully realized, and they should register the presence of both large minimum efficient scale and substantial disadvantages to suboptimal-scale production.[6] We employ a variable introduced in chapter 3.

> *MSU8* Average output of the largest plants accounting for 50 percent of employment in the U.S. counterpart industry, divided by industry sales (*MESU*), when the estimated cost disadvantage ratio for the industry (*CDRU*) is less than 0.8, and zero otherwise.[7]

A variable from industrial organization that has been included in previous studies of trade structure is seller concentration. Economic theory indicates that imports will be inflated by the profit-maximizing actions of either a monopolist who competes with imports that are an imperfect substitute for his own output or a risk-neutral monopolist who faces a stochastic price of perfectly substitutable imports. Baumann (1976) confirmed this relation for Canada, as did Pagoulatos and Sorenson (1976b) for the United States. Doubts arise about the wisdom of including concentration in its simple form, however, when we recall the determinants of concentration analyzed in chapter 3. Suppose that minimum efficient scale is the same in all industries and that total market demand in Canada has the same money value (at competitive equilibrium prices) for every industry. Concentration would then be higher in industries facing more import competition,

6. The variable used successfully by Baumann and taken from Hufbauer (1970) is essentially an estimate of the slope of the cost curve at suboptimal scales, and omits the minimum-efficient-scale component.

7. *CDRU* is defined in section 3.2. There is no theoretical basis for identifying the critical minimum cutoff for *CDRU;* the value of 0.8 gives slightly more significant results here than the value of 0.9 used elsewhere in this study.

simply because room is left for fewer domestic firms of efficient size. Imports and concentration may thus be positively related through the influence of costs and technology, and no market behavior need be involved. We therefore put the expected positive relation between imports and concentration to a more appropriate test by using the variable

$$C4AJ = C468/(1 + IMP),$$

which has the effect of deflating the four-firm concentration ratio ($C468$) on the assumption that imports function competitively the same way that a fringe of small domestic producers does. This test is stringent because errors in the measurement of imports tend to produce a negative statistical relation between $IMPD$ and $C4AJ$ and obscure any positive behavioral one.

Although explanatory variables derived from the theory of international trade are not a central interest for this study, we sought to include some in order to make the model as complete as possible. Canada's comparative advantage seems strongly influenced by its abundance of natural resources, so we would expect low imports and high exports in sectors heavily dependent on primary inputs. $IMPD$ should be negatively related to

   RAW Inputs from primary producing sectors as a percentage of total
         purchased direct inputs.[8]

Predictions are less easy to secure when we turn to other components of Canada's factor endowment. Should Canada have a comparative advantage in production processes that are highly capital intensive? Casual observation suggests that the nation's endowment of capital per worker is higher than for many of Canada's trading partners but probably lower than for the United States. We include a measure of capital intensity but without a clear prediction of its sign.

   KLU Assets of companies classified to the U.S. counterpart industry
         divided by its total number of employees (KLU is the inverse of
         $LAB2U$ in our data base).

Another relevant component of Canada's factor endowment is the skill mix of its labor force. Again, however, its influence is ambigu-

8. The industry's indirect requirements would be traced through the input-output table and included as was done by Carlsson and Ohlsson (1976), if we believe that the domestic prices of resource-using products generally reflect their abundance in Canada rather than being locked into the world prices of these goods. Our actual procedure is the appropriate one if primary inputs are deemed to sell in Canada at world prices.

ous because Canada appears better endowed with labor skills than some of its trading partners but less well endowed than others. We have no sign prediction for

> *PROT* Personnel in managerial, scientific, religious, teaching, medical, and artistic occupations expressed as a percentage of total personnel classified to the industry.

The final variables to be discussed deal with artificial and natural restrictions on trade. Tariff protection should reduce the fraction of consumption of a good supplied by imports on any reasonable assumption about the demand elasticity for imports. Tariffs are measured in our data base by two variables:

> *EFT* Effective rate of tariff protection.
> *NOT* Nominal rate of tariff protection.

The effective rate is theoretically superior, because it is designed to measure the extent to which the whole structure of Canadian tariffs enlarges the value-added slice that can be provided by an industry. On the other hand, the measurement of the effective rate involves various approximations and assumptions, and so it is not clearly superior to the nominal tariff rate in practice. One approaches a cross-sectional test of the effect of tariffs cautiously, because the political process determining tariffs probably takes account of an industry's competitive disadvantages; the industry with a great disadvantage seeks and gets high tariffs but may still face substantial imports, and so the effect of tariffs may not be apparent in cross section (Caves, 1976).

Transportation costs reduce the volume of international trade, just as they confine some domestic industries to regional submarkets. For lack of good data on the weight of transport costs, we simply employ the dummy variable designating regional industries in Canada (*REG*).

The results appearing in table 4.1 are somewhat disappointing. The TSLS regression (equation C) is not significant overall, and only three variables are significant at the 5 percent level—*RDIU*, *EFT*, and *REG*. Thus we find greater import competition for Canadian industries producing new and/or structurally differentiated goods, and tariffs and regionality have their predicted negative influence. *EFT* is significant only in equation C, confirming the simultaneity due to tariff rates themselves being determined by market structure.[9] The influence of scale economies (*MSU8*) is positive and significant at 5 per-

9. The nominal tariff rate (*NOT*) actually performs a little better than *EFT* in the TSLS equation, about the same in OLS equations.

Table 4.1 Determinants of imports as a proportion of domestic disappearance (*IMPD*).

Independent variable	Estimation method		
	A	B	C
ADI	−0.787	−1.44b	−2.12c
	(−1.22)	(−1.86)	(−1.49)
C4AJ	−0.001	−0.003a	−0.002
	(−1.18)	(−3.39)	(−0.99)
MSU8	2.43b	2.81b	5.46c
	(1.70)	(1.76)	(1.34)
RDIU	0.020c	0.019b	0.072a
	(1.62)	(1.87)	(2.65)
RAW	0.002b	−0.000	0.001
	(1.98)	(−0.12)	(0.44)
KLU	0.597	−0.379	−1.41
	(0.76)	(−0.41)	(−0.66)
PROT	0.003	0.002	−0.006
	(0.56)	(0.64)	(−0.75)
EFT	−0.020	−0.111	−0.221b
	(−0.12)	(−1.21)	(−1.84)
REG	−0.090b	−0.117a	−0.090b
	(−2.06)	(−2.75)	(−1.67)
Constant	0.157b	0.359a	0.320a
	(1.90)	(5.83)	(3.40)
$\overline{R}^2$	0.253	0.238	−
F	2.47	3.88	1.10
D.f.	30	74	74

Note: Levels of significance (one-tailed test) are a = 1 percent, b = 5 percent, c = 10 percent. The variables listed above the horizontal line are endogenous in our model.

cent in the OLS equations, although only at 10 percent in equation C. Advertising's influence is negative in each equation, but its significance is variable. As an alternative to *ADI* we tried *CONS*, the proportion of an industry's output passing into final household consumption; the results were not improved. Seller concentration takes a consistently negative sign, contrary to our hypotheses, and fluctuates considerably in its level of significance. The statistical bias is a sufficient explanation for the sign. We accept the null hypothesis that concentration is unrelated to imports.[10] The three factor-endowment variables (RAW, KLU, $PROT$) are insignificant and erratic in sign. Thus table 4.1 reveals the influence of impediments to trade and something of the influence of market structure on imports but essentially nothing about the traditional neoclassical forces of comparative advantage.

Share of Output Exported

We now consider the determinants of the share of output exported EXP. The variable is symmetrical with $IMPD$ in that it reflects both the comparative-advantage position of the Canadian industry vis-à-vis its foreign competitors and the extent to which natural and artificial barriers to trade limit the international movement of goods. Therefore some independent variables can be treated symmetrically. (If we wanted a pure indicator of Canada's comparative advantage in exports, we would take Canadian exports as a fraction of world exports as our dependent variable.) The determinants of EXP taken over from the equation for $IMPD$ include the comparative-advantage variables RAW, KLU, and $PROT$. RAW should be positive on a priori grounds. Theoretically KLU and $PROT$ should have signs opposite to those relating them to $IMPD$, but their inconsistent performance in table 4.1 leaves us without any firm predictions. The variables indicating the propensity of a good to enter into international trade should again be included, with $MSU8$ expected to increase the proportion of goods exported[11] and REG to reduce it.

The remaining variables in the export equation are not taken over from table 4.1. Rather than attempt to distinguish types of product differentiation in their influence on exports, it seems prudent to accept the commonplace observation that Canada exports few consumer goods and to include

CONS   Proportion of value of industry shipments going to final consumption.

10. If the negative relation has any behavioral significance, it might be from the following sources. Aspects of comparative disadvantage not captured in the equation might also be negative influences on seller concentration. Or concentration might proxy entry barriers that discourage importers' activities.

11. This prediction could be contradicted by foreign countries' trade barriers. Lacking a large domestic market, Canada is unlikely to develop exports subject to extensive scale economies if the exports face pervasive trade restrictions abroad. Wonnacott and Wonnacott (1967) argued that U.S. tariffs indeed have this effect.

There has been a good deal of interest in the relation between exporting and corporate size, seller concentration, and multinational activity. These tend to be correlated among industries; we shall consider them together, although their relations to exports have independent justifications. Exporting seems to involve significant economies of scale in gathering information about foreign markets, organizing distribution networks abroad, securing efficient means of shipment, and so on. We therefore expect that larger establishments will export a larger proportion of their output—both within industries and across the whole manufacturing sector.[12] The fraction of output exported should be related across industries to

VPE Value added per establishment.

as a measure of size. (Because multiplant development is relatively modest in Canada, plant and company size should be closely correlated.) The presence of multinational companies may also favor exports because the international administrative links within these enterprises reduce the associated costs of information. EXP would then be positively related to

FSE Sales by companies subject to 50 percent or more foreign control as a fraction of industry sales.

On the other hand, this effect could be cancelled by the tendency for multinational companies to invest in Canada to dodge the Canadian tariff, behavior that would carry their activities mainly into import-competing sectors. Finally, White (1974) argued that seller concentration could affect the proportion of output exported, but in diverse ways: if an exporting monopoly can price-discriminate against the domestic market, exports will be inflated; if not, they might go either way. No sign can be predicted for the relation between EXP and

$C468$ Share of shipments accounted for by the largest four sellers.

The difficulty in testing any or all of these hypotheses lies in the collinearity that we expect among the three variables. There are reasons for the collinearity, but for the moment its fact suffices: the correlation between VPE and $C468$ in our full data base is 0.402 (122 observations); between VPE and FSE, 0.252 (92 observations); and between $C468$ and FSE, 0.489 (92 observations). Because we can clearly

---

12. If there are scale economies in exporting, a greater proportion of large firms would do some exporting, but the proportion of output exported would not necessarily increase with size among firms that do some exporting. Data supporting this hypothesis are reported by Rapp (1976) for Japan and Auquier (1977) for France.

predict VPE's sign (as well as provide a more convincing rationale), we use it as our base variable among these three. We then examine the consequences of replacing VPE with either of the interaction terms

$$C4VE = C468 \cdot VPE,$$
$$FSVE = FSE \cdot VPE.$$

None of these variables, we stress, has an unambiguous one-way causal relationship with EXP. Companies with opportunities to serve an elastic export demand will expand in size, as we argued (with statistical support) in chapter 3, so that an industry's comparative advantage itself promotes large companies.

When these three variables are included as alternatives in regression equations explaining EXP, $FSVE$ is the clear winner.[13] The equations including $FSVE$ are shown in table 4.2. The results are better than those in table 4.1 but are still lackluster. $FSVE$, $CONS$, and RAW are all highly significant. Regionality has the expected negative sign in equations B and C but does not significantly discourage Canadian exports; border trade is a possible explanation. Scale economies ($MSU8$) do not significantly increase Canadian exports (though the variable is positive in equations B and C). The negative influence of foreign tariffs, especially U.S., may be to blame.[14] The employment of professional and technical manpower is a negative indicator of Canadian exports in the OLS equations, but it is not significant in equation C. Capital intensity has a positive though weak influence in the OLS equations but becomes insignificantly negative in the TSLS equation. We conclude that Canada exports primary products and goods not passing directly into consumption and that exports are fostered by some combination of scale economies in international transactions and the informational economies available to multinational companies. The lack of a positive direct influence of seller concentration on exports is consistent with the analysis of chapter 3, which suggested that the tendency of export opportunities to enlarge the scale of establishments is the source of higher nominal concentra-

13. Replacing $FSVE$ by VPE reduces the F-ratio for equation A from 6.68 to 5.91. The beta coefficient of VPE is 0.260, that of $FSVE$ 0.516. Replacing $FSVE$ with $C4VE$ provokes a larger deterioration.

14. Baumann (1976, p. 416) found that the proportion of Canadian output exported to the United States is negatively related to the U.S. rate of effective protection. He did not, though, replicate Wilkinson's (1968) result that U.S. tariffs increase Canadian imports from the United States by frustrating the achievement of efficient-scale production in Canada.

Table 4.2 Determinants of the share of Canadian production exported (*EXP*).

Independent variable	Estimation method		
	A	B	C
FSVE[1]	0.004[a]	0.001[a]	0.002[a]
	(3.78)	(4.19)	(4.06)
RAW	0.002[c]	0.003[a]	0.003[a]
	(1.52)	(3.24)	(3.23)
KLU	1.47	1.17[c]	−1.36
	(0.90)	(1.44)	(−0.91)
PROT	−0.006[c]	−0.005[b]	−0.005
	(−1.34)	(−1.74)	(−1.07)
MSU8	−0.633	0.786	2.46
	(−0.41)	(0.51)	(0.77)
REG	0.010	−0.031	−0.046
	(0.24)	(−0.77)	(−1.04)
CONS	−0.158[a]	−0.199[a]	−0.226[a]
	(−2.54)	(−3.49)	(−3.48)
Constant	0.098	0.144[a]	0.196[a]
	(n.a.)	(3.35)	(3.54)
$\overline{R}^2$	0.505	0.321	—
F	6.68	6.61	2.08
D.f.	32.	76	76

Note: n.a. = not available. Levels of significance (one-tailed test) are a = 1 percent, b = 5 percent, c = 10 percent. Variables listed above the horizontal line are endogenous in our model.

1. We have divided this variable by 100 in order to scale it conveniently.

tion in export industries. Other comparative-advantage factors remain obscure.

Net Exports and Comparative Advantage

The analysis of this chapter so far has left the determinants of Canada's comparative advantage in a murky state. Of the variables suggested by the neoclassical theory of international trade, only natural resources have emerged as a significant determinant of exports.

One possible reason is that the separate analysis of *IMPD* and *EXP* leaves comparative advantage entangled with at least two other sets of forces. One is the existence of natural and artificial barriers to trade, which reduce both of those ratios. The other is the phenomenon of intraindustry trade: the presence of high levels of balanced imports and exports in the same industrial category potentially obscures the influence of variables that should push exports and imports in opposite directions.

We can partially elude these entangling factors, especially the first, by analyzing the following measure of net exports:

$$NEXP = (EXP - IMP)/(EXP + IMP).$$

From the usual descriptions of Canada's economic structure, we would expect this variable to be positively related to *RAW* and probably to *KLU*, negatively related to *CONS, PROT*, and *RDIU*. It should also be positively related to the tariff-rate variables *EFT* and *NOT*. In general equilibrium tariffs depress a country's exports as well as its imports, because trade must be balanced overall. However, apart from particular input-output links, the high tariff that repels imports of a particular product has no specific tendency to diminish exports of that same product. Of course, a positive influence of tariffs on net exports may not survive if tariffs are put in place to keep out imports, and they take their highest values in markets where the protected producers' comparative disadvantage is the greatest. This endogenous character of tariffs would be affirmed by a negative relation between *EFT* or *NOT* and *NEXP*.

The equations shown in table 4.3 do much to clarify the structure of Canada's comparative advantage. For consistency with other tables significance levels are shown on the basis of one-tailed tests, although the two-tailed test of significance is appropriate for most of these variables. Nonetheless, *RAW, KLU, PROT*, and *CONS* are all significant at better than 5 percent in a two-tailed test. The capital intensity of Canada's export industries may be associated with complementarity between capital and natural resources in their production function, as is often suggested. Nonetheless, the two variables are both highly significant. An industry's use of professional and technical manpower (*PROT*) is negatively related to its net exports. Yet research intensity, which had a significant positive influence on imports (*IMPD*), displays a positive though variably significant influence on net exports. The finding suggests that, contrary to the Canadian self-image, the country is effective in applying modern technology even if the amount of R&D

Table 4.3 Determinants of net exports.

Independent variables	Estimation method		
	A	B	C
RAW	0.007[a]	0.012[a]	0.011[a]
	(2.46)	(3.03)	(2.51)
KLU	7.23[a]	9.44[a]	14.3[a]
	(3.68)	(2.75)	(2.66)
PROT	−0.036[a]	−0.073[a]	−0.108[a]
	(−3.51)	(−5.20)	(−4.39)
CONS	−0.560[a]	−0.621[a]	−0.662[a]
	(−3.50)	(−2.47)	(−2.38)
RDIU	0.026	0.110[a]	0.160[c]
	(0.84)	(2.44)	(1.58)
EFT	−1.37[a]	−0.357	−0.555
	(−3.92)	(−0.90)	(−1.22)
Constant	0.101	−0.103	0.078
	(n.a.)	(0.46)	(0.29)
$\overline{R}^2$	0.521	0.341	−
F	9.72	8.17	6.16
D.f.	42	77	77

Note: n.a. = not available. Levels of significance (one-tailed test) are a = 1 percent, b = 5 percent, c = 10 percent.

undertaken at home is moderate.[15] It also confirms that research-intensive industries tend to have high levels of intraindustry trade. Table 4.3 strongly confirms that Canada tends to import consumer goods and export those not destined for immediate consumption. Because this relation holds after we control for *RAW* and the other neoclassical determinants of comparative advantage, we may have support for Dreze's (1960) suggestion that small countries suffer diseconomies of small scale in developing the material trappings of a distinctive national culture and therefore tend to export producer goods and import consumption goods stamped with the marks of other national cultures.

The effective rate of tariff protection (*EFT*), which should be posi-

15. We cannot distinguish between Canada's absorption of technology developed abroad and that developed at home. When Canadian R&D as a percentage of sales (*RDIC*) is substituted for *RDIU* in the equation of table 4.3, the results are almost identical. *RDIC* and *RDIU* are very highly correlated.

tive if the variable is truly exogenous, turns up negative and indeed highly significant in equation A. If nominal tariff rates are substituted for *EFT*, the results are essentially the same. None of our statistical results contradicts the hypothesis that tariff rates should be viewed as politically determined endogenous variables within the system of industrial organization in an open economy.

4.2 Multinational Companies and Their Prevalence

The dominant role of foreign subsidiaries in many industries has eclipsed all other issues of Canadian policy toward business during the last two decades. Yet foreign investment is seldom treated as an element of market structure and, thus, one among many determinants of performance. In this section we relate the foreign subsidiary's prevalence to the other elements of Canadian structure and investigate some effects of foreign investment on performance.

Extent and Causes of Direct Investment

A high and rising proportion of Canadian manufacturing activity is accounted for by companies classified as foreign controlled. In 1970, 52 percent of manufacturing shipments originated in establishments classified as foreign controlled, 42 percent from establishments under the control of U.S. companies. The U.S. share had been 33 percent in 1961, 30 percent in 1953, and 22 percent in 1946.[16] Although the figures for these years were collected in ways that make them not completely comparable, they leave no doubt that U.S. control of Canadian manufacturing has risen substantially, and it seems likely that non-U.S. subsidiaries have expanded roughly in proportion. Since World War II foreign subsidiaries' shares may well have risen similarly in the markets of other industrial countries—the United States included.[17] That Canada's experience may not be unique, however, makes it no less worthy of study.

The distribution of foreign subsidiaries among Canadian manufacturing industries is quite uneven, and it has been shown that the

16. These data are presented and their sources described in Statistics Canada (1976, pp. 22–25).

17. For instance, U.S. investment in Canada rose faster than U.S. foreign investment in other countries during the 1950s but slower during the 1960s. See U.S. Department of Commerce data summarized by Scaperlanda (1974, p. 9). Rosenbluth (1970, p. 34) finds that non-U.S.-controlled subsidiaries in Canada were disproportionately responsible for merger activity in Canada during 1945–1961.

prevalence of foreign investment is systematically associated with elements of market structure. Two complementary hypotheses have been advanced and tested empirically. First, the firm that succeeds and earns rents from its activities in one national market is likely to possess some specific rent-yielding asset associated with its success. The asset may be an intangible property or skill that can be used in other markets—product or geographical. It might be applied to foreign markets in various ways—by exporting goods embodying the asset, licensing foreign producers to utilize it, or establishing a foreign subsidiary. The last choice is most likely when the relevant assets are associated with product differentiation—the firm's ability to present a product that a significant fraction of buyers consider preferable to those of its rivals. Unless scale economies are too important, production is then favored because the firm can support its marketing ability by adapting the product quickly to foreign preferences, providing reliable delivery and after-sales service, and so on. Other rent-yielding assets can better be used for diversification in a single national market (for example, general managerial ability) or traded at arm's length between independent businesses (proprietary production technology) and thus play an incidental role in the development of multinational companies. The second hypothesis starts from the observation that the multinational company is by definition a multiplant firm that overspills a single national market. If the economies of coordinating the activities of multiple plants (pooled reserves, common sourcing of inputs, common distribution network) do not stop at the national boundary, any industry that offers multiplant economies and contains multiplant firms in a large national market will also contain multinational firms. Empirically, these two hypotheses tend to dissolve into one another, because a firm with intangible assets that allow it to sell more than the output of a single efficient plant becomes multiplant, even if its "multiplant economies" are not those of the physical coordination of decentralized production.[18]

Both hypotheses have been confirmed statistically for Canadian manufacturing industries. The indicators of product differentiation were behavioral ones—rates of advertising and of research and development outlays as a percentage of sales. The latter proved the more robust predictor of foreign subsidiaries' shares. However, advertising is paradoxically a good predictor in producer-good industries, where the occurrence of some advertising probably distinguishes the relatively few industries possessing intangible assets that are exploited

18. See Eastman and Stykolt (1967), Caves (1971, 1974), and Baumann (1975) on these hypotheses and Scherer et al. (1975) on the economies of multiplant operation.

through direct foreign investment. There is also some evidence that multinational companies tend to be active in industries exhibiting significant barriers to the entry of new competitors into the national market. This is because the large company in another national market tends to enjoy advantages over other possible entrants to a market that places some entry barriers before all newcomers. Statistical evidence supports this hypothesis in regard to scale economies and product-differentiation barriers. Because industries with heavy foreign investment are populated by companies of large absolute size, it is probable that they also enjoy an advantage against absolute-capital-cost entry barriers (although this was not confirmed statistically).[19]

Foreign subsidiaries in Canadian manufacturing are typically larger than their domestic-owned competitors. The average-size figures by themselves are somewhat deceptive, however. For manufacturing establishments employing more than 100 persons, there is no systematic decrease in the proportion of value added accounted for by Canadian-controlled establishments as we observe larger and larger size classes.[20] Most small establishments, on the other hand, are under domestic control. Therefore the variation we observe from industry to industry in the relative average size of home- and foreign-controlled establishments is probably associated with differences in the relative number of small establishments (less than 100 employees) classified to the industry. This hypothesis is consistent with Thomas Horst's (1972b) analysis of the factors explaining which U.S. companies invest abroad. He found that the members of an industry investing abroad differ from their stay-at-home competitors only in their relative sizes—not their relative vertical integration, capital intensity, advertising or research effort, or product diversity. This result is explained by the substantial fixed costs of information and transaction associated with foreign investment, which can be absorbed only by the company prepared to stake a substantial investment. Also, a small but successful firm with a modest share of its home market is more likely to find that expansion in its base market provides the best use of the resources it plows back into growth. If firms that invest abroad are already large and successful in their home markets, it is not surprising that they can claim large shares in the foreign markets that they enter.

Two facts about foreign subsidiaries have vital implications for conduct and performance in Canada's industrial markets. Subsidiaries

19. Statistical results summarized here are from Caves (1974), Eastman and Stykolt (1967, chap. 4), and Gorecki (1976a).

20. Statistics Canada (1976, table 11, p. 10).

are frequently found in Canada's import-competing industries, and indeed many tariffs were first erected in order to induce foreign companies to invest behind the tariff wall. The multinational company chooses between exporting to a foreign market and supplying it through a subsidiary's production facilities in light of relative production costs, tariffs, and any favorable effect of local production on demand.[21] These conditions together indicate a distinctive brand of market structure and performance that may be characteristic of Canada's import-competing industries. Scale economies in production limit the firms in an industry to a number that lets oligopolistic interdependence be recognized. Price is elevated above a competitive level, but only up to the world price outside Canada plus the Canadian tariff (the natural focal point for oligopolistic pricing). If that price leaves a potential profit margin for the typical Canadian producer, entrants crowd in—especially multinational firms—producing the miniature replica of U.S. market structure described in chapters 1 and 3. Up to a point, subsidiaries can make more than normal profits even in inefficiently small scales of production, because an absence of price competition—and the insulation of companies' market shares provided by product differentiation—discourages any one seller from expanding to efficient scale and lowering price. Equilibrium in this environment can entail an undesirable combination of high concentration, inefficient scales of production (although little excess profit), and an elevated share of the market controlled by foreign subsidiaries.[22]

Another important structural trait of foreign subsidiaries is the diversity of their outputs relative to the output diversity of both their parent companies and their domestic competitors. We expect product diversification and foreign investment to be competing activities for large companies. They not only compete for the company's resources in the short run but also are alternative forms of risk spreading in the long run. The shares of U.S. multinationals' North American employment accounted for by their Canadian subsidiaries show significant negative correlations with measures of the diversification of their outputs in the United States. However, the output diversity of the Canadian subsidiaries is positively correlated with that of their U.S. par-

21. See Marshall, Southard, and Taylor (1936) and Horst (1972a). It appears that the statistical evidence that tariffs affect the behavior in U.S. firms exporting to and investing in Canada depends on the weight given to a small number of industries with either high tariffs and low exports or low tariffs and high exports. See Horst (1975) and Orr (1975).

22. This model was developed by Eastman and Stykolt (1960, 1967) and English (1964). It is discussed more generally in chapter 1.

ents (controlling for the size of the subsidiary) and increases with the size of the subsidiary relative to that of its parent. Output diversity is unrelated to multiplant operation (a predictor of direct investment, as we have indicated); for the U.S. parents there is actually a negative relation between the diversity of their U.S. outputs and the extent to which their primary outputs are produced in multiple U.S. plants. Foreign subsidiaries are more diversified than their Canadian competitors (at least partly a reflection of their larger size), although the secondary activities of Canadian firms tend to be spread out slightly more among industries.[23]

Any comprehensive analysis of Canadian industrial organization must come to terms with the high correlation (0.489) between foreign investment (*FSE*) and seller concentration (*C468*). Both are influenced by a number of common causal factors—economies of multiplant operation, product-differentiation barriers to entry, importance of research and development, transactional advantages of large firms that supply a sufficient explanation for the correlation.[24] However, causal relations can also run either way between the variables. Foreign investment can occur in oligopolistic industries as an imitative and defensive reaction (Knickerbocker, 1973); or foreign investment can increase concentration by elevating barriers to entry. We do not believe that a cross-sectional statistical analysis for a single country can sort out these complex causal links.

Because extensive research has already been done on the determinants of foreign investment (Caves, 1974; Baumann, 1976; Saunders, 1978, chap. 7), we did not undertake an ambitious analysis for this study. We can summarize briefly the determinants that have been isolated in these studies, before indicating the extensions that we attempt. Rates of expenditure on advertising and research and development (often measured from U.S. data) have proved highly significant predictors of foreign investment in Canada, as has the proportion of shipments in the U.S. industry emanating from companies that are multiplant within that industry. With multiplant operations controlled, an indication that industries are regionally fragmented by

23. See Caves (1975, chap. 4) and Statistics Canada (1978, pp. 43–45). Other aspects of diversification and foreign investment are discussed in chapter 8.

24. Rosenbluth (1970, pp. 19, 28) shows that the correlation between foreign investment and concentration can be accounted for by the size of foreign-controlled companies; he also concludes that over the period 1954–1964 there was no association between changes in concentration and changes in subsidiaries' share. An extensive analysis of the relations among concentration, corporate size, and foreign ownership appears in Statistics Canada (1978, chaps. 3, 4).

high transportation costs becomes a significant negative predictor of foreign investment. Consistent with Pugel's (1978, chap. 4) findings on U.S. investment abroad, Saunders (1978, chap. 7) found foreign investment in Canada to be related to managerial personnel as a proportion of total personnel in the U.S. industry—Servan-Schreiber's hypotheses about the superiority of American managerial talent. Caves (1974) found an independent positive influence for the absolute size of the largest companies in the U.S. industry, but in Saunders' study this variable is highly collinear with multiplant operation and proves insignificant. Other entry-barrier variables (scale economies, capital requirements) have no net influence on the multinationals, consistent with Gorecki's (1976a) finding that they do not significantly deter multinational entrants.

With these results established, we limited our statistical investigation to a few issues, mainly the effect on the equation of employing two-stage least squares and the relation of foreign investment to concentration. The following variables, all taken from previous studies, are simply listed here along with the expected signs of their coefficients.

ADI   Advertising-to-sales ratio, Canada (positive).

EXP   Fraction of output exported by the Canadian industry (positive).

RDIU   Research and development outlays as a percentage of sales, U.S. industry (positive).

EFT   Effective rate of tariff protection, Canada (positive).

PROT   Professional and technical employees as a percentage of total employees, Canada (positive).

RULC   Inverse measure of unit costs of production in Canada relative to United States: relative labor productivity in Canada (adjusted for Canadian tariffs) divided by relative wages in Canada (positive).

TRN   Transportation costs per unit wholesale value (based on U.S. data) (negative).

Table 4.4 presents a regression analysis of these determinants. Equation A is the nadir of our problem of missing observations; only 11 degrees of freedom survive, and so this equation must be ignored. In Equation B all variables are correctly signed, and ADI, EXP, RDIU, PROT, and MPLNT are significant. The use of two-stage least squares in equation C, however, produces a marked turn for the worse, with only MPLNT, PROT, and (weakly) RDIU retaining any of their influence. One can certainly argue that these variables theoretically enjoy better standing as ultimate independent factors than any of the

Table 4.4 Determinants of share of sales accounted for by foreign-controlled enterprises (*FSE*).

Independent variable	Estimation method		
	A	B	C
ADI	1.61	1.97[b]	−2.58
	(0.91)	(1.76)	(−0.99)
EXP	0.151	0.302[c]	−0.088
	(0.37)	(1.58)	(−0.32)
RULC	−0.034	0.008	−0.015
	(−0.73)	(0.67)	(−0.70)
RDIU	0.048[b]	0.041[a]	0.042
	(1.91)	(3.07)	(1.11)
EFT	−0.116	0.162	0.034
	(−0.22)	(1.18)	(0.18)
PROT	0.025[c]	0.007[c]	0.013[c]
	(1.56)	(1.58)	(1.32)
MPLNT	0.009[b]	0.005[a]	0.105[a]
	(2.28)	(3.05)	(3.24)
TRN	0.003	−0.003	−0.004
	(0.61)	(−1.00)	(−0.72)
Constant	−0.132	0.046	−0.000
	(−0.40)	(0.50)	(−0.00)
$\overline{R}^2$	0.564	0.462	–
F	4.07	9.1	2.56
D.f.	11	75	75

Note: Levels of significance (one-tailed test) are a = 1 percent, b = 5 percent, c = 10 percent. The independent variables listed above the horizontal line are endogenous in the model or contain endogenous components.

others, so one must suspect that advertising (measured in Canada, anyhow) and exports are not fundamental causal factors.

Working with the equation in table 4.4 as a base, we first tried adding a composite variable describing the height of entry barriers to the Canadian industry.[25] It has an insignificant positive relation to *FSE*, consistent with the evidence that multinational companies are not strongly deterred by the conventional sources of entry barriers.

We also investigated the interrelation between foreign investment

25. This variable, designated *BARR*, is defined in chapter 9.

and concentration by adding alternatively to the model the four-firm concentration ratio in the United States and Canada. Concentration in the United States might promote foreign investment because of imitative behavior in concentrated but imperfectly collusive industries (Knickerbocker, 1973). The causal relation between *FSE* and concentration in Canada might run either way. When U.S. concentration alone is added to the model, its coefficient is 0.0078 with a *t*-ratio of 6.02; adding the Canadian concentration instead yields a regression coefficient of 0.0055 with a *t*-ratio of 5.73. The relation of *FSE* to concentration in the United States is thus marginally stronger than to that in Canada. Also, when we shift to a quadratic relation, both U.S. concentration and its square are significant, and the squared term takes a negative sign; for the quadratic relation to Canadian concentration, neither term is significant. We read these results as providing weak evidence for Knickerbocker's hypothesis that foreign investment is promoted by high but incomplete collusion in the source-country market; otherwise, the correlation between foreign investment and concentration may rest largely on their common relation to underlying factors such as sources of entry barriers.

Relative Scale and Productivity of Domestic Establishments

We sought to extend this evidence on the multinational company in Canada by analyzing the differences in size and productivity between these enterprises and their domestic-owned competitors. Data are available for years since 1963 on enterprises 50 percent or more foreign controlled and their domestic competitors, classified by principal industry. In addition, since 1969, data on establishments collected in the annual census of manufactures have been subdivided by the ownership of the controlling enterprise, permitting many characteristics of manufacturing establishments to be compared. We investigated two such characteristics—the size (annual shipments) of domestically controlled establishments relative to those under foreign control, and the relative productivity of the domestic establishments (as indicated by the flawed measure of value added per employee). It is not difficult to explain half of the interindustry variance of each measure by variables that seem generally plausible from economic theory and independent empirical evidence. However, the specifications of both equations in the end seemed loose and conjectural enough that we shall present only a brief and informal report.

We know that, in Canadian manufacturing overall, the proportion of establishments under foreign control does not increase with establishment size beyond a fairly low threshold. If this pattern also holds for individual industries, interindustry variation in the relative average size of domestic companies should depend mostly on the relative prevalence of small (and thus domestic) establishments. This conjecture is strongly confirmed by the evidence: the more prevalent the working proprietors in the industry, and the smaller the average size of *all* establishments in the industry, the smaller the relative size of domestic establishments.

With the prevalence of small establishments controlled by these variables, one can attempt to isolate the forces that should favor foreign-controlled establishments—and thereby reduce the relative size or productivity (or both) of the domestically controlled ones. These forces should include indicators of the importance to an industry of the intangible assets that promote the spread of multinational companies, as well as any components of barriers to entry that should confront domestic entrants with greater disadvantages than multinational entrants. Exactly how the forces should affect domestic establishments' relative size and productivity is, however, difficult to predict theoretically, for the following reasons.

1. If an industrial setting confronts domestic establishments with disadvantages too great, they simply fail to appear. And where domestic establishments are viable, they must be able to command at least a normal rate of return (even if they fail to share in rents accruing to the market's multinational tenants). The disadvantages reflected in the size and productivity of actual domestic establishments, then, are only the moderate ones.

2. Entry barriers and special advantages of the multinational enterprise should adversely affect both the size and productivity of domestically controlled establishments. The effects on the two variables are joint, because of the economic processes by which domestic firms seek to minimize the disadvantages that they face. Economic theory does not (with any generality) predict how these adaptation processes should affect relative size and measured productivity.

3. Where domestic establishments are thought to face disadvantages associated with some economy of scale or size, it is not simple to generate predictions about the sign of the relation between the incidence of the entry barrier and the relative size and productivity of the domestic establishments that we actually observe. Does a scale-related entry barrier mean that domestic enterprises are viable only if they are as large and productive as their foreign-subsidiary rivals? Or does it imply that their best option is to hang on as fringe producers, suffering some disadvantage in both size and productivity? Theory is

capable of refining this issue, but the data requirements for testing the resulting prediction are extremely severe.

Because of these problems, we viewed our findings about statistical influences on domestic stablishments' relative size and productivity as strictly tentative. For what they are worth, the data suggest the following conclusions.[26] Statistical proxies for the advantages of multinational enterprises tend to show significant negative relations to both the relative size and productivity of domestic establishments. These proxies include the importance of nonproduction workers in an industry's labor force and its status as a supplier of consumer goods. Capital-cost entry barriers seem to have a significant negative influence on relative size. Finally, we sought to identify variables that might signify relative advantages of domestic firms against their foreign rivals—the regionality of an industry's markets and the variability of its sales. Relative productivity is positively related to these variables, as expected, but the coefficients are not significant. The only such variable indicating a significant advantage (or a minimum disadvantage) of domestic establishments is that suggesting the ease with which they opt for technologies that are less capital intensive than their foreign competitors'.[27]

4.4 Summary

The shares held by imports in domestic disappearance and exports in production are both made endogenous variables in our model, because they can be influenced by market conduct and because an industry's trade position is determined by some of the same underlying variables that determine its market structure. Imports' share of domestic disappearance is increased when scale economies (measured from U.S. data)

26. In the case of relative size, these conclusions are reached with small establishments' access to the industry held constant. This control was provided by measures of the prevalence of working proprietors, or simply the average size of all establishments in the industry, as we have mentioned. To analyze the relative value added per worker of domestically controlled establishments, we had to take account of any difference in capital intensity. This could not be measured directly independently, so we instead used the difference between the ratio of payroll to value added in the Canadian industry and in its U.S. counterpart. Our hypothesis is that this difference varies among industries with the elasticity of substitution between (nonhuman) capital and labor; hence if the Canadian industry as a whole is labor intensive relative to its U.S. counterpart, room exists for domestic establishments to be labor intensive relative to their foreign-subsidiary competitors. This variable wields a statistically significant influence on domestic establishments' relative value added per worker.

27. See footnote 26 for the construction of this variable.

are substantial and when research and development is important. They are reduced when the goods are heavily advertised—a status that promotes direct investment by foreign suppliers rather than exports. We found some evidence that imports are reduced by tariffs and transport costs, but none to associate them with features of the industry's input requirements indicated by the neoclassical theory of comparative advantage in international trade. Some theoretical considerations predict that imports will be higher in concentrated industries, but we found no relation after allowing for the fact that import competition leaves less room for Canadian sellers (making them appear more concentrated). The share of Canadian output exported is increased strongly by a group of collinear variables—size of plant, seller concentration, and extent of foreign ownership. Our efforts to disentangle their influences suggest that plant size and foreign investment are more important than seller concentration. The direction of causality between exports and plant sizes is not entirely clear. We also found that Canada exports goods requiring large inputs of raw materials, having light requirements for professional and technical manpower, and serving producers rather than consumers.

So far, our conclusions about import and export shares give little support to traditional views about the bases of Canada's comparative advantage, but these views are affirmed in the analysis of a different dependent variable—net exports divided by total trade. Net exports are high for capital-intensive industries, raw-material processors, makers of producer goods, and industries whose processes require little professional and technical manpower. Somewhat surprisingly, net exports are positively related to an industry's research intensity.

Previous studies of foreign direct investment have found its prevalence to be related to many features of a country's industrial organization and international trade, and accordingly it appears prominently as both cause and effect in our model. Foreign direct investment has been found to occur in industries whose firms possess intangible assets readily usable in foreign markets—assets created or indicated by advertising and research and development outlays. Multinational companies also enter the Canadian market to pursue economies of multiplant operation. They are attracted—or at least not much repelled—by entry barriers that exclude less well endowed firms. And because a company sees foreign investment as a substitute for exporting and licensing proprietary intangibles as ways to serve a foreign market, subsidiaries should be encouraged by factors such as tariffs that restrict these substitutes.

Our replication of previous tests supports both the intangible-assets and multiplant-economies explanations for foreign direct investment; it also finds that multinational companies are undeterred by entry barriers. We made a tentative investigation of the relation between foreign investment and seller concentration—a tricky business, because the causation could run both ways, and both variables are surely influenced by the same underlying forces. Some insight is gained by relating foreign subsidiaries' shares of Canadian industries' sales to seller concentration alternatively in the Canadian industry and in its U.S. counterpart. Both relations are statistically significant, but that between subsidiaries' shares and U.S. concentration is somewhat stronger. Furthermore, the relation to U.S. concentration is significant in a quadratic form, consistent with Knickerbocker's (1973) hypothesis that foreign investment is increased by imitative behavior in moderately concentrated oligopolistic industries.

The relation between entry barriers and foreign investment can be further developed by examining what determines differences from industry to industry in the size and productivity of domestically controlled plants relative to those under foreign control. Our exploratory effort, not reported in detail, suggests that market shares held by multinationals are negatively related to both the relative size and the relative productivity of establishments under domestic control. Relative size and productivity are also negatively related to variables that indicate the sources of the multinationals' advantages, and relative size is adversely affected by capital-cost entry barriers. The only offsetting advantage for domestic producers that proved a significant contributor to their productivity is an indicator of their ability to substitute labor readily for capital.

Overall, our findings on multinational companies support and extend a confluence of analysis drawn from many research studies. Broadly speaking, this consensus declares that production facilities are distributed among countries in ways that depend on comparative-advantage factors and the international mobility of factors of production—matters that are the central concern of international economics. Ownership of those productive facilities is consolidated among business units—multiplant and multinational companies—in ways that reflect the advantages (sometimes social, sometimes only private) of substituting administrative control for coordination of economic activity through the marketplace. In Canada the relative prevalence, relative size, and relative productivity of foreign-controlled establishments all reflect interindustry differences in these advantages. Where the advantages are potent (heavy advertising and research and development, heavy use of sophisticated managerial personnel and nonproduction workers generally) domestic-controlled establishments shrink to a competitive fringe. Conversely, the multinational presence shrinks where these assets are unimportant or where being small, local, and flexible affords a positive advantage. The multinational presence transmits effects of competitive conditions in the United States (we confirm Knickerbocker's hypothesis that imitative multinational expansion is encouraged by moderately concentrated oligopoly in the U.S. market) and may adversely affect the state of entry barriers and barriers to intraindustry mobility in Canada.

5 Comparative Structure of Retailing

The retail structure of an economy is the conduit between manufacturers of consumer goods and the ultimate buyer, and retailers are involved in transactions affecting a substantial proportion of a country's national income. In many studies of industrial organization, however, the retail stage has all but been ignored. Retailing is often pictured as a collection of small powerless enterprises beset with the infirmities of small business generally. In most countries there has been considerable resistance to the substitution of large retail organizations for small local retailers, often spearheaded by the politically powerful small retailers themselves.[1] Public policy measures have sought to preserve small business in retailing for its own sake and have not considered how the organization of the distributive sector affects the overall efficiency of the economy, especially the performance of manufacturing.

This picture of retailing is increasingly inadequate. The chain retail store has risen as the retailing sector's answer to the large manufacturing firm. Chain development has occurred in varying degrees in nearly all classes of retail stores, providing the retailing sector with some monopsony power against manufacturers in the national market. In addition, the retailer's strategic position between the manufacturer and the consumer yields the retailer substantial bargaining power through his influence on the consumer's decision to purchase certain types of consumer products. This bargaining power can shape the way that manufacturers distribute and market their products and can provide a check against manufacturers even without the exercise of con-

1. Palamountain (1958), Catena and Hess (1975, pp. 520–522).

ventional monopsony power. Thus the retail stage is of central interest insofar as it contains large enterprises and insofar as it has the power to influence significantly conduct and performance in the manufacturing sector.

This chapter examines the structure of the retailing system in a small open economy—using Canada as an example—with special emphasis on its comparison with a large economy like that of the United States. Two central questions are examined. First, how has the development of the large retail firm in the small, open economy compared with that in the United States, and how can we explain this development? This question involves both an examination of the aggregate concentration of the retail sector as a whole and the penetration of the large, chain retailers in individual classes of retail outlets. Second, how does the size of the retail establishment (or individual location) in a small, open economy compare with that of its counterpart in the United States, and what explains any differences? To provide this explanation and to make assessments of policy, it is necessary to present a theoretical framework for explaining retail structure. While our data do not permit complete statistical tests of our hypotheses, they provide a strong indication of the causes of basic differences in the retail structures of two economies.

The data base used for this chapter could not be integrated into our structural model of industrial organization in the manufacturing sector. However, the questions we investigate here are of great importance for specifying that system, since the structure of retailing can influence manufacturer behavior and performance. The analysis in this chapter has special significance for our study of advertising behavior, described in chapter 6, research and development (chapter 7), and profitability (chapter 9).

5.1 The Sources of Retailers' Market Power

A recent study by Porter presents a comprehensive theory of the sources of market power in the retailing sector.[2] Retailers' power derives from two basic sources, the structure of the retail system for a given product and the ability of the retailer to influence the buyer's choice among brands of consumer goods. The structure of the retail sector consists of the number and the size distribution of retail firms for a given product and the breadth of the retailers' product lines. As the retail distribution system for a product becomes more concentrated, the market power of the retail stage increases (other things

2. See Porter (1976b) for a more comprehensive discussion.

being equal). Market power at the retail stage leads to increased retail profits, extracted both from consumers and from the manufacturers who supply the retailers' product. The relevant concept of concentration differs between retailers and manufacturers, however. Concentration of sales of a given manufacturing industry's output in the largest retail firms is one important dimension of retail concentration. However, since most products are sold through many classes of retail outlets (cigarettes are sold through supermarkets, drug stores, and tobacco shops), the significance of concentration in the dominant retail outlet class for a product is modified by the presence of alternative retail channels for the product. In addition, since the retail market for a product is never national and usually local, the concentration of a product's retailers in the relevant retail market as well as in the national market is important. The breadth of a retailer's product line partly protects him against the manufacturer's threats to withhold a product and thus improves the retailer's bargaining position as well.

The presence of the large chain retail firm increases market power in the retail stage for a number of these reasons. Increased penetration by chain stores in a given retail outlet class raises concentration in that class and thereby increases its power vis-à-vis the industries that manufacture products it sells. If chain stores have broader product lines than independent retailers and/or if their presence reduces the number of alternative channels of distribution available to the manufacturer, this increases retailers' power against their supplying manufacturers. Finally, if the individual establishments of chain retailers are larger than those of independents, concentration in the local retail market may increase as well.

The retailers' power over product differentiation is derived from the information-gathering process that consumers go through in choosing among competing brands of products. If information were costless and subject to no uncertainty, the consumer would consider all product attributes in his purchase decision among brands of a product and would employ the full range of sources of information available about all the attributes. Because gathering information is costly, however, the consumer's buying behavior depends on the balance between his perceived benefits and the costs of additional product information. It costs more to gain information about some attributes (reliability) than it does about others (brand image). This trade-off, in general, varies among products, with the result that the weights assigned to attributes on which choice is based vary.

The retailer influences the consumer's purchase decision in two major and interacting ways. First, the retailer controls or embodies some of the attributes that the consumer may desire in the product. The store's reputation and image may reflect on the quality and image of the product. The physical amenity of the store as well as the quantity and quality of attendant services provided by the retailer (credit, billing, delivery, warranty, repair) are attributes of the product as relevant to a consumer's choice as are price, packaging, and advertised image. Second, as an important provider of information, the retailer can influence the sale of products. The salesperson in the store may influence the brand of product that the consumer buys. This influence is wielded through information contained in his selling presentation and personal recommendation, in the perceived expertise of the salesperson with respect to the product, and through other means. The retailer directly or indirectly conveys information about the product's reliability, features, and method of use that is difficult to obtain from other sources.

The importance of the retailer's selling efforts and his control of product attributes depends on the consumer's process of choice. The consumer rationally expends varying amounts of effort (cost) in selecting different products and considers varying sets of attributes. The retailer's influence in the purchase decision increases with (1) the importance of product attributes controlled by the retailer, (2) the perceived benefits of the range of product information disseminated by the retailer relative to the availability and cost of information from other sources, and (3) how large an investment in information the consumer chooses to make. If the amount of effort the consumer is willing to expend on selection is relatively large, he tends to shop in several retail outlets in order to compare brands and to solicit product information from the retailer. Here the retailing sector is influential in product differentiation.

Because consumer behavior varies from product to product, we need a way of identifying and measuring the economically relevant differences. Our discussion suggests that *the characteristics of the retail channels for a product reflect the relevant characteristics of consumer demand for that product.* Although the economically significant differences in buyers (and retailers) might be numerous, a principal dichotomy emerges between two types of retail outlets: convenience and nonconvenience outlets. *Convenience outlets* are retail stores in which little or no sales assistance (information transfer) in the form of interaction with a salesperson is provided with the sale, and the locational density of outlets is high. *Nonconvenience outlets* are retail stores in which sales assistance (information transfer) is provided with the sale, and outlets are selectively rather than densely located. Examples of convenience outlets are supermarkets, gasoline stations, and liquor stores. Examples of nonconvenience outlets are furniture stores, appliance stores, and automobile dealers.[3]

Products Sold through Convenience Outlets

The convenience outlet provides little or no information with sale and is located close to the buyer. For products sold through convenience outlets (convenience goods), low unit price and frequent purchase of the product reduce the motive of the consumer to expend effort on search.[4] As signaled by the characteristics of the outlet, the consumer demands a nearby retail outlet, is unwilling to shop around, and desires no sales help. Thus the consumer considers the purchase relatively unimportant and is willing to rely on inexpensive sources of information, such as advertising, in making his purchase. Relatively costly information sources such as sales assistance by the retailer and direct shopping and comparison are not used by the buyer.

In view of these buying characteristics, the manufacturer's prime strategy for differentiating his product is to develop a strong brand image through advertising. If the manufacturer can develop a brand image that encourages repeat purchases by consumers, the retailer has very little power. The retailer has little ability to influence the brand chosen by the consumer in the store, and a strong manufacturer's brand image creates consumer demand for the product which assures profits to the retailer from stocking the product and at the same time denies him the credible threat of not stocking the manufacturer's goods.

In view of the consumer's buying behavior, convenience outlets are densely located to be in close proximity to the consumer.

Products Sold through Nonconvenience Outlets

The purchase of a nonconvenience good is usually a relatively large outlay, postponable, and infrequent. The buyer views it as important

3. These two prototypes of retail outlets are an abstraction for the numerous types of retail outlets that occur in practice. See Porter (1976b, chap. 2) for a discussion of the differences in outlets within these broad categories.

4. Buying by the consumer in the home is the ultimate in convenience buying and may become feasible with new electronic technology. Mail order is a form of convenience buying, but mail order can arise either because the consumer desires convenience and low price or because the product assortment he seeks is unavailable in conventional retail outlets. Thus mail order retailing is a special case, and we do not consider it in this study.

and expends effort in comparing the alternative goods available. The buyer's intentions and plans to purchase are more likely made in advance of purchase. Although advertising and product-differentiating activities of the manufacturer can induce the consumer to consider a particular brand or to visit a store that carries it, the consumer's buying decision involves more: critical adjuncts to the information the consumer has from experience or media sources are physical demonstration and inspection of the product, the advice and counsel of the salesperson, and the reputation and attendant services provided by the retail outlet. Thus the nonconvenience retailer has substantial power to influence the buyer's choice among brands of the product.

The essential notion in product-differentiation strategies for nonconvenience goods is the necessity of sales promotion for both manufacturer and retailer. Even if the manufacturer advertises heavily, the policies of his retailers are critical to his success. The manufacturer must also direct his efforts toward convincing the retailer to stock and promote his product. For nonconvenience goods selective rather than intensive retail coverage of the market becomes important. The consumer is willing to travel to seek out alternatives, and hence the manufacturer needs to have a few well-chosen outlets rather than a large number of outlets.

The small size of the local retail market, constrained by the buyer's need to travel to the store, provides barriers to entry into retailing by implying that a local retail market can support only a few outlets. Thus the potential entry of new firms does not remove the bargaining power of nonconvenience retailers vis-à-vis manufacturers (Porter, 1976b, chap. 2).

Thus our analysis illustrates that substantial power accrues to the retailer from his ability to influence the differentiation of consumer goods, but this power differs markedly between convenience and nonconvenience goods. The two types of retail outlet classes also differ in a number of other dimensions, including the amount of personal service provided, locational density of outlets, and so on.

5.2 The Incidence of Chain Stores within and across Countries

Chain stores give rise to power in the retail sector, yet even casual observation suggests that the penetration of chain stores varies in two important dimensions. First, the penetration of chain stores varies markedly across retail outlet classes in a given country, and Canada is no exception. Second, the degree and pattern of chain-store penetration vary among different countries. As preparation for empirically examining the differences in the structure of retailing between a small, open economy such as Canada's and the economy of the United States, we must examine the theoretical reasons for expecting chain-store penetration to differ along these two dimensions. The factors that explain differences in chain penetration among outlet classes turn out to be closely related to those explaining international differences.

Chain Penetration among Classes of Retail Outlets

Since the size of an individual retail market is constrained by consumers' need to travel to the retail outlet (except for mail order), there are tight limits on the size of the individual retail establishment.[5] Retail firms become large only when a large number of retail establishments are grouped within a single administrative unit. There are generally two important consequences of such a grouping—the centralization of certain administrative functions at the firm rather than the establishment level and often vertical integration into the wholesaling function. The analysis of the incidence of chain retail firms is thus a problem in the theory of the scope of the firm and the relative efficiency of transactions via market mechanisms and administrative mechanisms. The extent of penetration of chain stores in a given retail outlet class depends on the balance between the pecuniary and the nonpecuniary economies of scale due to large firm size and the information, coordination, and transaction costs of administrative (versus market) operation.

This trade-off leads to conceptually separate conditions that give rise to chain stores, whose collective strength determines both the degree of chain penetration in a given retail outlet class and those retail classes in which chain penetration occurs first in an evolutionary sense.[6] Any one of these factors can lead to chains, although the factors often occur together.

Economies of mass physical distribution (vertical integration into

5. Our discussion focuses primarily on chain retailers in which individual units are linked by ownership. Another class of chains exists, called voluntary chains, which represent voluntary confederations of retailers to form buying groups or to yield other benefits. Our theory identifies situations in which the incentives to form voluntary associations are great by examining the motivations for chains generally. The analysis of the likely incidence of voluntary chains would combine an analysis of the contractual problems of voluntary association with the benefits of chains. We do not treat this problem here, and our data do not allow the testing of hypotheses about voluntary chains.

6. See Holton (1962), and Porter (1976b), for a discussion of some of these conditions.

wholesaling). By carrying out its own warehousing and distribution, the chain store can achieve economies of physical distribution unavailable to individual retail outlets. The chain's warehouses receive goods from manufacturers in higher volumes than the independent outlet's, and the chain is able to economize by shipping full loads of mixed merchandise from its warehouse to its individual locations. Even if the wholesaling sector is perfectly competitive, independent wholesalers may not be able to carry product lines corresponding exactly to that of a particular retailer and may not perform as efficiently as the manufacturer himself. In addition, the independent wholesaler may not be able to align the location of his warehouses and logistics system to the outlet configuration of a particular retail chain, making him a potentially inferior substitute for the retail chain's own warehouse and logistics system.[7] Contractual difficulties explain the unwillingness of a wholesaler to specialize in serving only one particular retail firm.[8]

Economies in centralized distribution by chains may be substantial in a retail outlet class that handles a large volume of standardized goods that are in widespread and standardized demand across geographic areas. High unit sales volumes of individual products and for individual stores reinforce the chain's advantage. Finally, centralized distribution by the chain gains in efficiency where goods have short life cycles due to fashion and lack established brand names, because the independent wholesaler who invests in sufficient inventories to achieve distributional efficiency runs too great a risk of their economic obsolescence. The chain retailer, with more knowledge of market conditions and of the salability of various types of merchandise, can invest more in inventory and distribute goods to his individual stores more efficiently at no greater risk.

Conversely, significant economies in vertically integrated distribution are probably lacking where low unit sales of individual products limit the volume shipped through chain warehouses, where a narrow retail line of goods is more efficiently distributed to retailers either directly by manufacturers or through independent wholesalers who can consolidate the flows of goods to a variety of retailers, or where market shares are low and a wholesaler can also potentially achieve

7. If a retailer's market share is modest in a particular area, an independent wholesaler may be able to distribute more efficiently. Also, if assortments of goods do not differ much from retailer to retailer, then once again the independent wholesaler becomes a feasible alternative. Thus the achievement of chain-store economies depends on these factors.

8. For analysis of such contractual problems see Williamson (1975).

advantages by consolidating. In addition, chain-store economies are limited where each geographic area requires a different assortment of goods. Differing assortments elevate the costs of coordination, information, and transaction within the mass distributor's administrative unit.

Nonlogistical economies of scale. Quite apart from economies in centralized wholesaling, the chain store may gain efficiencies by standardizing store design and operating procedures and by centralizing functions such as training, credit, merchandising, marketing, and top management. Standardization facilitates administrative control and consolidated personnel management and training, and it may lead to economies in planning and constructing new outlets. Centralization of functions can lead to economies by increasing the specialization of labor (for example, specialists in credit or advertising) as well as simply by spreading fixed costs. Potential economies of both standardization and centralization may be much greater for chain retailers than for multiunit manufacturers, since the large chain retailers encompass a very large number of individual outlets.

The available economies of centralization are closely limited by the possibilities for standardization. In retail outlet classes where individual locations (establishments) can be standardized across geographic areas, benefits from centralized training, credit, marketing, and so on are most pronounced. However, if outlets cannot be standarized because of differences in local market conditions, the cost of information and coordination reduces the efficiency of chain retailers relative to that of independent local stores.[9] Differences in local conditions also offset economies in centralization of these functions and reduce the efficiency of centralized training and management development. Thus chain penetration tends to be relatively less in retail outlet classes where local variations in taste or consumer buying behavior are great, such as in fashion-oriented goods. These variations are reflected in differences in the assortment of goods demanded, their styles and varieties, and the services expected of the retailer.

Low levels of personal service. The chain store gains efficiencies through standardization and routinization. Where personal service in selling is important in the retail outlet class, the opportunities for such efficiencies are reduced. There are few, if any, economies of scale in providing personal service, and if personal service is an important component of the retailer's services, it generally accounts for a sub-

9. Increasing sophistication of computer-based management-information and inventory-control systems is overcoming some of these difficulties.

stantial portion of the retailer's operating costs. Hence the economies gained by the chain retailer due to the efficiencies that we have discussed are reduced in relative importance. In addition, though there are exceptions, the importance of personal service in the retail outlet class is usually associated with the need to attune other nonlogistical functions such as marketing carefully to each store location. The scope for chain store economies in such retail outlet classes is further reduced.

Centralized control of pricing. Since competing retailers often sell identical products, pricing becomes a central aspect of marketing strategy for the retailer. While local market conditions vary and usually require some local responsibility for pricing, the efficiencies of chain-store operations are maximized where control over pricing can be centralized to optimize utilization of inventory, take advantage of buying conditions for merchandise, and so on. The ability to control pricing also facilitates the central administration of a multiunit system. Centralized control of pricing is facilitated by a stable assortment of goods, lack of demand fluctuations, and homogeneity of market conditions across individual selling locations.

Economies in purchasing. Following directly from our discussion of the sources of retailer power, chain retailing is promoted by the potential for achieving both pecuniary (quantity discounts) and nonpecuniary (monopsonistic) economies in purchasing through increasing size of the retail firm. The achievement of economies in purchasing is likely to be most significant for the retail outlet class that distributes a large proportion of the outputs of the manufacturing industries from which its goods are purchased. The chain store may also gain substantial economies in purchasing inputs other than the goods it resells, including capital, supplies, services such as computers and security, management talent, and so on.

The conditions supporting the development of chains are based largely on real economies of multiunit operation. Thus the market and buying power that chains acquire must be weighed against their social benefits. The conditions supporting the development of chains in a given economy are also closely related to the economy's logistics system, level of managerial sophistication, communication network, and so on.

Our two types of retail outlets—convenience and nonconvenience outlets—display the conditions facilitating chain stores in very different degrees. The power of convenience outlets to influence differentiation is low, and the personal service provided to the buyer is correspondingly minimal. Both conditions support the development of chains. Convenience outlets also have much to gain by achieving structural bargaining power due to size. They enjoy less power to influence the consumer's purchase decision than nonconvenience outlets. Their low component of personal service, coupled with the high unit volumes and broad product lines that reflect the convenience-motivated purchasing by the consumer, may enlarge the economies of centralized distribution. The small influence of convenience retailers on product differentiation and the associated presence of heavily advertised national brands also means that the design, operation, and product assortment of convenience outlets can generally be standardized across geographic areas, increasing the likelihood of nonlogistical economies of scale. The high locational density of convenience outlets enhances this potential, since the chain convenience retailer may have many locations even in a given geographic area.

Nonconvenience outlets present quite a different situation, however. Their key characteristic is a high degree of personal service, which limits the significance of multiunit distribution economies and tends to work against economies of standardization and routinization. We should expect to see chain stores confined to those nonconvenience outlet classes where the assortment of goods is broad (department stores), where unit sales volumes in individual products are high (shoe stores), and where personal selling is the least important. The efficiencies of chains are the greatest in these types of retail outlets. On the whole, chains should be less developed in nonconvenience goods than in convenience goods. Thus while the ability to influence product differentiation yields greater market power in nonconvenience goods, structural market power due to chain retailers should be generally less for these goods.

Chain Store Penetration and the Size of Chains

The conditions just described reflect a balance of the economies of large size in the retail firm with the need for local information and the coordination and transactions costs of operating multiple units. In addition to predicting the penetration of chains generally, these conditions also carry some implications for the size of retail chains and their geographic configuration.

A retail chain can consist of anything from two to thousands of individual stores and as many geographic locations. The economies of distribution and centralization are likely to increase monotonically with the number of locations that the retail firm operates, other things being equal, and so are economies in purchasing. Offsetting the growth of chains are the requirement for personal service and the diversity of consumer tastes and buying characteristics among locations. Although there are probably few economies or diseconomies in offering personal service as a function of the number of locations, the retail chain can minimize diversity by operating locations only in a relatively narrow geographic area or in areas carefully selected for homogeneity of their customer base though they may not be geographically contiguous. Although very large chains are generally not efficient in retail classes whose customers have highly diverse needs, small and medium-sized chains (in terms of number of units) may flourish if other conditions support their presence. Related to this, we may see chains with many units but divisionalized into subgroups, with each subgroup maintaining a separate name and some differences in operating philosophy. Without customer diversity, the economies of large, multilocation chains lead to their dominance over small and medium ones. Thus both the chains' overall share of sales and their size distribution reflect the balance of forces promoting and deterring the multiple-location retail firm.

The penetration of chains in department stores and clothing stores in the United States confirms these propositions. In both lines, especially department stores, chain stores hold significant shares. But because of the extreme importance of style and local tastes in these retail classes, department-store chains tend to be composed of fewer units than supermarket and drug chains. Chains in segments of the department-store industry catering to the broad middle- and lower-income market, such as Sears and Montgomery Ward, have a large number of locations, while firms emphasizing style and fashion and catering to the upper-income markets generally have fewer individual locations. Chains of discount department stores, selling nationally branded goods to a broad market based on price and deemphasizing style, also have more units than do the high-quality department-store chains. Many of the high-quality chains consist solely of a main downtown store with suburban branches, or locations only in selected cities or in areas of cities sharing common demographic characteristics, thereby minimizing diversity of consumer behavior and product lines and facilitating the achievement of the benefit of chains. To achieve further economies of chains while maintaining an ability to cope with diversity, some firms such as Federated Department Stores and Jewel have acquired a number of different small department stores and operate them under a corporate umbrella.

International Differences in Chain-Store Penetration

These conditions determine how the chain stores' share of sales and the size and geographic configuration of the chains vary among retail outlet classes in any country. Between countries, both the mean level of chain-store penetration and the distribution of individual retail classes around the mean are affected by underlying demographic, social, technological, and managerial factors that influence the degree to which the economies of chain stores can be realized and determine the size of coordination and transactions costs working against the development of chain stores. The key cross-country differences can be divided into four major categories:[10] consumer buying behavior, population location patterns, the nature of the logistical and communication system, and managerial techniques. In general, what might broadly be termed industrialization is favorable to chain-store penetration, though some demographic and geographic conditions seem to act as constants in determining the underlying potential for chain stores in every country.

Buyer behavior may vary markedly across countries along a number of dimensions important to the development of chain stores. The requirement for personal service varies depending on the expertise of the local consumer, the perceived value of the consumer's time spent shopping, the availability and accessibility of other sources of product information, and the consumer's risk aversion in making decisions to purchase. These traits reflect income levels, education levels, and other socioeconomic factors. They also reflect the degree of development of communications, particularly the advertising media, which provide an alternative or supplementary source of product information. The consumer's mobility and therefore confinement to a given geographic area for purchasing also vary. Chains do not flourish in countries where buyers are not mobile, have low income levels, shop frequently for small quantities, assign a low or negative cost to time spent shopping, and either do not have or cannot understand advertising. The buyer in such situations is risk averse, demands personal service, engages in extensive comparison among stores, and has a strong local orientation in purchasing, preferring the local merchant to the impersonal chain store. These same conditions imply that the importance of strong

10. Other country-specific noneconomic factors such as political philosophy and legal restrictions may also significantly affect chain-store penetration. Chain stores very often can be a politically sensitive issue, since they usually displace large numbers of small individual proprietors. Our theoretical discussion does not treat these factors, since they are idiosyncratic to the individual country. See footnote 1.

national brands, which promote the development of chain stores, may be less. A less developed country such as Nigeria provides a polarized example of these tendencies. There the retail sector is composed of a vast number of small merchants operating in stalls in local markets and a few chains catering to foreigners and wealthy Nigerians.[11]

Buyers' tastes and buying characteristics are more diverse in some countries than others. Some countries' households share common languages and backgrounds, while in other countries buying groups differ widely along cultural dimensions. The variance of income levels, education levels, mobility levels, and so forth, also differs among countries. The more diverse the population of buyers along all these dimensions, the less likely is chain store penetration.

Population density patterns, and hence store location patterns, affect the potential for economies in physical distribution as well as in standardization. High density of stores, reflecting dense population, allows the chain retailer to distribute goods cheaply to clusters of contiguous stores. The more numerous the stores in any given broad geographic area, the greater is the possibility that selling, marketing, and so on, can be standardized. If population is widely dispersed and stores of a given type are few and far between, distributing goods to stores through a chain organization may be no cheaper than the costs of serving them through independent wholesalers or by the manufacturer directly.

The potential for *logistical and communication efficiencies* relates to the state of transportation and distribution systems in a country. Logistical efficiencies are maximized by large transportation vehicles, well-developed highway and other transportation systems, and sophisticated refrigeration and storage techniques. Facilities for high-speed communication are also important for effective operation of a chain store. To the extent that a country lacks fully developed transportation and communication facilities, the potential economies of chain stores are reduced. The size of a country in national product terms affects the economies in distribution appropriable by chains. The chain store incurs a fixed cost in establishing the facilities to distribute goods internally throughout its system of locations, while distribution by manufacturers or wholesalers is a variable cost to the retailer. If the small size of the market means small sales in individual retail markets, the lack of physical volumes necessary to overcome these fixed costs may work against chain development.

11. See Baker (1965) and Munn (1966).

Finally, achieving the efficiencies of multiunit operation requires substantial *managerial sophistication* in areas such as inventory control, pricing, purchasing, and managing a logistics organization, all on a large scale. The ability to use electronic data processing and communication systems facilitates chain store economies. Because the state of managerial practice varies among countries in these areas, the potential for chain stores also varies.

We can explore these issues further by examining the likely differences between Canada and the United States. Canada differs from the United States in a number of these dimensions, though it differs far less than most other countries.[12] Table 5.1 compares a number of characteristics of the United States and Canada for the period under investigation. Canada has somewhat lower disposable income per capita and per household and lower levels of average education, both tending to lower the perceived cost of time spent shopping. Ownership of two or more automobiles per household is less common in Canada, and the percentage of females in the labor force is lower. These traits imply more time spent shopping and a more local orientation in shopping. Taken together, these buyer characteristics suggest that chain penetration will be lower in Canada.

In addition to differences in average buying characteristics, there is substantial evidence that buyer tastes are more diverse in Canada than in the United States. Numerous commentators point to fundamental language and cultural differences among Canadian regions, exacerbated by their geographic separation. Even within regions in Canada buyers may be more diverse, some authors argue, because ethnic groups are less assimilated.[13] Within Quebec, for example, there are strong language and cultural differences. Buyer diversity also suggests lower chain penetration in Canada, particularly of chains that operate in more than one region.

Canada's population is more geographically dispersed and dwells proportionately more in rural areas and less in urban areas with a population of 50,000 or over. This greater population dispersion re-

12. Differences in regulation of competition between the United States and Canada seem likely to worsen the relative benefits of chains in the United States. Antitrust restraints on concentration are more stringent in the United States, and the Robinson-Patman Act impedes the recognition of some chain-store economies. Thus the differences in chain-store penetration predicted by the theory in this section are probably not due to regulatory differences between the two countries.

13. See Mallen (1971), Thompson and Leighton (1973, p. 143), and M. S. Moyer, "Evolving Marketing Channels in Canada," in Thompson and Leighton (1973).

Table 5.1 Buyer and market profiles in the United States and Canada.

Characteristics	Canada	United States
Demographic		
Population, Canada as percentage of United States (1970)	10.4	100.0
Ten-year rate of population growth (1960–1970)	18.0	14.3
Percentage farm population (1966)	9.6	5.9
Percentage standard metropolitan area (50,000 population and over, 1970)	61.5	73.5
Percentage under 15 years (Canada 1969), under 16 years (United States 1969)	31.0	31.0
Persons per household (1970	3.7	3.2
Percentage single marital status (Canada over 14 years, United States over 13 years)	28.0	24.0
Percentage Roman Catholic (1960 United States, 1961 Canada)	45.7	26.0
Percentage labor force (male), completed 4 years high school only	8.7	24.6
Percentage labor force (male), completed university	5.6	11.1
Economic		
Effective buying power (1969)		
Per capita (personal disposable income	$2,481	$ 3,308
Per household (personal disposable income)	9,895	10,565
Median income of individuals completed 1–3 years high school (1960)	4,233	4,936
Median income of university graduate (1960)	7,956	7,693
1971 GNP (in billions of dollars)	94.4	1,061
Average annual percentage increase in Real GNP (1960–1967)	5.5	4.7
1971 over 1970 gross national product (estimate), %	6.7	7.0
1969 over 1965 disposable income, %	44.0	33.0
Households with 2 or more cars (1969), %	16.0	29.0
Consumption		
1969 per capita personal expenditures	$2,216	$ 2,834
Durable goods	520	441
Nondurable goods	854	1,200
Services	842	1,194
Percentage female population in the labor force (1962)	19.5	25.9
Number of radio sets in use (per 1,000 population, 1962)	504	1,006
Number of television sets in use (per 1,000 population, 1962)	235	322

Source: Mallen, 1971.

Note: The time periods of the data are chosen to be consistent with that of our empirical tests. Dollar amounts are in the currency of the country in question.

duces the potential logistical economies of chain stores in Canada relative to the United States. The smaller size of the Canadian economy and the fewer urban centers with concentrated volumes of retail sales further reduce the relative potential of chain stores. In addition, Canada's population is distributed along a long linear east-west band, so that the number of alternative transportation routes to major urban areas is less than in the United States.[14] The smaller number of alternative routes increases the risk of the disruption of transportation (due to weather and other reasons) and reduces the logistic flexibility in Canadian distribution arrangements, thus impeding the logistical efficiencies of chains versus a network of independent wholesalers.

While we expect the penetration of chain stores to be generally lower in Canada, the concentration of retail sales of the leading chains in a retail outlet class may be higher than it is in the United States for essentially the same reasons that we expect concentration in manufacturing to be greater in Canada. If economies of scale are present in chain-store operations, and proportionally no less in Canada, then the smaller absolute size of Canada's retail markets should lead to higher national retail concentration. Thus in retail outlet classes where chain-store economies are present, the top few chains should have a greater proportion of sales than in the United States, but independents should hold a larger share of retail sales relative to chains overall. The limits on chain economies are most severe in Canada's sparsely populated extreme eastern and western reaches, least severe though not absent within the provinces of Ontario and Quebec. Thus smaller intraprovincial chains may develop in many retail outlet classes, though the percentage of total retail sales that all chains command in the outlet class nationally should be less than in the United States.

A number of differences point to greater chain penetration in the United States than in Canada, but some of these differences between the two countries have been narrowing steadily over the last two decades.[15] For example, as table 5.1 shows, disposable income increased faster in Canada than in the United States between 1965 and 1969. Thus, while we should expect chain-store penetration in Canada to be generally less than that in the United States, we should also expect the differential to be narrowing in some areas.

14. J. D. Forbes, "Some Managerial Implications of Canada's Unique Distribution System," in Thompson and Leighton (1973, pp. 150–151).
15. Moyer, in Thompson and Leighton (1973, p. 198).

5.3   Chain-Store Penetration in Canada and the United States

To examine the incidence of chain stores in the Canadian economy and the comparative penetration of chain stores in Canada and the United States, we assembled data on the sales of chain stores as a percentage of total sales in a matched sample of Canadian and U.S. retail outlet classes. Data on Canadian chain-store penetration was compiled from the Canadian Census and the Dominion Bureau of Statistics, *Retail Trade: Revisions to Postcensal Estimates*; data on U.S. chain-store penetration was taken from the U.S. Bureau of the Census, *Census of Business*. While data on chain-store penetration in the United States is quite complete, Canadian data on multiunit development in retailing disaggregate no category finer than chain stores of four units or larger. Thus census sources reveal the proportion of sales of Canadian retail classes accounted for by all chains but not the concentration in the very largest chains. Because we expect the concentration of sales in the largest chains to differ in Canada and the United States, we also analyzed the proportion of retail sales accounted for by the top 20 retailers in Canada and the United States. Although the leading firms in many retail outlet classes fall outside this group, it is suggestive of the relative top-end concentration in Canadian and United States retailing.

Comparative Penetration of All Chains

We examined the penetration of chains in matched retail outlet classes in the two countries to control for differences in the mix of retailing activity and, more important, to control for the basic nature of the retail channel and the buying characteristics of its shoppers that should affect the relative efficiency of chain stores and independents. Retail sectors are not classified identically in Canadian and American data on the matched sample of retail outlet classes, and so small differences in some classifications that we constructed remain and should temper the interpretation of the results.[16] The U.S. classification is generally less aggregated, though the Canadian system has become less aggregated over time at a faster rate than the U.S. one. Different Canadian data are presented at different aggregation levels. As a result, our sample of matched outlet classes varies from year to year.

Besides the differences in classification, another difficulty arises in

16. Classification differences for the reported outlets, though always relatively minor, were greatest for candy, nut, and confectionary stores, accessory tire and battery stores, and lumber and building materials stores.

constructing comparative retail data because the Canadian and U.S. census years do not coincide. Although some Canadian data are available for each year and can be exactly matched to the U.S. census data, other statistics could be obtained only for Canadian census years. Thus some of the comparisons employ data for closely adjacent though not identical years.

Table 5.2 gives comparative sales penetration by chain stores of matched retail outlet classes in Canada and the United States during the period 1954–1967. Table 5.2 compares sales of chains with four or more units with those of all other retail firms for each retail outlet class. All available data have been presented even if the data for a given retail outlet class were not available throughout the entire period.

The data clearly show the substantial degree of chain-store penetration in Canadian retailing, greatest in food, general merchandise, variety stores, and clothing. Despite the geographic and cultural diversity of Canada, its retailing system exhibits a degree of concentration comparable to that of the United States. Nonetheless, chain penetration is marginally lower in Canada than in the United States, as we predicted. For the 14 matched retail outlet classes in table 5.2, 9 have greater chain-store penetration in the United States than in Canada throughout the period for which data were available, and in one case the ratios are similar though the United States holds a slight edge. Canada has greater chain-store penetration in 4 retail outlet classes: variety stores; general merchandise stores; furniture, television, and appliance stores; and jewelry stores. This general pattern is reinforced by more detailed data not reported here. Thus chains have achieved less penetration in Canada's retail sector, consistent with the factors suggesting lower chain-store economies in the Canadian economy.

The trends in the data, though subject to only imprecise measurement, do not show Canada catching up with the United States in chain-store penetration except in other food stores and fuel dealers. The United States appears to be gaining on Canada in furniture, television, and appliance stores and in jewelry stores and is getting further ahead in most other retail classes, as Canada's chain penetration appears to be leveling off. While Canada's chain-store development has closely followed that of the United States, it appears to be reaching its peak sooner or at least reaching a plateau sooner.

The retail outlet classes where Canada has greater chain-store penetration are primarily of the nonconvenience type, especially the nonconvenience outlet classes where personal service is relatively im-

Table 5.2 Comparative sales penetration of chain retailing in matched retail outlet classes for the years 1954, 1958, 1963, and 1967: Percentage of chain sales to total sales.

Class of retail outlet	1954		1958		1963		1967	
	Canada	United States	Canada	United States	Canada	United States	Canada	United States
Total retail	26.6	23.7	28.6	26.8	30.8	30.1	33.9	34.0
Grocery stores	37.9	43.3	43.8	48.2	46.0	51.9	45.9	56.1
Other food stores	4.6	6.8	52.51	10.1	5.7	15.4	10.7	14.5
General merchandise stores	–	–	–	–	–	–	73.72	8.6
Variety stores	83.2	79.7	38.9	81.0	82.3	81.0	87.4	81.4
Motor vehicle dealers	1.0	1.1	1.0	1.2	1.1	1.2	1.5	3.2
Service stations3	0.8	8.1	0.5	9.1	1.1	11.5	3.9	12.8
Men's clothing	12.2	–	12.3	18.8	12.2	22.9	12.5	26.2
Women's clothing	24.8	–	29.5	34.6	29.9	36.6	30.3	38.0
Family clothing	11.5	–	19.8	31.6	20.5	36.4	19.7	42.2
Shoe stores	37.6	46.3	43.7	48.2	42.9	51.0	45.6	53.2
Furniture, TV, and appliance	19.7	10.6	22.7	12.7	15.9	14.1	17.8	16.2
Fuel dealers	1.3	9.8	2.0	10.5	7.8	13.36	14.0	18.4
Drug stores	12.7	19.9	13.0	23.0	12.2	26.1	13.7	33.7
Jewelry stores	33.7	13.5	35.3	15.7	28.9	20.1	33.3	20.9

Sources: U.S. Bureau of the Census, *Census of Business*, chap. 4, pp. 1–7 (1954), chap. 4, pp. 1–32 (1958), chap. 4, pp. 1–37 (1963), chap. 4, pp. 9–33 (1967). Canada, Dominion Bureau of Statistics, *Retail Trade*, p. F-10 (1954), p. 8 (1958), pp. 6–9 (1961–1964); Canada, Dominion Bureau of Statistics, *Retail Trade: Revision to 1966–1970 Postcensal Estimates*, July 1971, pp. 16–18.

1. Figure for 1958 is not comparable due to classification change.

2. Prior to 1967 general merchandise stores and variety stores were lumped together.

3. Service stations often operate under oil company names though they are independently owned. Chains here are groups of stations under one owner.

portant. These include jewelry stores, general merchandise and variety stores, hardware, lumber and building materials, and furniture and appliances. The United States has greater chain-store penetration in all the convenience retail classes in addition to classes such as shoe stores and clothing stores, where the buyer's selection is heavily based on style and the role of the salesperson is diminished as a source of technical information. The United States also leads in some of the outlet classes offering extensive personal service, such as motor vehicle dealers and tire, battery, and accessory stores.[17]

Canada's lower chain penetration in the convenience outlet classes is consistent with behavioral differences in buying convenience products and Canada's lower potential for achieving economies in physical distribution and centralization. These traits can also explain why the United States has pushed further in chain-store penetration in the nonconvenience outlet classes most susceptible to such economies, and in nonconvenience classes where the effects of Canada's cultural diversity are more pronounced, such as style-sensitive clothing items.

Canada's lead in some of the other nonconvenience classes may reflect a number of factors. First, the greater geographic dispersion of the Canadian population may put greater emphasis on the general or department store than in the United States. (Unfortunately, all department stores were classified as chains in Canada, and no finer data are available to make the comparison between U.S. and Canadian department-store chains directly.) With general or department stores selling proportionally greater volumes in Canada than in the United States, conditions may be more favorable for chain penetration in these types of stores. This conclusion is supported by the data in table 5.3, which compares the ratios of sales of matched retail outlets classes in Canada and the United States to each country's total retail sales. Though the United States appears to be catching up, broad-line general stores have historically accounted for a greater percentage of total retail sales in Canada, especially relative to total nonfood retail sales (which is important since the proportional retail sales of food in Canada are substantially higher than in the United States).

Second, similar reasoning could apply to hardware and building material stores. In a more rural, agriculturally oriented economy, these retail classes may have generally broader product lines and may sell higher volumes of merchandise than similar outlets in the United States, factors that promote chain penetration in Canada. This con-

17. In these industries style and image through advertising loom quite large as purchase criteria as well.

Table 5.3 Proportion of total national retail sales accounted for by retail outlet classes, matched in Canada and the United States, 1954–1967.

Retail outlet class	1954 Canada	1954 United States	1958 Canada	1958 United States	1963 Canada	1963 United States	1967 Canada	1967 United States
Grocery	18.9	20.3	20.2	21.9	22.6	21.5	23.5	21.0
Other food	1.3	1.3	7.3[1]	2.7	3.7	1.9	2.4	1.7
Drug	2.2	3.1	2.5	3.3	2.8	3.4	2.9	3.3
Total broad-line general stores	10.7	8.0	10.7	8.5	12.0	10.3	13.9	14.0
Department stores	8.8	6.2	8.7	6.7	9.7	8.4	8.9	10.4
General merchandise[2]	–	–	–	–	–	–	2.8	1.9
Variety	1.9	1.8	2.0	1.8	2.3	1.9	2.2	1.7
Motor vehicle	16.8	14.8	15.6	12.7	17.5	15.3	18.4	14.7
Gasoline service stations	5.2	6.3	6.7	7.1	9.3	7.3	8.3	7.3
Men's clothing	1.7	–	1.5	1.3	1.6	1.2	1.5	1.1
Women's clothing	1.8	–	1.7	2.3	1.9	2.2	2.0	2.0
Family clothing	1.6	–	1.5	1.4	1.4	1.3	1.5	1.1
Shoes	1.0	1.1	1.0	1.1	1.2	1.0	1.2	0.9
Furniture, TV, appliance	1.6	3.2	3.7	2.4	3.4	2.2	3.3	2.1
Jewelry	1.0	0.8	0.9	0.8	0.9	0.6	0.9	0.7
Fuel	2.1	1.7	2.1	1.7	2.1	1.4	1.9	1.3

Sources: See table 5.2.

1. Figure for 1958 is not comparable because of a change in classification.
2. Prior to 1967 department stores and general merchandise stores were not distinguished in the data.

clusion is supported by our analysis of the relative size (sales) of retail establishments as well as Moyer's observation that Canadian lumber and building material and hardware stores were moving very aggressively into broader product lines.[18]

Third, data in table 5.1 show that durable goods are a proportionally greater component of consumption expenditures in Canada than in the United States, and this is supported by the greater relative sales of furniture, television, and appliance stores in Canada than in the United States (table 5.3). Though Canadian prices may be high, and thus proportional unit volumes of goods could be the same, some of the economies of chains relate to dollar volumes as well as to unit volumes of goods, particularly in areas such as capital, credit, and billing. Thus this greater proportional volume could help explain the relatively greater chain-store penetration in Canada in these areas.

5.4 The Relative Concentration of Sales in the Largest Retail Firms

While the chains' national share of sales in retail outlet classes is generally less in Canada than in the United States, we had reason to suspect earlier that the concentration of sales in the very largest retail firms might be greater in Canada. This is confirmed by the data in table 5.4, which gives the concentration of retail sales in the largest retail firms in Canada and the United States for selected years. The top-end concentration in retailing increased steadily in the United States throughout the period 1955–1975 and in Canada for at least the brief period measured (1972–1974). This trend is consistent with rising incomes, education levels, mobility of buyers, and other factors reducing the local orientation of the buyer and his demand for personal service from the retailer. Rising population has increased the volume and variety of goods sold by retailers, enhancing the potential economies of chains. Improvements in the logistics infrastructure, in the ease and cost of communication, and in management to coordinate complex operations and to process information to manage them have improved distribution efficiencies. Urbanization of the population has played a similar role.

Analysis of the product lines of the largest Canadian retail firms revealed no extensive diversification into operating outlets in several retail classes. Thus the large retail firm has by and large taken increasing market shares of its retail outlet class. When viewed in the

18. Moyer, in Thompson and Leighton (1973).

Table 5.4 Comparative concentration of sales in the largest retail firms in Canada and the United States, selected years (sales in billions of dollars and percentage of total retail sales).

Number of largest firms		1955	1958	1961	1964	1967	1970	1971	1972	1973	1974	1975
						United States						
Top 10	Sales	15,499	18,645	20,609	24,579	29,632	39,460	42,619	47,810	54,085	60,311	66,189
	% Total	0.083	0.093	0.094	0.094	0.095	0.105	0.104	0.107	0.107	0.112	0.113
Top 20	Sales	20,019	24,224	27,511	32,773	40,418	53,347	57,887	64,567	72,993	82,320	89,586
	% Total	0.108	0.121	0.125	0.125	0.129	0.142	0.142	0.144	0.145	0.153	0.153
Top 25	Sales	21,635	26,293	29,856	35,650	44,117	58,297	63,330	70,861	79,841	89,777	97,170
	% Total	0.117	0.131	0.136	0.136	0.141	0.155	0.155	0.158	0.159	0.167	0.166
Top 50	Sales	25,610	32,112	37,262	45,189	54,961	73,572	80,439	89,895	100,494	111,587	121,682
	% Total	0.138	0.159	0.170	0.173	0.175	0.196	0.197	0.200	0.200	0.207	0.208
						Canada[1]						
Top 10	Sales								3,440	10,169	12,574	
	% Total								0.249	0.266	0.286	
Top 20	Sales								10,082	13,102	15,855	
	% Total								0.297	0.342	0.362	

Sources: "The Fifty Largest Merchandising Firms," *Fortune*, July issue, various years; "The 200 Largest Companies," *Canadian Business*, July issue, various years; U.S. Bureau of the Census, *Retail Trade*; Dominion Bureau of Statistics, *Retail Trade*, various years.

1. These data were unavailable in Canada prior to 1972.

context of the more stable concentration in manufacturing industries, concentration in retailing is rapidly becoming a question of importance for public policy. Since weighted-average concentration ratios in manufacturing industries have not increased significantly since 1945, the relative power due to concentration of the retail sector vis-à-vis manufacturing is generally increasing.

The largest retailers in food and general merchandise hold larger shares in Canada than in the United States, just as do the top 10 and 20 retailers overall. The 4 largest food chains in Canada accounted for 63 percent of food sales in 1975, while the 4 largest U.S. chains account for only 19 percent. Evidence developed by Mallen[19] yields a similar conclusion in general merchandise: the 4 largest Canadian department stores accounted for 21 percent of department-store sales in 1970, compared with 11 percent for the 4 largest U.S. chains (Sears Roebuck, J.C. Penney, Montgomery Ward, Federated Department Stores).

While overall penetration of all chains is lower in most Canadian retail outlet classes, then, there is evidence that the penetration of the largest chains is greater in Canada, in at least these two important retail outlet classes. In addition to the factors discussed earlier, the greater top-end concentration in Canadian retailing may reflect in part a somewhat looser Canadian antitrust policy toward retail chains. While large U.S. chains have encountered some antitrust limits, including the Robinson-Patman Act, there is little evidence that similar constraints affect the large Canadian chains. Otherwise the regulation of retailing appears to be generally similar in Canada and the United States.[20]

The higher top-end concentration in Canadian retailing and the greater general impediments to chain-store development in Canada together imply a three-tiered structure in retailing. One group is a few very large chains that have reaped the economies of chain stores and who serve the mass-market customer on products where little diversity of needs is present. The second group is a relatively larger number of small and medium-sized chains, most probably operating in a single Canadian province or region within a province. The growth of these chains is constrained by cultural diversity and other impediments to chain-store development. They operate in a single area to minimize these impediments. Finally, a large proportion of retailers consists of

19. Mallen (1971).
20. R. G. Wyckham and M. D. Steward, "Canada," in Boddewyn and Hollander (1972, pp. 81–99).

small independent outlets, emphasizing product lines tuned to the buyers in their particular areas and offering high levels of customer service.

Chain-Store Penetration and Private-Label Merchandise

Private-label goods are products sold under the retailer's brand name rather than the brand of the manufacturer who produced them. Their presence is a manifestation of retailer power,[21] often coupled with the existence of strong manufacturer-branded goods. The manufacturer gives up identification with the product and the bargaining power this yields over the retailer (and also foregoes the expense of achieving identification) in exchange for the volume of sales of the product that can be attained under the retailer's own label. Depending on the nature of the product, chain stores may be a prerequisite for private-label merchandise. Unless the retailer can influence product differentiation (nonconvenience goods), he must offer a lower price to compete against manufacturer-branded goods and to do this requires chain purchasing economies. Manufacturing technology also has a role in private-label selling. The economies of scale in producing a good dictate the volume of retail sales that is necessary for that product to compete successfully in private label.

Although no systematic data were available to confirm such a conclusion, a number of observers have suggested that private-label goods are significantly less prevalent in Canada than in the United States. This is clearly consistent with the lower overall penetration of chains in Canada but not with the greater top-end concentration in Canadian retailing. The question is, Why have the large Canadian chains not adopted private labels faster?

Other characteristics of the Canadian economy bear on the use of private label. First, greater diversity of tastes may impede standardization on a single private-label variety all over Canada to allow volume production. Second, large imports of branded goods tend to work against private label in Canada. If these are manufactured subject to economies of scale abroad, the chances that Canadian manufacturers (or imported private-label goods) can match production efficiencies to yield a discount price for private-label merchandise are reduced. Third, while top-end concentration in retailing is greater in Canada, so is concentration in manufacturing, as we saw in chapter 3; more-

21. See the study of vertical relations in consumer goods in Porter (1976b, chaps. 2, 3).

over, we shall also find in chapter 10 that much Canadian manufacturing may be at inefficiently small scale due to the relatively small size of the Canadian economy. The combination of these two factors makes it difficult for the Canadian chain retailer to secure efficient Canadian production of private-label merchandise to compete with the leading manufacturers' brands.

5.5 The Size of Retail Establishments in Canada and the United States

In view of the smaller size of the Canadian economy and the difference in the penetration of chain stores in retailing, it is of interest to compare the size of retail establishments (or individual retail loca-tions) in the two countries as measured by sales. The importance of this issue is reinforced by the fact that Canadian manufacturing plants operate at an inefficiently small scale relative to the United States. Table 5.5 presents data on the sales per establishment of retail establishments in a variety of matched Canadian and U.S. retail outlet classes.

U.S. retail establishments are indeed bigger than Canadian establishments in the overwhelming majority of retail outlet classes, and this conclusion holds both for the overall data shown in table 5.5 and for data broken out by chain and nonchain retailers, which are not reported. This result is consistent with the generally lower chain-store penetration in Canada, since chain stores with inhouse logistical systems tend to increase their relative distributional efficiency by distributing broad lines of merchandise to establishments that are thereby large. The result is also consistent with lower population density and consumer mobility in Canada, both of which shrink the size of the effective market for Canadian retail establishments relative to that of the United States. Finally, smaller establishments are a result of the lower Canadian income levels and greater diversity of tastes, which lower the retail sales in the effective retail markets and work against sales of standardized product lines by higher-volume outlets. The larger sales volume per establishment in the United States appears to be particularly significant in clothing, shoe, and drug retailing. This may explain (though in part reflect) the fact that chain penetration in these areas is increasing faster in the United States than in Canada, and this result in the case of style-sensitive clothing and shoes supports the hypothesis of greater diversity of tastes in Canada. Canadian retail establishments are larger in general merchandise, where Canadian

COMPETITION IN THE OPEN ECONOMY

Table 5.5 Comparative size of establishments (sales) in matched retail outlet classes 1971–1972 (thousands of dollars).

Retail class	Sales per establishment in Canada, 1971	Sales per establishment in the United States, 1972
Bakery	45.5	82.5
Candy and nut	41.7	50.7
Dairy	77.8	140.1
Fruit and vegetable	81.9	78.0
Grocery stores	239.9	471.2
Meat	130.4	230.7
Fish	77.2	153.9
Department stores	5482.4	6589.2
General merchandise	526.7	242.9
Variety	255.9	332.3
New car	1399.7	2219.6
Used car	199.0	134.3
Tire, battery accessory	179.7	240.3
Home and auto supply	611.9	252.5
Service stations	132.7	138.6
Men's and boys' clothing	138.4	233.9
Millinery	17.8	74.8
Fur	104.6	97.2
Children's and infants' wear	67.9	105.3
Family clothing	181.8	261.3
Piece goods	52.6	78.0
Men's shoes	57.1	167.5
Women's shoes	108.8	182.3
Children's shoes	75.3	121.8
Family shoes	96.0	162.3
Hardware	127.4	145.1
Paint, glass, wallpaper	91.74	166.6
Household appliances	125.3	183.6
Television, radio, hi-fi	103.6	222.6
Floor covering	183.5	234.0
Draperies	106.8	111.6
Pharmacies	195.6	326.0
Patent medicine	132.3	196.6
Government liquor	1,072.8 ⎫	
Brewer's retail	582.7 ⎬ 929.4	225.9 (liquor stores)
Wine	159.9 ⎭	
Jewelry	89.7	119.7
Tobacco	90.8	91.7
Book and stationery	95.8	
News	81.6	122.6

Table 5.5   (cont.)

Retail class	Sales per establishment in Canada, 1971	Sales per establishment in the United States, 1972
Florists	52.9	63.0
Sporting goods	95.9	107.9
Boats	189.8	349.1
Motorcycle	135.1	335.7
Gift and souvenir	46.8	46.6
Cameras	135.1	158.0
Pianos	124.3 ⎫ 103.3	186.3
Music stores	97.7 ⎬	
Luggage and leather	63.7	106.8

Sources: Dominions Bureau of Statistics, *Retail Trade*, 1971; U.S. Bureau of the Census, *1972 Census of Retail Trade*, Special Report, "Establishment and Firm Size."

chain-store penetration is greater, and marginally larger in a few other outlet classes.

As Canadian consumers become more mobile and as population concentration in urban areas increases, Canadian retail establishments seem likely to increase in size. When these factors are controlled for, however, our data support the view that increased chain-store penetration in Canada would improve the sales per retail establishments. Since the diversity of consumer tastes is one of the factors limiting chain-store penetration in Canada, this diversity in Canada's consumer population has its costs in the size of Canadian retail establishments.

5.6   Summary

We have developed a framework for explaining the variation of retail structure across industries and countries and tested its hypotheses with data on the comparative penetration of chain stores in a sample of matched Canadian and U.S. retail outlet classes, on the comparative concentration of sales in the largest Canadian and U.S. retail firms, and on the relative size of retail establishments in the two countries. As predicted by our theory, chain store penetration is generally lower in Canada than in the United States, particularly in convenience-good retail outlet classes. Chain-store penetration in Canada and the United States increased similarly over time. Penetration of chain stores is higer in Canada in some nonconvenience outlet classes, though the United States appears to be catching up. Consistent with the lower penetration of chains in Canada, the incidence of private-label goods appears to be lower in Canada.

The concentration of overall retail sales in the largest retail firms, on the other hand, is considerably higher in Canada than in the United States. There is also some evidence that the concentration of sales by the very largest chains in several Canadian retail outlet classes (supermarkets and department stores) is higher than in the United States. Thus there appears to be a multitiered structure to Canadian retailing that is more differentiated than in the United States. The average sizes of Canada's retail establishments are almost always smaller than those in matched U.S. retail outlet classes. The key exception occurs in the few retail outlet class where chain penetration is greater in Canada.

The nature of the data in this chapter has precluded statistical tests of the many hypotheses advanced. Since many variables influencing retail structure could not be measured accurately, we have used observed partial association between variables predicted by our theory as an indication of the usefulness of that theory. Yet our findings confirm a general pattern of differences between Canadian and U.S. retailing and a consistent set of explanations for many of these differences. Thus even though complete tests could not be performed, we have some confidence in the general pattern of results as an input to policymaking and also to the discussion in later chapters.

6 Advertising Expenditures

The advertising outlays of the large firm have been the subject of intense debate among students of social policy toward business. In a purely competitive economy no firm has the incentive to advertise since products are undifferentiated and competitors numerous. Where firms command significant shares of their markets, however, even the firm with an undifferentiated product can benefit from advertising. When the prevalence of concentrated industries is combined with the pervasive differentiation of products in many industries, there is ample reason to expect the large amounts of advertising actually observed in every industrialized free-enterprise economy. For example, total outlays on advertising in Canada were estimated at $909 million in 1965, an increase of 128 percent in the ten-year period from 1954 to 1965.[1] One estimate of total advertising expenditures in the United States for the same year put outlays at $15.3 billion.[2]

Although the substantial resources expended on advertising may be sufficient justification for examining it as part of our system of characteristics of a small, open economy, there are other reasons for its inclusion. First, there is substantial though controversial evidence that advertising may have a pivotal influence on market power and hence performance, especially in consumer-good industries. Second, advertising is a major source of product information used by consumers in their choice of goods and thus plays a central role in matching buyers and sellers. The amount and nature of information transmitted by advertising is not innocent of social implications. Third, although most previous research in industrial organization has treated adver-

1. Dominion Bureau of Statistics (1968, p. 6).
2. Scherer (1970, p. 326).

tising in isolation, it is clearly linked to other aspects of industry structure and firm behavior, including some that go well beyond market power. Advertising is but one part of the firm's marketing strategy and thus must be considered in conjunction with research and development on new products. Advertising and product differentiation are potentially linked to trade flows and foreign investment (chapter 4) and may play a role in firms' diversification decisions (chapter 8). Advertising may also be related to concentration through any entry barriers it may erect and may support technically inefficient manufacturing facilities (chapter 10). Thus advertising is clearly imbedded in the interrelated set of industry structural relationships. By considering the complex simultaneity surrounding advertising, this study promises to advance our understanding of its role and significance.

This chapter examines advertising in the small, open economy from two points of view. First, we develop and estimate an advertising equation to imbed in our simultaneous system of industrial organization relations. This equation will take us a good distance in exposing the determinants of advertising-to-sales ratios in Canadian manufacturing industries and in understanding how advertising fits into the broader system of industrial-organization traits. However, in view of the many complex and hard-to-measure factors that enter any comprehensive theory of the optimal level of advertising for firms, we confront certain limitations in specifying a cross-industry equation for the level of advertising. In view of these, the second part of this chapter examines the comparative advertising behavior of a matched sample of Canadian and U.S. industries. Examining comparative advertising behavior for matched industries provides a control for some of the determinants of advertising most resistant to measurement, in the process exposing the influence of other determinants whose importance may be masked in a cross-industry study of absolute advertising rates.

The analysis provides some guidance for how a broad range of policy changes in a small, open economy such as Canada's might affect advertising behavior in its industries and yields predictions about the future patterns of advertising in consumer-good manufacturing industries in such countries.

6.1 Optimal Advertising for the Firm

The starting point in seeking to explain differences in advertising rates across manufacturing industries is a theory of the optimal adver-

tising level of the firm for a particular product. Despite a great deal
of research on advertising, comprehensive models of its determinants
are still in their infancy. Dorfman and Steiner (1954) present the logical conditions for optimal firm advertising,[3] but their model is not
operational since the determinants of the advertising elasticity of
demand are unspecified. Much attention has been placed on the relationship between advertising and competition, one factor that should
influence advertising elasticity, but the erratic nature of the results in
this area belies the partial nature of this relation. Other determinants
of advertising have been similarly proposed in a piecemeal fashion.

A recent study by Porter (1976b, chap. 5) has proposed general
framework for the determination of advertising behavior. The optimal
advertising level of the firm can usefully be viewed as the result of the
equilibrating reactions of individual transactors in the markets for
product information to parameters of the information markets they
face and the clearing of the market as a whole. The firm's decision to
supply advertising is derived from the buyer's demand for information to make his choice among competing brands of the product. In
the buyers' information equilibrium are determined the size and the
composition of his investment in gathering information about brands
from the available sources, including the advertising media. The determinants of informational equilibria for buyers in the market are
important inputs to the determination of the seller's outlay on advertising. The other input is the seller's cost function for disseminating
information messages (such as advertising) to buyers. The demand of
the buyer for the information that the seller controls and the seller's
cost of disseminating messages jointly determine the partial equilibrium of information outlays for the individual seller. Finally, advertising outlays of individual sellers interact in the market, with the
revenue productivity of one seller's outlays dependent on the outlays
of competing sellers. In addition, patterns of mutual dependence
recognition among sellers influence the degree to which advertising
competition occurs. The market equilibrium of information outlays
reflects the reconciliation in the market of individual sellers' advertising preferences.

Buyer Information Equilibrium

The buyer has access to numerous sources of product information—his
own experience, salespersons, advice from friends, physical comparison

3. Arrow and Nerlove (1962) extend this basic framework to make advertising
a capital good with effects extending beyond one period.

of competing brands, independent technical information such as *Consumer Reports,* and advertising in the various media. He invests in costly information to make the optimally informed choice of the brand of a product that best meets his needs. Each source provides information about differing sets of product attributes and involves differing acquisition costs to the buyer in time and utility. Advertising is a particularly low cost source of product information because it comes embedded in media and obtaining it requires little outlay of time and money.

In addition to its content and cost, each information source is of different "quality," where perceived quality increases with the source's flexibility in adapting information to the buyer's particular preferences or needs, the expertness of the source with respect to the brand and the product, and the likelihood that the source's information is uncolored by objectives (economic or otherwise) that may conflict with the buyer's. Advertising messages are the same for all recipients and are controlled by the seller; hence advertising's low cost is balanced against its lower quality.

A product possesses a set of product attributes, and buyers can be viewed as having a preference ordering of these attributes. This ranking of product attributes that affect buyer choice varies across products (for example, for some products taste is ranked high, for others it is unimportant). Similarly, the desire of the buyer to make an informed choice varies across products. As products vary in cost and other utility-affecting attributes, the optimal investment in information designed to increase utility by selecting the best brand changes in general. Combining this with the differing costs of the information sources and their differing capabilities in informing about particular product attributes, it is clear that not only the buyer's optimal outlay on information but also the portfolio of sources that he selects differ from product to product.

This analysis suggests that advertising is most important where the buyer is less willing to expend resources in gathering information from more expensive, higher-quality sources. This is true for frequently purchased, low-priced products where the risks of a poorly informed choice are modest and the low cost of the product does not justify large outlays on information gathering.

Partial Equilibrium of Information Outlay for the Single Seller

The seller faces buyers who select their strategies for gathering information as outlined. The buyer demands messages from the sources;

the seller controls some of these messages directly (advertising media), others indirectly (presentations by the independent retailer's salespersons), and others not at all. The cost of supplying or influencing messages to buyers varies by information source. Unit prices for transmitting a message differ among information sources, as do the sources' efficiencies in placing their messages before potential buyers of the particular product. For example, the cost per message of a salesperson's presentation may be higher than the cost per reader of a magazine advertisement. But the salesperson makes this presentation only to carefully selected (or self-selected) potential buyers, while the magazine advertisement is placed before many persons not planning to purchase the product at the time. Thus the number of messages placed before potential buyers per dollar of outlay on sales promotion varies among the media. Since the density of potential buyers, the frequency with which they are in the market, and the ease with which they can be identified all vary among products, the number of messages per dollar outlay placed before potential buyers also varies among products for a given medium.

The prices of messages sent by the information sources, including the advertising media, are central data in the firm's optimization process. If they could discriminate freely in price, the media could set prices to different advertisers to capture all the rents that the advertisers derive from the transmission of messages through the media. However, the media supply their services in markets that are to some degree competitive. This competitiveness is enhanced by the largely fixed nature of production costs of print and broadcast media, which creates strong pressures to cut prices in order to fill advertising space or air time. In addition, a given advertising slot on a medium is priced the same to all advertisers, so that price discrimination does not eliminate the variation among products in the efficiencies of different information sources. Another important issue in media pricing is whether competition among media eliminates their differing efficiencies to different advertisers. Given the diversity of advertisers' situations, this would require elaborate price discrimination, which we do not observe.

The responsiveness of buyers to messages from information sources and their cost per message to potential buyers jointly determine the seller's optimal outlay on that source, under the assumption that there are no reactions of competing firms. Equalization of marginal returns from outlays on each information source controlled or influenced by the seller characterizes his optimal portfolio of information, of which his outlay on advertising is a major part.

Market Equilibrium

The presence of existing and potential competitors affects the revenue productivity of information outlays by the firm. There are three major market influences on sales-promotion equilibrium. First, rivalry among firms affects the profit-maximizing level of advertising and other forms of sales promotion. Competing outlays may reduce the response of buyers to messages of the firm. In addition, recognition of mutual dependence in the market may limit the extent to which sellers bid up advertising outlays competitively. Recognition of mutual dependence may shift rivalry from price to nonprice forms such as advertising. Seller concentration and other structural determinants of oligopolistic rivalry therefore influence the level of information outlays in a market. Second, the model of manufacturer-retailer interaction summarized in chapter 5 implied that retail enterprises possess bargaining power. Advertising directed to the ultimate buyer can improve the manufacturer's relative power vis-à-vis the retail stage; hence retailer power provides a motivation for advertising. Third, if advertising increases entry barriers, then advertising may be increased beyond the point at which its influence on demand equals its cost.

This theoretical framework indicates many factors that should determine the variation of advertising rates across our broad sample of Canadian industries. First, it implies a set of simultaneous relations explaining buyer behavior, seller behavior, and the market equilibrium. Our single advertising equation is a reduced form of this system. The framework also calls for including many characteristics of the product, buyer group, media cost functions, and market structure. The bulk of these are quite difficult to measure.

The richness of the theoretical determinants of advertising rates has led to serious difficulties in previous empirical research. Although we cannot survey this literature here, a few observations will motivate our own empirical tests. No known study has attempted to explain cross-industry variations in the ratio of advertising to sales across a broad sample of manufacturing industries. Previous work has confined itself exclusively to consumer-good industries despite the presence of advertising in many producer goods, albeit at generally lower levels. The many studies of advertising-concentration relationships have failed to show consistent results, because they have either ignored the other theoretical determinants of advertising rates or have controlled for them in different ways.[4] Telser (1964), Doyle (1968), and

4. For a critique see Porter (1976b, pp. 122–124).

Comanor and Wilson (1974) examine the relation between advertising and concentration in broad samples of consumer-good industries and find no significant relation. These studies either do not control for product, buyer, and other traits at all or, in the case of Comanor and Wilson, control for them relatively crudely. Greer (1971), Mann et al. (1973), and Cable (1972) obtain positive and significant relations between advertising and concentration (Greer and Gable find nonlinear ones), which are exposed by the fact that their samples of industries are constrained to low-priced consumer nondurables, which share many product and buyer traits.[5]

Previous work on the determinants of advertising has paid little or no attention to the link between advertising and other aspects of firms' competitive strategies. The buyer's demand for advertising information should be affected by the number of brand names in the market, the rate of new product innovations, and the like—aspects of a firm's competitive posture that are simultaneously determined. Several studies (Porter, 1978; Cable, 1972; Else 1966) find a positive relation between advertising rates and the number of brand names offered in the market, for example. A recent study by Porter (1978) exploring the link between advertising behavior and other aspects of firm strategy in a sample of firms within one industry finds a positive relation between new product innovation and advertising-to-sales ratios (as do Buzzell and Farris, 1977). The promise of these results suggests that the link between advertising and other aspects of firm behavior such as research and development expenditures needs to be explored in a simultaneous-system context such as the one presented here.

Finally, a number of observers have noted that advertising is caught up in other potential simultaneous systems, with the direction of causality uncertain. A case can be made that advertising causes concentration through the enhancement of entry barriers, as well as concentration acting as one determinant of advertising (Greer, 1971). Similarly, many have argued that high profits or gross margins lead to high advertising rather than vice versa.[6] Comanor and Wilson test this assertion in a two-equation model of profitability and advertising rates, finding that profitability has a significant positive impact on advertising rates but that the advertising rate continues to have a strong positive impact on profitability (1974, chap. 7). This is a starting point, but a more complete system of relations is clearly needed.

5. Lapp (1976) finds a positive relation between advertising and concentration in an intraindustry test using local savings and loan markets. This procedure clearly controls for many aspects of the product and buyer group.

6. See, for example, Comanor and Wilson (1974, pp. 153–154).

To these previously discussed areas of possible simultaneity involving advertising rates we add two others. Product differentiation and advertising play a role in determining foreign-trade patterns and foreign direct investment, but foreign competition may affect industry-rivalry patterns and hence advertising. Finally, the rapidity of product innovation is likely to increase advertising spending, but the ability to advertise may also determine firms' propensities to invest in research and development (see chapter 7). Our simultaneous system of relations is clearly needed to explore these complex interdependencies.

6.2 Advertising Rates in Canadian Manufacturing Industries

We seek to explain the variation in ratios of advertising to sales in our broad sample of Canadian manufacturing industries.

> *ADI* Ratio of reported total advertising costs (both internal and external to the firm) to the value of industry shipments, 1965.

The theoretical framework presented earlier serves to identify the important factors that must be specified. The primary determinants of advertising rates are the numerous product and buyer traits that determine the buyers' demand for advertising and the sellers' cost of providing advertising information vis-à-vis other forms of product information. While we cannot measure these precisely, we can employ two variables to taxonomize industries according to major differences in their information equilibrium.

> *CNPR* Dummy variable; equals one if the industry is judged to manufacture primarily consumers' goods, zero if it manufactures primarily producers' goods.[7]
>
> *CONO* Dummy variable; equals one if the consumer-good industry is judged to sell a convenience good, zero otherwise.

Together these two variables summarize a wide variety of product and buyer characteristics. *CNPR* differentiates consumers' from producers' goods, the latter purchased by buyers who are generally quite well informed and tend to base purchases on objective features of the product. Given our theory, their demand for product information in the form of advertising is likely to be considerably lower than that of consumers, and they are likely to demand information in the form of salespersons, technical literature, and the like. Also, buyers of pro-

---

7. *CONS*, a continuous measure of the percentage of industry sales to end consumers, proved a less satisfactory variable in this analysis.

ducer goods tend to be small in number relative to the number of households and often purchase large dollar amounts of goods, spending heavily on search and making it less costly to supply them product information through the manufacturer's salespersons than to supply customers with such information. These message costs also argue for lower ratios of advertising to sales in producer goods than in consumer goods.[8]

While this reasoning suggests that advertising rates are generally higher in consumer than in producer goods, the theory summarized in chapter 5 combined with our framework of determinants of advertising suggest an important distinction within consumer goods in explaining advertising rates. Advertising rates should be considerably higher in convenience goods where low unit price and frequent purchase suggest high buyer demand for advertising information, and where broad sales of small dollar amounts to nearly all households suggests low relative costs to sellers of advertising versus other forms of product information. Furthermore, for convenience goods, advertising becomes a prime strategy for product differentiation and holds the key to the manufacturer-retailer bargain.[9] For nonconvenience goods, advertising is proportionally less important to other forms of sales promotion. Thus the convenience-nonconvenience distinction should capture several key aspects of the product, buyer, and market in consumer goods that determine optimal advertising levels.[10]

To capture the patterns of market rivalry that may influence advertising we introduce a series of variables:

C868   Percentage of industry shipments accounted for by the largest eight firms, 1968.

C8CV   Product of C868 and CVC, where CVC is the coefficient of variation of the market shares of the eight largest firms, 1968. The rationale for this interactive measure of concentration is discussed in chapter 9.

These two variables are alternative measures of industry concentration. Previous research has suggested that the relationship between

8. Product and buyer traits will clearly vary *within* producer goods (Porter, 1976b, pp. 108–109), though a usable proxy capturing within-group variance was not available for this investigation.

9. Porter (1976b, pp. 19–35).

10. Any one product trait, such as "durability" or unit price, only incompletely captures the fundamental differences in buyer behavior embodied in the convenience-nonconvenience distinction, taken from the nature of the retail distribution channels for the product.

advertising and concentration may be nonlinear; hence these variables were entered in a variety of nonlinear specifications. Concentration may also be a proxy for the presence of scale economies in advertising.

In a small, open economy such as Canada's simple measures of home-industry concentration are inadequate to completely capture the degree of industry rivalry due to the presence of foreign trade. A number of measures of foreign trade exposure were tested.

IMP   Imports divided by value of shipments, 1961.
EXP   Net exports divided by value of shipments, 1961.
EFT   Effective rate of tariff protection, 1963.

As we discussed in chapter 4, market rivalry should be inversely related to the rate of effective tariff protection and positively related to the extent of import competition. Thus advertising should increase with tariff protection and decrease with imports, though the relation might be nonlinear.

Exports, the other major dimension of international trade, have a more complex impact on market rivalry in the home country. If the country's home market is assumed to be uninsulated from competition for imports, then high exports should signal the presence of a world market with correspondingly greater rivalry than recorded by the home country's concentration ratio. Greater rivalry implies lower advertising outlays. If the home market is assumed to be protected by tariffs or transportation costs, however, high exports signal the opportunity for profitable price discrimination and an outlet for competitive behavior that does not destabilize the home market. Evidence for this later view is found in a recent paper by Caves and Porter (1978), which finds that the presence of exports tends to stabilize market shares among leading firms.

Exports raise an additional problem of interpretation, due to measurement problems. The advertising data for the Canadian sample does not include expenditures on advertising outside Canada; thus for industries with heavy exports the measured advertising-to-sales ratios are biased downward. A negative association between EXP and ADI could reflect this measurement rather than any behavioral relation, but EXP should be included in the analysis as a control variable at the very least.

Profitability was included in the model to test the possibility that it was a determinant of advertising rather than vice versa.

ROI   Net profit (loss) after taxes divided by total equity, averaged over 1968–1971.

PCADRD   Value added less payrolls, divided by value of shipments, 1967, less ratios of advertising to sales (1965) and research and development expense to sales (1969). Advertising and R&D are subtracted from margins to approximate the margins available for expenditures on product differentiation, of which both are a part.

Three more variables were included in the analysis. The first was the nominal rate of industry growth.

GSI   Slope coefficient from the regression of the logarithm of total industry shipments on time, 1961–1971.

Rapid industry growth could affect advertising in a number of ways. If growth implied less rivalry (because firms could expand in a rapidly growing market without need to fight for market share), then growth could be positively associated with advertising. With less rivalry on price, competition may shift to nonprice grounds for reasons indicated by the usual advertising-concentration hypothesis. However, in stating this hypothesis, we should point out that rapid growth does not necessarily increase mutual dependence recognition—in fact it may decrease it but reduce the incentive to compete. Under these circumstances it would be unclear why competition should shift to nonprice grounds.

Another more promising cluster of hypotheses for the impact of growth on advertising behavior can be derived from a life-cycle model of industry development. Rapid growth implies that industries are in an early stage of their development. Here heavy advertising in proportion to sales is necessary to create and build the consumer's product and brand awareness. With any intertemporal interdependence of demand, firms would rationally invest early in brand-name creation, to reap the benefits as the industry matures. Comanor and Wilson argue, consistent with this view, that advertising is more effective for newer products with which the consumer has less experience.[11] It has also been argued in the literature on the product life cycle that physical differences in products erode as the industry matures,[12] again implying higher advertising rates in the earlier, more rapid growth years of industry development, while later competition is based more on price. This latter set of hypotheses links advertising positively to industry growth through the use of industry growth as a proxy for the industry's state of maturity.

Our earlier discussion of the relationship among elements of firm

11. Comanor and Wilson (1974, p. 141).
12. See, for example, Theodore Levitt (1965).

strategy suggests that advertising rates may be associated with outlays on research and development.

> *RDIC*   Research and development expenditures divided by total sales of firms performing R&D, 1969.

R&D, like advertising, has its structural and behavioral components. However, high levels of R&D reflect underlying technological opportunities to innovate, as well as the motivation of firms to expend resources on innovation given the market environments in which they compete.[13] R&D can be directed toward product or process improvement. Here we associate R&D with product innovation, consistent with the evidence that most R&D has a product orientation. High rates of new product introduction should be associated with high rates of advertising, since introduction of a new product implies increased buyer demand for information as previously gathered information about market alternatives is made obsolete.[14]

A final variable introduced into the analysis was the proportion of output in the Canadian industry accounted for by foreign-controlled firms.

> *FSE*   Value of shipments and other revenues of establishments classified as belonging to enterprises 50 percent or more foreign controlled, divided by the value of shipments by all establishments in the industry, 1969.

Foreign-controlled firms with preferences and objective functions different from those of domestically controlled firms could increase rivalry, thus lowering advertising. However, it seems more likely that they bring to the industry different marketing abilities and a higher propensity to advertise than Canadian firms. Our earlier discussion of the incidence of foreign firms implies that advertising rates would increase with the extent of foreign ownership.

FSE also provides one possible mechanism for measuring the much-discussed condition that advertising by U.S. firms operating adjacent to the Canadian border spills over to reach consumers in the Canadian market. Since Canadian firms not operating in the United States do not have sales to the U.S. border markets over which to amortize

---

13. Evidence in chapter 7 suggests that much Canadian R&D is directed to adaptation and imitation rather than to original research. However, this does not change the link between Canadian R&D expenditures and product innovation essential to this test.

14. See Porter (1976b, pp. 110–112). Alemson (1970) found that advertising is related to the rate of new brand introduction in cigarettes. Cable (1972) also argued that advertising and new brand introductions should be positively related.

their advertising outlays, their advertising costs for achieving given message volumes to Canadian consumers would be higher than those of firms operating in both countries (whether U.S. based or otherwise). Since advertisers taking advantage of spillovers would have lower advertising costs per message per Canadian household, other things being equal they would purchase more advertising messages than Canadian firms. The effect on advertising dollar outlays depends on the elasticity of consumer demand for messages. If demand is inelastic, lower spending on advertising would be the result. If demand is elastic, the key to the effect of greater spending on Canadian advertising in a given industry relative to U.S. advertising would depend on where firms did this additional advertising. If the additional outlays were spent through the firms' Canadian subsidiaries on Canadian media, then Canadian advertising would increase, though this seems unlikely given the much smaller size of the Canadian market. If the additional advertising was done on the U.S. border media, as many Canadian observers seem to imply, advertising on Canadian media by foreign subsidiaries might even decrease. Thus the classic interpretation of the spillover problem would imply lower advertising in industries dominated by foreign subsidiaries, other things held equal.

Table 6.1 presents simple OLS, filled-in OLS, and TSLS regression equations explaining *ADI* in our broad sample of Canadian manufacturing industries. The first group of equations contains linear specifications of the independent variables. *CNPR* and *CONO,* our two summary measures of underlying product and buyer traits, are positive and significant as expected.[15] *EXP* is negative and significant, indicating support either for the hypothesis that high exports indicate international competition or for the hypothesis that *ADI* is biased downward in high-export industries. *IMP* has the expected negative sign but is never significant either alone or in a variety of unreported interactive specifications. *GSI* is positive though not significant, the positive sign supporting the industry life-cycle interpretation of the growth-advertising link. *RDIC* is positive, as expected, but not significant. *ROI* proved positive and insignificant, and these results are not reported. *PCADRD*, however, is positive and highly significant, consistent with Comanor and Wilson's (1974) results, which employed profits on sales as the measure of profitability. *FSE* is positive and highly significant, supporting the different marketing propensities of foreign-controlled firms and going directly against the existence of

15. *CNPR* and *CONO* alone explain approximately 25 percent of the variation in *ADI*. *CNPR* performed somewhat better than a continuous measure of the percentage of industry sales to the final consumer, *CONS*.

Table 6.1 Determinants of advertising-to-sales ratios.

Independent variables	Estimation method					
	A	B	C	A	B	C
C868	−0.0002051c (1.361)	−0.0002967a (2.847)	−0.0004745b (2.287)	—	—	—
EXPC	−0.02249c (1.346)	−0.02403b (2.048)	−0.01623 (0.893)	−0.0236b (1.783)	−0.02660a (2.679)	−0.01906 (1.173)
IMPC	−0.00837 (0.910)	−0.005515 (0.877)	−0.01278 (0.853)	—	—	—
RDIC	0.18227 (0.838)	0.1783c (1.329)	0.08636 (0.200)	—	—	—
PCADRD	0.08483b (2.163)	0.07204a (3.062)	0.06953b (1.827)	0.06816b (2.057)	0.06534a (3.120)	0.06868b (1.896)
FSE	0.03512b (2.141)	0.03293a (3.058)	0.05791b (1.863)	0.02290a (2.500)	0.01548b (2.278)	0.01156 (1.019)
RDICCONO	—	—	—	0.6993a (2.291)	0.8669a (3.606)	1.3045a (2.565)

	(1)	(2)	(3)	(4)	(5)	(6)
CPNR	0.01274[b]	0.01306[a]	0.01329[b]	0.01326[b]	0.01142[a]	0.01241[a]
	(1.675)	(2.629)	(2.266)	(2.220)	(2.694)	(2.494)
CONO	0.02143[b]	0.01260[b]	0.008274	–	–	–
	(2.309)	(2.001)	(0.788)			
GSI	0.03802	0.02642	–0.01821	–	–	–
	(0.447)	(0.509)	(0.262)			
GSICONO	–	–	–	0.3025	0.1686[b]	0.05902
				(2.751)	(2.155)	(0.579)
MEDCONC	–	–	–	0.002848	0.008068[b]	0.02333[b]
				(0.561)	(2.214)	(2.100)
Constant	–0.01472	–0.004068	0.002509	–0.01854[b]	–0.01527[a]	–0.01992[b]
	(0.997)	(0.458)	(0.190)	(2.156)	(2.661)	(2.136)
$\bar{R}^2$	0.459	0.458	0.458	0.603	0.555	–
F	5.804	8.779	2.349	12.058	15.776	5.732
D.f.	42	74	74	44	76	76

Note: Levels of statistical significance (one-tailed test) are a = 1 percent, b = 5 percent, c = 10 percent. The independent variables listed above the horizontal line contain components that are endogenous in our model.

spillover effect.[16] Finally, contrary to expectations, concentration is negative and generally significant in linear form, with or without the inclusion of *FSE* with which it is collinear. Interacting concentration with imports to test for mismeasurement of concentration due to the presence of foreign trade yields inferior results.[17]

The linear specification provides substantial support for the hypotheses presented earlier and explains approximately 45 percent of cross-industry variation in *ADI* in our simple OLS equation (45 percent in the larger filled-in sample). This compares with approximately 50 percent in Comanor and Wilson's (1974) sample of 38 consumer-good industries and 40 percent to 50 percent in Cable's (1972) tightly constrained sample of 26 consumer nondurables. We can improve our results, however, by returning to the theory to derive a number of nonlinear specifications of the relations described before.

A prime candidate for examining nonlinear specifications is the relationship between advertising rates and competition. Previous researchers have argued that this relationship may well be nonlinear, with advertising increasing with concentration until firms recognize their mutual dependence enough to bring advertising competition under control and lower advertising rates.[18] This hypothesis can be refined by noting that at very low levels of concentration, problems of appropriability imply little advertising, the problem becoming more marked the more homogeneous are the products of competing sellers. Once a threshold level of concentration is reached, appropriability of advertising increases, and in addition recognition of increased mutual dependence may imply that advertising competition begins to replace price competition. However, it is not clear from theory that advertising rates will increase continuously with concentration, and hypotheses can be formulated in which advertising decreases with concentration under certain conditions.[19] Above a high concentration threshold, advertising rivalry indeed seems likely to be brought under control as recognition of mutual dependence becomes very high. Thus advertising should probably be highest for medium-concentration industries,

16. Unless one believed that spillover advantages held by foreign-controlled firms in the industry forced Canadian firms to increase their advertising more than proportionally.

17. *EFT*, the variability of industry sales and our various measures of diversification were all insignificant, though these results are not reported.

18. See Greer (1971), Porter (1976b, pp. 121–122). See also Ferguson (1974, chap. 5), for a survey.

19. See Comanor and Wilson (1974, pp. 144–150); see also the survey in Ferguson (1974, chaps. 2, 5).

very low for unconcentrated industries, and somewhere between for highly concentrated industries, other things held equal, though the precise functional form of the relation is ambiguous.

Nonlinear specifications of concentration were tested in two ways. One involved quadratic and cubic specifications of the concentration variable, and the other employed a series of dummy variables dividing concentration into classes.

LOCONC   Dummy equal to one if $C468 < 40$; zero otherwise
MEDCONC   Dummy equal to one if $40 \leq C468 \leq 70$; zero otherwise
HICONC   Dummy equal to one if $C468 > 70$; zero otherwise.

The quadratic specification proved somewhat erratic and not significant, unlike results reported by Greer (1971) and Cable (1972). The linear term was negative and the squared term was positive. A cubic specification, while not significant in the A equation, was nearly significant in the filled-in equation and the TSLS equations. The linear term was positive, the squared term negative, and the cubed term positive. However, the best results, and those reported, are obtained with the discontinuous, dummy variable specifications. MEDCONC alone is positive and significant (reported), and HICONC alone is negative and significant. In specifications combining the concentration dummies, HICONC proves significantly lower than MEDCONC.[20] Thus the impact of concentration on advertising rates may be more discontinuous than the smooth relationships implied in previous research. While clearly not a potent determinant of advertising rates relative to the other variables in the model, concentration does add to the level of explained variance.

Theory suggests that two other variables in the model may affect advertising rates nonlinearly across the sample. RDIC is the clearest candidate. Our earlier hypothesis argued that advertising would be associated with new product innovation, proxied by RDIC. Yet Porter (1976b, pp. 43–45) suggests that the association between advertising and product innovation should be strongest in convenience-good industries. Here advertising is a virtual necessity to bring new or improved product features to the attention of buyers unwilling to engage in costly information gathering. In nonconvenience goods and producers goods, better informed purchasers are more willing and able to

20. All three dummies are not properly included in the equation simultaneously. Where two are included, their coefficients measure their differences from the third. LOCONC has almost zero simple correlation with ADI, while MEDCONC has a simple correlation of +0.19 with ADI in the filled-in sample and HICONC a simple correlation of −0.18.

seek out improved products, and new products can be brought to their attention by nonconvenience retailers or manufacturer salespersons. This suggests that *RDIC* is a positive determinant of advertising rates primarily in consumer-good industries.

RDICCONO   *RDIC* if the industry is classified as a convenience-good industry, and zero otherwise.

RDICCONO indeed proves to be a positive and highly significant determinant of *ADI* in all equations in which it appears.

Industry growth may not have equal significance in the entire sample, when growth is viewed as a life-cycle proxy. If advertising leads to the creation of brand identities and habit persistence in purchasing, then the present value of a given share increases with the growth rate of the market. As with R&D, however, the incentive to advertise heavily to build brand preference in the early years of an industry's development is greatest for convenience goods. For these products buyer behavior does not include substantial information gathering and comparison shopping, and hence the firm whose strategy is to overcome early established brand preferences faces a more significant problem than a manufacturer of nonconvenience or producer goods. For these latter product categories, the manufacturer with a better product (broadly defined) is more likely to attract buyers from other brands on the basis of their search for information and comparison shopping. But there is a premium to early creation of brand loyalties among buyers of convenience goods that are early in their life cycles. So we expect the relation between *GSI* and *ADI* to derive primarily from convenience-good industries.

GSICONO   *GSI* if the industry is a convenience-good industry; zero otherwise.

Once again the interactive specification greatly improves the performance of the variable, with *GSICONO* highly significant and positive in all runs. With *RDICCONO* and *GSICONO* in the model, the *CONO* variable becomes afflicted with multicollinearity and its sign reverses; hence it is omitted from reported specifications.

Overall, then, we find that advertising rates are higher in consumer goods and higher still in convenience goods. Convenience-good industries that have high research outlays and are growing rapidly are the largest advertisers. Heavy exports are negatively associated with advertising intensity, though the effect may be due to mismeasurement. With these other product and industry traits controlled, advertising rivalry is greatest in moderately concentrated industries, lower in industries with low and high concentration. Finally, industries with heavy foreign ownership advertise more, other things equal. The equation explains 55 percent or more of the cross-industry variation in advertising rates.

The TSLS equations prove to be remarkably similar to the OLS equations. While the efficiency of the estimates declines as expected, the signs of the independent variables remain the same, and many retain statistical significance. Industry growth is the variable most affected by simultaneity, losing its significance in the TSLS runs. Since growth seemed to be acting as a proxy for industry maturity, we might expect this sensitivity.

It is instructive to note that advertising behaves quite predictably in Canadian manufacturing industries, even though Canada is a relatively small open economy. If anything, the evidence is against any important spillover effect, and import competition is insignificant, though foreign ownership does play a role. However, underlying determinants of advertising predicted by our theory and applicable to a wide range of economies produced the lion's share of the explained variance in the model.

6.3 Comparative Advertising Rates in Matched Canadian and U.S. Industries

The cross-industry analysis of advertising rates in Canada has yielded strong results in directions suggested by theory. Yet we were forced to rely on summary proxies for the key product and buyer characteristics which, though powerful as we have seen, do not completely control for cross-industry differences in these product and buyer traits and the interaction among them and market characteristics. As a result, we cannot yet have full confidence that the impact of concentration, foreign trade, and other elements of market structure on advertising rates were fully revealed.

To explore the relation between competition and advertising further, and to investigate some other theoretical aspects of advertising, we employ a complementary research methodology that takes advantage of the similarities between certain key aspects of the Canadian economy and the U.S. economy. Advertising behavior of firms is compared in a sample of matched U.S. and Canadian industries. If we compare advertising behavior in matched industries in two countries with similar demographics and tastes, many product and buyer characteristics that influence advertising are controlled, and the effect on advertising of competitive rivalry is highlighted. In addition, a cross-country test introduces variance in the sample in some variables that influence advertising but do not change within a given country, such as the nature of the advertising media and retail distribution systems.

In view of the differences between interindustry and international tests, we must begin the comparative analysis by adapting our theoretical framework to specify the determinants of differences in advertising rates for given industries in two countries, a question that previous research has considered little if at all.

Variation in Advertising between Countries

Our model of advertising's determinants yields clear predictions for the causes of differences in advertising rates between countries. The factors identified in our model that can affect advertising rates when they vary between products wield the same influence when they vary between countries. International differences in an industry's advertising rate should reflect differences in buyers' behavior (associated with variations in the amount of advertising information that they acquire), in the costs of supplying advertising messages to buyers, and in the patterns of competitive rivalry in the market. Differences in any one of these areas can cause the producers of a good to advertise it at different rates in two countries. We first examine the way that each of the model's components in general terms may vary internationally, then briefly consider the specific differences between Canada and the United States (saving the details for the statistical analysis).

Buyers' Behavior

Virtually all the components of the buyer's information equilibrium can vary between countries for a given product. Where income levels are higher, so is the utility cost of time spent in shopping. The desire to make an informed choice among brands decreases as the product represents a smaller part of the buyer's budget. In a less developed country, on the other hand, consumers with very low income levels purchase goods in very small quantities, and every good is selected by risk-averse buyers only after considerable shopping and comparison.[21] There is evidence that the perceived cost of time increases with education levels, reducing the propensity to shop. It should also decline as the percentage of women in the labor force increases. As the willingness to shop and the desire to make an informed choice decrease, we should observe increases in the rate of advertising by sellers.

21. See Baker (1965) and Munn (1966).

Other demographic and cultural factors should affect advertising levels as well. The subjective disutility of time spent in shopping or the risk aversion on purchase decisions may change with culture—indeed, there is evidence from the United States that some individuals shop to a disproportionate degree. In addition, countries with a population dispersed in geographically (or economically) isolated areas may place greater faith in the local merchant than in a manufacturer's advertising.

In Canada the parameters underlying buyer behavior are very similar to those in the United States, perhaps more so than in any other country. Despite the high degree of similarity, however, a number of factors suggest that Canadian buyers demand less information in the form of advertising relative to other forms than buyers in the United States demand. Canadian income and education levels are lower, and there are proportionally fewer women in the labor force. More of the population are geographically isolated. And some studies have identified cultural differences implying less advertising as well. One study argues that the Canadian consumer is more cautious about buying, given his more recent affluence, which is reflected in a more skeptical attitude toward advertising.[22] Mallen argues that Canada's ethnic groups have a slower rate of assimilation than those in the United States, with the consequence that there are more pockets of different heritages, philosophies, and social structures.[23] These differences should reduce the demand for advertising, with its mass message, vis-à-vis shopping and reliance on the local retailers. They should also reduce the number of nationally branded and advertised goods in favor of local, less advertised varieties.

Cost of Advertising Messages

The cost of supplying messages about a product varies internationally with the geographic dispersion of population, the diversity of buyers, the ease of targeting messages to consumers who are potential buyers, the availability and cost of advertising media, and the size of leading firms. As the cost of supplying advertising messages to potential buyers increases (other things held constant, including the responsiveness of the buyer to these messages), the rational seller purchases fewer messages. If the seller's derived demand for advertising messages is elastic, the seller spends fewer total dollars on advertising.

22. Sutherland (1963).
23. B. Mallen (1971).

Increasing geographic dispersion of population increases the cost of supplying messages, since the seller who uses local media must purchase space in increased numbers of them in order to reach all buyers. Although media prices clearly reflect the number of households they reach, any fixed element in the cost of media is sufficient to generate this conclusion.

Other things being equal, greater diversity in the preferences of buyers forces a product's sellers to choose between supplying more numerous advertising messages to meet buyers' diverse needs for information and accepting their lower responsiveness to a common message. If each advertising message supplied incurs a fixed cost, the cost of eliciting a given response of buyers to advertising increases with buyers' diversity. Sellers find that the advantage in transmitting product information shifts toward devices such as the salespersons' presentations, which can be tailored to individual buyers. Thus the seller pursuing diverse buyers diverts his promotional resources toward persuading the retailer to feature his product.

The seller who can identify potential buyers has a chance to avoid wasting advertising messages on media consumers who are currently not potential buyers of the product. The easier they are to identify, and the larger the proportion of households who consume the product, the lower the cost of supplying advertising messages. For example, while nearly all Americans purchase automobiles, only a small fraction of the population in a less developed economy may buy them. The unit cost of reaching these scattered consumers may be much higher than the unit cost of beaming advertising across national media with low costs per message in the United States.

The structure of a country's advertising media also plays a central role. In an economy like that of the United States, a wide variety of specialized publications and other specialized media cater to small but highly select elements of the buying population. The proliferation of magazines for photography enthusiasts, apartment dwellers, gourmets, and so on is staggering, and these media allow the seller to confine advertising outlays to those who might buy their products. In less industrialized or smaller economies, such media may be much less prevalent, increasing the cost of using advertising to reach select groups of buyers.

In some countries advertising media that are important elsewhere may be unavailable or less efficient for transmitting information. A lack of media that can achieve low costs per message per household may cause fewer advertising messages to be purchased. While most countries have television, for example, the number of television sets per household varies markedly among them. In some countries television exists but is state owned or controlled, and advertising on it is restricted or forbidden. The prevalence of radio broadcasting and the number and advertising policies of magazines and newspapers vary a great deal from country to country with literacy rates, government policies, and other factors. National media such as network television and wide-circulation magazines, which reach large segments of the population at low cost, differ in availability and price.

The sizes of firms may be important to international differences in advertising rates if markets differ in size but similar economies of scale are present in supplying advertising messages. Comanor and Wilson (1974), Porter (1976a, b), and others argue that such economies exist, but much controversy has surrounded the issue. If they do, the large firm supplying a greater total volume of messages achieves a lower cost per message than the smaller firm. This effect of relative size depends critically on whether media economies of scale are the same in each country, however. If small firms generally populate a small country's markets, those that use its national media may enjoy lesser economies over users of local media than users of national media in a country such as the United States. Thus the level and shape of the advertising-supply cost function may vary internationally, making it hard to interpret the effect of international difference in sizes of firms on advertising behavior.

The factors determining the cost of supplying advertising messages are more similar between Canada and the United States than between the United States and the majority of other countries. Once again, however, some differences are worth noting. Supplying advertising messages in Canada should be more costly because the population is more dispersed geographically and less urbanized. Buyers' preferences are more diverse, and the smaller size of the Canadian economy may mean fewer specialized media than in the United States. The leading firms in Canadian industries may be smaller and less able to reap any scale economies in advertising, though this conclusion depends formally on the shape of the advertising cost curve. In addition, as table 5.1 illustrated, the number of television and radio sets in use per thousand of population is somewhat less in Canada than in the United States.

A factor running counter to these tendencies toward lower advertising is the greater proportion of income that Canadians spend on durable goods. If we assume that prices of durable goods are comparable, this may mean that proportionally more Canadians purchase durable goods per period, reducing the amount of advertising information wasted and raising its efficiency relative to other sources of information on these goods. This factor may promote proportionally more advertising of durable goods in Canada.

Patterns of Market Rivalry

Two dimensions of market rivalry hold particular importance when we examine international differences in advertising. First, for a given product, the pattern of mutual dependence recognition may vary between countries with such factors as seller concentration, the total number of rival sellers, and public policies (and industry norms) toward interfirm collusion. Second, the bargain struck between manufacturers of a product and the wholesalers and retailers who distribute it may vary between countries with the nature of buyers' behavior, extent of chain-store penetration, concentration in retailing, and so forth.

Where mutual dependence is recognized more fully in one country than another, perhaps because seller concentration is higher, the ratio of advertising to sales should be higher unless the relation between advertising and concentration is nonlinear.[24] If the relation is quadratic, then higher concentration implies higher advertising up to the neighborhood of the advertising maximum, which is usually posited to occur at high levels of concentration (Greer, 1971).

In chapter 5 we argued that advertising holds the key to the bargaining relation between manufacturers and retailers in convenience goods and is influential in nonconvenience goods as well. Thus if chain-store penetration in a product's retail channels is higher in one country than in another, manufacturers spend less on salespersons to persuade the retailer and more on advertising appealing directly to the consumer. In addition, where consumers' incomes and thus their costs of shopping are higher, the retailer loses influence on the buyer's choice of brand, and the manufacturer advertises more in order to gain bargaining power against the retailer.

Of the three sources of international variation in the determinants of advertising, patterns of mutual dependence and retail structure should vary the most between Canada and the United States. The lower prevalence of chain stores in Canada found in Chapter 5, except in some classes of nonconvenience outlets, should exert a downward in-

---

24. This conclusion also depends on the absence of offsetting shifts in the shape and position of the advertising-concentration relation across countries.

fluence on advertising rates in Canada. In addition, the levels of concentration in given industries differ substantially between the two countries, as does the importance of foreign competition.

6.4 Statistical Analysis of Comparative Canadian and U.S. Advertising Rates

The aggregate advertising data provide some evidence that advertising is proportionally less important in Canada than in the United States. In 1965 aggregate advertising in Canada amounted to 1.75 percent of GNP and 2.34 percent of manufacturers' shipments while it represented 2.25 percent of GNP and 3.16 percent of shipments in the United States.[25] To examine comparative advertising rates in Canada and the United States more closely, we assembled a sample of 46 matched industries for the two countries. Since intrinsic characteristics of the product and the process by which buyers select it are important determinants of the firm's optimal advertising rate, the traits of the sample of industries chosen for study have an important impact on the advertising behavior that we observe. The procedure of working with a sample of matched industries controls for differences in the distribution of output between consumer and producer goods and among types of consumer-good industries. These differences could bias aggregate comparisons. In addition, comparing advertising rates in matched industries should control quite well for the gross characteristics of buyers' behavior, despite some international differences in buyers.

The sample of matched industries for the comparative test was smaller than the set used elsewhere in part II of this study because of a lack of comparable U.S. advertising data. The matched sample used here was at approximately the three-digit level of the Canadian standard industrial classification or the IRS Minor level of aggregation in U.S. data. The construction of the sample, sources of data, definitions of variables used in the analysis, and some of the limitations of the data are described in detail in appendix B. Of the 46 industries, 15 were producer-good industries and 31 were consumer-good industries, of which 15 were convenience-good and 16 were nonconvenience good industries. In the statistical tests the analysis of comparative advertising behavior was carried out on these subgroups of industries as well as for the sample as a whole.

25. Data on GNP and shipments in the U.S. and Canada were taken from Statistics Canada, *Canada Year Book* and U.S. Bureau of the Census, *Statistical Abstract of the United States.*

COMPETITION IN THE OPEN ECONOMY

The variables used in the study were as follows:

CAS   Ratio of industry advertising to industry sales in the Canadian industry, 1965.

USAS   Ratio of industry advertising to industry sales in the matched U.S. industry, 1965.

RAS   Ratio of CAS to USAS, the proportional difference in advertising.

CCR4   Four-firm concentration ratio in the Canadian industry, 1965.

CCR8   Eight-firm concentration ratio in the Canadian industry, 1965.

USCR4   Four-firm concentration ratio in the matched U.S. industry, 1963.

USCR8   Eight-firm concentration ratio in the matched U.S. industry, 1963.

RCONC   Ratio of CCR4 to USCR4, the ratio of four-firm concentration.

RCONC8   Ratio of CCR8 to USCR8, the ratio of eight-firm concentration.

EFT   Rate of effective tariff protection in the Canadian industry, 1963.

IMP   Imports as a percentage of shipments in the Canadian industry, 1961.

EXP   Net exports as a percentage of shipments in the Canadian industry, 1961.

FSE   Sales by enterprises 50 percent or more foreign controlled divided by industry sales in the Canadian industry, 1967.

CSIZ   Average value of shipments for the leading four firms in the Canadian industry, 1965.

USIZ   Average value of shipments for the leading four firms in the matched U.S. industry, 1965.

RSIZ   Ratio of CSIZ to USIZ, the ratio of average firm size.

CGROW   Ratio of 1965 value of shipments to 1958 value of shipments in the Canadian industry.

UGROW   Ratio of 1965 value of shipments to 1958 value of shipments in the matched U.S. industry.

RGROW   Ratio of CGROW to UGROW, the ratio of growth rates.

Bivariate Analysis of Comparative Advertising Rates

The incidence of advertising in both Canadian and U.S. industries follows the predictions of our model of advertising determination by firms. As shown in table 6.2, mean advertising rates are by far the highest in convenience-good industries, where the consumer's demand for advertising information is the greatest and where average concentration ratios tended to be the highest. It is lowest in producer-good industries where advertising should play a minor part in buyer choice. It takes an intermediate value in nonconvenience goods, where adver-

Table 6.2 Means and standard deviations for selected Canadian, U.S., and comparative industry variables.

Variable	Full sample (N=46)		Consumer goods (N=31)		Producer goods (N=15)		Convenience goods (N=15)		Nonconvenience goods (N=16)	
	Mean	Standard deviation	Mean	Standard deviation	Mean	Standard deviation	Mean	Standard deviation	Mean	Standard deviation
USCR4	2.53%	3.12%	3.43%	3.45%	0.69%	0.46%	4.89%	4.23%	2.06%	1.56%
USCR8	2.50%	2.77%	3.34%	3.01%	0.75%	0.45%	4.85%	3.56%	1.89%	1.34%
RAS	0.972	0.423	0.985	0.375	0.945	0.508	0.890	0.312	1.07	0.406
CCR4	49.3%	23.6%	49.2%	24.4%	49.7%	21.9%	55.9%	23.6%	42.8%	23.3%
CAS	38.0%	16.8%	39.0%	17.6%	35.9%	14.9%	40.7%	15.1%	37.4%	19.6%
USAS	63.7%	25.7%	63.8%	26.6%	63.5%	23.7%	70.3%	22.9%	57.8%	28.3%
CCR8	50.3%	19.4%	51.6%	20.3%	47.8%	17.3%	54.1%	18.1%	49.2%	21.9%
RCONC	1.32	0.49	1.28	0.47	1.42	0.50	1.39	0.47	1.17	0.46
RCONC8	1.28	0.34	1.24	0.33	1.36	0.36	1.32	0.26	1.17	0.37
CGROW	1.61	0.41	1.58	0.45	1.69	0.30	1.41	0.20	1.74	0.56
UGROW	1.43	0.29	1.39	0.26	1.50	0.33	1.33	0.26	1.45	0.24
RGROW	1.14	0.23	1.14	0.23	1.16	0.23	1.08	0.17	1.19	0.26
RSIZ	0.108	0.063	0.098	0.043	0.129	0.087	0.115	0.045	0.081	0.034

Note: The sources of data and the variables are described in appendix B.

COMPETITION IN THE OPEN ECONOMY

tising information is combined with shopping and information gathered from other sources to reach purchase decisions.

Before continuing with table 6.2, we examine the correlation between advertising to sales in matched industries in the two countries. Correlations between CAS and $USAS$ for the entire sample of matched industries and the subsamples are as follows: full sample, 0.969; consumer goods, 0.964; producer goods, 0.817; convenience goods, 0.971; nonconvenience goods, 0.874. The correlations are extremely high and highly significant. They support the view that buyer behavior is the dominant influence on observed advertising levels, because we suspect buyer behavior to be relatively similar in the two countries while industry concentration and retail structure are known to differ somewhat, as do factors affecting the cost of messages supplying advertising (such as firm size and the diversity and dispersion of buyers).

The only known previous international comparison of advertising rates was Kaldor and Silverman's comparison of U.S. and U.K. advertising rates for the year 1935.[26] Matching data they compiled to an earlier study by Borden (1942, pp. 66, 442), they found a correlation of 0.93 between advertising rates in a sample of 18 matched consumer-good industries. This is quite consistent with our results, whose higher correlation is even more significant in view of the greater number of industries in our study.[27]

We were able to roughly match 13 of Kaldor and Silverman's industries to the matched Canadian and U.S. industries in our sample. As shown in table 6.3, mean advertising rates have fallen substantially (and proportionally across industries),[28] but the correlation among advertising rates across the thirty-year period is remarkably high.[29]

26. Kaldor and Silverman (1948, pp. 30–31).

27. Kaldor and Silverman's sample of matched industries was more heavily weighted toward convenience goods than ours and of course was composed solely of consumer goods.

28. The substantial drop in advertising levels suggests increasingly efficient advertising media, economies of scale due to the large increase in population, and efficiency in information transmitted due to the urbanization of the population. These factors apparently outweighed the effect of rising incomes and education levels, the rise of chain retailers, and so on.

29. While the construction of Borden's and Kaldor and Silverman's advertising-to-sales ratios was based on methods and data sources somewhat different from ours, there appears to be no difference that would explain the significant drop in advertising rates between 1935 and 1965. Kaldor and Silverman excluded sales to other manufacturers from the denominator of their advertising-to-sales ratios, but Borden apparently did not (nor did our data). In any event, this difference would not explain the large international differences in the observed advertising-to-sales ratios.

Table 6.3 Relationships among advertising rates in 1935 and 1965 for matched samples of consumer-good industries.

Country	Year	Mean advertising to sales	Standard deviation
United Kingdom	1935	9.1	10.2
United States	1935	10.0	9.8
United States	1965	5.0	3.7
Canada	1965	5.3	4.3

Correlations among advertising rates

		United Kingdom 1935	United States 1935	United States 1965	Canada 1965
United Kingdom	1935	—	0.93	0.68	0.65
United States	1935	—	—	0.77	0.79
United States	1965	—	—	—	0.97

Sources: For 1935, Kaldor and Silverman (1948, pp. 30–31); for 1965, appendix B.

This again supports the importance of the stable underlying characteristics of buyer behavior in determining advertising rates.

Table 6.2 presents means and standard deviations of *CAS, USAS,* and *RAS,* in addition to the independent variables to be discussed later. The mean value of *RAS* is always less than 1 except for non-convenience goods, where it is greater than 1. Generally, then, advertising rates in Canadian industries are less than those in the United States, as we predicted. The mean ratio is lowest in convenience goods, where chain-store penetration is less than that in the United States and where the higher durable-good purchases of Canadian consumers would show up. These relationships are consistent with our theory of advertising determination.

Multiple Regression Analysis of Comparative Advertising Rates

To examine comparative advertising more closely, we conducted a multiple regression analysis explaining the ratio of Canadian to U.S. advertising rates, as a function of ratios of market-structure traits in the two countries. High values of explained variance in the bivariate analysis illustrated that the underlying buyer choice processes for matched industries were quite similar in the two countries. Under the assumption that the underlying product and buyer traits determining buyer choice are similar in the two economies, advertising rates should vary between them because of differences in competitive rivalry, foreign trade, the size of firms, and other determinants of the supply cost of advertising messages in the matched industries.

In measuring differences in market rivalry in the two countries, differences in concentration ratios provide the appropriate starting point. Our international research design using matched industries allows us to perform a test of the relation between advertising and concentration somewhat different from the test with the Canadian sample reported earlier. Previous work that examines the relation between advertising and concentration in a given country has been plagued by the inability to control for the myriad of determinants of the underlying buyer choice process. Since the determinants of buyer choice are the dominant influence on advertising behavior, as our earlier empirical tests illustrated, the advertising-concentration relation has not been clear, and indeed previous results have been erratic.[30] By examining the proportional difference in Canadian and U.S. advertising rates for matched industries, we control for the most important elements of the buyer choice process. But we lose control over differences between the two countries in advertising scale economies. which affect the result if they are not the same for all media.

To explain the relationships between advertising and rivalry in a small, open economy such as Canada's, the Canadian industry concentration ratio is an incomplete measure of the pattern of rivalry. Thus, as in section 6.2, we included measures of tariff protection, import competition, and export competition. Since imports and exports and also tariff rates are generally very much less in U.S. manufacturing industries than in Canada, we are justified in introducing *EFT*, *IMP*, and *EXP* into the model directly rather than using ratios to the U.S. variables. The measurement bias with *EXP* remains in the comparative research design because of Canada's proportionally higher export sales and the fact that the U.S. advertising data include advertising expenditures outside the U.S. while the Canadian data do not.

In addition to the measures of market rivalry, we developed comparative Canadian-U.S. measures of some additional determinants of advertising behavior. Relative size of sales by the leading four firms in the matched industries (*RSIZ*) should control for economies of scale in advertising which apply to both Canada and the United States. Since leading firms in Canadian industries are in every case substantially smaller than their U.S. counterparts (table 6.2), the relative size effect would reduce the mean value of *RAS*. Whether the variation in rela-

30. See Ferguson (1974, chap. 5) for a survey.

tive size we observe across matched industries (from 0.02 to 0.33, with most values near the mean of 0.11) should lead to variation in *RAS* depends on the shape of the advertising cost function and the elasticity of demand for advertising messages. Even if our basic hypothesis about the effect of size differences on advertising is true, the observed variation of relative sizes could occur in a range in which the advertising cost function is relatively flat and thus the regression coefficient of relative size may not be statistically significant. In addition, the hypothesis depends critically on the presence of economies of scale in advertising that apply to both countries. Given the smaller Canadian market, economies of scale in national versus local media could be less pronounced in Canada, a supposition that our analysis of media differences supports. Finally, while economies of scale would unambiguously yield differences in the cost of providing a given level of advertising, the effect on advertising spending (what is being measured) depends on the elasticity of demand for advertising messages.

Two more variables were included in the analysis. One was a measure of the relative nominal rates of growth in the Canadian and U.S. matched industries over the period of 1958–1965 (*RGROW*). If Canadian and U.S. matched industries were growing at different rates, this might imply the same differences in advertising rates suggested by our earlier analysis. As shown in table 6.2, however, Canadian industries generally grew faster than their American counterparts. This is consistent with Canada's faster rate of population growth and faster growth in disposable income (table 5.1), and such causes may not reflect the same life-cycle or rivalry implications.

A final variable introduced into the analysis was the proportion of output in the Canadian industry accounted for by foreign-controlled firms (*FSE*). Foreign-controlled firms with preferences and objective functions different from those of Canadian national firms could increase industry rivalry, reducing advertising, or they could increase it by bringing different marketing abilities to the market. Since the proportion of foreign-controlled firms is smaller in the United States than in Canada, the lack of a corresponding variable for the matched U.S. industry was not believed to affect the results.

FSE is also a possible proxy for the spillover effect, which would influence relative Canadian-U.S. advertising. Since Canadian firms not operating in the United States would not have sales to the border U.S. market over which to amortize their advertising outlays, their advertising costs for achieving given message volumes to Canadian consumers would be higher than those of firms operating in both countries, whether they are U.S. based or otherwise. Since advertisers taking advantage of spillovers would have lower advertising costs per message per Canadian household, other things being equal they would purchase more advertising messages than Canadian firms. (The effect on advertising dollar outlays again depends on the elasticity or demand for messages.) The existence of the spillover problem would imply lower advertising in industries dominated by foreign subsidiaries, other things held equal.

Statistical Results

Table 6.2 presents means and standard deviations of the variables included in the analysis for the full sample and subsamples, and table 6.4 gives simple correlations between selected independent variables and *RAS*. Concentration is generally higher in Canada than in the United States, growth in shipments is higher, and the average size of leading firms is greatly lower. As in the United States, Canadian concentration tends to be higher in convenience goods than in nonconvenience goods, perhaps reflecting the potent role of advertising as an entry barrier in convenience goods.

Mean *RSIZ* is lowest for nonconvenience goods, which also have the highest value of mean *RAS*, thus providing some limited support for the view that small relative size leads to advertising cost disadvantages. While *RSIZ* is generally quite collinear with *RCONC*, for nonconvenience goods *RCONC* takes on the lowest mean value of any subsample. Thus the association between high-mean *RAS* and low-mean *RSIZ* does not appear to reflect the collinearity of *RSIZ* with high relative concentration, which we expect also to drive up *RAS*.

One difference among the subsamples is striking: the clear ranking

Table 6.4 Correlations between Relative advertising rates (*RAS*) and comparative industry structural variables.

Variable	Full sample	Consumer goods	Producer goods	Convenience goods	Non-convenience goods
RCONC	0.35	0.21	0.57	0.16	0.39
RCONC8	0.34	0.28	0.45	0.25	0.41
IMP	−0.08	−0.01	−0.20	0.08	−0.21
EXP	−0.13	−0.03	−0.42	−0.05	−0.07
EFT	−0.00	0.23	−0.51	0.44	0.02
FSE	0.20	0.43	−0.17	0.39	0.44
RSIZ	0.27	−0.08	0.58	−0.05	0.09
RGROW	0.07	0.08	0.05	−0.08	0.08

among subsamples of industries in the association of *RAS* with *RCONC* and *RCONC8*. Relative concentration explains a higher proportion of relative advertising in producer goods and nonconvenience goods than it does in convenience goods. But this is not surprising. In producer goods advertising is generally a relatively unimportant element of marketing strategy, reflected in the low mean levels of *CAS* and *USAS* in producer goods. As such, advertising rates are less sensitive to variations in buyer behavior and message supply costs and more sensitive to factors affecting the balance between price and nonprice competition such as concentration. The same reasoning holds to a lesser degree for nonconvenience goods. Relative to convenience goods, advertising is a less central element of marketing strategy in nonconvenience goods, and cross-country variations in buyer behavior should affect it less than variations in convenience goods.

Table 6.5 presents multiple regression equations explaining *RAS* in the full sample of 46 matched industries. *RCONC* and *RCONC8* are positive and always highly significant, with *RCONC* yielding somewhat better results. The comparative research design clearly uncovers a robust relation between concentration and advertising rates. *FSE* is positive and always highly significant, consistent with our earlier results, as is the case with *EXP*, which is negative and sometimes significant. A dummy variable registering when the industry was a producer or consumer good (*CNPR*) improves the fit of the model, its sign signifying that *relative* advertising is higher in consumer goods, other things held equal. Thus with product and buyer characteristics controlled for, the broadest results are that advertising increases with concentration and with the presence of foreign subsidiaries in the Canadian industry, the latter result countering the usual spillover hypothesis. The other variables were not significant for the sample as a whole but become significant when the differences among the subsamples are accounted for.

We constructed two additional classes of specifications for the relative concentration variable in an attempt to clarify the nature of the relationship. The first was a nonlinear specification of *RCONC* (and *RCONC8*) which assigned greater importance to high and low values of *RCONC* in determining *RAS*.

RCONC2   The value of *RCONC* raised to the second power.
RCONC3   The value of *RCONC* raised to the third power.
RCONC82   The value of *RCONC8* raised to the second power.
RCONC83   The value of *RCONC8* raised to the third power.

Table 6.5 Multiple regression equations explaining the ratio of Canadian to U.S. advertising rates for 46 matched industries.

	Constant	Independent variables				R^2	$\overline{R}^2$
1.	.5720[a] (3.299)	+ .30210[a]*RCONC* (2.457)				.121[b]	.101
2.	.4404[b] (1.911)	+ .41594[a]*RCONC8* (.2387)				.115[b]	.095
3.	.7622[a] (7.818)	+ .10540[a]*RCONC2* (2.702)				.143[a]	.123
4.	.8366[a] (10.987)	+ .04036[a]*RCONC3* (2.794)				.151[a]	.131
5.	.3426 (1.491)	+ .34314[a]*RCONC* (2.750)	+ .0001486*EFT* (.403)	+ .0003363[b]*FSE* (1.782)		.188[b]	.130
6.	.4057[b] (2.097)	+ .34812[a]*RCONC* (2.905)	− .0003864[b]*FSE* (2.074)	− .0006011 *EXP* (1.456)		.224[b]	.169
7.	.5978[a] (4.562)	+ .12433[a]*RCONC2* (3.275)	+ .0004296[b]*FSE* (2.334)	− .0005610[c]*EXP* (1.393)		.258[a]	.205
8.	.6707[a] (5.846)	+ .04811[a]*RCONC3* (3.415)	+ .0004510[a]*FSE* (2.457)	− .0005138 *EXP* (1.289)		.271[a]	.219
9.	.5899[a] (4.019)	+ .04971[a]*RCONC3* (3.491)	− .0004632[a]*FSE* (2.510)	− .0005306 *EXP* (1.326)	+ .10692*CGPG* (.887)	.284[a]	.215
10.	.7372[a] (7.545)	+ 1.2021[a]*ARCONC* (4.148)	+ .0004116[b]*FSE* (2.394)	+ .0002806 *EXP* (.782)		.339[a]	.292
11.	.6143[a] (4.725)	+ 1.2906[a]*ARCONC3* (4.402)	− .0004305[a]*FSE* (2.526)	− .0002892 *EXP* (.764)	+ .16203*CGPG* (1.411)	.370[a]	.308

Note: Figures in parentheses are *t*-values. Levels of statistical significance (one-tailed test) are a = 1 percent, b = 5 percent, c = 10 percent. The significance of the coefficients of multiple determination is tested using the *F*-test.

The nonlinear specifications of the relation of relative concentration to relative advertising performed generally better both in the full sample and in subsamples. Thus higher (greater than 1) values of relative (not absolute) concentration have a disproportionately positive influence on *RAS*. In the full sample *RCONC83* yielded the best fit, performing modestly better than *RCONC82*. Both the nonlinear relative concentration specifications substantially improved the performance of the model relative to *RCONC8*.

It is important to relate the nonlinear specifications in these equations explaining relative advertising to the quadratic specification that proved significant for explaining the level of advertising in Canada. While the results of table 6.5 establish the direction of the causal relationship, one cannot directly compare the functional forms estimated in tables 6.1 and 6.5. Even if one believes that the functional forms of the relation between advertising and concentration in Canada and the United States are identical, the ratio of these functional forms is a complicated expression. The result of table 6.5 probably indicates the position of the quadratic advertising-concentration relation in Canada relative to the corresponding relation in the United States. The presence of scale economies in advertising seems to explain the overall lower level of advertising in Canada, if the demand for advertising messages is indeed elastic. However, the assumption of elastic demand may not apply to the nonprice rivalry undertaken by highly concentrated Canadian industries, and the nationwide media they use are likely to suffer particularly great inefficiencies in the small Canadian market.

Another class of specifications recognized the possibility that import competition should be allowed to interact with concentration rather than being entered as a separate variable. To adjust concentration for imports directly we constructed the following additional variables:

ARCONC   The value of *RCONC* divided by *IMP*.
ARCONC8   The value of *RCONC8* divided by *IMP*.
ARCONC82   The value of *RCONC82* divided by *IMP*.
ARCONC3   The value of *RCONC3* divided by *IMP*.

Imports, because they signal that measured Canadian concentration is overstated, should decrease effective relative concentration and are implicitly given a heavy weight in the specifications shown. Generally, these specifications differentiate strongly between industries with some imports and industries with nearly none. Alternative specifications not reported did not materially affect the results.

In the full sample *ARCONC* performed about the same as *RCONC*,

Table 6.6 Multiple regression equations explaining the ratio of Canadian to U.S. advertising rates in subsamples of industries.

	Intercept	Concentration measures	EFT[1]	FSE[1]	CONO	RSIZ	EXP	IMP[1]	TRAD	R^2	Corrected R^2
Consumer-good industries (N=31)											
1.	0.306 (1.27)	0.758ᵃRCONC8 (2.79)	—	0.470ᵃ (2.52)	—	-4.10ᵇ (-2.04)	—	—	-0.133 (-1.06)	.402ᵃ	.310
2.	0.717ᵃ (4.22)	0.332ᵃRCONC82 (3.20)	—	.449ᵃ (2.61)	-0.104 (-0.86)	-4.19ᵇ (-1.93)	—	—	—	.448ᵃ	.363
Producer-good industries (N=15)											
3.	0.608ᵃ (4.84)	0.084ᵃRCONC3 (4.03)	—	—	—	—	—	—	—	.566ᵃ	.522
4.	1.53ᵃ (2.54)	-0.625 RCONC +0.139ᵇRCONC3 (-1.22) (2.54)	-0.503 (-0.61)	—	—	—	-0.001ᶜ (-1.60)	—	—	.751ᵃ	.651
Convenience-good industries (N=15)											
5.	0.051 (0.12)	0.505ᶜRCONC8 (1.69)	—	0.486ᵇ (2.09)	—	—	—	—	—	.313	.199
6.	-0.379 (-0.86)	1.47ᵃRCONC82 -4.33ᶜARCONC82 (2.84) (-1.60)	—	0.344ᶜ (1.56)	—	-5.24ᵇ (-2.00)	—	—	—	.535ᶜ	.348
Nonconvenience-good industries (N=16)											
7.	0.406ᶜ (1.46)	0.476ᵇRCONC8 (2.14)	—	0.753ᵃ (2.72)	—	—	—	-0.481ᵇ (-2.38)	—	.538ᵇ	.423
8.	0.800ᵃ (3.44)	0.339ᵇRCONC82 (2.46)	—	0.719ᵇ (2.67)	—	-4.31 (-1.19)	—	-0.440ᵇ (-2.26)	—	.616ᵇ	.477

Note: Figures in parentheses are *t*-values. Levels of statistical significance (one-tailed test) are a = 1 percent; b = 5 percent; c = 10 percent. The significance of the coefficients of multiple determination is tested using the *F*-test.

1. We have divided these variables by 1,000 in order to scale their coefficients conveniently.

but *ARCONC3* performed significantly better than the best unadjusted specification of relative concentration (*RCONC3*), with its *t*-value improving from 3.4 to 4.4 in the best equation and corrected R^2 increasing from 0.215 to 0.308. This result supports the view that imports increase effective competition and thereby have a negative influence on advertising, an effect that was submerged in our earlier test in the sample of Canadian manufacturing industries.

Table 6.6 presents multiple regression equations explaining *RAS* in subsamples of the population of industries. The signs of individual variables are largely consistent with the results using the entire sample. Relative concentration is positive and significant in all the subsamples. However, there are important differences among them in the significance levels of the other variables as well as in the explanatory power of the model as a whole. *FSE* is positive and significant and *RSIZ* negative and significant in all consumer-good industries and in convenience and nonconvenience goods separately, but not in producer-good industries. These results are consistent with the hypothesized differences between producer-good and consumer-good industries. The negative result for *RSIZ* is consistent with diseconomies of small scale in the advertising media used by consumer-good industries, coupled with patterns of market rivalry that generate an effectively inelastic demand for advertising messages.

In producer goods, international variations in the pattern of market rivalry appear to dominate the determination of relative advertising levels, and international variations in buyer behavior and the cost of advertising messages exert proportionally less influence. Relative concentration is an extremely powerful determinant of relative advertising, and *EXP* and *EFT* (measures of rivalry) are significant or nearly significant. Our model yields corrected R^2 of 0.64 in producer goods, higher than for nonconvenience goods and much higher than for convenience goods. This result is in accord with our model of advertising determination, which assigns great importance in consumer-good industries to buyers' processes of choice. In producer goods advertising has little effect on buyer choice, so its use reflects the balance between price and nonprice rivalry more than small differences in the nature of buyers. Because advertising matters so little in producer-good industries, it is not surprising that *RSIZ* becomes insignificant, since its rationale turns on scale economies in advertising. Similarly, multinational companies in producer-good industries rely on assets other than their advertising skills, and so *FSE* is predictably insignificant.

The proportion of variance in *RAS* explained is much less in convenience goods than in the other subsamples. This supports the view that advertising is the critical element of marketing strategy in these industries, and even small international variations in buyer behavior or uncontrolled differences in the productivity of advertising media play a major role in determining the relative advertising levels observed. The impact of market rivalry on advertising appears to be proportionally less important in convenience-good industries.

It is of interest to examine the residuals from the regression analysis of RAS in convenience goods for clues about the causes of the unexplained variance and to relate the residuals to our analysis of the retail sector in chapter 5. For convenience goods the model overestimates RAS in meat products and underestimates RAS in soft drinks, tobacco products, and confectionery and related products. Soft drinks are a regional industry in both countries, and differences in the effect of regionality on measured concentration might explain the poor performance of the model there. Confectionery and tobacco products were the only convenience industries for which there was some evidence that chain-store penetration in Canada was greater than that in the United States. Since greater chain-store penetration should induce convenience-good manufacturers to advertise more heavily, the failure of our advertising model to control for the generally lower chain-store penetration in Canada would cause RAS to be underestimated.

These explanations provide some support for the impact of retailing structure on advertising behavior and may rationalize some of the poor performance of the model. However, the low percentage of variance in RAS explained signals important remaining differences in buyer behavior for convenience goods in the two countries.

The model explains somewhat more of the variance in RAS for nonconvenience goods than for convenience goods. This difference is consistent with our finding that advertising is less important to marketing strategy in nonconvenience goods than in convenience goods. Examination of the residuals in the nonconvenience-good model provides further support for the influence of retailer structure on relative advertising behavior. The model overestimates RAS in tires, appliances, and especially jewelry, three industries in which Canadian chain-store penetration exceeds that in the United States. In the presence of powerful chain nonconvenience retailers, lower relative advertising in the Canadian industries may reflect the enhanced industry rivalry that these buyers induced. Unlike convenience goods, where the manufacturer's primary strategy for dealing with chains is advertising, chain penetration may induce the manufacturer of nonconvenience goods to shift toward nonadvertising devices such as persuasion of the retailer. The substantial bargaining power of the nonconvenience chains, which is not present to nearly the same degree for convenience chains, appears to have a substantial destabilizing influence on rivalry among manufacturers, thereby potentially reducing advertising. The nonconvenience model underestimates *RAS* in the radio and television industry, for which we have no explanation, and in men's clothing, where Canadian chain-store penetration is less than that in the United States.

Our comparative research design has allowed us to supplement our earlier results from the cross section of Canadian industries. Controlling for product and buyer traits, we find concentration exerting a strongly visible influence on advertising, with its influence varying among convenience, nonconvenience, and producer goods in an explainable manner. In addition, import competition which was submerged in the earlier tests proves to be a robust and significant variable in the expected way. *FSE* remains associated with heavy advertising while relative average firm size plays a role only in consumer goods, where advertising is heavy enough to confront scale economies. Predictably, the strongest impact of relative size is in convenience goods.[31]

6.5 Summary

This chapter has examined the level of advertising as a percentage of sales in Canada from both a theoretical and an empirical standpoint. Two complementary research designs were utilized. One estimated multiple regression equations to explain advertising-to-sales ratios in a sample of Canadian manufacturing industries as part of our simultaneous system of industrial organization relations. The other approach

31. It is of interest to review briefly the results of a recent study of the comparative media mix of advertising in Canada and the U.S. (Caves et al., 1977). Media mix in Canada was broadly similar to that in the United States, with heaviest use of television advertising in convenience goods and heaviest use of print media in nonconvenience goods. Industries with very heavy advertising were heavy users of network television advertising and television advertising generally, and the presence of foreign subsidiaries was associated with use of television advertising as well. However, Canada's media mix differed from that of the United States in some respects that were predicted by theory, and exposed in our study of comparative media mix in matched Canadian and U.S. industries and in a sample of firms operating in both Canada and the United States. Canada's firms utilized proportionally less network television advertising, but more spot television advertising and radio advertising. Newspaper advertising is proportionally more important in Canada, and magazine advertising proportionally less.

utilized the comparison of advertising rates in matched Canadian and U.S. industries to expose other aspects of advertising behavior in Canada.

In the cross-sectional regressions explaining advertising-to-sales ratios in Canadian industries, the most potent determinants of advertising were the underlying traits of the product and the buyers, proxied by dichotomies between consumer and producer goods and between convenience and nonconvenience goods. Industry concentration had a positive and nonlinear impact on advertising, with advertising greatest in medium-concentration industries and significantly lower in high-concentration industries. Exports exerted a negative influence on advertising, probably because of measurement errors, while imports had a negative influence which was exposed more clearly in the comparative research design. Industries with heavy expenditures on R&D were heavy advertisers, especially if they were sellers of convenience goods, and advertising was associated with industries with high profits as a percentage of sales (price-cost margins). Rapid industry growth, an inverse proxy for the state of maturity of the industry, was associated with high advertising, with the effect deriving primarily from convenience-good industries. Finally, industries with heavy proportions of foreign subsidiaries had higher advertising, directly contrary to the often-repeated advertising spillover hypothesis. These results were verified in our simultaneous estimation procedure, and the equations explained over half of the variance in advertising rates in the samples of 52 and 84 industries.

The comparative research design reinforced the cross-sectional results. Using the comparative research design to control effectively for product and buyer traits, the positive relation between concentration and advertising that has been so elusive in previous research came through even more strongly. Imports, indicating greater rivalry than is apparent in measured concentration ratios, had a strong negative influence on advertising, and the presence of foreign subsidiaries remained a strong positive influence on advertising. Comparative advertising rates were examined in producer-good, convenience-good, and nonconvenience-good subsamples of the matched industries, yielding further insights into advertising behavior when combined with the earlier results. In producer goods, where advertising is not the central element of marketing strategy, the dominant determinant of advertising appeared to be the degree of market rivalry which set the balance between price and nonprice competition. In nonconvenience goods and especially convenience goods, product, buyer, technological, and industry life-cycle traits played a proportionally greater role in determining advertising behavior. The relatively small size of Canadian firms compared with U.S. firms exerted a depressing influence on Canadian advertising only in consumer goods, where advertising was heavy enough to confront economies of scale. Finally, differences between Canadian and U.S. retailing described in chapter 5 could be used to explain otherwise inexplicable differences in advertising.

Taken as a whole, the results illustrate that the determinants of advertising in a small, open economy such as Canada's are broadly similar to those in a larger economy such as that of the United States. Nevertheless, foreign trade and foreign investment do affect Canadian advertising, as do differences in the Canadian consumer, media, and distribution system.

7 Research and Development Spending

Technological innovation, spurred by expenditures on research and development, is one of the most significant forces causing economic growth and a major determinant of social welfare. In fact, in the range of market-performance variables usually considered in the field of industrial organization, technological innovation or progressiveness probably carries the greatest weight in terms of market performance.[1] Furthermore, since Schumpeter and even before, it has been recognized that innovation can be the great competitive equalizer, creating new industries and new large firms while causing the decline and even disappearance of others. In any economy, including Canada's, the study of innovation must take on major importance.

Given the large stakes involved with innovation, it is not surprising that the study of innovation has become a large field in itself, including branches in economics, business management, organizational behavior, and sociology. In the field of industrial organization, interest has centered on the market characteristics that determine the level of innovation by firms and on the impact of innovation on competition. Or put another way, how does competition affect innovation, and how does innovation affect competition?

The impact of innovation on competition has been examined primarily because it was hypothesized that there may be scale economies in research and development that would create barriers to entry and solidify market power. The impact of competition on innovation has been of interest because, beginning with Schumpeter, some economists have believed that large firms with market power were necessary to

1. Harberger (1954). Many studies have built on this early foundation.

assure the highest level of innovation.[2] Size and market power yielded, according to this view, a stable base from which to undertake risky R&D, the financial resources to fund R&D projects, the ability to spread risk by undertaking a portfolio of R&D projects, the size of R&D effort required to reap economies of scale in R&D, and greater appropriability of the fruits of R&D because of market share.

Many of these arguments apply to the absolute size of the firm as well as to its market share, while some are more applicable to just one. Related to these hypotheses, because large corporations are likely to be diversified, is the thesis that diversification increases R&D spending by presenting a variety of businesses in which the output of innovative activity can be marketed.[3] This argument rests on the premise that it is difficult to anticipate the results and market applications of innovative activity ahead of time and that an innovation may have applicability to a variety of different businesses. The Schumpeterian hypotheses and its relatives have been intensely debated because much evidence suggests that industrial R&D projects are in many cases neither very large nor very risky and that economies of scale in R&D are far from clear.[4]

In addition to examining the effects of size, concentration, and diversification on innovation, previous work has investigated the impact of product differentiability, growth, the presence of technical entry barriers, and government subsidy on innovation. Each of these factors can be hypothesized as either an indicator of the intrinsic ability to innovate (often termed "technological opportunity" in the literature) or the incentive of a firm to innovate.

It is immediately apparent from even this brief survey that innovation is inherently caught up in the system of simultaneous relations in industrial organization that is the subject of this study. Indeed, whether innovative activity is determined by competition, itself determines competition, or both, is a problem in sorting out this system of simultaneous relations. Also, many of the variables that have been posited in the literature to affect innovation are themselves endogenous to the system. Yet few of the previous studies of innovation have recognized these simultaneous elements and none has examined the

2. Schumpeter (1950). See Scherer (1970) for an excellent survey of the literature, as well as a more recent survey by Kamien and Schwartz (1975).

3. See Nelson (1959), Scherer (1965), and the survey in Scherer (1970).

4. Mansfield's (1968, 1969) evidence suggests that the cost of the average industrial R&D project is less than $300,000 and has a high prior probability of success. Industrial R&D seems to be more development than breakthrough innovations, with many of the latter made by individual inventors.

determinants of innovation in a simultaneous-system format, a deficiency that we shall remedy here.

In addition to examining innovation in a simultaneous-system context, we shall be faced with another set of issues that stem from investigating innovation in a small, open economy such as Canada's. Since innovations create intangible assets that can be transferred internationally through licensing, imitation, and by internal transfers in multinational companies, it is not necessarily the case that the determinants of innovative activity in Canada are the same as those in a large economy much less exposed to foreign trade, such as the U.S. economy, the site of most of the previous research on this subject. The model that has been used in U.S.-based research is implicitly closed and rests on the assumption that to enjoy the fruits of innovation a country must spend its resources on discovery. In a small, open economy most new productive knowledge comes from abroad. R&D undertaken for domestic application uses resources efficiently only if it is cheaper than buying the information from abroad or if it efficiently modifies and adapts information available from abroad. On the other hand, the payout of domestic R&D may also be affected by the possibility of collecting rents on its output from the rest of the world.[5]

This chapter presents the results of two empirical studies of the determinants of innovative activity in Canada, using R&D expenditures as a percentage of sales as the measure of innovative effort. After presenting a theoretical framework of the determinants of R&D in an open economy, we estimate a model explaining R&D as a percentage of sales in our sample of Canadian manufacturing industries. This model will take its place in our system of simultaneous industrial organization relations in Canada.

In estimating the basic model, however, we confront a problem analogous to the one we faced in chapter 6 when we explored the determinants of advertising. As previous literature has consistently shown, R&D spending is heavily influenced by the underlying technological opportunity of the industry. Industries such as electronics and chemicals offer inherently richer possibilities for innovation than industries such as textiles and dairy products. Controlling for this technological opportunity in a cross-industry study presents difficult measurement problems, and thus once again we take advantage of comparisons between a matched sample of U.S. and Canadian industries as an alternative research design that will illuminate issues untestable in the cross-industry design.

5. Mansfield, Romeo, and Wagner (1978) illustrate the degree to which R&D would be reduced if the firm could not collect foreign rents.

7.1 The Determinants of Industrial Research and Development Spending in a Small, Open Economy

We take as our measure of innovative activity the average research and development expenditures of firms in an industry as a percentage of total industry sales. R&D as a percentage of sales is a measure of the inputs to innovation, or the intensity of innovative effort. While it has shortcomings as a proxy for innovation, it is a workable measure of the degree to which firms seek to innovate and has proven illuminating in previous empirical work.[6]

The firm's optimal level of spending on R&D depends broadly on four factors: the a priori probability that expenditures on R&D will yield innovations in products or processes, the resources available to innovate, the competitive incentives to innovate, and the availability and cost of any alternative means of gaining access to innovations besides doing R&D.

The a priori probability that R&D spending will yield innovation will increase with the absolute level of R&D expenditures, though it may increase more or less proportionally. Increases in the productivity of R&D inputs with the scale of these inputs would imply a more than proportionate increase. The a priori probability that expenditures on R&D will yield commercially significant innovations is also heavily influenced by what we have called technological opportunity. Technological opportunity is imbedded in the underlying technology of an industry. However, the intrinsic technological opportunity is not as important to the R&D decision as is the firm's a priori perception of this opportunity. In a small economy the firm's a priori probability that R&D spending will result in innovation may be heavily determined by the presence of innovations elsewhere in the world, even if they are not perfectly applicable to the small economy's setting. This contrasts with the decision of firms in countries such as the United States and Japan to commit their larger total R&D resources to undiscovered possibilities for innovation.

Investments in innovation depend on the opportunity cost and availability of funds of sufficient quantity. Though the resources rationally invested in innovation clearly depend on their expected profitability, the usual lag of commercial sales due to an innovation from the R&D spending that uncovered it forces the firm to finance R&D from operating profits, from excess working capital, or with

6. For a discussion of the pros and cons of the various measures of the inputs to and outputs of innovative activity, see Scherer (1970, chap. 15).

outside capital. It may be quite difficult to borrow or raise equity to finance uncertain R&D investments with little or no salvage value. For these reasons, it has been posited that profitability or cash flow is a determinant of R&D spending.[7] Not only might the profit margin or return on investment of the firm determine R&D spending, but the absolute size of the firm influences the absolute amount of resources available for R&D. Finally, government subsidies for R&D in Canada may play a role in determining R&D spending if they ease resource constraints that limit Canadian firms from engaging in R&D that yields returns in excess of their opportunity cost of capital.[8]

A third factor influencing R&D spending is the incentive to innovate. The incentive to innovate depends on the size of the benefits appropriated by the firm from innovation, or conversely the reduction in the firm's performance due to lack of innovation. One determinant of the size of the benefits appropriated from innovation is the ability of the firm to protect the innovation from imitation by other firms. The patent system provides a mechanism for appropriating the benefits of innovation, but patents rarely prevent other firms from defensive imitation of innovations. Thus appropriability is also likely to depend on a number of industry characteristics, one of which is the differentiability of the product. Differentiability allows the firm to attach innovation to its particular product variety or image or, conversely, provides the firm with the incentive to innovate to enhance the differentiation of its product.[9] However, isolating these effects of differentiability on innovation may be difficult because it is also probably a component of technological opportunity for product (though not process) innovation.[10] And differentiability may create an umbrella that protects firms from competitive erosion due to innovations by others, thus reducing the incentive to innovate.

A firm's market share and diversification also influence the appropriability of the benefits of innovation and hence the incentive for R&D spending. A large market share increases the absolute benefits to a given innovation, and thus the presence of firms with large shares

7. For a recent theoretical examination see Schwartz and Kamien (1978). See also Scherer (1970, pp. 363–364).

8. For a discussion of these subsidies see McFetridge (1977). McFetridge's results suggest that subsidies do not have a major impact on company-funded R&D; our results are somewhat different.

9. See Comanor (1967).

10. Comanor (1967) did not recognize this, and hence his results could be measuring the fact that technological opportunity is highest in durable goods and investment goods rather than establishing that differentiability is positively associated with R&D.

(high concentration) may be positively associated with R&D spending. Conversely, in unconcentrated industries the number of potential imitators is large and the absolute benefits to innovation are likely to be smaller.[11] Diversification has been posited to increase appropriability.

While R&D spending reflects the gains to the firm of innovating, it should also reflect the probable loss of cash flow if the firm does not innovate and its rivals do. Competition in R&D is a dimension of market rivalry just as is advertising or price competition. In unconcentrated industries competitive rivalry is great, but low appropriability and possibly more rapid imitation may imply little R&D spending. As concentration increases, the impact on R&D spending is mixed. On the one hand, in an analogy to the hypotheses about advertising competition, competition may shift from price to nonprice grounds, implying greater R&D. Following this line of reasoning, we can see that increasing concentration should eventually result in mutual dependence recognition sufficient to bring R&D competition under control, so that the relationship between R&D and concentration would have an inverted U shape. However, the appropriability of R&D investments may increase with concentration, working toward a monotonic increase of R&D activity with concentration throughout.

In a small, open economy such as Canada's another category of incentives to innovate that is not usually considered in U.S.-based treatments takes on potential importance. The incentive for a firm to innovate depends on the gains to marketing the innovation anywhere in the world as well as in its own country. Where the home market is small, the ability to capture rents from an innovation from outside the home market would be a major stimulus to innovative spending. Despite this, however, there are reasons to suspect that the incentive to innovate in Canada is fundamentally less compared with that facing firms in large economies.

While Canadian firms can capture the rents of an innovation elsewhere in the world, there are costs to doing so. There are information costs of finding opportunities to exploit innovations overseas, including the costs of finding foreign licensees. Greater uncertainty is created by the need to market an innovation overseas compared with marketing it in the home country. Restrictions on foreign patents may discourage full overseas exploitation of innovations. And in a small coun-

---

11. Working in the other direction would be Arrow's (1962) point that innovation lets a small competitor who monopolizes the market gain more than an established monopolist already collecting monopoly rents. The accuracy of this statement clearly turns on the vulnerability of either type of firm to imitation of its innovation.

try firms may lack the resources for foreign direct investment or a worldwide distribution system, forcing the adoption of licensing and other methods less likely to capture the full rents of innovation. Finally, any cost of adapting an innovation to an overseas market must be charged against the returns from exploiting it overseas.

For all these reasons, producers in a smaller country such as Canada may find the rents to innovation restricted to those available through product sales in the small Canadian market. Firms in large economies have much larger home markets over which to capture the rents of innovations and greater resources to overcome the costs of capturing rents to these innovations elsewhere in world markets. Hence we would expect the preponderance of spending on original innovative activity to occur in large markets or to be undertaken by firms whose multinational operations provide low-cost mechanisms for capturing the rents of innovations in large markets. This conclusion is reinforced if there are any costs of adapting innovations to new markets or benefits to be gained by carrying out the innovative process in proximity to the market. These will reinforce the tendency for spending or innovation to occur in large markets and not in Canada, even by multinational firms.[12] Large Canadian firms in heavily export-oriented industries or in industries where Canada's production of a good is large relative to the world market are probably the only exception to the rule that few original innovations occur in a small, open economy because of insufficient incentives.

The final major category of determinants of R&D spending is the availability and cost of innovations from other sources. This determinant has fundamental importance for an economy such as Canada's, where there are limited incentives for original innovation and where the large proportion of Canadian companies that are subsidiaries of multinational companies implies that they will rationally spend on innovation in larger markets.[13] Since innovations are intangible assets, potential alternatives to R&D spending are to imitate innovations created abroad by other firms or to license them (and pay

12. The incentive for firms to do R&D and to introduce new products in the large markets is amply supported by the literature on the life-cycle theory of international trade. See Wells (1972, chap. 1). This conclusion is also supported by the finding of an Economic Council of Canada (1971) study that the greatest majority of Canadian patents are issued to non-Canadian residents. A similar conclusion is reached by Johns (1978) for Australia.

13. The few previous studies of Canadian R&D behavior have all but ignored this, by and large replicating the conventional U.S.-based studies. See Howe and McFetridge (1976).

a royalty fee).[14] For a subsidiary of a multinational company, a third alternative is to use innovations created by components of the company located elsewhere.[15]

In all three alternatives the level of R&D spending required by the firm in Canada is presumably lower than that of the original innovator. Since imitation requires some R&D outlays, this is particularly true where the firm licensed the innovation or acquired it through its parent company. However, the availability of these latter options does not eliminate the need for R&D spending by Canadian firms. While the Canadian firm can obtain the innovation through these means at lower cost than the cost of creating the innovation, it will have to expend some R&D resources in adapting the innovation if necessary and in learning how to assimilate the innovation into its operations. Indeed Safarian (1969) found that foreign subsidiaries engaged in substantial research in Canada despite their access to parent-company research, which they viewed as highly important to them, but that the rate of research spending in Canada was less than in the subsidiaries' parent companies and that the research was directed less at conceiving new products than was research by parents. Teece (1976) found that even intracorporate transfers of technology with adaptation involved significant costs to physically move it. Finally, R&D spending is probably required as a "listening post" to learn of innovations elsewhere, even if the R&D spending is not required to adapt them.[16] Thus all three alternatives potentially available for gaining access to innovations without original research demand some R&D spending by the receiving Canadian firm or subsidiary, with the most R&D spending required when the innovation must be imitated or adapted for Canadian use.

If many Canadian companies lack the size and resources to be the original creators of new innovations, then many firms will employ these alternative mechanisms to obtain innovation. However, since no alternative is costless and all three require R&D spending and royalty payments in the case of licensing, we must inquire into the determinants of this different form of R&D across industries.

It is apparent that many of the interindustry differences in determinants of R&D spending by Canadian firms or subsidiaries will be similar to those just described even though the spending is on imita-

14. Safarian (1969). Dunning's (1958, chap. 5) evidence is similar.

15. Safarian (1969) found that many nonsubsidiaries made arrangements with nonaffiliated firms or industry associations outside Canada to get similar access to outside knowledge.

16. See Peck (1968).

tion or adaptation rather than innovation. Technological opportunity is a determinant of the likelihood that innovations exist elsewhere to be imitated or adapted to Canada. The resources available for innovative activity are a determinant of the ability to imitate or adapt. And the incentives to innovate determine the competitive benefits and pressures to imitate or adapt. Thus, paradoxically, a model explaining determinants of industries' R&D spending in Canada may look a lot like one explaining the determinants of industries' R&D in a large economy like that of the United States, despite the fundamental differences in the character of the uses for R&D funds.

The key differences between a Canadian and a U.S. model should be measures of Canadian firms' ease of access to innovations through imitating, licensing, of obtaining them from a corporate parent. Each alternative has its cost, including some R&D outlay in Canada, but each should generally be associated with lower rates of R&D spending in Canada than when Canadian firms themselves seek to innovate. With the other determinants of R&D held constant, R&D spending will probably be greatest where Canadian firms are themselves innovating, less when they are imitating, licensing, and adapting, and least when they are obtaining innovations from a parent and adapting them to Canada. The last two strategies are ranked as they are because the process of adaptation is probably facilitated by having successfully introduced the innovation elsewhere within the same company.

In industries in which Canadian firms compete in world markets, both the presence of resources available to innovate and the inability for competitive reasons to imitate or adapt may require Canadian firms to innovate. Firms that compete directly with other firms possessing the resources to innovate may not have opportunities to license or obtain innovations from parent companies elsewhere or the time delay of imitation or adaptation may be unacceptable. This explains why U.S. firms cannot often pursue strategies of imitation or adaptation despite the lower R&D resources required.

The availability and relative cost of the options to license and to imitate and adapt foreign innovations depend on the degree to which innovations must be altered to fit Canadian industry. In some industries Canada's institutional, cultural, or economic characteristics may render innovations created elsewhere of limited value. The degree to which the Canadian industry's requirements for marketing an innovation differ from the industry's requirements in the country where the innovation originated will vary. For example, in some consumer-good industries innovations may need significant adaptation to fit Canada's consumer tastes and retail distribution system. In countries very different from the Western industrialized countries, the option to imitate or adapt innovations flowing from large economies like the U.S. and Japan may be severely constrained by such differences and hence their determinants of R&D spending may be quite different from those of Canada. Since Canada is in many ways similar to the United States, we would expect the imitation and adaptation possibilities to be extensive, though not costless.

Whether the option of obtaining innovations from a parent firm is available depends on the presence of subsidiaries or branches of multinational companies in Canadian industries. The higher the foreign subsidiaries' percentage of sales in the Canadian industry, the more extensive will be the intracompany flow of innovations. A final issue is raised by the unlikely possibility that a multinational company will choose to do its R&D spending in Canada and shift the innovation elsewhere, rather than vice versa. This would mean that Canadian R&D spending would be high even though there were foreign subsidiaries in the Canadian industry and would imply that R&D spending would be positively associated with the prevalence of foreign subsidiaries in the Canadian industry.

Where a multinational chooses to conduct R&D would probably depend on the importance of the particular national market to its overall operations, the degree to which the national market was similar to or dissimilar from other major markets, and the benefits of proximity to the market for the expected success of the R&D effort. This seems to imply that multinationals would choose to do R&D in Canada only where Canada was an important source of raw materials or productive assets, where Canada was otherwise a power in world markets for the product, or where Canada offered some advantage in terms of lower cost or more effective R&D personnel or lower product-testing costs.[17] Otherwise, any difference between the Canadian market and large markets such as that of the United States or Western Europe would cause the rational multinational to conduct the R&D in those markets, particularly if the R&D effort benefited from proximity. Thus many of the same factors that determined the likelihood that Canadian industries would seek to create innovations rather than obtain them from elsewhere would determine the likelihood that multinationals were conducting original research in their Canadian subsidiaries. With these factors controlled for, the presence of extensive foreign subsidiaries in the Canadian industry should imply lower R&D spending.

17. This latter point was suggested by F. M. Scherer.

The hypothesis that small size constrains the ability of Canadian industries to innovate, but that they often imitate and adapt innovations, is supported by comparative data on R&D spending as a percentage of sales in matched Canadian and U.S. industries. Comparing our sample of Canadian industries to their U.S. counterparts, we found that the mean ratio of average R&D to sales in the Canadian industry to the ratio in the U.S. industry was 0.68. However, the correlation between ratios of R&D to sales in the two countries is approximately 0.8, consistent with our hypothesis that although the levels and characteristics of the R&D spending are very different, Canadian R&D spending behaves similarly to that of a large economy in its variation across industries.

7.2 Statistical Determinants of R&D Spending

These hypotheses were employed to specify a regression equation explaning R&D spending in our sample of Canadian manufacturing industries, as part of our simultaneous system of industrial-organization relations in Canada. Our model can be viewed as an estimate of the reduced form of the relations defining the benefits and cost of R&D spending. The dependent variable was

> RDIC   Sum of internal and external (contracted) research and development expenditures divided by the total sales of firms performing R&D, 1969.[18]

The first major specification problem was developing a measure of technological opportunity. Previous studies have either employed arbitrary classes of industries grouped by supposed technological opportunity or estimated models within broad sectors of the economy to attempt to control for technological opportunity (Scherer, 1970, chap. 15). The latter procedure was not feasible in our broad cross section of industries, and the former procedure was unsatisfying. However, we had available a measure of R&D spending in a matched sample of U.S. industries.

> RDIU   Funds for R&D expressed as a percentage of net sales for companies performing R&D, United States, 1969.

Since the United States is the world's largest economy and is in an advanced state of development, R&D spending in the United States

18. An important issue in examining R&D behavior in a sample of industries is the level of aggregation, since differences in R&D spending could be masked by overly broad industry definition. We are forced to rely on the standard industrial classification, as were most other researchers.

should reflect underlying technological opportunity and be relatively unaffected by the international inflow of technology. However, U.S. spending on research and development should be influenced by competitive conditions and other measures of incentives to conduct R&D that are similar to conditions in Canada, in which case including *RDIU* in an equation explaining *RDIC* will obscure the impact of certain variables. Thus we must be careful in interpreting equations that include *RDIU*, and we shall always present identical equations without *RDIU* for comparative purposes. In these latter equations we must accept the bias of a lack of control for technological opportunity in order to avoid obscuring important relationships.

To measure incentives to engage in R&D in the form of competitive rivalry, we employed a number of measures.

> *C468*   Percentage of shipments accounted for by the largest four enterprises, 1968.
>
> *C868*   Percentage of shipments accounted for by the largest eight enterprises, 1968.

To test for the presence of nonlinearities, we also employed the square of *C868* (*C8682*), and *C468* (*C4682*) as well as a discontinuous measure of concentration.

> *LOCONC*   Dummy variable equal to one if four-firm concentration in 1968 is less than 40 percent, zero otherwise.
>
> *MEDCONC*   Dummy variable equal to one if four-firm concentration in 1968 is less than or equal to 70 percent but greater than or equal to 40 percent, zero otherwise.
>
> *HICONC*   Dummy variable equal to one if four-firm concentration in 1968 is greater than 70 percent, zero otherwise.

To capture the presence of industries with regional or local character we employed

> *REG*   Dummy variable equal to one if the industry is judged subject to significant regional fragmentation, zero otherwise.

Regionally fragmented industries are industries in which each local or regional market is distinct and noncompetitive with other regions. In this sort of industry, transfer of R&D across regions through imitation and adaptation is possible within the same country, not to mention across national borders. The transfer is aided by the fact that the same firms often have operations in a number of regional markets, and thus R&D can be spread at very low cost through this mechanism. These arguments all suggest relatively low R&D spending in regionally fragmented industries.

Since Canada's economy is small and open, the degree of rivalry and the likely international flow of technology were also influenced by the presence of international competition.

IMP   Imports divided by the value of shipments, 1961.
EXP   Net exports divided by the value of shipments, 1961.
TRAD   Sum of *IMP* and *EXP*.
EFT   Effective rate of tariff protection, 1963.

To test the effect of industry size on R&D spending we included

ECA67   Number of employees in the industry, 1967.

ECA672, equal to the value of *ECA67* squared, was included to capture the presence of nonlinearities.

We included industry size rather than firm size in the model because of the different character of Canadian R&D in relation to R&D in a large economy. Firm size has been investigated extensively in many U.S.-based studies, to measure hypothesized economies of scale in R&D. While such economies may be plausible in conducting original research, it is far from clear that significant economies of scale will exist in adapting and imitating R&D done elsewhere. Industry size, on the other hand, should be a key determinant of R&D in a small, open economy such as Canada's, given our theory. It measures the extent to which the comparative advantage or size of the home market make Canada a likely site for original research.[19] A large Canadian industry would imply a greater likelihood that original research, and high R&D spending, were occurring in Canada.

Since R&D spending is hypothesized to be influenced by profitability, we included

ROI   Net profit (loss) after taxes divided by total equity, 1968–1971.
PCAD   Value added minus payroll and advertising expenditures, divided by the value of shipments, 1967.

ROI is measured after R&D expenditures have been substracted and hence is not a perfect measure of the profits available for R&D. Unfortunately, *ROI* data were unavailable for years before our dependent variable, and thus we could not examine lag effects. *PCAD* is a measure of margins after advertising but before R&D is deducted, though it includes interest expense and other expenses that should be deducted in measuring true price-cost margins.

19. This likelihood is not adequately captured by the extent of exports because high exports may occur in a market that is tiny in Canada and small relative to world markets.

Growth of the industry was included as a measure of the incentive to engage in R&D and potentially as a measure of technological opportunity.

GSI   The slope coefficient of the regression of the logarithm of industry shipments on time, 1961–1971.

High industry growth might reduce the incentive for rivalry for market share and perhaps also reduce the incentive for R&D spending. But growth might also proxy the future payout to R&D, with greater benefits expected if the industry is expanding. Rapid growth usually signals the presence of an industry relatively early in its development. In a less mature industry the future payout to innovation could be greater than in a more mature industry. Finally, growth proxying an industry early in its development could imply more technological opportunity for innovation and hence a positive relation between growth and R&D spending.[20]

To test for the impact of product differentiation we included

ADI   Ratio of total advertising costs as a percentage of sales, 1965.
DADI Dummy equal to one if ADI is greater than 1 percent, zero otherwise.

The latter measure was intended to discriminate between industries in which differentiation through advertising was possible and those in which it was not.

To test the relation of diversification to R&D spending we employed a number of measures of diversification (the second and third are inverse measures).

DCC   Concentric measure of diversification, described in chapter 8. Weighted average of the measure for all the enterprises classified to the industry.
DE3C Fraction of employees in manufacturing establishments engaged in activities classified to the enterprise's principal three-digit industry. Weighted average of the measure for all the enterprises classified to the industry.
DE4C Fraction of employees in manufacturing establishments engaged in activities classified to the enterprise's principal four-digit industry. Weighted average of the measure for all the enterprises classified to the industry.

20. The appropriate variable is industry growth, not firm growth, as had appeared in some studies (for example Rosenberg, 1976). Firm growth is less likely to be a causal variable than an outcome of R&D spending, unless it is lagged. Firm growth is also associated with firm profits and some of the underlying variables determining R&D spending and hence produces misleading results even if lagged.

Finally, we included measures of the importance of foreign subsidiaries in the Canadian industry and of the degree of government-financed R&D in the industry.

FSE   Value of shipments and other revenues of establishments classified as belonging to enterprises 50 percent or more foreign controlled, 1969, divided by the value of shipments by all establishments in the industry, 1969.

GRDC   Government-financed research and development expressed as a percentage of all internal and external R&D outlays, 1969.

As was the case elsewhere in our simultaneous system of equations, we estimated multiple regression equations explaining *RDIC* in three ways: using simple OLS in the basic sample of Canadian manufacturing industries, using simple OLS in our sample of industries with missing observations filled in, and employing two-stage least squares (TSLS) on the filled-in data base. We employed *RDIU* as a proxy for technological opportunity, but we recognize that it may obscure the impact of some significant variables. Thus in the regression equations we estimate the model including *RDIU* but also report the identical equation without *RDIU*.

In the estimation of the model a difficulty became apparent in examining the impact of *FSE*. While theory identifies *FSE* as a potentially important variable in determining R&D spending, *FSE* is also associated with R&D spending for reasons that are not causal. One of the factors determining foreign direct investment in an industry is the presence of intangible assets, of which innovation is clearly one. Thus foreign investment is associated with industries engaging in high levels of R&D spending, even though industries with heavy proportions of foreign subsidiaries probably also have lower R&D spending than would similar industries without foreign investment, though the latter are rare. Thus it is difficult to empirically separate the causal role of foreign ownership from its effects on R&D spending in a model explaining the rate of R&D spending across industries, though use of TSLS should improve the state of affairs.

When *FSE* was included in our *RDIC* equations, it had a positive sign and was highly significant with *t*-values of 5 and higher. This is consistent with the association between *FSE* and industries with higher innovation.[21] However, inclusion of *FSE* introduced substantial collinearity into the model, including of course the TSLS equations. Since its primary role in an *RDIC* model is evidently not causal,

21. This result was conclusively demonstrated by Safarian (1969). See his chapter 5.

we chose to omit it from the *RDIC* equations. Later in this chapter when we examine R&D spending in matched U.S. and Canadian industries, we shall be able to devise a test that better captures *FSE*'s causal significance.

Table 7.1 presents multiple regression equations explaining *RDIC* in our sample of Canadian manufacturing industries. In the equations including *RDIU, RDIU* is uniformly positive and highly significant and is the largest contributor to explained variance. The inclusion of *RDIU* has effects on a number of the other variables in the analysis.

C868 always has a positive effect on R&D spending, with a *t*-ratio hovering around 1, consistent with U.S. studies that find a positive though not robust effect of concentration on R&D. The inclusion of *RDIU* generally reduces the significance of concentration, similar to the results of Scherer (1965), who found that concentration lost significance if technological opportunity was controlled. However, since Canadian and U.S. concentration are quite highly correlated (Chapter 3), adding *RDIU* to the equation may be including some of the effect of concentration and biasing the results.

The performance of the concentration variable does not improve with nonlinear specifications including *C868* and *C8682*, though the linear term is always positive and the squared term negative while neither is significant (these results are not reported). The discontinuous dummy measures of concentration produce some interesting results, however. In a simple correlation analysis *LOCONC* is negatively and significantly correlated with *RDIC*, while *MEDCONC* and *HICONC* are positively correlated with *RDIC*. In a regression equation *LOCONC* and *MEDCONC* are signed the same way, though multicollinearity between the concentration variables and other variables in the equation appears to hold their significance below 90 percent. *HICONC* is positive and performs marginally better than *C868* in some runs. Although the results are not robust in the regression equations and hence are not reported, concentration thus appears to have a nonlinear influence on *RDIC*, with *RDIC* low in unconcentrated industries and highest in highly concentrated industries, controlling for industry size and the diversity of firms in the industry.[22]

22. The *HICONC* result is different from Scherer's (1967) U.S. result that R&D increases with concentration only up to moderate levels of concentration (approximately 50 percent). The difference reflects the different character of R&D in a small, open economy. In Canada the overall small size of the economy means that the most concentrated industries are in the best position to engage in the most original research rather than to adopt the alternatives of imitation and adaptation. Our result is also not supportive of Romeo's (1975) finding from U.S. data that concentration is inimical to the diffusion of innovation.

Table 7.1 Determinants of research and development expenditures as a percentage of sales.

Independent variable	Estimation method					
	A	A	B	B	C	C
C868	0.0090026	0.0039221	0.010162[c]	0.0035871	0.0027920	0.0024958
	(0.868)	(0.644)	(1.134)	(0.785)	(0.258)	(0.361)
DCC	1.9501[a]	0.55850[c]	1.1805[a]	0.32644[c]	2.5688[a]	1.1425[c]
	(3.5299)	(1.575)	(3.153)	(1.415)	(3.381)	(1.595)
ADI	24.626[a]	11.330[b]	15.813[b]	6.9335[c]	20.746[b]	10.118
	(2.663)	(2.028)	(2.107)	(1.554)	(1.754)	(1.207)
EXPC	-1.8819[c]	-1.1034[c]	-1.2868	-1.0667[b]	-1.8584[b]	-1.9708[b]
	(1.401)	(1.396)	(1.281)	(1.810)	(1.752)	(1.842)
IMPC	1.5700[b]	-0.11628	0.93347	-0.016905	1.3195	-0.28988
	(2.150)	(0.252)	(1.714)	(0.051)	(1.056)	(0.294)
ROI	-9.0212[b]	-7.7195[a]	-8.3348[b]	-6.3995[a]	-11.982[c]	-10.439[b]
	(1.731)	(2.529)	(1.976)	(2.581)	(1.321)	(1.888)
DADI	—	—	—	—	—	—
REG	-0.83748[c]	-0.52025[c]	-0.44887	-0.28250	-0.38156	-0.42408
	(1.446)	(1.529)	(1.023)	(1.097)	(0.683)	(1.218)
RDIU	—	0.71680	—	0.70992	—	0.50542
		(9.556)		(12.081)		(2.651)
ECA67	—	—	—	—	—	—
ECA672	—	—	—	—	—	—
EFT	—	—	—	—	—	—
GSI	—	—	—	—	—	—
GRDC	—	—	—	—	—	—
Constant	-0.6466	0.07567	0.05259	0.2559	-0.4245	0.4657
	(0.538)	(0.107)	(0.067)	(0.555)	(0.360)	(0.577)
$\bar{R}^2$	0.332	0.771	0.208	0.728	—	—
F	4.831	23.766	4.108	28.693	5.269	11.297
D.f.	47	46	76	75	76	75

Table 7.1 Determinants of research and development expenditures as a percentage of sales (continued).

Independent variable	Estimation method					
	A	A	B	B	C	C
C868	0.010970 (0.979)	0.0013295 (0.200)	0.010509 (1.185)	0.001716 (0.347)	-0.0004122 (0.024)	-0.0025491 (0.261)
DCC	1.8175[a] (3.181)	0.76619[b] (2.173)	1.0785[a] (2.697)	0.41249[b] (1.818)	2.5354[a] (3.004)	1.2766[b] (2.038)
ADI	-	-	-	-	-	-
EXPC	1.4891 (0.896)	0.40884 (0.418)	0.20644 (0.164)	-0.20439 (0.293)	0.58186 (0.169)	0.24424 (0.124)
IMPC	-	-	-	-	-	-
ROI	-10.931[b] (2.088)	-6.7831[b] (2.178)	-8.2160[b] (1.822)	-4.3334[b] (1.727)	1.4261 (0.166)	-0.076300 (0.011)
DADI	1.6622[a] (3.437)	0.90938[a] (3.093)	0.69486[b] (1.799)	0.41426[b] (1.932)	0.77357 (1.177)	0.57750[c] (1.519)
REG	-1.5113[a] (2.821)	-0.66277[b] (2.032)	-0.65695[c] (1.518)	-0.2829 (1.175)	-0.84122[c] (1.558)	-0.47955[c] (1.458)
RDIU	-	0.68184[a] (9.268)	-	0.74726[a] (12.932)	-	0.55961[a] (3.143)
ECA67	0.000091908[b] (1.717)	0.000023152 (0.720)	0.00003560 (0.968)	0.000019041 (0.935)	0.00006437 (0.661)	0.000032124 (0.568)
ECA672	-0.15883E-08[b] (2.258)	-0.55082E-09 (1.172)	-0.72593E-09[c] (1.410)	-0.38176E-09[c] (1.336)	-0.13022E-08 (0.925)	-0.69153E-09 (0.837)
EFT	2.5419[c] (1.520)	0.93575 (0.943)	0.94534 (0.943)	0.3096 (0.557)	1.5054 (1.065)	0.71229 (0.842)
GSI	10.989[c] (1.354)	-5.7594 (1.135)	3.6546 (0.758)	-7.4084[a] (2.650)	-1.2964 (0.196)	-7.2927[b] (1.722)
GRDC						
Constant	-2.555[b] (1.756)	-0.2014 (0.227)	-0.4314 (0.434)	0.2398 (0.435)	-1.951 (1.034)	-0.5976 (0.515)
$\bar{R}^2$	0.417	0.801	0.188	0.752	-	-
F	4.863	20.759	2.918	23.896	2.511	10.889
D.f.	44	43	73	72	73	72

	(1)	(2)	(3)	(4)	(5)	(6)
C868	-0.011018 (0.611)	0.014147 (0.614)	0.00027804 (0.056)	0.012420c (1.513)	0.00048208 (0.073)	0.011127 (1.029)
DCC	1.6415b (1.745)	1.1982 (0.777)	0.51417b (2.216)	0.53759c (1.496)	0.89491a (2.468)	1.3349b (2.232)
ADI	—	—	—	—	—	—
EXPC	-0.36018 (0.146)	1.5237 (0.394)	-0.13533 (0.196)	-0.11550 (0.099)	0.48484 (0.499)	1.1204 (0.695)
IMPC	—	—	—	—	—	—
ROI	1.6444 (0.193)	-2.5497 (-0.183)	-3.5218a (1.395)	-9.5943b (2.294)	-5.9646b (1.913)	-11.902b (2.347)
DADI	0.089926 (0.097)	1.5734c (1.527)	0.37707b (1.771)	0.72963b (2.045)	0.89869a (3.083)	1.5491a (3.299)
REG	-0.35517 (0.827)	-0.88150c (1.487)	-0.23798 (0.994)	-0.68919b (1.723)	-0.68929b (1.975)	-1.4096a (2.716)
RDIU	0.71842b (2.147)	—	0.81562a (11.639)	—	0.73687a (8.789)	—
EC467	-0.000030963 (0.250)	0.000016425 (1.165)	0.000014919 (0.736)	0.000043474 (1.276)	0.000023689 (0.744)	0.00007816b (1.502)
ECA672	0.35537E-09 (0.179)	-0.29199E-08c (1.361)	-0.30570 (1.070)	-0.86051E-09b (1.804)	-0.49910E-09 (1.178)	-0.13938E-08 (-2.035)
EFT	0.26420 (0.216)	1.9184 (1.203)	0.26271 (0.478)	0.91123 (0.984)	0.8945 (0.909)	2.3423c (1.449)
GSI	-3.1500 (0.373)	-12.119 (0.982)	-6.8306a (2.455)	-1.14151 (0.247)	-3.4264 (0.643)	2.6628 (0.303)
GRDC	-0.086499 (0.598)	0.16018 (1.084)	-0.024604b (1.681)	0.074281a (3.680)	-0.023845c (1.330)	0.058881b (2.075)
Constant	0.3867 (0.183)	-3.063c (1.327)	0.2523 (0.643)	-0.2839 (0.309)	-0.4010 (0.449)	-1.675 (1.143)
$\bar{R}^2$	—	—	0.758	0.307	0.805	0.458
F	0.750	3.392	22.696	4.339	19.517	5.145
D.f.	71	72	71	72	42	42

Note: Levels of statistical significance (one-tailed test) are a = 1 percent, b = 5 percent, c = 10 percent. The independent variables listed above the horizontal line contains components that are endogenous in our model.

These results survive the inclusion of $RDIU$ as a measure of technological opportunity.

REG has a negative and nearly always significant influence on $RDIC$, with its significance generally improving when technological opportunity is controlled. If regionality was acting as a correction to the concentration variable, signifying that measured national concentration understated true concentration in regional industries, then our other results would imply a positive sign for regionality. On the other hand, regionality may be picking up some of the effect of concentration, since it is somewhat collinear with $LOCONC$ which has a negative influence on $RDIC$.

Industry size, measured by $ECA67$, has a consistent, nonlinear impact on $RDIC$. $RDIC$ increases with size, when the other variables in the model are controlled for, but reaches a maximum and diminishes ($ECA672$ is negative and significant or nearly significant). This result is consistent with our proposition that large Canadian industries would be ones in which original research, and high R&D spending, will occur. It will be supported by our comparative analysis. The negative sign for $ECA672$ indicates that the effect of size on R&D spending is most significant for medium-sized industries. For very large industries R&D spending as a percentage of sales falls off, perhaps because of economies of scale in conducting original research. We also tested various measures of average firm size for their impact on R&D spending, for comparative purposes with previous U.S.-based studies.[23] None of the numerous measures of average firm size tested proved even marginally significant, supporting our hypothesis that average firm size is not likely to play a role in Canada, given the different character of much Canadian R&D.

International trade has an erratic effect on R&D intensity in Canadian industries. IMP is positive and significant without $RDIU$ but becomes negative and not significant when $RDIU$ is included in the model to control for technological opportunity. This is not because $RDIU$ is capturing the effect of imports, which are proportionally quite low in the United States. Rather, IMP is in part a measure of technological opportunity. Imports into a country such as Canada occur in industries with relatively high technological opportunity. The life-cycle theory of international trade suggests that countries such as the United States will export high-technology goods in developing industries to countries such as Canada, though later they may establish subsidiaries to produce these goods in Canada. Thus

23. For a discussion see Scherer (1970, chap. 15).

the positive association of imports and *RDIC* probably reflects the higher technology of the high-import industries and the requisite need for Canadian-based producers in these industries to conduct R&D. When technological opportunity is controlled, the results indicate that import competition has a negative effect on R&D spending, a result that is confirmed later in this chapter by the use of an alternative research design. Such an association is consistent with the view that import-competing industries have greater opportunities for licensing and other lower-cost mechanisms to gain technology and hence spend less on R&D than industries without international competitors also serving the Canadian market. *EXP* has a negative and nearly significant influence on *RDIC* which disappears when the industry-size variables are included in the model. Industry size and exports should be and are highly correlated; when size is controlled, the theoretical impact of exports is much weaker since it runs through the relation of exports to industry rivalry.

EFT, the effective rate of tariff protection, has a positive and significant influence on R&D, which retains most of its significance when *RDIU* is included. Daly and Globerman (1976, chap. 5) have argued that tariffs slow technological innovation and diffusion. However, our results imply that tariff-protected industries have higher R&D spending, other things equal, perhaps because protection from foreign competition shifts firms away from imitation and adaptation to meet this competition and toward more original research aimed particularly at the Canadian market, raising the total R&D outlays. Daly and Globerman's hypothesis evidently fails to consider the underlying nature of Canadian R&D and the choice that Canadian firms face among different approaches to R&D activity.

Differentiation, measured by *ADI*, has a strong positive and significant influence on *RDIC*. With the variable specified as a dummy measuring either the presence or absence of differentiation (*DADI*), it becomes even more significant, and hence it appears that potential for differentiation rather than the extent of differentiation or advertising is what matters for *RDIC*. Differentiation may be a partial proxy for technological opportunity, yet the result holds when *RDIU* is included. Differentiation could also be signifying greater incentives to engage in R&D through allowing more appropriability of the results of R&D. However, including *RDIU* in the model would once again embody this effect; and if it was the primary influence of differentiation on R&D, including *RDIU* in the model would presumably drastically worsen the performance of *DADI*. Since this was not the case (though the performance of *DADI* does fall slightly with the inclusion of *RDIU*), it seems most likely that *DADI* is capturing the need to adapt foreign R&D for the Canadian market. If differentiation is present, it is likely that products must be specially adapted to the Canadian market, thereby requiring more significant R&D outlays than is the case for undifferentiated products. Thus differentiation is a key measure of the cost to the industry of converting foreign R&D to Canadian uses. We get the same basic result as Comanor (1967) and Shrieves (1978) but for very different reasons.

Industry growth (*GSI*) is a positive and significant or nearly significant influence on *RDIC* where *RDIU* is not included. A positive sign is consistent with growth indicating the presence of a developing industry with either greater technological opportunity or greater incentives to engage in R&D in view of increasing future size, or both. However, an industry's state of development and hence its relative growth rate are similar in the United States and Canada, and so this effect is embodied in *RDIU* when it is included.[24] Thus the fall in significance of *GSI* is to be expected. We explore the negative sign that results from the inclusion of *RDIU* later in this chapter through our alternative research design.

Profitability is negative and always significant as a determinant of *RDIC*, with or without the inclusion of *RDIU*. *ROI* performs somewhat better than *PCAD*. The opposite sign is predicted theoretically by most previous research, though most studies have failed to find a significant relationship between profitability (or cash flow) and R&D spending in U.S. data.[25] The negative impact of *PCAD* on *RDIU* could occur because high profits signify the presence of some rent-yielding asset which implies the absence of competition and thus the lack of competitive pressure to innovate. Or high profits, with the other variables in the model controlled, could be picking up those industries that have patented technologies developed elsewhere and require little ongoing R&D under the patent umbrella (such as photographic equipment with Polaroid and Kodak and duplicating equipment with Xerox). With the other variables in the model controlled, whatever causes the high profits must also reduce the need for ongoing R&D in Canada to adapt technology and hence lower Canadian R&D spending.

24. We would expect growth to be positive and significant in U.S. studies, particularly if the proxy employed to measure technological opportunity was crude.

25. If the relation has been significant in previous studies, it has been positive. See Scherer (1970, pp. 363–364) for a survey. Howe and McFetridge (1976) get erratic results for the relation between firm profits and firm R&D in three Canadian manufacturing industries.

A major variable in the model is diversification, measured in a variety of ways. Diversification is always a strong positive and significant determinant of *RDIC* with or without the inclusion of *RDIU*, though its significance falls with the inclusion of *RDIU*. The positive result in the equation not controlling for technological opportunity is consistent with U.S. studies.[26] However, these studies find that when technological opportunity is controlled, diversification is no longer a significant determinant of R&D except where technological opportunity is low. Our results suggest a greater role for diversification in a small, open economy such as Canada's; indeed diversification is one of the most robust variables in the model, because of Canada's smaller size and the differing character of its R&D. Diversification in such a setting may enable the Canadian firm to innovate rather than to adapt innovation, through partially overcoming the scale economies of innovation that push Canadian firms to licensing and imitating. Previous research suggests a modest threshold firm size for effective R&D in relation to the size of leading firms in U.S. industries; it is thus not surprising that diversification has a much smaller positive impact on R&D in the United States when tests are properly controlled.

The final key variable to be discussed is the extent of government financed R&D, *GRDC*. *GRDC* is the fraction of *RDIC* that was financed by the Canadian government. Where *RDIU* is not included, *GRDC* proved to be a positive and quite significant determinant of *RDIC*. Thus government-subsidized R&D does not cause company-funded R&D to fall proportionally; rather it increases the total amount of R&D spending. When *RDIU* is included in the equation, however, *GRDC* becomes negative and significant or nearly significant. Evidently *RDIU* reflects the greater R&D expenditures in industries in which government subsidy is broadly practiced, such as defense-related industries and critical natural resources. With these controlled, subsidy by the Canadian government is associated with lower overall R&D expenditures. This result may or may not reflect a causal connection. Controlling for industries in which government subsidy is common through the inclusion of *RDIU*, we see that high *GRDC* may signify industries for which structural conditions that determine R&D but are not captured in the model are very unfavorable. Here government financing is a large percentage of total R&D because little R&D is done at all. Government R&D financing is made available to all firms on comparable terms regardless of their industry environments—in environments unfavorable for R&D, little R&D

---

26. See Grabowski (1968), Scherer (1965).

would be done without financing. If the structural variables in the model are incomplete, therefore, the presence of a high percentage of government subsidy in R&D expenditures may be proxying unmeasured structural considerations.

A dummy variable measuring whether the industry was a nonconvenience industry had a positive and significant simple correlation with $RDIC$, though its marginal significance in the regressions (probably due to collinearity) did not justify reporting its regression results in view of space limitations.[27] Work by Porter (1976b, chap. 2) suggests that the incentive to engage in R&D in consumer-good industries should be greatest in nonconvenience industries, because more careful buyer behavior and the information-providing function of the retailer should insure that innovation is assimilated into the marketplace. Nonconvenience goods, which include consumer durables, may also be richer in opportunities for innovation. Innovations in convenience goods may not be successful in the market without heavy advertising. Recall the results in chapter 6, which found that $RDIC$ was positively associated as a causal variable to advertising intensity in convenience goods, though not in nonconvenience goods. The causality is established because advertising in convenience goods is not a significant determinant of $RDIC$. Nonconvenience buyer behavior is causally related to R&D spending.[28]

Finally, a variable that interacted $C868$ and $DADI$ performed marginally better in some cases than the two variables entered separately, though these results are not reported. This better performance supports some role for the effect of differentiation-based incentives for R&D. Increasing concentration implies increasing appropriability of the benefits of an innovation, but only if product differentiation allows the firm to capture these benefits by associating the innovation with itself. Product differentiation makes imitation more difficult. This result is inconsistent with Comanor's (1967) result, recently confirmed by Shrieves (1978), that concentration has the greatest impact on R&D in differentiated industries. In any event, the interaction effect appears much less important than the separate effects of the two variables in Canada, perhaps because firms in Canadian industries with high concentration and high differentiation are probably heavily multinational, with access to low-cost sources of R&D done elsewhere.

27. The nonconvenience dummy is not acting as a proxy for advertising, since advertising is lower in nonconvenience industries. The simple correlation between the dummy and $RDIC$ is +0.24.

28. Not surprisingly, the nonconvenience dummy loses significance when $RDIU$ is included, since $RDIU$ embodies the convenience-nonconvenience distinction.

The two-stage least-squares results are generally quite similar to the *OLS* results, with the usual difference that the efficiency of the estimates falls. Thus the basic results hold. Establishing the absence of simultaneity bias is especially noteworthy with respect to concentration and differentiation. Concentration still has a causal, albeit weak, relation to R&D when simultaneity is controlled. There are a few differences worth noting, however. First, the shape of the implied relation between concentration and R&D in Canada is altered. In the TSLS equations *C868* is negative while *C8682* is positive; *LOCONC* and *HICONC* are positive and nearly significant (despite the efficiency loss of TSLS), and *MEDCONC* is negative and nearly significant. This could suggest that at low levels of concentration, scale economies in imitation and adaptation of R&D mean that firms must spend a greater proportion of their sales on it, outweighing potentially low appropriability. Medium levels of concentration combine relatively low appropriability with the lack of this problem. *GSI* is the variable that is affected by the simultaneous-equation methods, sustaining a marked loss in significance in the equations not controlling for technological opportunity and becoming negative and significant in the equations that do. Evidently, in a simultaneous model the incentive and life-cycle effects of growth are minor or captured elsewhere in the system.

Taken as a whole, our results show that it is possible to explain a substantial proportion of the variation in R&D across industries even in a small, open economy, and the results consistently support the theoretical framework. Our equation is able to capture more influences on R&D spending than was possible in previous research. Carefully specified, the model withstands estimation by simultaneous methods in the much larger system represented by our system of equations. While the results are robust, however, we can benefit by pushing our analysis further in certain areas. With a number of variables, it was difficult to separate their causal effects from their effects as proxies for technological opportunity or other things. A complementary research design allows us to make progress toward doing so.

7.3 Differences in R&D Spending for Matched Canadian-U.S. Industries

To control for technological opportunity and certain other aspects of industry structure such as growth, convenience versus nonconvenience, and the incentive effects of differentiation in a different way, we estimated a model explaining the differences in R&D spending between matched Canadian and U.S. industries. Unlike our advertising data in chapter 6, R&D data were available for a sample of U.S. industries that matched our basic Canadian manufacturing industry sample.

The difference-equation formulation controls for technology and other exogenous variables that we believe will affect U.S. and Canadian R&D behavior in the same way, because they are eliminated from the equation by subtraction.[29]

$$R\&D_c = A_c + Bx + C_c y + \mu,$$
$$R\&D_u = A_u + Bx + C_u y + \gamma;$$

thus

$$(R\&D_c - R\&D_u) = (A_c - A_u) + B(x - x) + (C_c - C_u) y + \mu - \gamma$$

where

$u =$ United States,
$c =$ Canada,
$y =$ variables that vary between Canada and the United States,
$x =$ exogenous variables,
$\mu, \gamma =$ error terms.

Such a procedure will thus control for the component of technological opportunity captured in variables such as *IMP* and for the properties of the differentiation, buyer-behavior, and growth measures that will affect both countries equally. Thus we shall be able to examine directly the impact of concentration, profits, growth, trade, differentiation, and other variables while separating out these elements.

The dependent variable for the analysis was

DIFFR&D   *RDIC* minus *RDIU.*

In addition to the variables already defined, we computed a number of other differenced and ratio variables.

DIFFCON   *C868* minus *US868.*
DIFFROI   *ROI* minus *ROIU,* the latter the rate of return on equity capital in the matched U.S. industry, 1968–1971.
RATROI   *ROI* divided by *ROIU.* This variable allows a test of another functional form of the relation between *ROI* differences and R&D differences.

29. This formulation also assumes a functional form of the relation where the absolute difference in the ratio of R&D to sales is proportional to absolute differences in the independent variables, in contrast with the formulation in chapter 6, where we examined proportional differences. This yielded superior results here.

DIFFSIZ   *ECA67* minus *EUS67*, the latter the number of employees in the matched U.S. industry in 1967. This variable is a measure of comparative industry size.

DIFFGS   *GRDC* minus *GRDU,* the latter the percentage of government-financed R&D in the matched U.S. industry, 1969.

Table 7.2 presents OLS regressions explaining *DIFFR&D*, which we interpret mindful of the generally greater difficulty of achieving significant results in differenced models as compared with levels models. *DIFFCON* has a positive and nearly significant impact on *DIFFR&D*,

Table 7.2 Determinants of differences between Canadian and U.S. research and development.

Independent variable	Estimation method			
	A	B	A	B
DIFFCON	0.0116	0.008295c	0.00189	0.00760
	(1.055)	(1.343)	(0.206)	(1.252)
RATROI	−16.706a	−18.051a	−14.48a	−17.159a
	(2.710)	(3.507)	(2.957)	(3.394)
REG	−0.3518	−0.2308	−0.3081	−0.1885
	(0.932)	(0.942)	(0.931)	(0.777)
TRAD	−0.5107c	−0.2628	−0.8942a	−0.2634
	(1.383)	(1.033)	(2.595)	(1.036)
FSE	−0.4159	−0.6561c	−0.4130	−0.6687c
	(0.623)	(1.565)	(0.634)	(1.591)
DADI	0.3070	0.3925b	0.0718	0.3547c
	(0.887)	(1.720)	(0.231)	(1.565)
GSI	−8.5814c	−9.4702a	−7.930c	−8.555a
	(1.440)	(3.585)	(1.415)	(3.159)
DIFFSIZ	−	−	0.5376	0.6046
			(0.581)	(0.755)
DIFFGS	−	−	−0.0281	−0.0310b
			(1.228)	(2.181)
Constant	0.6712	0.7865b	1.096b	0.9050a
	(1.180)	(2.399)	(2.336)	(2.769)
$\bar{R}^2$	0.250	0.297	0.482	0.329
F	3.048	6.003	4.412	5.526
D.f.	36	76	24	74

Note: Levels of statistical significance (one-tailed test) are a = 1 percent, b = 5 percent, c = 10 percent.

which becomes only marginally more so when the coefficients of *C868* and *US868* are allowed to differ, giving them unequal impacts on the dependent variable (these results are not reported). This result supports the earlier finding that concentration has a positive impact on R&D spending. *DIFFROI* has a negative and usually significant impact on *DIFFR&D* (not reported) and *RATROI* has a negative and highly significant impact. Thus differences in Canadian and U.S. R&D spending for matched industries are related more to the proportional differences in return on investment than to the absolute differences.

With technological opportunity controlled, *EXP* and *IMP* both have a negative and nearly significant impact on *DIFFR&D* (not reported), with the best specification using the combined *TRAD* variable. This supports our earlier assertion that the presence of foreign trade is generally associated with lower costs and/or better opportunities to adapt or easily imitate innovation; this result may also support the hypothesis that the presence of trade signifies that the difficulty of adaptation of R&D is less since the sale of foreign goods in Canada may imply less peculiarly Canadian requirements for these goods. This is contrary to the view of Johns (1978) and others who argue that imports signify international competition, which causes higher R&D spending. Our negative sign for imports coupled with a positive impact of tariff protection solidifies the importance of access to foreign technology as a key determinant of R&D spending in Canada.

DADI retains its positive sign even under the controls for technological opportunity and industry characteristics embodied in this research design, supporting our earlier interpretation that one of its properties is signaling the degree to which foreign R&D had to be adapted for Canadian use. The more differentiation, the more likely is significant adaptation necessary, other things held equal, and hence the positive sign.

GSI is a negative and highly significant influence on the difference in R&D, contrasted with its positive and significant influence in the *RDIC* equation. We argued that *GSI* was a proxy for industry maturity, with high growth implying a newer industry where the expected payout to R&D spending was greater. However, when we are comparing R&D spending in matched industries, the state of industry maturity is likely to be controlled. The negative sign obtained in this test (as well as earlier when we included *RDIU* in the model) is consistent with the other hypothesis linking growth and R&D spending. Rapid growth, controlling for industry, maturity, and concentration, reduces the incentive for rivalry and competition in R&D.

DIFFSIZ has a consistent positive sign, though its significance is not robust. Thus if the Canadian industry is large relative to the matched U.S. industry, it tends to spend more on R&D as a percentage of sales. The positive sign supports our earlier result that large Canadian industries are more likely to be conducting original research and to be spending heavily on R&D.

DIFFGS has a negative and significant influence on *DIFFR&D*. Thus a high percentage of Canadian subsidy relative to U.S. subsidy is associated with lower Canadian R&D relative to U.S. R&D in matched industries. These results are consistent with our earlier ones in the model explaining R&D in Canada. Either Canadian government subsidy actually discourages R&D in industries where it is high relative to U.S. industries, or in such situations high Canadian subsidy is acting as a proxy for a poor Canadian industry environment for R&D that is incompletely captured in our model.

A final result of great interest is that *FSE* enters with a consistent negative sign and is nearly significant. Although we could not unscramble the effect of foreign subsidiaries in our *RDIC* equations because of *FSE*'s role as a proxy for other variables, in this controlled test we see that high foreign subsidiary share indeed lowers R&D intensity in Canadian industry. Thus the presence of foreign subsidiaries facilitates the lowest-cost mechanism for obtaining R&D by allowing intrafirm transfer of technology into Canada.

7.4 Summary

We have examined the determinants of R&D spending in Canadian manufacturing industries, employing two complementary research methodologies. One estimated a cross-sectional equation explaining R&D spending as part of our simultaneous system of industrial-organization relations and allowed a test free of possible simultaneity biases that have clouded previous research. We also examined comparative spending on R&D in a matched sample of Canadian and U.S. industries, a procedure that remedied the difficult problem of controlling for technological opportunity to innovate.

When we investigated the particular determinants of R&D spending by firms in a small, open economy such as Canada's, our theory suggested that the characteristics of the R&D done in Canada would be markedly different from that in a large economy. Nevertheless, theory suggested that the cross-sectional determinants of R&D spending would be quite similar to those in an economy such as the U.S. economy, though for very different reasons, and this was verified in our empirical tests. The most potent influence on R&D spending was technological opportunity to innovate. Concentration had a positive influence on R&D spending, most significant at high concentration levels. Regional industry fragmentation had a negative influence, while industry size had a nonlinear positive impact which reached a maximum and became negative. Firm size in Canada was not of the same theoretical significance for R&D spending as it was in the United States, and firm size proved an insignificant influence on R&D in Canada. Imports had a negative influence on R&D once technological opportunity was well controlled, while tariff protection had a positive influence. Product differentiation had a strong positive influence on R&D spending, as did diversification. Unlike U.S. studies, *ROI* had a negative influence on R&D that was explicable given the particular Canadian context. Industry growth, after controlling for technological opportunity and industry maturity, had a negative influence on R&D spending. High government subsidy is associated with greater R&D spending overall but with lower R&D spending in industries where U.S. subsidy is not also high. Several other variables yielded interesting though not robust results.

The results reported persist in the TSLS equations, confirming their freedom from simultaneity bias. The comparative research design reinforced the positive influence of concentration and differentiation and the negative role of profitability on R&D. It also confirmed the negative roles of foreign trade and growth, variables for which it was difficult to separate their causal significance from their roles as proxies for other things. Finally, in the comparative research design we were able to perform an unbiased test of the impact of heavy foreign ownership in the industry on R&D spending, finding its influence to be negative as our theory suggested.

8 Diversification

Diversification is said to influence market performance in many ways. Diversified firms can dip into their "deep pockets" to intimidate or expel rivals and dampen competition. But they can also arbitrage resources from declining sectors and provide a supply of well-endowed potential entrants to markets in which entry barriers deter newborn firms. Because of diversification's significance for performance, we seek to explain its level—both the amount of diversification undertaken by firms based in an industry and the amount flowing into it by firms based elsewhere. We propose and describe measures of diversification, then apply them to show how diversification varies with the size and nationality of firms. We attempt to explain diversification outbound from and inbound to an industry. We return to the subject in chapter 11, where the large firm becomes the unit of observation.

8.1 Data Base and Measurement of Diversification

The economic theory of diversification does not provide a strong basis for determining how diversification should be measured, and there are many measures to choose from. For that reason, and because special properties of our data qualify the analysis significantly, we first consider the data and ways of measuring of diversity. Dun and Bradstreet offer a commercial service known as Dun's Market Identifiers, a continually updated file of information on manufacturing and other industrial establishments in Canada as well as the United States. Each establishment's record shows the corporate headquarters to which it reports, the number of employees at that location, and the principal product or activity—and as many as five secondary products or activities—described by four-digit numbers of the U.S. standard industrial classification. No figures are given for total sales or production of individual product lines, but the four-digit numbers describing the product mix always place the principal product first; the secondary products are arrayed in decreasing order of value of shipments for nearly all establishments. The coverage of establishments appears to be quite complete, although the file at any one time must contain a few records of establishments that have ceased operations and must omit others that have just started up.

We secured from Dun and Bradstreet (hereafter D&B) a tape containing the records for all Canadian establishments employing 50 or more and engaged principally in manufacturing, which should account for about three-fourths of value added in manufacturing. We received a total of 4,497 usable plant records. Using D&B's system of code numbers, we aggregated these establishments into enterprises by following all channels of ownership—branch and subsidiary relationships—until an ultimate parent was reached. This process yielded 2,117 companies, including 15 that were engaged primarily in nonmanufacturing activities.

One consequence of the continual updating of the D&B file is that its information does not pertain to any particular date. Probably most of the records on our tape (received in 1975) were secured or checked during 1974 or 1975. However, there is apparently an older residue, for we uncovered some product information in the records based on the version of the U.S. standard industrial classification that was superseded in 1972.

Can a descripion of a plant's activities in terms of the U.S. standard industrial classification be taken to convey any useful information on diversification? A moment's reflection reveals that any comparison of output diversity across sectors of the economy must depend on the homogeneity and regularity of some system for classifying and subdividing products. The standard industrial classification system used by the United States is in fact reasonably well suited for this purpose. It distinguishes products on the basis of differences in production technology and inputs as well as on the basis of physically and legally independent production facilities. The census industry is typically a "branch of a trade," perhaps inappropriate for the economic definition of a market because it ignores the existence of close substitute products based on different technologies, or because it couples end products that are poor substitutes for one another in use (Conklin and Goldstein, 1955). But these features of the industrial classification become an advantage for the study of diversification, a concept that depends—at least when considered at the plant level—on physical differences among production facilities and processes. The U.S. classification (SIC) contains 20 two-digit industries in manufacturing which are subdivided into 142 three-digit industries and further into 451 four-digit industries. This four-digit classification, used by Dun and Bradstreet, is probably as reasonable as any that could be secured. It is somewhat finer than the classification of three- and four-digit industries used by Statistics Canada for reporting production data.

If we accept the classification scheme used in the D&B files to describe the diversity of plants' outputs, the next question is how to assemble these data to summarize the output diversity of their parent firms. The actual value of shipments resulting from each activity carried on in each plant is not revealed; only the ranked list of the plant's primary activity and up to five secondary activities is reported. Thus some activities may be omitted for plants that report the maximum number of secondary activities and actually carry on more, and we do not know which weights to attach to the ones that are listed. On the basis of previous experimentation with the D&B data (Caves, 1975, chap. 3), we used the rankings of establishments' activities in the following way. Employees in each of a company's plants were assigned to its various products according to a geometric series, giving the least important a weight of 1, the next a weight of 2, then 4, 8, 16, and 32. Thus if one primary and one secondary activity are listed for a plant, we assume that its primary activity accounts for 67 percent ($2/3$) of its total production; if five secondary activities are listed, the assumed share of the primary activity drops to 51 percent ($32/[32 + 16 + 8 + 4 + 2 + 1]$). This assumption permits us to aggregate the activities of a firm's plants and to calculate measurements of the diversity of the firm's output as a whole.[1] The guidance of economic theory is too

1. The only comprehensive aggregated data known to us that permit checking the assumption are Utton's (1977) figures for the largest 200 U.K. manufacturing corporations. The weighted-average proportions of employment in the industries ranked first through fifth for these firms are 0.567, 0.126, 0.090, 0.050, 0.035. Utton's industry classification is the U.K. Minimum List Headings, which includes many fewer categories than the four-digit level of the U.S. standard industrial classification. The numbers are similar enough at the three-digit level, however, to make a comparison meaningful. Our Canadian companies show a *simple* average proportion of employment classified to their chief three-digit industry of 74.3 percent, which can be compared with Utton's 56.7 percent *weighted* average. The weighted average should be lower than the simple average if large companies are more diversified than small ones. Thus the two figures seem reasonably similar. Utton's data do suggest, though, that a "tail" of minor products may exist but not be observed in our data. Gorecki (1978) offers direct data on diversification by Canadian food-

general to derive a single measure of diversity appropriate to our hypotheses about diversity's causes or effects. Furthermore, different hypotheses about diversity suggest different considerations for the appropriate construction of the measure. We therefore proceeded in an eclectic manner to calculate six measures of output diversity, described here starting with the simplest. Earlier studies of diversity in U.S. manufacturing industries often used a simple count of product to measure diversity (for example, Gort, 1962), and we included such a measure although we felt it could be improved. Specifically, we calculated

> NS Number of unduplicated SIC output categories reported by all plants classified to a company.

NS makes no use of our information on the rankings of activities carried on by a firm's various plants.

The next measure was only slightly more complex. One relevant dimension of diversity is the proportion of a company's activity that lies outside its principal or base market. Using our estimate of the employees associated with each of a firm's activities, we identified the activity accounting for more employment than any other and then calculated

> $DE4$ Employment assigned to the U.S. four-digit SIC industry accounting for more of a firm's activity than any other industry, divided by total employees in the firm's manufacturing establishments.

We also computed the related measure $DE3$, which is based on the proportion of employees assigned to the firm's principal three-digit industry (determined by pooling all industries whose first three digits were identical). Both $DE4$ and $DE3$ measure diversity inversely; in the statistical analyses we usually subtracted them from unity to secure positive measures of diversity $VDE3$ and $VDE4$.

$DE3$ and $DE4$ take no account of the number of activities in which the firm engages, just as NS takes no account of its concentration on its chief activity. The final three measures employed were designed to capture both dimensions of diversity. All three were calculated from

---

processing enterprises within the food-processing sector. His research suggests that our assumption overstates the diversification of this sector, although the proxy variable constructed using our assumption produces only modest distortion in his regression results. It is anyone's guess whether Gorecki's finding can be generalized to all of Canadian manufacturing.

the vector of estimated numbers of employees assigned to each of a firm's activities expressed as proportions of the firm's total employment. The first measure used is the Hirschman-Herfindahl index, commonly used to measure concentration in both its aspects of small numbers and unequal size. Here we employ it inversely as a measure of diversification.

$$DH = 1 - \sum_i p_i^2.$$

Use of the Herfindahl index to measure diversity was first proposed by Berry (1975). Because the employment proportions are squared, the Herfindahl index gives the firm's top few four-digit activities a great deal of weight in determining the extent of measured output diversity. The index ranges from zero, when the firm produces a single product, to one, approached when it produces many products.

The remaining two indexes share two properties. Neither employs the squares of the proportions of employment, in contrast to the Herfindahl measure, and both take account of the "distance" between parts of products turned out by a diversified firm. The concentric index of diversification is

$$DC = \sum_j p_j \sum_i p_i d_{ij}.$$

The employment fraction p_i is defined as before; d_{ij} is a weight whose value depends on the relations between products i and j in the standard industrial classification system. That is, d takes a value of zero if i and j are four-digit products within the same three-digit industry, one if they are in different three-digit industries but the same two-digit industry, two if they are in different two-digit industries. The index increases with diversity and ranges in value from a minimum of zero when the firm's products lie within a single three-digit to a maximum of four approached when there are many four-digit products, no two in the same two-digit industry.[2]

The weighted index is similar to the concentric index but measures diversity in terms of distance out the branches of the classification tree from the three-digit industry assigned a larger fraction of the firm's employment than any other—the same base as that identified for calculating DE3. The weighted index is defined as

$$DW = \sum_i p_i d_{ih}.$$

2. For simplicity, the program for computing DC did not eliminate duplications; each pair is counted twice, i with j and j with i.

In this index d_{ih} is a weight that equals zero if the four-digit product i is included within the three-digit base industry, one if it is in a different three-digit industry within the same two-digit industry, and two if it lies within a different two-digit industry. The weighted index thus assigns a significance to the firm's base activity that the concentric index does not. But the concentric index takes account of the distance of secondary products from one another, which the weighted index does not. The weighted index increases with diversity from a value of zero, when the firm's outputs all lie within a single three-digit industry, to a maximum of two, approached when it produces many products, none lying in the two-digit industry that contains the base three-digit industry.[3]

These measures of diversification calculated from the Dun and Bradstreet file were supplemented by two taken from the Canadian census of production. They describe the extent to which manufacturing establishments classified to an industry and companies classified to that same industry fail to overlap. Diversified companies in the industry can own establishments whose primary products are classified to other industries. Or establishments classified to the industry can belong to diversified companies based in other industries. From published data we can secure the following variables:

SPL One minus enterprise industry specialization ratio (enterprise industry specialization ratio is defined as value added by establishments classified to the industry divided by value added by all establishments belonging to enterprises classified to the industry).

OWN One minus ownership specialization ratio (defined as the ratio of value added of the primary establishments of the enterprises classified to the industry to value added of all establishments classified to the industry).

SPL measures diversification outbound from a base industry, as do the indexes developed from our D&B data. OWN indicates diversification inbound to an industry. Both indexes pertain to the industry as a whole (as defined in the Canadian standard industrial classification) and not to the individual enterprise. The six measures of companies' diversity taken from the D&B data were also aggregated to the level of the Canadian industry[4] in order to permit comparison with SPL

3. Some other properties of the indexes, DH, DC, and DW are developed in Caves (1975, chap. 4).

4. Each diversity measure was calculated for an industry as the employment-weighted average of measures for firms classified to that industry as their principal business.

Table 8.1 Correlations between measures of diversification of companies classified to 79 Canadian industries.

	NSI	DE4I	DE3I	DHI	DCI	DWI	SPL
DE4I	−.706						
DE3I	−.612	.747					
DHI	.536	−.708	−.535				
DCI	.709	−.924	−.809	.667			
DWI	.618	−.819	−.799	.588	.942		
SPL	.582	−.406	−.299	.399	.396	.317	
OWN	−.118	−.196	−.112	.075	.131	.075	.002

Note: All correlations are significant at 1 percent except those involving OWN. The correlation between OWN and DE4I is significant at 5 percent.

and OWN and, more important, to explore their behavioral relation to other characteristics of these industries. The symbol I added to a variable name indicates that it has been aggregated to the industry level.

How similar are these measures of output diversity? Examples are easily constructed of firms or industries that would differ in their ranking by any pair of these measures. It is an empirical question whether the differences that can make these rankings diverge actually prevail among Canadian industries. In table 8.1 we present the matrix of zero-order correlation coefficients for these variables at the industry level—including OWN, although it measures diversification into rather than from an industry. The number of observations underlying each correlation coefficient is 79 for all coefficients utilizing D&B-derived variables, 123 for SPL and OWN (because we used the full sample of Canadian manufacturing industries, not just those matched to their U.S. counterparts).

Each pair of diversity measures is significantly correlated well beyond the 1 percent confidence level. The highest correlations are among DCI, DWI, DE3I, and DE4I, a natural result because they all measure to some degree the proportion of the activity of enterprises classified to an industry that is carried on in other sectors. Less highly correlated with other variables and with each other are DHI, NSI, and SPL. Each is "more different"; the Herfindahl measure involves the use of squared proportions, NSI neglects output shares entirely, and SPL recognizes diversified outputs only when they are produced as primary products of separate plants. SPL is more highly correlated with NSI than with any other measure, perhaps because both tend to take high values in industries populated by large enterprises.[5] A big company could be relatively undiversified by (say) *DH*, yet make a large number of products (*NS*) in plants specially set up for them (*SPL*). The indexes of outbound diversity of industries are largely uncorrelated with diversification inbound to them (*OWN*), but the negative correlation with *DE4I* is significant at 5 percent.[6]

8.2 Output Diversity and Industrial Base

Because we shall attempt to explain interindustry variations in these measures of diversity, we must first examine how diversity varies among industries. Theoretical approaches to the diversified firm leave room for doubt how well we can predict a firm's level of diversity from knowledge of its base industry. On the one hand, diversity may be a response to risks common to all firms operating in an industry (if investors cannot themselves diversify costlessly in the capital markets or if risk avoidance gives utility to companies' managers).[7] Diversification may result from joint production or specific complementarities that are imbedded in the production function of an industry, again affecting all firms in common. But other phenomena thought to affect diversification are specific to the firm or have only a weak probable relation to conditions common to its base industry. A company may diversify in order to utilize more fully some lumpy, fixed factor of production or to reuse an intangible asset at no opportunity cost.[8] As

5. Michael Gort (1962, pp. 20–22) reported no correlation between the diversity of the principal outputs of a company's plants (our *SPL*) and the average diversity of outputs within its plants. Our measures of diversity based on D&B data all contain both aspects of diversity. Their correlations with *SPL* in table 8.1 are significant at the 1 percent level. Although they do not provide a clean test, our data do not seem to support Gort's result. Nor does our theory lead us to expect it: a company with many opportunities to diversify trades off the advantages of multiple specialized plants and larger diversified ones.

6. An important limitation of our diversity measures is that they do not distinguish between vertically integrated activities and those diversified in the sense of lacking a vertical relation to the base industry. Measures making this distinction could be constructed by combining the information from Dun and Bradstreet with that of the input-output table, but our resources were inadequate to develop them.

7. See Fisher (1961). We shall study the relation between companies' diversity and their cost of capital in chapter 13.

8. See Weldon (1948), Rubin (1973). Case studies of the expansion of the diversified firm stress that diversification is undertaken to make further use of "capabilities" developed by the firm, meaning excess capacities in some combination of tangible and intangible assets. For Canada this is demonstrated by Lemelin (1978).

a use of funds, diversification may respond to an excess of internally generated funds relative to investment opportunities within the base industry—a relation that varies somewhat among an industry's member firms as well as over time. It is therefore an empirical question whether the base industry significantly influences companies' output diversity.

The number of firms for which we could measure output diversity is large, but not so large that substantial numbers are classified to many of the industries in our data base. Therefore the companies were sorted according to a coarse classification—the two-digit level of the U.S. standard industrial classification, and weighted averages were calculated (employment weights) for each of the diversity measures defined in the preceding section. Table 8.2 shows the ranks of the two-digit industries on six measures of diversity and on the extent of multiplant development (NP).[9]

Before considering those rankings, we ask whether classifying firms to their base industries explains a significant proportion of the variance of their diversity. Gort, Arora, and McGuckin (1972) reached a negative conclusion, finding only three two-digit industries whose tenants' diversity measures could not be viewed as randomly drawn from the population of companies. Because our concern is with inter-industry variance in diversity, an analysis of variance is appropriate to test the null hypothesis that the industry mean levels of diversity within the sample are equal to each other and contribute nothing to explaining the overall variance of the population.[10] This test was performed on unweighted data for the firms' values of diversity index DH, and we concluded that the hypothesis that industry means are equal can be rejected at the 1 percent level of confidence. The calculated F-statistic is 3.38, whereas $F_{0.01} = 1.87$.

In table 8.2 there appears a fairly strong consistency in the ranking of two-digit manufacturing sectors by the six indexes of diversity. Tobacco and pulp and paper generally stand at the top of the list; apparel, printing, and the miscellaneous industries at the bottom. The primary industries (textiles, wood products, metal) tend to be less diversified than the secondary industries (food processing, paper,

9. The means themselves and standard deviations appear in Caves et al. (1977, table 4.2). NP is the employment-weighted average number of plants per company, and it includes plants classified to the company's primary industry and also plants whose primary outputs are classified to other industries.

10. We are not concerned whether each industry's mean differs significantly from that of the whole population; even if there is substantial dispersion in the industry means, some of them are likely to differ little from the population average.

COMPETITION IN THE OPEN ECONOMY

Table 8.2 Rankings of 20 broad Canadian industries by average extent of diversification on seven measures of diversification.

Industry	Diversification measure						
	NS	DE4	DE3	DH	DC	DW	NP
Food	2	9	12	8	11.5	16	2
Tobacco	3	1	1	1	1	1	8
Textiles	11	15	13	16	18	17.5	10
Apparel	20	19	20	20	20	20	19
Wood	14	16	11	17	16	15	13
Furniture	12	6	9	9	11.5	11	15
Paper	1	2	2	2	2	2	1
Printing	17	20	18	19	19	19	14
Chemicals	7	4	4	4	7	7	6
Petroleum	5	17	10	12	4	6	4
Rubber	9	11	5	6	3	4	9
Leather	18	5	19	7	15	17.5	16
Stone, clay, glass	8	8	7	10	8	8	7
Metals	6	14	14	13.5	13.5	12	3
Metal fabricating	10	7	6	5	5	3	11
Nonelectrical machinery	16	12	15	13.5	10	10	20
Electrical machinery	4	3	3	3	6	9	5
Transport equipment	12	10	16	11	13.5	14	12
Instruments	15	13	8	15	9	5	18
Miscellaneous	19	18	17	18	17	13	17

Source. Caves et al. (1977, Table 4.2)

Note: Identical fractional rankings indicate ties; for example, two industries ranked 13.5 tied for thirteenth place.

tobacco). Some industries evidently appear diversified just because of the technical heterogeneity of their main lines of products (chemicals, electrical machinery).

Differences in rankings, related to differences in the construction of the diversity measures, provide further insights. The food sector ranks much lower and the instruments sector much higher on *DW* than their positions on other measures. The food processors' diversification is mostly within that two-digit sector, whereas the instrument sector wanders far afield. This pattern is supported by comparison of the rankings on *DE3*; food appears less diversified on the three-digit measure, as do the furniture, leather, and machinery industries—all sectors that probably diversify close to home on the basis of common raw materials and/or distribution channels, so that vertical integration is also involved. Conversely, the wood-products, petroleum, rubber, and instruments sectors tend to diversify relatively far along the standard industrial classification tree; part of their diversification is nonetheless technology determined because common raw materials are converted into finished products that are classified to different two-digit sectors.[11] The tobacco firms also diversify far from their primary base; tobacco's excess of diversity over other industries is much greater for the DW measure than for the others.

Some useful information emerges from the ranking of sectors on the extent of their multiplant development (NP). A sector can have extensive multiplant development either because it contains diversified firms or because its base activity entails economies of multiplant operation. The food and primary metals sectors show extensive multiplant development but are not highly diversified. A highly diversified sector with low multiplant development must produce many products per plant. The furniture, metal fabricating, nonelectrical machinery, and instruments sectors fall into this category—probably a reflection of technical complementarities in their production processes.

8.3 Market Size, Company Size, and Diversity of Outputs

Output diversity is related to the sizes of companies and establishments, and their size in turn is related to the size of the market in which they operate. In chapter 3 we discovered the important influence wielded by scale economies and market size on the number and size distribution of Canadian producers. Because the sizes of companies (and establishments) and their diversity should also be related, we need to examine the theory and empirical evidence on these relations.

Students of industrial organization in Canada have often spoken of output diversity—short production runs, excessively full product lines produced for the small market—as if output diversity compounded a problem already created by the small size of the market.[12]

11. See Gilbert (1971, chap. 3). The rank correlation between $DE3$ and $DE4$, 0.692, is lower than the rank correlations between a number of other pairs of measures. The highest rank correlations are between DH and $DE4$ and between DC and DW—a result that accords with similarities in the construction of these pairs.

12. See Fullerton and Hampson (1957, pp. 72–74, 90–92), Daly, Keys, and Spence (1968).

COMPETITION IN THE OPEN ECONOMY

However, in an important sense diversity mitigates the consequences of the small size of production units. Given the outputs to be produced, one can have a small diversified enterprise—or several companies smaller still, each producing a homogeneous product. We need to consider the process by which the multiproduct company determines the output diversity of its plants. Given that the firm produces multiple products, what forces determine whether it crams them into one plant or spreads them over several? Let the costs of production include the following components.

1. Capacity costs for the physical plant and its supporting services are subject to scale economies, so that total costs of plant (per square foot of capacity, say) increase with size less than proportionally over a significant range.

2. Each line of output that could be produced in the plant incurs a fixed cost of production facilities that generally increases less than in proportion to the output capacity for the line.

3. Each line of output also involves short-run variable costs specific to the line that we shall assume independent of the scale of output up to a capacity constraint. (The exact behavior of these costs does not affect the analysis.)

4. Supervisory and related costs of coordination within the plant that depend on the scale of each output but also on the diversity of output, increasing as the output mix grows more complex.

Now consider the firm that can profitably diversify into several products but faces a downward-sloping demand for each of them, so that its desired output of each product is to some extent limited by demand factors. It will build a specialized plant for each output—to avoid the extra costs of supervising diversified plants—if it can produce each on a scale large enough to exhaust economies of scale in physical plant construction and operation. However, as the diseconomies of operating suboptimal specialized plants increase, it may become more economical to combine some lines in a single plant, accepting the higher supervisory costs that result in order to get lower unit costs of plant capacity. Thus the extent to which firms opt for diversified plants depends not only on forces making diversification profitable but also on forces making the operation of small, specialized plants unprofitable.

Because the assumption that supervisory costs increase with diversity is crucial to this argument, we should give some attention to its empirical content. If diversified outputs literally involve separate production facilities, they may interfere with one another because of different requirements for cleanliness, temperature, and other physical conditions. They complicate the scheduling of input arrivals, inventories, and shipping of outputs. Experts on industrial engineering such as Skinner (1974) have noted the many subtle ways in which increasing the complexity of a plant's output can increase its coordination costs or impose increased costs on outputs already produced. A form of coordination cost often noted in Canada is that of changing over a single production line to produce different varieties of the output. This is a coordination cost in the sense of our model, in that it could be avoided if the firm chose a smaller-capacity production line that could produce a single specialized output full-time.

These considerations imply that larger plants are typically more diversified than small ones, because some large plants turn out diverse outputs as a result of this optimization process. This conclusion would not follow if diversification were purely a matter of joint products: lamb chops and sheepskins are produced jointly, whether with one sheep or a thousand.

The diversity of Canadian plant and company outputs should also be related to the size of the national market. Where products are differentiated or simply heterogeneous, the potential demand perceived by each producer becomes dependent on the size of the national market. In industries enjoying a strong comparative advantage, this constraint is relaxed by exports, and so we expect export-oriented industries' plants to be less diversified than others. For nonexporting industries, however, the relevant market is no larger than the Canadian national market. This small market thereby creates an incentive for plants to be either small or diversified. One implication is that plants of a given size in Canadian manufacturing industries should be more diversified than plants of similar size in U.S. industries. This prediction was confirmed in a previous study of diversification (Caves, 1975, chap. 5), although the result was somewhat qualified because base industry and size of plant could not be controlled simultaneously in making the Canadian-U.S. comparison.

It does not follow from this, though, that the leading firms in a given Canadian industry should be as diversified as the leaders in a larger national market. On the contrary, we expect that specialized goods will not be produced in Canada, being secured instead through international trade. With fewer varieties being produced than in a larger national market, the typical Canadian enterprise should be less diversified than its U.S. counterpart unless small size in the national market somehow shrinks the enterprise population more than proportionally. This hypothesis finds support in the evidence that the outputs of Canadian subsidiaries are less diverse than the U.S. operations of their American parents. Because foreign subsidiaries' plants of a given scale are more diversified than those belonging to Canadian domestic companies, we can state the following conclusion: Given companies with similar market shares in the U.S. and Canadian branches of a given industry, the Canadian company should be less diversified (Caves, 1975, chaps. 4, 5).

Previous research on output diversity and scale has suffered from inadequate control over the industry bases of the sampled enterprises, needed because both are affected by industry-specific traits. The data base available for this project permits a somewhat improved analysis of how companies' diversity varies with their size and other character-istics in principal sectors of Canadian manufacturing. We use regres-sion analysis, although the relations are not clearly causal. The Dun and Bradstreet tape provides several indicators of the size of each company. The first is simply

> NE   Number of employees at all manufacturing establishments classified to the company.

NE omits employees in any establishment not primarily engaged in manufacturing even if it belongs to a manufacturing enterprise, and it includes employees in manufacturing establishments not engaged in manufacturing activities. Nonetheless, it is probably a good measure of the scale of a company's manufacturing activities.[13] We included both employment and its squared value as factors explaining diversi-fication. Output diversity is not likely to increase linearly with a firm's size, and we generally expect a positive relation between diversity and NE, a negative relation between diversity and NE^2.

Because many manufacturing processes are subject to different loca-tional pulls or are technically incompatible within the same plant or both, we expect output diversity to be positively associated with

> NP   Number of manufacturing establishments controlled by the com-pany and reported in the D&B file.

Like the number of employees, the number of plants is not a cause of diversification but a possible correlate of the degree of diversity chosen by the firm. With NE controlled, our hypothesis of a positive relation between diversity and NP amounts to a prediction that the more diversified of two firms of equal size will choose, technology per-mitting, to carry on its activities in more plants. If the hypothesis

13. Sales would be a better measure, obviously, but it is not included in the D&B data.

holds, we have some support for the assumption that a company faces increased marginal costs of coordination when it expands the lines of output produced in a plant.

A final variable included in the analysis is

> FD   Dummy variable, equals one if the company is a subsidiary of a
> U.S. parent, zero otherwise.

American parentage can be identified from the code numbers assigned to companies by Dun and Bradstreet; unfortunately, subsidiaries of enterprises based in other foreign countries cannot be thus identified, and so FD is a faulty indicator of a company's status as the subsidiary of a multinational enterprise. Economic theory and statistical evidence both suggest that a multinational subsidiary will be more diversified than an otherwise comparable company of domestic ownership (Caves, 1975, chap. 5; Statistics Canada, 1978, chap. 2). This is because the incremental cost of installing an additional activity is reduced for a subsidiary, if its parent already carries on the activity elsewhere and can provide it with know-how, depreciated equipment, and associated intangibles at lower cost than they can be secured by an independent firm. In the present analysis we can test the hypothesis while imposing a more effective control for differences in company size than has previously been possible.

As we have explained, it would be ideal to test hypotheses on firms within an industry, to control for base industries' differing potentials for diversification. However, not enough Canadian companies represented in our D&B data fall into individual, narrowly defined industries to permit such a test, and so we control partially for our companies' primary or base industries by assigning them to the 20 two-digit families in the U.S. standard industrial classification. Only one of these industries—tobacco—was represented by too few firms to carry out a regression analysis. For the other 19 we regressed each of the six company-specific diversity measures on NE, NE^2, NP, and FD, yielding 114 regression equations. Because all six diversity measures behave similarly, the general pattern is easy to summarize: the coefficients of NE and NP are usually positive and significant, the coefficient of NE^2 negative and significant, and the coefficient of FD positive and not statistically significant. Table 8.3 summarizes the distribution of the 114 coefficients of the independent variables between positive and negative sign, significant and insignificant.[14]

The coefficients of NE and NE^2 take opposite signs in all but three

14. Details can be found in Caves et al. (1977, table 4.4).

COMPETITION IN THE OPEN ECONOMY

Table 8.3 Summary of signs and significance of regression coefficients of diversity measures on four independent variables.

| | Number of regression coefficients | | | |
| | Positive | | Negative | |
Independent variable	Significant	Not significant	Significant	Not Significant
NE (number of employees)	53	50	1	10
NE² (number of employees squared)	1	11	58	44
NP (number of plants)	80	27	0	7
FD (foreign subsidiary)	9	63	7	35

Note: Significance is based on 5 percent confidence level, one-tailed test.

of 114 regressions, and in those three neither is significant. The only sector for which NE^2 regularly takes a positive sign is petroleum, in which the number of companies is relatively small. For diversity measure NS, which we noted tends to emphasize the diversity of large companies, the coefficient of NE is negative and that of NE^2 is positive for four other sectors, but that pattern prevails for no other measure of the diversity of any of these four industries. Therefore we conclude that the general pattern is for diversity to increase with the size of companies, although at a diminishing rate.

The number of plants per company shows a strong positive relation to diversity, even though it is surely collinear with NE, so that the standard errors of both variables' coefficients are inflated. NP is a more significant influence on the NS measure of diversity than any of the others, consistent with that measure's emphasis of diversity in large (and more likely multiplant) companies.

Although a company's status as a subsidiary of a U.S. enterprise generally increases its output diversity, the relation is usually not significant statistically once size and multiplant operation are controlled. Thus a considerable amount of the subsidiaries' apparently greater diversity of output may be due to their relatively large size. Nonetheless, regressions for the individual sectors show that subsidiary status exhibits a significant positive influence on diversity in sectors where foreign-controlled companies account for large proportions of sales—chemicals, metal fabrication, electrical machinery, and instruments; negative signs appear in industries hosting relatively little foreign investment, with the substantial exception of petroleum.

A somewhat complex relation is apparent between the variation of diversity with scale and the average diversity of sectors indicated in table 8.2. In some sectors such as food and electrical machinery the average level of diversity is high, but the relation between diversity and size of company is not very close (regression coefficients are relatively small and tend to be insignificant). Technical characteristics of these product groups and their channels of distribution probably induce all companies engaged in them to diversify somewhat, so that diversity does not strongly increase with company size. By the same token a weak relation of diversity to size goes with a low average level of diversity in other sectors—apparel, printing, petroleum, and leather —where most firms are undiversified. The industries in which the diversity-size relation is strong and significant include both those in which the average level of diversity is high (paper, and to a lesser degree chemicals and metal fabrication) and those in which it is on the low side (textiles, nonelectrical machinery). The latter industries are ones in which the technical bases for diversity are relatively weak, but the larger firms find it profitable to plow their retained earnings into diversification rather than into expansion of their primary activities.

8.4 Interindustry Differences in Diversity

The researcher does not approach the task of explaining differences among industries in the average diversity of their member firms with optimism. Measured at the industry level, diversity reflects technical complementarities that are buried in the technology of production and distribution, and the data available are generally insufficient to dig them out. The decision to diversify may often rest on factors specific to the diversifying company but not characteristic of all firms in its industry. We return to that question in chapter 11, where we present a parallel analysis of the output diversity of the large companies in the data base.

Our dependent variables in the following analysis are the company-based measures of each industry's output diversity, described in section 8.1. We also use as a dependent variable *SPL*, the complement of the industry enterprise specialization ratio, taken from census data.

Some independent variable must be included to control for the relation between diversity and size of firm. The form of the variable is influenced by our discovery that diversity increases with the number of a company's manufacturing plants, even after we controlled for its total number of employees. Therefore our control is the average size of establishments classified to the industry, measured by value added, multiplied by the employment-weighted average number of plants per company. These variables, designated *VPE* and *NPI* respectively, are defined more fully in appendix A. Thus we use the variable

$SIZE \equiv VPE * NPI.$

Because *NPI* is an employment-weighted measure of multiplant operation, it varies among industries more than an unweighted average if the multiplant companies have larger plants than single-establishment firms—as is likely.[15]

The variables that can potentially explain diversification outward from an industry, once we have controlled for company size, deal mainly with competitive conditions and the rate of return to resources allocated to expansion within the primary activity. A company is more likely to diversify when it is profitable (or at least not too unprofitable) and faces a downward-sloping demand curve in its primary activity, so that funds are available for expansion but expansion in its base industry is not attractive because of the ensuing struggle with its rivals over market share. This situation is unlikely unless sellers are at least moderately concentrated. Several measures of concentration are available in our data base. The one that proved most effective here and in other uses is a product of two terms.

$C4CV \equiv C468 * CVC$, where *C468* is the four-firm concentration ratio for the industry in 1968 and *CVC* is the coefficient of variation of the sizes (shipments) of the largest eight firms.

Concentration is a sufficient condition for diversification only where the industry's profits are high in relation to the rate of growth of market demand. Therefore we combine these three elements into the following interaction term:

$C4GR \equiv C4CV(1 + ROI)/(1 + GSI)$, where *ROI* is the average (1968–1971) rate of return after taxes on equity capital for companies classified to the industry, and *GSI* is the compound annual rate of growth of industry shipments 1961–1971.

One more influence that should interact with those already rolled into *C4GR* is the industry's access to foreign markets. The exporters selling an undifferentiated product on world markets should not face

15. As a check we also employed an unweighted measure of multiplant operation in an alternative version of *SIZE*, calculated as $VPE * (NCA67/NENT)$, where *NCA67* is the number of establishments classified to the industry and *NENT* is the number of companies. It performed slightly less well than the version discussed in the text and is not reported.

a downward-sloping demand curve, individually or jointly, if as is likely the Canadian industry accounts for a modest fraction of world output. The exporting industry might diversify to spread risk, but it should not be pushed to diversify by limitations of demand in international markets. Export exposure hence should mitigate the incentive to diversify of firms in industries with high concentration of production in Canada. Export status is positively correlated across Canadian industries with both size of enterprise and level of seller concentration, especially the former. If concentration measured from Canadian production overstates the effective level of concentration in the markets faced by exporting industries, and if risks associated with exporting do not induce too much diversification, there should be a negative interaction between concentration and exports.[16] To detect this interaction we formed the variable

$CGRX \equiv C4GR * EXP$, where EXP is the fraction of output exported.

It should be negatively related to diversification.

Diversification may be positively associated with an industry's level of research and development activity. The nature of the relation between these variables is clear, although the direction of causality is not. Research adds to an industry's stock of salable products and can readily cast up a new product that is technologically related to other outputs of the industry but serves a different function and reposes in a different SIC category. If the industry produces the good that it discovers instead of licensing it to others, its diversification is increased. The existing level of diversification should positively influence the productivity and hence the volume of R&D activities, because the chances are increased that a company can use some new discovery without incurring heavy start-up costs. Because the hypothesis is concerned with productive knowledge accessible to an industry and not just with the R&D undertaken in Canada, we use the proxy

> RDIU   Research and development expenditures as a fraction of industry sales, U.S. counterpart industry.

It should be positively related to diversification.

On the other hand, a form of intangible asset that may be hostile to diversification is advertising. Many companies apply a brand name to

16. Import competition is not treated symmetrically with export opportunities because of the evidence (chapter 4) that imports are characteristically differentiated goods. In the preliminary version of this study (Caves et al., 1977, chap. 5) we considered the possibility that an industry's net export position has a negative (additive) influence on diversification and found no statistical support.

a line of products and advertise them jointly, but these product lines nonetheless often seem to fall within a single four-digit industry and thus would not register as diversified in our indexes. The intangible assets of companies that advertise heavily do not seem to transplant readily to remote branches of the standard industrial classification tree. A more likely form of diversification for companies successful in high-advertising industries is foreign investment, which has been found to be closely associated with rates of advertising outlay (Caves, 1974), and they may be effectively diversified within SIC categories. Hence we expect a negative relation between diversity and

  ADI Advertising expenditures as a fraction of industry sales.

We predict a negative relation to diversification.

A familiar motive for diversifying is to reduce the variability of a firm's activity—its reported profits, cash flow, or utilization of common fixed facilities—and thereby avoid risk. The more variable are shipments by establishments classified to an industry, the more would we expect firms classified principally to that industry to have diversified into other industries. The modern theory of financial portfolios suggests that the relevant measure of variability is actually some sort of covariance: the less positively correlated is an industry's primary activity with output fluctuations in the economy generally, the more readily can it find a variance-reducing activity into which to diversify. On the other hand, the profit-maximizing firm dealing in a perfect capital market would not increase its market value by diversifying and could even reduce that value by destroying its status as an outlier for portfolio balancers. Therefore it makes sense to think about risk as perceived by the firm's management rather than by its owners. The managers cannot diversify their jobs, and so the variability of real activity in the base industry should induce them to follow a policy of diversification.[17] Hence our instability measure is

  SSI Standard deviation of base-industry shipments around their trend value for 1961–1971.

Its relation to diversification should be positive. However, insofar as companies have diversified merely by adding outputs to plants classified to their principal industries, the diversification washes out the variability of the base industry and obscures the statistical relationship.

17. Surveys of company behavior strongly support this interpretation, although statistical research so far has not (Gilbert, 1971; Bond, 1974).

A final indicator of an industry's prospects for diversification is whether its markets are regional. A modest-sized company that operates in a single regional market may be discouraged from diversifying by its relatively poor access to national capital markets. A company that operates in a number of regional markets is already diversified to the extent that the profit prospects in these regions are imperfectly correlated, and the risk-spreading value for it of product diversification is reduced. Hence we expect diversity to be reduced if an industry's markets are judged to be regionally fragmented in Canada (*REG* is a dummy variable equal to one for regional industries, zero otherwise).

Table 8.4 presents regression equations for three of our available measures of diversification, *DHI*, *DWI*, and *NSI*. Unlike the others, *NSI* and *SPL* tend to register more diversity for larger companies, and they behave similarly here. *DCI* and *DE3I* differ too little from *DHI* and *DWI* to be worth reporting separately. Previous statistical studies of outbound diversification have turned up relatively poor statistical results,[18] and table 8.4 is not really an exception. First, both base-industry instability (*SSI*) and regionality (*REG*) are without regularity in their statistical relation to the diversity measures. They are correctly signed in the equations where they are significant, but their nonrobust behavior inclines us to accept the null hypothesis. A further disappointment is that the TSLS results deteriorate markedly for the *DHI* and *DWI* variables although not for *NSI*. The independent variables in this model are not thought to serve as proxies for unobserved forces in the system, so we did not expect this deterioration and cannot explain it. We take equations C for *DHI* and *DWI* as a qualification to the positive results for the remaining variables. The control for company size (*SIZE*), *RDIU*, and the exports interaction variable *CGRX* always take the predicted signs and are nearly always highly significant. As we expected, the size variable is more significant for *NSI* than for *DHI* and *DWI*. Also, research and development (*RDIU*) contributes substantially more to explaining the variance of *DWI* than of *DHI* or *NSI*; this is consistent with the proposition that new discoveries can be products distant in the SIC tree from the company's base industry (*DWI* reflects this distance). The variable combining concentration, profitability, and growth is almost always positive in sign and occasionally significant (especially with *NSI* as expected), so that we bow to the null hypothesis rather than embrace it. If the components of *C4GR* are entered additively, each is completely insignificant and irregular in sign. Finally, the advertising variable

18. See Caves (1975, chap. 6), Hassid (1975, p. 387), Berry (1975, chap. 5).

Table 8.4 Determinants of three measures of outbound diversification (DHI, DWI, NSI).

Dependent variable	Estimation method	Independent variables							Constant	$\bar{R}^2$	F/D.f.
		ADI	C4GR[1]	CGRX[1]	SIZE[1]	RDIU	SSI	REG			
DHI	A	−1.65c (−1.45)	0.566 (0.566)	−6.92a (−2.62)	0.001b (2.06)	0.017 (1.24)	4.82 (0.68)	−0.075 (−1.10)	0.419a (5.36)	0.092	1.84 / 51
	B	−1.13 (−1.12)	0.884 (1.15)	−5.24b (−2.35)	0.001b (2.08)	0.021b (1.73)	−1.80 (−0.32)	−0.081c (−1.44)	0.393a (6.03)	0.079	2.02 / 76
	C	−0.820 (−0.56)	−0.124 (−0.10)	−1.02 (−0.18)	0.001 (0.93)	0.067a (2.70)	−3.82 (−0.54)	−0.042 (−0.64)	0.340a (4.16)	—	1.92 / 76
DWI	A	−1.30 (−1.18)	0.160 (0.16)	−7.67a (−3.00)	0.001b (2.31)	0.035a (2.68)	14.6b (2.12)	0.005 (0.08)	0.278a (3.67)	0.219	3.37 / 51
	B	−1.27 (−1.13)	1.32c (1.54)	−6.23a (−2.52)	0.001c (1.49)	0.039a (2.80)	0.959 (0.15)	−0.020 (−0.32)	0.314a (4.34)	0.100	2.31 / 76
	C	−2.18c (−1.37)	1.12 (0.85)	−5.95 (−0.95)	0.001 (0.96)	0.090a (3.25)	−1.75 (−0.23)	0.020 (0.27)	0.254a (2.86)	—	2.07 / 76
NSI	A	−8.80 (0.57)	12.4 (0.91)	−127a (−3.53)	0.042a (5.06)	0.312b (1.69)	134c (1.39)	0.841 (0.91)	2.80a (2.63)	0.297	4.50 / 51
	B	−6.82 (−0.50)	19.7b (1.90)	−101a (3.36)	0.038a (5.06)	0.365b (2.18)	55.1 (0.73)	0.492 (0.65)	2.66a (3.03)	0.260	5.17 / 76
	C	−23.0 (−1.26)	27.8a (1.86)	−133b (−1.85)	0.047a (3.78)	0.565b (1.83)	44.0 (0.50)	0.744 (0.91)	2.22b (2.18)	—	1.22 / 76

Note: Levels of significance (one-tailed test) are a = 1 percent, b = 5 percent, c = 10 percent. The three independent variables listed to the left of the space are endogenous in our model or contain endogenous components.
1. We have divided these variables by 1,000 in order to scale them conveniently.

(*ADI*) always has the predicted negative sign and teeters on the edge of being significant at 10 percent.

In conclusion, we must point to the low explanatory power of the equations in table 8.4. The TSLS equations are not significant overall, on the basis of their *F*-ratios, and only three equations have values of R^2 (adjusted for degrees of freedom) over 0.2. In section 11.3 our analysis of the diversity of large companies' outputs is somewhat more successful. The diversity of all companies in an industry reflects both technical factors that we can model poorly, if at all, and competitive factors for which economic theory is a more suitable instrument. The importance of the latter is surely modest for the smaller companies whose diversity is reflected in our industrywide measures, but should emerge more strongly for large companies that tend to operate in relatively concentrated industries and to dominate those industries.

8.5 Diversification into an Industry

The extent of diversification into an industry holds great interest because it allows us to analyze what attracts the entry of companies already established in other industries. The dependent variable measures the accumulated stock of inbound diversification.

> *OWN* The proportion of an industry's value added that originates in establishments belonging to companies whose primary activity lies in another industry.

Inspection of the dependent variables's values for our sample of industries reveals a distinctive pattern: high values appear for industries that either sell most of their output to, or buy their chief input from, another industry that is concentrated and has larger firms and establishments than the industry in question. Diversification inbound to such industries in the main represents vertical integration by large enterprises in the adjacent industry. Vertical integration for them is feasible, because risks are low and capital-cost entry barriers are unimportant, and it might carry various advantages.[19] To detect situations ripe for this form of inbound diversification we followed a very simple procedure. Using variables in our data base describing seller concentration (*C468*) and the size of establishment (*VPE*), as well as the input-output table (Dominion Bureau of Statistics, 1969), we constructed judgmentally a dummy variable set equal to one when an industry buys the bulk of its purchased inputs or sells the bulk of its out-

19. See the discussion by Williamson (1971) of the reasons for vertical integration.

put to another industry which has substantially higher concentration and establishment sizes. We settled for a dummy because a continuous variable embodying these influences could not be constructed for many industries whose leading supplier or customer industries lie outside manufacturing, due to lack of data on concentration. The variable is designated $VRTD$, and should be positively related to OWN.

Because inbound diversification involves entry by established companies, its occurrence should be related to barriers to entry into the industry. Entry impediments for going firms differ from those facing newly organized companies; the going firm is generally better equipped to hurdle entry barriers but still faces some disadvantage against the standard sources of entry barriers.[20] Our strategy is not to consider the sources of entry barriers directly but rather to employ the proposition that an industry's level of concentration in the long run must reflect the ease of entry: very low concentration should indicate easy entry; very high concentration, difficult entry. Entry into highly concentrated industries is thus presumed difficult—for the going firm as well as for the newborn company. We expect low values of OWN in highly concentrated industries. On the other hand, a diversifying firm should generally pass over an atomistically competitive industry in which no more than a normal competitive rate of return can be expected. The implied nonlinear relation between OWN and concentration can be specified in many ways, and no theoretical guidance is available as to the right one. Experimentally we found the relation between OWN and four-firm seller concentration to be apparently linear up to quite high levels of concentration, then to drop sharply. Therefore we captured the nonlinear relation by entering $C468$ as a linear variable along with

$C490$ $C468$ if $C468 \geq 90.0$, zero otherwise.

A negative coefficient for $C490$ would support the hypothesis that established firms face substantial entry barriers into highly concentrated industries and hence avoid them. (We also experimented with a quadratic form, but it had less explanatory power than the discontinuous form just proposed.)[21]

The concentration variables are supposed to summarize the ex post

20. See Bain (1956) and Caves and Porter (1977).

21. In the preliminary version of this study we also used as an indicator of easy entry PRB, the industry's number of working proprietors per establishment. A high value of PRB should signal easy entry by small enterprises and an absence of potential excess profits that would attract established companies. The variable was significant, but it reduces the significance of the concentration variables and does not increase the overall explanatory power of our regression equations.

effects of entry barriers. Is there any point, then, in employing direct measures of structural barriers to entry? The answer is not clear. Our ability to measure entry barriers statistically is imperfect, and the standard sources of entry barriers imperfectly measured by statistical proxies do not comprehend all the mechanisms by which entry can be deterred in particular industries. Therefore, at the risk of distorting the estimates of some coefficients, we included two measures of structural entry barriers, defined to pick off only the high values of entry deterrents that should affect going firms. That is because low to medium entry barriers might actually encourage entry by established firms by protecting them against new enterprises. Our indicator of capital-cost barriers to entry is

> CAPC   The absolute size (sales) of the plant of estimated minimum efficient scale (MABC; see chapter 3) multiplied by the industry's average ratio of assets to sales. CAPC is set equal to zero when the productivity disadvantage of suboptimally scaled establishments in the U.S. counterpart industry is no more than moderate (CDRU ≧ 0.9).

The coefficient of CAPC is negative if high capital-cost barriers deter going firms as well as new ones. We also investigate the effect of advertising outlays in those industries where they are capable of building high entry barriers—the convenience-good sector. The variable is

$$ADIC \equiv ADI * CONO,$$

where ADI is the industry's ratio of advertising to sales and CONO is a dummy variable equal to one if the industry is classified as a convenience-good industry. Empirical evidence (Porter, 1976b) identifying advertising as a source of entry barriers in these industries points toward a negative sign.

Research activity was hypothesized to promote diversification from an industry, and it should promote inbound diversification as well. Imperfect markets for proprietary technology (and technicians) may incline companies to enter high-technology industries in order to acquire technical and research capabilities. This behavior would produce a positive relation between inbound diversification and

> RDIC   Research and development outlays as a percentage of sales by the Canadian industry.

We also employed as an alternative the corresponding measure based on U.S. data.

> RDIU   Research and development outlays as a percentage of sales, U.S. counterpart industry.

It is not clear whether firms diversifying into an industry should pursue its general stock of technology (proxied by the U.S. variable) or the research facilities active in Canada and the knowledge they have produced.[22]

Another sort of indicator of entry to an industry is the presence of import competition, which functions like new-firm entrants to limit the maximum rate of return expected in an industry and to reduce its attractiveness to the diversifying enterprise. Also, an industry exposed to international competition may pose a greater risk for the going-firm entrant because international-trade linkages provide another channel for disturbances to the market. Therefore we expect OWN to be negatively related to

IMP Imports as a percentage of shipments by the domestic industry.

In table 8.5 the determinants of OWN are analyzed in two specifications. The first three equations omit the potentially redundant entry-barrier variables $CAPC$ and $ADIC$ and employ $RDIC$; the second trio include $CAPC$ and $ADIC$ and substitute $RDIU$ for $RDIC$. $VRTD$ is highly significant throughout and by itself explains 30 percent of the variance of OWN, so we conclude that much inbound diversification represents backward or forward vertical integration of the sort designated by $VRTD$. The two variables describing the nonlinear relation to concentration are also significant. The entry-barrier variables $CAPC$ and $ADIC$ take the expected signs (with one exception) but are not significant, and as we expected they somewhat lower the regression coefficient of $C490$ and its statistical significance. They also reduce the F-ratio for the equation. We accept the hypothesis that the nonlinear relation of OWN to concentration takes full account of the influence of entry barriers on the diversifying behavior of established firms. The research and development variable is generally significant and positive as expected, with the U.S. version ($RDIU$) performing somewhat better than the Canadian. Finally, import competition (IMP) has a significant deterrent effect in the OLS regressions, but it is no longer significant when TSLS is employed.

8.6 Summary

Because economic theory does not identify a single best measure of diversity, we computed a number of them that give varying weight to

22. The predicted positive sign is not entirely certain because R&D is alleged to impose an entry barrier, at least in mature industries where it serves chiefly to support nonprice competition (Mueller and Tilton, 1969).

Table 8.5 Determinants of inbound diversification (OWN).

Independent variables	Method of estimation					
	A	B	C	A	B	C
C468[1]	0.237a (2.65)	0.195a (2.41)	0.147c (1.37)	0.209b (2.11)	0.190b (2.33)	0.146c (1.34)
C490[1]	−0.269a (−2.61)	−0.261a (−3.63)	−0.374a (−3.09)	−0.169 (−1.09)	−0.236a (−2.98)	−0.382a (−2.50)
ADIC	—	—	—	−0.640 (−0.83)	−0.665 (−0.93)	0.412 (0.40)
RDIC	0.019b (1.83)	0.015c (1.49)	0.025 (1.20)	—	—	—
IMP	−0.142a (−2.50)	−0.103b (−2.05)	−0.034 (−0.38)	−0.160b (−2.36)	−0.118b (−2.30)	−0.053 (−0.47)
VRTD	0.322a (5.02)	0.306a (5.80)	0.315a (5.41)	0.333a (5.02)	0.299a (5.62)	0.316a (5.25)
RDIU	—	—	—	0.021b (2.05)	0.018b (1.96)	0.025c (1.31)
CAPC[1]	—	—	—	−0.164 (−0.51)	−0.026 (−0.32)	−0.006 (−0.05)
Constant	0.062 (1.29)	0.073c (1.58)	0.075 (1.22)	0.074c (1.58)	0.074c (1.59)	0.069 (1.09)
$\bar{R}^2$	0.426	0.389	—	0.430	0.392	—
F	10.96	11.58	14.58	7.45	8.64	9.54
D.f.	62	78	78	62	76	76

Note: Levels of significance (one-tailed test) are a = 1 percent, b = 5 percent, c = 10 percent. The independent variables listed above the horizontal line are endogenous in our model or contain endogenous components.
1. We have divided these variables by 100 in order to scale them conveniently.

the number of a firm's activities, the proportion lying outside its base activity, and how far apart the activities lie in the standard industrial classification. These measures were averaged for the firms classified to three-digit manufacturing industries, and the averages for the different measures were found to be quite highly correlated among industries. The ranks of industries differ somewhat on these diversity measures, however, and the differences give insight into the varying technical and economic bases for their diversification.

Theoretically, we expect diversity to increase with plant size. Although excess diversification and small size are often bracketed as twin ills of Canadian industry, under certain assumptions diversification mitigates the elevation of cost that would result if plants were more specialized and as a result smaller still. We analyzed the diversity levels of companies within 20 Canadian manufacturing sectors and found that diversity generally increases with company size (although at a diminishing rate) and with the extent of multiplant operations. Although foreign subsidiaries are on the average more diversified than their domestic competitors, this relation does not prove statistically significant once we control for companies' size and multiplant operations.

We also sought to determine what explains the variation of diversity among our sample of three-digit manufacturing industries. Research-intensive industries tend strongly to diversify, while industries that advertise heavily show a weak tendency to avoid diversification. We found some support for the hypothesis that companies tend to diversify out of industries that are concentrated and yield profits that are high relative to the growth rate of the base market. Highly concentrated production does not support this motive, however, when the industry sells extensively on export markets.

If the diversification outbound from an industry reflects its inducements to diversify, inbound diversification reveals the ease of entry by firms established in other industries. We tried a two-pronged approach to measuring barriers to entry by established firms—including direct proxies for conventional entry barriers and utilizing the theorem that the level of seller concentration in the long run reflects the height of these entry barriers. We found a strong nonlinear relation of inbound diversification to concentration, rising linearly to rather high levels of concentration but then dropping abruptly. We conclude that diversifying firms avoid industries with either very high or very low entry barriers and that (for this purpose, at least) concentration depicts entry barriers rather better than do the standard statistical proxies themselves. We also found that research and development activities attract diversifying firms and that much inbound diversification is actually vertical integration.

9 Profits, Wages, and Market Power

Few topics have held as great a fascination for observers of industrial organization—or adduced as much controversy—as the causes of industries' profitability. High profits to some are the ultimate symbol of market power, while to others they represent the fruits of efficiency and capable management. Profits are highly visible and relatively easily measurable and as a result have probably been the most studied dimension of market performance.

Although the work of Harberger (1954), Leibenstein (1966), and others deprecates welfare losses due to allocative inefficiency relative to those from technical inefficiency or deficient innovation, there are convincing reasons for studying industries' profitability. Theory and evidence suggest that the sources of market power leading to excess profits are also among the determinants of market performance along other dimensions. Market power creates the potential for survival of technically inefficient firms. There is also substantial evidence that market power affects the incentives for firms to innovate, the relative success of innovations by large and by small firms, and the diffusion of innovation within and across industries. The rents due to market power offer a ripe target for bargaining by labor, and hence market power may be related to wage rates as well.

The analysis of market power in our model differs in several ways from its treatment in the single-equation models that have dominated the literature. We shall recognize that potential monopoly rents can materialize in several forms—actual excess profits, wages elevated above the opportunity cost of labor (when the rents are captured by the labor force), and excessive inputs per unit of output (when the rents are squandered in technical inefficiency). Theory leads us to expect that some potential rents are dispersed into each of these pockets, and so our model must take each into account. In this chapter we explore three dependent variables—actual excess profits, wages, and trade-union membership (the force presumed to divert excess profits from shareholders' to workers' pockets).

We shall also be concerned with modeling market power in an open economy and identifying the fundamental determinants of allocative inefficiency in a multiequation model. These two problems turn out to be closely interdependent. Finally, our data base allows us to formulate the profit variable in several ways; most studies of allocative performance have seized a single specification for the dependent variable, leaving the reader uncertain how robust the results might be to its replacement by another defensible measure of allocative performance.

9.1 Industries' Profits in the Open Economy

Although studies of differences in industries' profitability have been undertaken for many countries and with a dizzying variety of specifications, most research has employed a model appropriate to a large, closed economy such as that of the United States. There one can suppose that market size imposes no barrier to the attainment of efficient scale by the leading firms and that the competitive restraint of foreign trade is minor except in a few industries. The intangible assets due to product differentiation or production know-how can be legitimately attributed to past and present expenditures on these intangibles by firms operating in the market under study rather than being imported via foreign-controlled firms or through other processes of international diffusion such as technology licensing.

The U.S. economy provides the exception rather than the rule,[1] however, for markets in most industrialized countries are considerably more exposed to foreign influences. When we consider a smaller, more open economy, our hypotheses about profit determinants become increasingly vulnerable to the erroneous assumption of a closed economy. Where foreign trade is substantial, exposure to trade should significantly affect industries' profitability. Trade flows should not only influence competition but also render suspect the use of unadjusted measures of home-industry concentration. Likewise, it may be inappropriate to use the standard statistical proxies for scale economies, because they depend on the observed size distribution of plants. In a

1. And, apparently, not even the exception; see Pugel's (1978) findings of international influences on market power in the United States.

small economy many plants may be below minimum efficient scale, and at the least the relation among plant scale, trade flows, and multi-product plant operation must be considered (see chapters 3 and 10). The influences on profits of product differentiation and research and development must be reconsidered because of the possibilities for transferring skills and intangible assets across national boundaries.

Most previous research on industries' profits in Canada has taken over hypotheses and single-equation methodology from research done on the U.S. economy. It has reached consistent conclusions in some areas but failed to confirm relationships in others. McFetridge (1973) examined the relationship of price-cost margins to industry structure in 43 Canadian three-digit manufacturing industries for the years 1965–1969. He related price-cost margins to growth in demand, various measures of seller concentration, economies of scale measured as by Comanor and Wilson (1967), effective tariff protection, local or re-gional industry fragmentation, advertising intensity, and capital in-tensity. The last two variables are needed as controls because price-cost margins inappropriately include advertising and payments to capital in addition to profits.

McFetridge finds that the squared value of the Herfindahl index of the size distribution of firms in the industry is statistically significant, as are his two control variables. The significance of the squared Herfindahl coefficient implies that the shares of the top few firms are very important while the shares of the remaining firms have little effect on profits. The coefficient of the Herfindahl index is larger for consumer-good industries than for producer-good industries. Adver-tising's coefficient is not significantly different from the value expected from advertising's presence in value added, and hence McFetridge does not find advertising significant as a behavioral variable. Coefficients of the balance of his variables are not significant, though the measure of regionality is nearly so. The scale-economies proxy is highly collinear with concentration and may be insignificant because the two effects cannot be separated.

In a similar study Jones, Laudadio, and Percy (1973, also 1977) in-vestigate the determinants of net profit on equity and profit before taxes plus interest on total assets in a sample of 30 consumer-good in-dustries. The sample is restricted to industries defined consistently in the data sources used. As independent variables they employ seller concentration, advertising-to-sales ratios, the industry's rate of growth, minimum-efficient-scale (MES) measures similar to those of Comanor and Wilson (1967), absolute capital requirements determined as the capital cost of the MES plant, a regional dummy variable, and dummy variables indicating whether the import share of the market lies between 15 and 30 percent or over 30 percent.

Jones and his colleagues get better results with profit plus interest on total assets than with net profit on equity as the dependent variable. Scale economies are not significant. Concentration is significant only when scale economies are omitted (one would expect substantial collinearity between the two). Capital requirements are significant only when MES and concentration are omitted. The advertising-to-sales ratio, the industry's growth rate, and the regional dummy are all significant, though not strongly so. Finally, the dummy indicating strong import competition is unexpectedly positive and significant (the authors report that nominal and effective tariff rates were tried and found insignificant).

An earlier test of determinants of profitability in Canada was provided by Schwartzman (1959), who related the differences in the ratio of price to direct cost in matched Canadian and U.S. industries to differences in their seller concentration. He found that high relative concentration in Canada is associated with a high ratio of price to direct cost. The result did not hold in industries with heavy export trade but was unaffected by the presence of imports. A methodological descendant of Schwartzman is Bloch (1974), who argues (in parallel with our own analysis) that the influence of market power on performance should be evident only in industries not closely exposed to international competition. He indeed finds that Canadian prices are high relative to the prices of U.S. counterpart industries only in those highly concentrated sectors protected by high tariffs. The source of this asymmetrical price performance in concentrated industries turns out to be elevated production costs, however. Bloch's concentrated industries report higher profit margins than the less concentrated ones, but the level of tariffs makes no difference.

A recent study of profitability in Canadian industries by Gupta (1977) uses a simultaneous-equation format. Gupta finds that advertising and a measure of scale economies are positive and significant determinants of price-cost margins (averaged for 1966–1970). Concentration's coefficient is significant only when scale economies are excluded and becomes insignificant in the two-stage least-squares (TSLS) equation. Measures of foreign trade are erratically significant, though the tariff rate's coefficient always has a positive sign while imports and exports are negative. Finally, a measure of the extent of foreign direct investment in the Canadian industry is negative and sometimes significant but loses significance in the TSLS equation.

Taken together, these studies agree on a number of points. First, seller concentration proves significant, but its effect is weak and sensitive to choice of specification, data set, and estimation method. Second, advertising and the industry's growth rate are not such powerful influences in Canada as they are over the profits of U.S. industries. Third, foreign trade appears to matter, but its influence is quite sensitive to specification. Fourth, scale-economies and capital-requirement proxies drawn in the same way as used in U.S. studies are seldom significant—perhaps because they themselves determine seller concentration, perhaps because they were measured in a way that makes them close reflections of the observed level of concentration. The results are fairly consistent with our general interpretation of industrial organization in a small, open economy, but they do leave a number of puzzles.

9.2 Determinants of Return on Investment

Economic theory clearly indicates that three conditions are necessary for a monopolistic distortion of a market in an open economy. Sellers must be few enough to recognize their mutual interdependence in short-run (pricing) and long-run (investment) decisions affecting the quantity sold in the market. Entry barriers must deter entry even when profits are persistently elevated above a normal competitive level.[2] And international competition must not constrain the domestic price to a closed-economy competitive level. The joint necessity of these conditions implies that they should interact with each other in the statistical specifications. Which aspects of international competition should be interacted is a question that can receive various answers. Other determinants of allocative distortion either should clearly enter in additive fashion or can be wedded interactively to the independent variables already mentioned only on rather shaky reasoning.

The researcher attacking the determinants of profitability is plagued by the incrustation of past controversy in this field. Must he settle, or even take a position on, all the outstanding issues, while testing his own pet hypothesis? To lighten our burden of argumentation, we decided to avoid entering into certain controversies on statistical specification by simply trying the competing procedures rather than choos-

2. Collusive sellers protected by entry barriers may maximize the present value of their long-run profits by charging a price high enough to induce some entry and giving up market share (Gaskins, 1971). This behavior may well occur, but we give it little attention in our statistical specifications because it violates our general assumption that industries are in long-run equilibrium.

COMPETITION IN THE OPEN ECONOMY

ing and defending one.[3] One such controversy is over the choice of a dependent variable among net profits on equity, the price-cost margin, and excess profits on sales. We use and report on all these variables.

ROI   Net profit (loss) after taxes divided by total equity, averaged over 1968–1971.[4]

PCAD   Price-cost margin: value added minus payroll and advertising outlays, divided by value of shipments. Data are for 1967 except for advertising, which is available only for 1965.

ATPS   Profits before interest but after direct taxes divided by total sales, 1968–1971.[5]

We find ourselves in the same position in choosing a measure of seller concentration, because neither economic theory nor previous empirical research on Canada identifies a clearly superior variable. Three conventional options are available.

C468   Proportion of shipments controlled by the four largest sellers, 1968.

C868   Proportion of shipments controlled by the eight largest sellers, 1968.

HFL   Herfindahl coefficient of concentration, 1968.

The former two enjoy the most convincing theoretical justification in Saving's (1970) proof that the n-firm concentration correctly predicts the extent of allocative inefficiency if the n largest firms form a collusive core and the remaining firms behave as a competitive fringe.[6] Within the n-firm core, however, one can argue that the presence of a dominant firm facilitates the formation and policing of a stable agreement. Therefore we formed the composite measure

3. This does not mean that we view the issues as moot either theoretically or empirically—only that they are peripheral to our concern with market size and openness and hence would distract us from the main show.

4. In any economy with a high proportion of foreign subsidiaries, transfer-price and investment-valuation issues may well create noise in return on investment data to some extent. Thus our test is a more stringent one than is the case with U.S. data, and any relationships exposed are likely to be robust.

5. Qualls (1974), who has promoted this measure, also removes an estimate of the opportunity cost of capital to convert the variable into excess profit. We follow Pugel (1978), instead placing the ratio of interest-bearing debt to sales on the right-hand side of the equation in order to determine the opportunity cost of capital inductively rather than by assumption.

6. Cowling and Waterson (1976) justify the Herfindahl coefficient on the assumption of Cournot oligopoly, but to assume that no mutual dependence is recognized strikes us as discarding the essence of the problem of oligopoly behavior.

>
> C4CV Product of C468 and the coefficient of variation of the sizes of the eight largest firms.

This measure would give nonsensical results in the limiting case of a concentrated industry with leading firms of identical size (it goes to zero). In fact, the coefficient of variation has a skewed distribution with a few high values and most observations clustered comfortably above zero. C4CV leans in the direction of the Herfindahl coefficient but is less dominated by the shares of the top one or two firms.[7]

Seller concentration measured at the national level understates effective concentration if the market is regionally fragmented, and evidence available for Canada (Department of Consumer and Corporate Affairs, 1971) shows that regional concentration in such Canadian industries is higher than in their national counterparts. We were unable to construct a set of average regional concentration ratios, and so we simply used as an additive variable

>
> REG Dummy variable equal to one if the industry is judged to be subject to significant regional fragmentation, zero otherwise.

It should be positively related to profits if concentration measured at the national level understates concentration in the relevant regional market.

The theoretically appropriate indicator of import competition is an elasticity of excess supply at prices in the neighborhood of equilibrium with a competitive domestic industry. Like most other investigators, we lack a direct measure of this elasticity and must rely simply on

>
> IMP Imports as a proportion of domestic shipments, 1961.

We did attempt to allow for weakening of the force of import competition when products are differentiated, by means of

>
> IMAD $IMP(1 - 5 * ADI)$ where ADI is the industry's ratio of advertising to sales in 1965.

The values of ADI are distributed so that IMAD is always positive, but the value that IMP would take is proportionally much reduced in industries that advertise heavily. When import competition is interacted with concentration, it will be done by forming the following variables:

---

7. We also computed this composite measure using C868. As it turns out, it makes no difference which is used. Note that the specification is consistent with studies of U.S. industries that confirmed the negative influence on profits of a high marginal concentration ratio given the four-firm concentration ratio.

$$CONM1 = CON/(1 + IMP),$$

$$CONM2 = CON/(1 + IMAD),$$

where CON is any of the concentration measures. This formulation assumes that imports function as a competitive fringe, which is logical if one accepts Saving's (1970) theoretical justification of the n-firm concentration ratio.

Our treatment of entry barriers differs somewhat from the usual one, partly for conceptual reasons and partly because of our view that entry barriers, concentration, and insulation from foreign rivals are jointly necessary to permit allocative inefficiency. We indicate first how we model the standard (Bain, 1956) sources of entry barriers individually, then explain the assembly process.

1. *Scale economies.* An entry barrier is created where minimum efficient scale is a substantial proportion of the market and the cost disadvantage of suboptimal-scale plants is relatively high (Caves, Khalilzadeh-Shirazi, and Porter, 1975). The analysis presented in chapter 3 makes it certain that the cost disadvantage of small firms should not be inferred from Canadian data and at least doubtful that minimum efficient scale should be so constructed. We did utilize a Canada-based measure in the regressions reported but ascertained that the choice between a Canada-based and a U.S.-based measure made no difference to the results. Specifically, we use

MESD   The average size (shipments) of the largest plants accounting for 50 percent of industry employment, divided by industry shipments (*MESC* in our data base), if the cost disadvantage ratio for the U.S.-counterpart industry is less than 0.9,[8] zero otherwise.

2. *Absolute capital costs.* The usual proxy is the estimated capital cost of the minimum-efficient-scale plant. Like scale economies, however, this entry barrier should operate only where the cost disadvantage of suboptimal-scale establishments is significant. Hence our variable is the estimated assets of the minimum-efficient-scale plant when the small plant's cost disadvantage is deemed significant, zero otherwise.

MABD   Shipments by the average-size plant among the largest plants accounting for 50 percent of industry shipments (*MABC* in our data base) multiplied by the industry's assets-to-sales ratio (*ATS*) if *CDRU* is less than 0.9, zero otherwise.

8. The cost disadvantage ratio (*CDRU*) equals value added per worker in the smaller plants accounting for half of employment in the U.S. industry divided by value added per worker in the larger plants accounting for the other half.

3. *Product differentiation.* The usual proxy for entry barriers created by large-scale advertising outlays is simply the industry's ratio of advertising outlays to sales. On the basis of Porter's (1976b) work, we expect heavy advertising to create an entry barrier only in convenience-good industries. Hence our measure is

ADIC   The ratio of advertising to sales (*ADI*, in our data base) multiplied by a dummy variable (*CONO*) equal to one if the industry is judged a convenience-good industry, zero otherwise.

In order to interact these entry-barrier components with concentration and exposure to trade, we need some way to aggregate them. The choice is necessarily somewhat arbitrary. We chose to express each as a ratio to its mean value in our sample of industries. With average values denoted by a prime, we calculated

$$BARR = 1 + MESD/MESC' + ADIC/ADI' + MABD/(MABC' * ATS'),$$

with one added to insure positive values. Previous statistical research on allocative efficiency in Canada found no influence of scale economies, and our own analysis (chapter 3) warns that their complex interactive effect on concentration leaves little room for an independent influence of scale economies and concentration on market performance. So we also subdivided *BARR* into

$$BARSC = 1 + MESD/MESC' + MABD/(MABD' * ATS')$$

and

$$BARAD = 1 + ADIC/ADI'.$$

Our most fully interactive specification of concentration, entry barriers, and import competition is

$$CBARR = CONM1 * BARR \text{ or } CONM2 * BARR,$$

and we also use $CBARSC = CONM1 * BARSC$ and $CBARAD = CONM1 * BARAD$. It would be preferable to estimate weights of the components of *BARR* rather than assume them, as we have done, but multicollinearity in the data make this impractical.

International competition can affect allocative efficiency through an industry's exposure to export opportunities as well as import competition (Caves, 1974), but the export relation is not a simple one. One can defend a negative relation of profits to

EXP   Exports as a proportion of industry shipments.

This relation could also be positive under reasonable theoretical conditions, notably if the exporters are able to segment the foreign from the domestic market and thereby profit from price discrimination (dumping). Empirical studies of profit determinants in other countries have reported correspondingly diverse results. We tried to disentangle these relations by adding an indicator of circumstances in which this market segmentation should be possible. A condition that is probably sufficient (though not necessary) is that the industry advertise significantly, in which case it probably can control the distribution of its output among markets. Besides EXP we also include

$$EXAD = EXP * ADI.$$

Research and development activity has not generally been included in statistical analyses of profit rates, although the literature contains the suggestion that R&D may serve as an entry barrier in at least some types of industries.[9] However, the conclusions of chapter 7 suggest that research activities of the sort carried out in Canada do not create economies of scale or raise product-differentiation entry barriers. Rather they serve the defensive purpose of adapting knowledge originated abroad to Canadian conditions or fortifying Canadian companies against international competition. The need to make these defensive outlays actually implies that Canadian producers' profits may be lower than they otherwise would be and that they are thus negatively related to

$RDIC$ Research and development outlays as a proportion of industry sales.

This specification does less than full justice to the role of multinational companies in Canadian industry, and for that reason we shall return to it later.

Analyses of the determinants of profits normally include a measure of the rate of growth of output, expecting (and getting) a significant positive coefficient. Several hypotheses support this specification; one is that actual growth is positively correlated with deviations of actual from expected growth and hence positively correlated with windfall profits (losses). Our variable is

GSI Slope coefficient from regression of logarithm of total value of industry shipments on time, 1961–1971.

Our final independent variable, the industry's ratio of capital to sales, has a different significance for each of our three versions of the

9. See Mueller and Tilton (1969) and Orr (1974).

dependent variable. *ATPS* and *PCAD* both include in their numerators interest on borrowed capital and the opportunity cost of equity, and *PCAD* contains depreciation allowances as well. For them the capital-to-sales ratio must be included to remove these components of the opportunity cost of capital. The regression coefficient of the capital-to-sales ratio should be positive, of course. On the other hand, there is a behavioral relation between capital intensity and excess profits that should carry a negative sign: the more capital-intensive the industry, the more likely is marginal cost to fall below average cost at any output short of capacity, and the more fragile should be any oligopolistic consensus. The capital-to-sales measures that we use are

> *ATS* Total assets divided by total income, 1969.
> *KTS* Total interest-bearing debt (equity, debt, and current liabilities to banks) divided by total income, 1969.

We use *ATS* with dependent variables *ROI* and *ATPS*, *KTS* with *PCAD*. A ratio of fixed assets to sales would actually be more appropriate with *ROI*.[10] That refinement was not available here but is employed in an analysis of companies' profits in Chapter 12.

Principal Statistical Results

Only by resort to the data can we resolve several issues left open in our a priori specifications—the "best" measures of seller concentration and import competition, the degree of interaction among the central determinants of market power (concentration, entry barriers, import competition), and the sensitivity of the results to the choice of the dependent variable. Space limitations preclude reporting the competing regression equations in detail; the most revealing single specification appears in table 9.1. First, a glance at the equations in the table quickly reveals that the statistical results generally match the theoretical predictions for dependent variables *ROI* and *ATPS* but diverge considerably for *PCAD*. (The puzzles raised by the equations for *PCAD* are addressed later.) If we compare the equations for *ROI* and *ATPS* in table 9.1 to alternative specifications, we reach the following conclusions.

1. Among our concentration measures, *C4CV* is modestly but robustly superior to the alternatives. It apparently gives the most appropriate weight to top-end concentration and to the presence of dominant firms among an industry's leaders.

10. That refinement was not available here, but is employed in an analysis of companies' profits in chapter 12.

Table 9.1 Determinants of three measures of industries' profitability.

Independent variables	Profit on equity (ROI)			Profit on sales (ATPS)			Price-cost margin (PCAD)		
	A	B	C	A	B	C	A	B	C
CONMI[1]	0.526a	0.355a	0.460b	22.6a	14.5a	20.5b	−0.720b	−0.184	−0.319
	(2.81)	(2.63)	(1.86)	(2.75)	(2.62)	(2.11)	(−2.25)	(−0.64)	(−0.60)
BARAD	0.003	0.002	0.007b	0.190b	0.194b	0.370a	0.011a	0.010b	0.011c
	(1.04)	(1.06)	(1.87)	(1.77)	(2.12)	(2.69)	(2.71)	(2.11)	(1.41)
EXP	−0.029	−0.017	−0.027	0.044	−0.301	−1.16	−0.144a	−0.102b	−0.196b
	(−0.96)	(−0.79)	(−0.66)	(0.03)	(−0.34)	(−0.73)	(−2.82)	(−2.22)	(−2.21)
RDIC	−0.007b	−0.006a	−0.007	−0.283b	−0.194b	−0.276	0.004	−0.002	0.017c
	(−2.38)	(−2.79)	(−1.25)	(−2.27)	(−2.18)	(−1.25)	(0.74)	(−0.31)	(1.39)
ADEX	0.476b	0.317a	0.025	9.11	12.4a	4.06	0.184	0.479a	0.187
	(2.07)	(5.00)	(0.14)	(0.90)	(4.81)	(0.58)	(0.47)	(3.55)	(0.48)
ATS[2]	−0.026b	−0.024b	−0.023c	0.042	0.047a	0.046a	0.125a	0.101a	0.120a
	(−1.98)	(−2.15)	(−1.63)	(7.25)	(10.7)	(8.62)	(5.56)	(4.17)	(3.95)
REG	0.007	0.006	0.002	−0.063	−0.162	−0.359	0.002	−0.017	−0.005
	(0.69)	(0.65)	(0.18)	(0.13)	(−0.44)	(−0.77)	(0.10)	(−0.88)	(−0.18)
GSI	0.145	0.263a	0.298b	5.03	3.31	4.74	−0.046	0.145	0.180
	(1.13)	(2.78)	(2.44)	(0.89)	(0.86)	(0.99)	(−0.21)	(0.73)	(0.69)
Constant	0.090a	0.087a	0.079a	0.664	1.33a	1.15b	0.111a	0.120a	0.092a
	(6.01)	(6.88)	(4.99)	(1.02)	(2.80)	(1.98)	(4.37)	(4.49)	(2.70)
$\bar{R}^2$	0.224	0.355	—	0.661	0.717	—	0.408	0.296	—
F	2.99	6.72	0.96	14.4	27.3	12.8	5.74	5.36	1.48
D.f.	47	75	75	47	75	75	47	75	75

Note: Levels of statistical significance (one-tailed test) are a = 1 percent, b = 5 percent, c = 10 percent. The variables listed above the horizontal line are endogenous in our model.
1. We have divided this variable by 1,000 in order to scale it conveniently.
2. When the dependent variable is ATPS, ATS is replaced by KTS.

2. We confirm the finding of previous studies that the scale-related components of entry barriers have no power to explain profits in Canada—even when (as in our case) the proxies used employ data from outside Canada and when simultaneous methods are used that could potentially isolate the independent influences of these barriers and concentration. Only *BARAD*, the product-differentiation component of entry barriers, appears in table 9.1.[11] We argued in chapter 3 that scale economies wield a rather complex influence on the number and size distribution of firms in Canada; apparently the concentration measure summarizes that influence in the equations of table 9.1.

3. When concentration (*C4CV*) and import competition (*IMP*) are entered separately, both are correctly signed but only the former is significant. The replacement of the separate terms with the interaction shown in table 9.1 always appreciably improves the *F*-ratio of the equation. There is no systematic difference in statistical fit between *CONM1*, which utilizes *IMP*, and *CONM2*, which incorporates *IMAD*. Although we have cited evidence that imports generally behave as if they were differentiated from competing domestic output, the advertising levels of Canadian industries are apparently not associated with the extent of this differentiation.

4. For the dependent variables *ROI* and *ATPS* the overall fit of the equation is not improved by allowing concentration to interact with entry barriers (either *CBARR* or *CBARAD*). The failure to confirm this interaction hypothesis can be interpreted in several ways; one is that industries are not always observed in limit-price equilibrium and that concentrated industries are more likely to pursue the short-run profits associated with entry-inducing prices. Before we discard the interaction hypothesis, however, we must note that it is strongly confirmed when the dependent variable is *PCAD*. If we replace *CONM1* and *BARAD* in table 9.1 with *CBARR*, the following equation B results for *PCAD*.

$$PCAD = 120 + 0.121\ CBARR - 0.128\ EXP + 0.401\ ADEX$$
$$(4.84)\ (3.24) \qquad\qquad (-2.93) \qquad\quad (3.03)$$
$$- 0.000\ RDIC + 0.095\ ATS - 0.008\ REG + 0.106\ GSI,$$
$$(-0.01) \qquad\quad (4.37) \qquad\quad (-0.46) \qquad\quad (0.55)$$

$$\overline{R}^2 = 0.353,$$
$$F = 7.46.$$

11. If *BARSC* is also included, it takes an insignificant negative sign, and the significance of the other variables is left unaffected.

The F-ratio generously exceeds that for the corresponding B equation in table 9.1, and *CBARR* takes a positive and highly significant coefficient. The A and C equations differ from this one approximately as those in table 9.1. Because *PCAD* is less subject to measurement errors (due to diversification, and to arbitrary reporting of the profits of foreign subsidiaries) than the other variables, we give significant credence to this result.

Table 9.1 taken by itself reveals various other conclusions. The complex influence of exports embodied in variables *EXP* and *EXAD* is confirmed as all the expected signs in all equations, although the negative coefficient of *EXP* is significant only for the dependent variable *PCAD*. The positive coefficient of *EXAD* tends to be significant, often highly so, in OLS equations, but its significance invariably collapses in TSLS equations. Because the other term that incorporates advertising, *BARAD* (advertising entry barriers), becomes more significant in the TSLS equations, we tentatively conclude that the favorable effect of advertising on profits comes about through the creation of entry barriers more than through allowing export industries to segment the domestic market.

The capital-intensity variables perform as expected, with *KTS* and *ATS* respectively taking highly significant positive signs in the equations for *ATPS* and *PCAD*, and *ATS* exerting a significant negative influence on *ROI*. *REG*'s expected positive influence is not confirmed; its coefficient is erratic in sign and never significant. Growth *(GSI)* is significant for profit measure *ROI* but not for those that include sales in their denominator. Recall our hypothesis that *GSI* indicates windfall components of profits associated with deviations of actual from expected growth of sales. Because these deviations also affect the denominators of profit measures *ATPS* and *PCAD*, it is logical that the windfall effect should fail to be significant for them.[12]

12. This is only one of several hypotheses that have been put forward about the relation between growth and profits. We can mention a failed attempt to test another. Several lines of reasoning imply that growth should have a weaker behavioral influence on profits in competitive industries than in those with significant entry barriers and some elements of oligopoly. In the latter, fast growth can shore up an oligopolistic consensus and create windfalls that are not immediately eroded by entry. We trifurcated our industries by level of *C468* and allowed the coefficient of *GSI* to take a different value in each third. *GSI* sometimes took a higher and significant coefficient for the most concentrated group, sometimes for the middle group, but the results were not robust. We conclude that the hypothesized interaction between growth and concentration is not confirmed.

Supplemental Hypotheses

Besides the hypotheses already reviewed, we tested certain others that are supplemental in the sense that their justification depends on hypotheses already tested. The variables indicated by these new hypotheses were added to the regression equations shown in table 9.1 or used to replace variables included therein. Equations A, B, and C were then estimated for each of the three profit measures. To avoid presenting a surfeit of regression equations, we report only the B equations that test these hypotheses in table 9.2. The A and C equations generally differ from the B equations in about the same way as in table 9.1, and exceptions are noted in the text.

1. *Unionization.* In the next part of this chapter we shall develop and test the hypothesis that trade-union organizations are formed (among other reasons) for the purpose of capturing potential monopoly rents as wages for their members. The hypothesis implies that profits should be negatively related to union bargaining power, which we represent by

> *PWUN* Proportion of production workers covered by collective-bargaining agreements.

Neither theory nor our subsequent empirical inquiry gives a definite answer to the question whether *PWUN* should interact with concentration and entry barriers or simply wield an additive effect. It is included as an additive variable in equations 1–6 of table 9.2. Its sign is negative, and it is always significant for dependent variables *ATPS* and *PCAD*. However, its significance collapses in any TSLS equation. We attribute its collapse to the conclusion that the extent of union membership itself depends on entry barriers, concentration, and other variables (such as plant size) closely correlated with them. Union membership is thus a proximate determinant of profits, but ultimately it and reported profits are both determined by an overlapping set of underlying forces.

2. *Rents from technology.* Our hypothesis about research expenditures in Canada—only weakly confirmed in table 9.1—was that they amount to defensive outlays that enable Canadian producers in research-intensive industries to compete against goods originating elsewhere in the world market. This hypothesis, which indicated a negative sign for *RDIC*, flies against certain hypotheses pointing toward a positive sign. Orr (1974) found that R&D outlays act as an entry barrier in Canada. Technology developed by foreign multinational companies and applied by their subsidiaries in the Canadian

Table 9.2 Extensions of analysis of determinants of three measures of industries' profitability, OLS equations using filled-in data base.

Independent variables	Dependent variables								
	ROI (1)	ATPS (2)	PCAD (3)	ROI (4)	ATPS (5)	PCAD (6)	ROI (7)	ATPS (8)	PCAD (9)
CONMI[1]	0.439a (2.92)	20.4a (3.37)	0.113 (0.36)	0.398a (2.64)	21.0a (3.40)	0.044 (0.14)	—	—	—
DCP	—	—	—	—	—	—	−2.31c (−1.33)	−122c (−1.60)	2.77 (0.72)
DCC	—	—	—	—	—	—	−5.74c (−1.36)	−144 (−0.78)	−15.2c (−1.63)
DCN	—	—	—	—	—	—	−10.6a (−4.06)	−355a (−3.06)	−1.10 (−0.19)
BARAD	0.001 (0.27)	0.079 (0.76)	0.004 (0.75)	0.001 (0.19)	0.082 (0.78)	0.004 (0.69)	0.002 (0.80)	0.168c (1.60)	0.015a (2.79)
PWUN[1]	−0.326 (−1.25)	−22.4b (−2.15)	−1.16b (−2.13)	−0.299 (1.16)	−22.8b (−2.18)	−1.11b (−2.05)	—	—	—
RDIC	−0.006a (−2.67)	−0.177b (−2.02)	−0.001 (−0.13)	−0.011a (−2.81)	−0.095 (−0.57)	−0.010 (−1.19)	−0.013a (−3.39)	−0.167 (−1.00)	−0.014c (−1.60)
RDFS	—	—	—	0.008c (1.62)	−0.112 (−0.59)	0.013c (1.33)	0.008b (1.87)	−0.068 (−0.35)	0.014c (1.47)
EXP	−0.012 (−0.54)	0.074 (0.09)	−0.084b (−1.53)	−0.021 (−0.92)	0.201 (0.22)	−0.100b (−2.10)	−0.033c (−1.54)	−0.450 (−0.49)	−0.111b (−2.38)
ADEX	0.319a (5.04)	12.6a (4.98)	0.485a (3.68)	0.328a (5.22)	12.4a (4.88)	0.501a (3.81)	0.363a (6.00)	13.4a (5.06)	0.505a (3.77)

ATS²	−0.023ᵇ	0.048ᵃ	0.105ᵃ	−0.020ᵇ	0.047ᵃ	0.110ᵃ	−0.022ᵇ	0.048ᵃ	0.089ᵃ
	(−2.03)	(11.0)	(4.45)	(−1.78)	(10.7)	(4.62)	(−2.15)	(10.8)	(3.84)
REG	0.007	−0.095	−0.013	0.009	−0.120	−0.010	0.004	−0.325	−0.007
	(0.77)	(−0.26)	(−0.70)	(0.97)	(−0.33)	(−0.53)	(0.42)	(−0.81)	(−0.36)
GSI	0.287ᵃ	4.99ᶜ	0.231	0.220ᵇ	5.96ᶜ	0.117	0.166ᵇ	2.72	0.021
	(2.99)	(1.30)	(1.16)	(2.13)	(1.42)	(0.54)	(1.74)	(0.66)	(0.10)
Constant	0.105ᵃ	2.66ᵃ	0.187ᵃ	0.107ᵃ	2.63ᵃ	0.190ᵃ	0.124ᵃ	2.63ᵃ	0.125ᵃ
	(5.37)	(3.44)	(4.57)	(5.51)	(3.38)	(4.66)	(8.77)	(4.47)	(3.98)
$\overline{R}^2$	0.360	0.730	0.328	0.374	0.728	0.335	0.438	0.716	0.334
F	6.19	26.0	5.50	5.95	23.2	5.18	6.89	20.0	4.78
D.f.	74	74	74	73	73	73	72	72	72

Note: Levels of statistical significance (one-tailed test) are a = 1 percent, b = 5 percent, c = 10 percent. The variables listed above the horizontal line are endogenous to our model.

1. We have divided these variables by 1,000 in order to scale them conveniently.

2. When the dependent variable is *ATPS*, *ATS* is replaced by *KTS*.

market should leave some rents on the subsidiaries' books. We tested for this latter influence by forming the variable

> *RDFS*   Product of *RDIU* (research and development outlays as a proportion of sales, U.S. counterpart industry) and *FSE* (proportion of sales in the Canadian industry accounted for by companies under 50 percent or more foreign ownership).

RDFS should take a positive sign and increase the significance of the negative coefficient of *RDIC*. In equations 4–6 of table 9.2 *RDFS* behaves as expected and achieves a modest level of significance with dependent variables *ROI* and *PCAD*, and it strengthens the negative influence of *RDIC* with these same variables. The hypothesis is not confirmed in OLS equations for the dependent variable *ATPS*; however, in the TSLS versions of the equations in table 9.2 it is confirmed (10 percent significance) for *ATPS* and is generally significant at 5 percent for *ROI* and *PCAD*. We conclude that the profit equations support the characterization offered in chapter 7 of research and development in relation to industrial organization in Canada.

3. *Uncertainty and oligopolistic coordination.* Spence (1978) has urged that the theory of tacit coordination implies a sharp falling off of the ability of sellers to maintain mutual understandings as seller concentration drops from high levels, as the variability of demand increases, and as buyers become more concentrated. He proposes that profits should be negatively related to an interaction of (1) the shortfall of concentration from high levels—$1 - (C468/100)^2$, where *C468* is the simple four-firm concentration ratio; (2) the standard deviation of annual shipments around their trend—*SSI*; and (3) buyer concentration. Because we were unable to construct a satisfactory measure of buyer concentration for an acceptably large proportion of our sampled industries, we followed Spence (1978) and simply allowed the product of terms (1) and (2) to take a different slope for producer-good, consumer convenience-good, and other consumer-good industries. We also maintained our assumption that imports should be counted as a competitive fringe for the purpose of adjusting concentration ratios and constructed the following three variables.

$$DCP = (1 - (C468/100)^2) * SSI * (1 - CNPR)/(1 + IMP),$$
$$DCC = (1 - (C468/100)^2) * SSI * CONO/(1 + IMP),$$
$$DCN = (1 - (C468/100)^2) * SSI * (CNPR - CONO)/(1 + IMP),$$

for the producer, consumer convenience, and other consumer-good industries respectively. All should be negatively related to profits, but the characteristics of buyers should make collusion more difficult to sustain for the producer-good and consumer nonconvenience industries. Therefore we expect larger negative coefficients for *DCP* and *DCN* than for *DCC*. The results in equations 7–9 confirm the difference between the two groups of consumer-good industries proposed by Porter (1976b) and exhibit negative signs for the coefficients of all three variables, but the result for producer-good industries is not as expected. Some producer-good industries successfully differentiate their products or sell to atomistic buyers (such as agriculture and construction) or both.

Multinational Companies and Profit Determinants

Given our emphasis on multinational companies in this study, readers may wonder that they have played no more prominent role in specifying the profit equations. The reason is that no model serves to forge a direct and unambiguous causal connection between foreign-subsidiary activity in an industry and its level of profitability. The forces promoting foreign investment are also the stuff of which entry barriers are made, but it is the entry barriers and not the foreign investment that should yield excess profits. The multinational company may actually augment the effective level of entry barriers, but it also offers a supply of potential entrants to a barrier-protected market, and these effects imply opposite signs for the profits variable.

Even if one accepts that the prevalence of foreign investment itself is not a primary determinant of profits, many possible reasons explain why the profits of foreign subsidiaries and domestic-controlled companies should not be determined by identical models. In some industries domestic and foreign companies may compose different strategic groups, and entry barriers may not protect them equally from competitive forces (Porter, 1979) . Of course, the foreign subsidiaries could simply be subject to large errors of observation because of the accounting practices of their parents. We split the profits of our sample industries into those accruing to foreign-controlled companies and those accruing to domestic-controlled companies and calculated the following counterparts of *ROI*:

FROI   Net profits after taxes on equity capital, companies subject to 50 percent or more foreign control, 1965–1967.

HROI   Net profits after taxes on equity capital, companies classified as subject to domestic control, 1965–1967.

Table 9.3 Determinants of rates of return on equity for domestically controlled companies $(HROI)$ and companies under 50 percent or more foreign control $(FROI)$.

Independent variables	Domestic-company profits			Foreign-subsidiary profits		
	A	B	C	A	B	C
$CONMI$[1]	0.914a	0.687a	0.284	−0.492	0.102	0.151
	(2.76)	(3.24)	(0.76)	(−0.69)	(0.31)	(0.23)
$BARAD$	−0.003	0.001	0.006	0.008	0.006	0.015c
	(−0.89)	(0.23)	(1.14)	(1.08)	(1.09)	(1.60)
EXP	−0.066c	−0.012	0.052	−0.189b	−0.074c	−0.204b
	(−1.56)	(−0.36)	(0.84)	(−2.09)	(−1.38)	(−1.89)
$RDIC$	0.004	0.001	0.011	−0.006	−0.001	−0.005
	(0.95)	(0.26)	(1.34)	(−0.64)	(−0.18)	(−0.36)
$ADEX$	0.357	0.634a	0.728a	−1.06c	0.042	−0.742c
	(1.04)	(6.36)	(2.68)	(−1.44)	(0.27)	(−1.56)
ATS	0.008	0.006	0.009	−0.008	−0.029	−0.006
	(0.42)	(0.32)	(0.41)	(−0.20)	(−1.02)	(−0.16)
REG	0.015	0.019c	0.026c	−0.019	−0.009	−0.025
	(0.87)	(1.34)	(1.45)	(−0.52)	(−0.42)	(−0.81)
GSI	0.338c	0.389a	0.261c	0.801c	0.532b	0.701b
	(1.44)	(2.63)	(1.42)	(1.59)	(2.29)	(2.19)
Constant	0.108a	0.094a	0.085a	0.184a	0.186a	0.173a
	(4.47)	(4.79)	(3.56)	(3.84)	(6.02)	(4.16)
$\bar{R}^2$	0.151	0.432	—	0.078	0.028	—
F	1.91	8.87	2.09	1.43	1.30	0.55
D.f.	33	75	75	33	75	75

Note: Levels of statistical significance (one-tailed test) are a = 1 percent, b = 5 percent, c = 10 percent. The variables listed above the horizontal line are endogenous in our model.

1. We have divided this variable by 1,000 in order to scale it conveniently.

When these two variables are regressed on the independent variables shown in table 9.1, we secure the equation shown in table 9.3. Clearly the two regression planes differ a great deal. The profits of the foreign subsidiaries are very poorly explained, while the explanatory power for domestic-company profits is quite good. This fact suggests that transfer-pricing and accounting practices may substantially distort the reported profits of foreign subsidiaries. (The differing variances also preclude applying the standard statistical test that the regression relations for $HROI$ and $FROI$ are the same; Rao and Miller,

1971, pp. 90–93.) The foreign firms show weak signs of enjoying the benefits of product-differentiation entry barriers, as one would expect. On the other hand, the profits of domestic companies are much more closely tied to concentration (*CONM1*) and to the dummy indicating regional markets (*REG*). Many explanations for this difference suggest themselves, such as that mutual dependence recognized among the subsidiaries depends on relations among their parents in a market larger than Canada. Capital intensity (*ATS*) is not significant for either group, signifying that its influence rests on differences between the two. The influence of the growth of industry shipments seems somewhat stronger on the profits of foreign than domestic companies. The same is true of the negative influence of unionization, if that variable is included in the equation.

9.3 Determinants of Unionization

Economists have often voiced the suspicion—while contemplating the modest proportion that they could explain of the variance of industries' profitability—that some of the rents associated with market power are captured by factors of production other than equity capital. A leading candidate is the trade union that exerts the monopoly power of an industry's labor force. Therefore this chapter should logically include an examination of the determinants of the degree of unionization and wages in Canada's manufacturing industries. Incorporating these variables befits a study that emphasizes the simultaneous determination of industrial structure and performance. A central failing of much previous research on the effect of unionization on wages is the neglect of the fact that workers rationally join trade unions only in market structures in which the expected gain in wages repays the cost of their organization.[13] The relative effect of seller concentration and unionization on wages cannot be accurately assessed in a single-equation format if, for example, the rise of unions is itself explained by the existence of seller concentration.

Organizing and maintaining a trade union is costly to its members, and a "free rider" problem must be overcome. We expect that the extent of union membership depends on the perceived benefits to organizers and members relative to the costs incurred. Data are available for a number of Canadian manufacturing industries on the proportion of workers covered by collective-bargaining agreements (*PWUN*),

13. The simultaneous determination of wages and unionization has, however, been explored by Ashenfelter and Johnson (1972). Our analysis here follows a line suggested by Marie-Paule Donsimoni.

and that fraction is the dependent variable that we seek to explain.[14] The benefits take the form of the potential rents that can be appropriated by the union for its members, and these in turn depend on the sources of market power for the buyers of labor. In the long run market power demands the presence of entry barriers, and this is true for workers as well as for entrepreneurs. Trade unions in the manufacturing sector generally lack the power to prevent new workers from entering the industry if a new enterprise stands ready to hire them. Hence the competitive erosion of monopoly rents to labor can be avoided only if entry barriers exclude new enterprises. We include the standard variables, already described, to designate entry barriers.

$MSU9$ Scale-economy entry barriers as inferred from U.S. data; $MESU$ in industries for which the cost disadvantage ratio ($CDRU$) takes a value of 0.9 or less, zero otherwise.

$CAPC$ Estimated capital cost of the minimum-efficient-scale plant in industries for which diseconomies of small scale discourage entry at smaller scales (where $CDRU$ takes a value of 0.9 or less), zero otherwise.

$ADIC$ Advertising-to-sales ratio in convenience-good industries, where high levels of advertising in national media are likely to impose a significant barrier to entrants, zero otherwise.

Some workers covered by collective-bargaining agreements are not union members, and so our analysis pertains only indirectly to the effect of union organization. The effect of union membership may be diluted where union-induced collective-bargaining agreements also cover many nonunion members. All three variables should be positively related to unionization.

Independent of entry barriers, the short-run level of market power of the employing enterprises may affect unionization. Without entry barriers, concentrated sellers would not enjoy any rents that could be annexed through union bargaining power; with such barriers, unions could in principle raise wages and gather monopoly rents even if the

14. This information is available for both production ($PWUN$) and nonproduction workers ($NPUN$). The variables specified in the text pertain primarily to production workers, and we did not inquire seriously into possible explanations for the unionization of nonproduction workers (because of their diverse skills and interests). We did check to see whether nonproduction union membership is explained by the variables advanced to explain membership by production workers; the results were negative. Some workers covered by collective-bargaining agreements are not union members (Mulvey, 1976), and so our analysis pertains only indirectly to the effect of union organization. The effect of union membership may be diluted where union-induced collective-bargaining agreements also cover many nonunion members.

employing enterprises were purely competitive. Hence the hypothesis that concentration influences unionization is a tentative one, and its confirmation might reflect features of the employment contract other than the division of monopoly rents. Our measure of concentration is interacted with import competition, as in the analysis of industries' profit rates, on the assumption that concentration is associated with market power only where import competition is low or product differentiation is present; the variable is *CONM1*.

Even with entry barriers and concentration controlled, the presence of multinational companies may increase the degree of unionization because it signals the existence of rents to the multinationals' special assets that can potentially be shared under collective bargaining. Furthermore, international unions operating in Canada appear on casual observation to operate in industries containing many foreign subsidiaries, and it seems plausible that the structure of wage bargaining in the United States has spread to some Canadian industries. Although multinationals do not claim that as a matter of policy they pay higher wages than other firms (Safarian, 1966), their presence could still affect wages in their industries. Therefore we include

FSE Percentage of sales accounted for by companies under 50 percent or more foreign control.

The extent of union organization of an industry should also depend on the relative costs of organizing its employees. Large plants are less costly per worker to organize, and for this as well as for sociological reasons unionization should be greater in industries with larger numbers of employees per average plant, *EPE*. Unfortunately, *EPE* is likely to be collinear with seller concentration, and so isolating their separate influences may prove impossible.[15] Two other variables related to the benefits and costs of union organization are regionality (*REG*) and the female proportion of the industry's work force (*PWFM*). The dummy variable indicating regional industries should be negatively related to unionization because organization becomes more costly when plants are dispersed across the country. Union membership should be lower in industries with large female proportions of employees because the shorter average term of employment expected by women in most occupations reduced the expected returns to them from investing in union organization. Finally, slow growth in a

15. Furthermore, if the scale economies in organizing plants' work forces are apparent only for medium and large plants, plant concentration might be a better indicator than average plant size. Plant concentration may be more highly correlated with company concentration than with average plant size.

market, especially if it results in an actual decline in the number of establishments, should reduce the perceived long-run benefits from union membership; we therefore expect a positive relation between union membership and the long-term growth rate of the number of establishments (*GNE*, calculated over the period 1961–1971).

Although the hypotheses as stated are additive in their effects, the known high collinearity among *EPE*, *CONM1*, and *FSE* leaves us with no hope of disentangling their separate effects. We used the same device used in section 4.1, where a similar cluster of variables was considered, adding them in multiplicative combinations and accepting the combination that yields the highest *F*-ratio. This procedure leads to the equation shown in table 9.4. The fit secured by our three methods of estimation unfortunately varies widely; equation A, with only 22 degrees of freedom, nonetheless explains 71 percent of the

Table 9.4 Determinants of the proportion of employees covered by collective bargaining agreements (*PWUN*).

Independent variable	Estimation method		
	A	B	C
ADIC	−442[a]	−317[a]	−404[a]
	(−5.63)	(−4.34)	(−4.05)
MCFSE	0.446[b]	0.294[a]	0.418[a]
	(2.32)	(3.90)	(3.83)
PWFM	−0.292[b]	−0.164[b]	0.022
	(−2.35)	(−2.15)	(0.17)
GNE	99.1	39.2	126[c]
	(1.23)	(0.85)	(1.60)
MSU9	167	−145[c]	−264[b]
	(1.10)	(−1.69)	(−2.01)
CAPC	0.269	0.050	0.040
	(0.74)	(0.64)	(0.45)
Constant	73.4[a]	72.7[a]	67.9[a]
	(18.9)	(25.3)	(17.5)
$\bar{R}^2$	0.709	0.374	—
F	12.4	9.27	1.87
D.f.	22	77	77

Note: Levels of significance (one-tailed test) are a = 1 percent, b = 5 percent, c = 10 percent. The variables listed above the horizontal line are endogenous in our model or contain endogenous components.

variance of *PWUN* after correction for degree of freedom. In equation B, although the significance of the regression coefficients does not change much, the explained variance drops by half (37 percent). Finally, the TSLS equation C exhibits an *F*-ratio markedly lower than that of equation B, estimated from the same data.

Although *EPE* is statistically significant if used in an equation lacking *CONM1* and *FSE*, the best statistical explanation is obtained when we employ *MCFSE*, which is the product of *CONM1* and *FSE*. The interaction is theoretically appropriate because any wage-increasing tendency of multinational companies should be feasible only if the product market is not too competitive. *MCFSE* is highly significant in all equations. Because of *EPE*'s absence, we must assume that part of the effect is due to workers' discontentment with large plant environments and the ease of organizing unions in them. The entry-barrier variable *CAPC* is positive throughout but not significant; *MSU9* turns out to be wrongly signed and indeed significant in equations B and C; and *ADIC* is wrongly signed and significant throughout. The last result is quickly explained by inspection of the list of convenience-good industries: they tend to seasonal production in geographically decentralized facilities, and and so *ADIC* inadvertently turns out to be a good proxy for plant conditions obviously hostile to union organization. The performance of *CAPC* and *MSU9*, however, leaves us without support for the hypothesis that product-market entry barriers determined unionization; evidently the somewhat collinear forces wrapped up in the variable *MCFSE* are more potent. This result parallels our findings about the determinants of profits. Union membership appears sensitive to market-structure variables but not in ways neatly in accord with our hypotheses. The negative effect of the female percentage of the work force (*PWFM*) is significant in the OLS equations, and the expected positive influence of *GNE* is weakly significant.[16]

9.4 Determinants of Wages

Production workers' average wages should depend on labor's bargaining skill and the rents available to be annexed by it, as well as skill and locational characteristics. The dependent variable to be explained in this section is

16. When the dependent variable is union membership among nonproduction workers, the signs of the coefficients are generally the same but the level of statistical significance is abysmal.

WPW   Average wages paid per hour to manufacturing production and
related workers, all establishments classified to the industry,
averaged over 1961–1971.

Wages are only one term of the employment contract, and unions may
choose different mixes of benefits in different industries (Kochan and
Block, 1977) or choose overall a different mix of benefits from those
that nonunion workers receive (Donsimoni, 1978). Thus our results
may be distorted because we lack information on some terms of the
employment contract.

We expect wages to be positive related to the proportion of workers
covered by collective agreements (PWUN). Although workers who
are not union members are covered by collective agreements, the
collective-agreement coverage measure has been found to reflect union
bargaining power (Mulvey, 1976). A positive linear relation seems
reasonable on either of two conjectures: that unionized workers gain
higher wages for themselves, thus raising the average wage of all production workers in their industry, or that unionized wages are elevated and that the threat of unionization in addition raises wages in
nonunionized establishments in proportion to the industry's share of
unionized workers.

How much wages can be elevated through unions' bargaining efforts
depends on how much surplus is available for expropriation, over the
opportunity cost of all other factors of production. Pugel (1978) points
out that the theoretically appropriate variable is the amount of pretax
excess profits per production-worker hour—pretax because all wages
are deductible before the assessment of the corporate income tax, so
that tax payments as well as reported profits are affected. The variable is

XPROF   Pretax profits minus 6 percent of the average level of interest-
bearing debt (equity, debt, and bank loans), 1968–1971, divided
by number of production-worker hours.

Pugel shows that the positive regression coefficient of WPW on
XPROF can be transformed into a measure of the proportion of pretax
profits appropriated as wages. If the regression coefficient is b, that
proportion is $q = b/(1 + b)$.

Controlling for the influence of PWUN and XPROF on wages may
leave no room for any further effect of the structure of the product
market. Our model treats entry barriers not as a direct cause of high
union wages but as a stimulus to the organization of unions which
then bargain away barrier-protected profits. If this hypothesis is correct, entry barriers should not appear as determinants of wages.

Whether to include seller concentration, however, is a more intricate question. Various hypotheses have been advanced about how seller concentration might affect wages; some implicitly invoke concentration as a proxy for entry barriers, but others do not. Concentration would have a negative influence on wages if monopoly in the product market is correlated with monopsony in the industry's market for labor. On the other hand, a positive relation may emerge between product-market monopoly and wages because the entrepreneurs in a concentrated industry know that surplus lost to labor can be partly recouped through joint action to raise product prices, whereas the pure competitor by definition assumes that he lacks this escape hatch (Segal, 1964). Hence we include *CONM1* without a confident prediction about the sign or significance of its coefficient.

It has been argued that concentration and union membership may interact in determining wages—but the sign again is in doubt. A negative interaction is predicted on the reasoning that a single lump of surplus exists (on certain narrow assumptions) in a chain of vertically related markets. It could be captured by either a monopolist of labor or a monopolist of output (positive signs for these), but the presence of one diminishes the surplus available to others (negative interaction). Empirical results in several studies have in fact supported this hypothesis,[17] although the most satisfactory ones for the United States confirm a positive influence for union membership but find no significant influence of concentration, either by itself or interacted (Weiss, 1966; Masters, 1969). A positive interaction can be predicted either if unions can block the monopsony power that concentrated employers would otherwise exert or if concentrated industries are particularly vulnerable to labor's ability to mobilize public opinion or governmental influence behind its demands. We shall include interactions between *PWUN* and concentration measures among the determinants of *WPW*, but with no confident prediction about the signs of their coefficients.

Other variables besides concentration may affect the bargaining power of workers or employers' willingness to offer high wages. If the output of a production process can be held in inventory, the bargaining power of a union to raise wages through strikes is presumably reduced. We lack information on inventories of an industry's output held by its customers, but we can include its own holdings.

17. Hood and Rees (1974) using British data, obtained a negative interaction along with positive signs for union membership and concentration. Jenny's (1975, chap. 3) analysis for France found wages positively related to concentration in industries with low unionization but unrelated in unionized industries.

    FIN   Finished-good inventories as a percentage of total inventory, averaged over 1961–1971.

FIN should be negatively related to wages. Wages, like profits, may include a windfall component related to the growth of activity in the industry, if there are lags in the inflow or outflow of workers. The appropriate growth measure here might be either *GNE*, the growth rate of the number of establishments, or *GSI*, the growth rate of the value of industry shipments.

To complete the model we should include measures of the interindustry variation in the quality of labor and of the supply price of labor as influenced by the disutility of working conditions in the industry. Canadian data do not reveal interindustry variations in the skills of production workers, and so we resorted to

    SKIL   Index of the effect on production-worker wages of the mix of production-worker skills observed in the U.S. counterpart industry, 1969.

The index is constructed for each industry by multiplying the U.S. average national wages in manufacturing industry of foremen and craftsmen, operatives, and laborers by their respective proportions in that industry's labor force. The U.S. variable is available only for rather aggregated industries, and it might prove insignificant even without this problem because skill mixes in Canada and the United States differ. We also include the variable *PWFM*, the female percentage of production workers. Female production workers probably have lower skill levels on average and, of course, may also be subject to discrimination.

Also included are variables indicating the disutility or supply price associated with work in each industry. Other things equal, a less pleasant job should command a higher wage. An industry offering cyclical or unstable employment should have to pay more per manhour, and so we include alternative measures of output instability.

    SSI   Standard deviation of value of shipments around its time trend, 1961–1971.
    SMCI Mean of absolute values of proportional annual change in output, 1961–1971.

Either should be positively related to wages.[18] Labor's supply price should also depend on the cost of living, which varies substantially

    18. But Kumar (1975) did not find the predicted positive relation for either output instability or accident rates.

among Canada's provinces, as do manufacturing wages themselves. We calculated

> GEOG Index of the effect on production-worker wages of the geographic distribution of the industry among Canada's provinces, calculated by multiplying the proportion of the industry's employment by province, 1969, by the average hourly wage in all manufacturing in that province.

Its coefficient should take a positive sign.

Table 9.5 presents two equations with WPW as the dependent vari-

Table 9.5 Determinants of wages per production-worker hour (WPW).

Independent variable	Estimation method					
	A	B	C	A	B	C
XPROF	0.032c	0.019a	0.036a	0.002	0.014a	0.028c
	(1.51)	(4.37)	(3.14)	(0.96)	(3.08)	(1.60)
CONM1	—	—	—	0.003	0.004a	0.003
				(1.06)	(2.90)	(0.53)
PWUN	0.008b	0.006a	0.006	0.006c	0.003	0.003
	(2.14)	(2.52)	(1.03)	(1.55)	(1.14)	(0.44)
SKIL	0.993a	0.892a	1.66b	1.07a	0.869a	1.58b
	(2.67)	(3.53)	(1.75)	(2.84)	(3.60)	(1.71)
GEOG	0.368	0.400	3.52c	0.475	0.458	3.71c
	(0.55)	(0.96)	(1.48)	(0.71)	(1.15)	(1.60)
GNE	4.33b	4.15a	4.95	3.66b	3.85a	3.74
	(2.20)	(3.48)	(1.13)	(1.78)	(3.37)	(0.78)
SMCI	−2.29	−2.95a	−5.15b	−2.34	−2.23b	−4.27c
	(−0.70)	(−2.74)	(−2.30)	(−0.73)	(−2.10)	(−1.57)
FIN	0.257	−0.022	−0.728	0.186	−0.082	−0.759
	(0.82)	(−0.11)	(−1.00)	(0.59)	(−0.42)	(−1.07)
PWFM	−0.008b	−0.011a	−0.004	−0.007b	−0.011a	−0.004
	(−2.48)	(−5.55)	(−0.46)	(−2.42)	(−5.60)	(−0.49)
Constant	−2.18	−1.58	−12.5c	−2.65	−1.63	−12.8b
	(−1.00)	(−1.14)	(−1.59)	(−1.19)	(−1.24)	(−1.67)
$\bar{R}^2$	0.710	0.656	—	0.712	0.686	—
F	9.27	20.7	6.72	8.42	21.2	5.39
D.f.	19	75	75	18	74	74

Note: Levels of significance (one-tailed test) are a = 1 percent, b = 5 percent, c = 10 percent. The variables listed above the horizontal line are endogenous in our model or contain endogenous components.

able, one including $CONM1$, the other excluding it. Consider the first three independent variables listed in the table, which are endogenous in our model. Excess profits are a significant determinant of wages, although their significance shrinks as expected when $CONM1$ is added in the second set of equations. In the B equation $CONM1$ is significant and increases the F-ratio, but otherwise it does not add to the model's explanatory power. We conclude that most of the effect of monopoly on wages is captured by $XPROF$. However, the proportion of potential monopoly profits captured as wages is quite small, only around 3 percent.[19] Union membership is quite significant in the OLS equations when $CONM1$ is omitted but drops to insignificance when $CONM1$ is added or when the TSLS estimation is used. This result seems consistent with our view that union membership is itself an endogenous variable in the model and rests on more fundamental structural determinants.

The results for the remaining variables in table 9.5 can be discussed briefly. The measure of finished-good inventories is insignificant and erratic in sign; apparently this short-run bargaining factor has no substantial effect. The control variable for labor-force skills ($SKIL$) is quite significant (despite the variable's poor quality), and the control for an industry's geographic distribution ($GEOG$) has the right sign but is weak. Growth (GNE has more explanatory power than GSI) seems to confer windfalls to wage earners as well as to profit recipients.[20] On the other hand, there is no evidence that wages are elevated where workers must incur the disutility of unstable employment; the sign of $SMCI$ is unexpectedly negative and indeed significant in the B and C equations. The female percentage of the work force is a significant negative influence on wages in the OLS equations but, puzzlingly, not in the TSLS equations. Our model may not have succeeded in sorting out the complex interrelation among wages, union membership, and the female proportion of the work force.

In additional equations (not reported) we tested further hypotheses about the interaction between concentration and unionization as de-

19. Pugel (1978) estimated as much as one-quarter for the United States. Kumar's (1975) study of the determinants of selected wage categories in Canadian manufacturing seems to attribute rather more leverage to seller concentration.

20. Under certain assumptions, this relation between wages and growth could emerge from the construction of the dependent variable, which is averaged over a period of time that includes but also antedates the independent variables. That the dependent variable covers a decade's experience makes a significant windfall component somewhat unlikely.

terminants of wages. When *CONM1* in the equations of table 9.5 is replaced by interactions between concentration and entry barriers used in the explanation of profits, the coefficient of determination and the *F*-statistic for the equation deteriorate. We conclude that entry barriers do not affect wages directly. We also failed to find any strong influence of entry barriers on unionization. We added to the equation an interaction between concentration (or concentration interacted with entry barriers) and union membership. Neither the concentration term nor the interaction with union membership was significant in any specification; the concentration term and the interaction term always take opposite signs, but not the same pair in every specification. We conclude that the ability of unions to raise wages depends simply on the excess profits to be annexed (the *XPROF* variable) and not on whatever forces caused those profits to be at hand in the industry.

Another supplemental test concerns the hypothesis that higher wages are paid to workers in larger establishments, either to compensate for the disutility of working in a big plant or because the managers of such plants hire "better" workers in order to reduce the costs of supervision. The measure of employees per establishment, *EPE*, is so collinear with concentration that there is no hope of testing the two as independent hypotheses in the same regression. When we replace *CONM1* with *EPE* in the equations of table 9.5, *EPE* proves highly significant; its *t*-statistic is 3.05 in equation A, 4.50 in equation B, and 2.78 in equation C. In table 9.5 we found that adding *CONM1* to the model contributes significantly to its explanatory power; the *F*-statistic for the reduction in the sum of squared residuals due to adding *CONM1* is 8.38, significant at the 1 percent level. (The reduction is significant at 5 percent in the C equation, not significant in the A equation.) If *EPE* instead of *CONM1* is added to the B equation, the reduction in the sum of squared residuals is much greater, and the *F*-statistic is 20.25. Furthermore, the significance of the variable *XPROF* increases in two of the three equations; its *t*-statistics become 0.99, 4.36, and 3.00 in the A, B, and C equations respectively. We are quite skeptical that concentration has any direct influence on wages (except through *XPROF*) but do find that wages are significantly elevated for workers in large establishments (for one of the reasons mentioned before).[21]

21. Previous studies of wages and union membership have treated concentration as strictly a proxy for the effects of large sizes of establishment (Masters, 1969; Hood and Rees, 1974). However, they have not employed any control such as *XPROF*.

9.5 Summary

An industry's potential monopoly rents can accrue as excess profits to its shareholders or as wages in excess of labor's opportunity cost, or they can be squandered in technical inefficiency. This chapter presents our analysis of the first two destinations for the surplus, as well as of the determinants of trade-union membership.

Our analysis of the determination of profits (as an indicator of allocative efficiency) is built around the proposition that three conditions are necessary for the exercise of monopoly power in a small, open economy: high seller concentration, entry barriers, and the absence of strong import competition. Procedurally, we differ from most other analyses in employing alternative measures of profits (profit on equity, excess profit on sales, and price-cost margin) and of seller concentration; the inductive procedure is justified because there is no theoretical model that decisively narrows the alternatives. We conclude that imports act like a competitive fringe in limiting the market power of concentrated industries but that (on the testimony of two of our three dependent variables) concentration and entry barriers do not interact. The best-performing concentration measure modifies the conventional four-firm ratio to give some weight to size inequality among the leading firms. We also find support for a hypothesis that associates market power with the uncertainty surrounding collusive arrangements, and some indication that market power is less readily exercised in sectors where the buyers enjoy some market power of their own. And there is weak evidence that profits are reduced when trade unions are present to bargain them away.

Our study echoes previous ones in finding little evidence that profits in Canada are directly influenced by those components of entry barriers that are related to economies of scale. This finding is consistent with our analysis (chapter 3) of the complex influence that scale economies wield. For example, they decrease the number of Canadian sellers but also reduce their size inequality, with opposing effects on the chances for collusive understandings. The findings of this chapter should not be taken as apportioning excess profits between efficiency rents to firms enjoying scale economies and "outright" monopoly rents. Our conclusion is simply that scale economies wield their influence on profits through concentration and not as the separable influence hypothesized by the traditional theory of entry barriers.

Other hypotheses about allocative efficiency were also tested. We expected and found a negative effect (of weak significance) of export-market activity on profitability except where the Canadian market can be segmented from the world market (this offset is strongly significant in OLS equations). Research and development in Canada may be a defensive activity and shows weak evidence of bearing a negative relation to profits, whereas the rents from R&D done abroad and collected in Canada by foreign subsidiaries contribute positively to reported excess profits. Capital intensity is positively related to two of our profit measures for reasons inherent in their construction but shows a negative behavioral relation to profits on equity capital (because the feasibility of collusive arrangements is reduced). Market growth affects only profit rates on equity capital but not our other profit measures— again an expected result.

We confirmed our expectation that the profits of foreign subsidiaries and of domestically controlled companies are not determined by the same influences. Indeed, the subsidiaries' profits can hardly be explained at all, suggesting that their measured profits may poorly reflect their actual profit streams. The subsidiaries benefit from product-differentiation entry barriers and from market growth but respond significantly to no other influences. The profits of domestic companies, however, are strongly sensitive to seller concentration and to the existence of regionally fragmented markets (which causes national concentration ratios to understate effective market concentration).

Our model of trade-union membership is based on the benefits and costs of forming a union organization. Higher benefits should be indicated by the existence of high entry barriers and concentration in the product market, low costs by large plants, absence of regional fragmentation, and a low female percentage of the work force. Our results do not confirm the entry-barrier hypothesis, but they do suggest that seller concentration (interacting with the presence of multinational companies) is associated with higher levels of trade-union membership. These findings are consistent with our failure to uncover a direct relation between companies' profits and entry barriers of the scale-economies variety. Union membership is negatively related to the female proportion of the work force and to an indicator that production is seasonal and geographically dispersed.

The average wages of production workers are significantly and positively related to the excess profits appropriable by the labor force, although only a thin slice is taken. Wages are increased by trade-union membership, according to our OLS equations; but the relation collapses in two-stage least squares, consistent with our view that union membership itself is determined by more fundamental influences. Seller concentration in the product market does not have a robust influence on wages once excess profits are controlled, and we cannot reject the hypothesis that any apparent influence of seller concentration is due to the tendency for workers in larger establishments to be paid more. Wages are affected by the skill level of the labor force, but (like Kumar, 1975) we found little significant influence for other factors that should affect the disutility of work or the supply price of labor.

Overall, this chapter's results lead us to conclude that market power varies significantly among industries even in small, open economy such as Canada's, that it makes a substantial contribution to explaining interindustry variations in profits for both domestic firms and foreign subsidiaries, and that workers capture a significant though small slice of monopoly rents through trade-union activity or other mechanisms.

10 Technical Efficiency

Technical efficiency refers to the extent to which the costs of producing a given output have been minimized. It is usually contrasted with allocative efficiency, which refers to the quantities of various products that are sold in relation to some welfare optimum. The latter involves not only prices but also product attributes and product differentiation. Our concern here is with the failure to achieve the lowest possible costs for a given level of output. Because the term *technical efficiency* is sometimes used loosely, we shall take care in defining it.

10.1 Components of Technical Efficiency

An industry can fail to be efficient in at least four ways. Suppose that the production function is $f(k,l,m)$ where k is capital, l is labor, and m is materials. If the industry's output is x and $x < f(k,l,m)$, then the industry is not on the production frontier—the first and most elementary way to be inefficient.

Second, let the cost function be

$$c(x) = \min wl + rk + m,$$
$$subject\ to\ x = f(k,l,m), \tag{10.1}$$

where w is the wage and r the cost of capital. The price of materials is set equal to one. It is possible for an industry to be on the production function but to have higher than minimum costs because it employs the wrong input combination given prevailing input prices. This is a second dimension in which an industry can be technically inefficient.[1]

---

1. The classic treatment of this topic is Farrell (1957).

The third and fourth dimensions of technical efficiency overlap with allocative efficiency, but for reasons associated with measurement problems, it is necessary to include them in this discussion. The third aspect of efficiency is the following. An industry may have successfully minimized costs, given the factor prices, but it may have faced (or set, depending on its power in the factor markets in relation to the power of the factors themselves) inappropriate factor prices. The sharp distinction between technical and allocative efficiency breaks down to some extent, when the industry has a role in setting its input prices, or when other factors of production cause their own input prices to be inappropriate. For example, monopsony power, unions, and imperfect capital markets may produce distortions of this type.

The fourth dimension of technical efficiency relates to scale economies. Let us define the minimum average costs for the total market to be

$$A = \min_{x} \frac{c(x)}{x}. \tag{10.2}$$

An industry may fail to achieve minimum average costs because of small scale. This is of particular concern in Canada. The market is small compared with that of the United States, roughly one-tenth the size. It is also possible that Canadian costs are higher than those in the United States because of higher transportation and distribution costs associated with the large geographic area and relatively low population density.

Publicly available data do not permit one to measure these separate aspects of technical efficiency directly. On the other hand, the standard measures, usually some variant of value added per worker, do not directly measure technical efficiency either. Value added per worker has several problems as a measure of technical efficiency. First, value added per worker reflects capital intensity, which in turn is responsive to relative input prices.

Thus if one wants to compare technical efficiency across countries, some attention to factor proportions and input prices is imperative. If the prices of its output reflect an industry's possession of monopoly power, then its value added includes monopoly rents. Ideally they should be subtracted out in a measure of technical efficiency.

In view of these facts it is necessary to exercise some care in measuring technical efficiency and to make some assumptions about the relationship between output prices and costs.

10.2   The Measurement of Technical Efficiency

Let $\overline{w}$ and $\overline{r}$ be the appropriate shadow prices for labor and capital in the country. The levels of these prices may diverge from the actual levels in a particular industry because of entry barriers and other aspects of structure that inhibit competition. We lump the first two categories of technical efficiency together and define the following measure of efficiency:

$$S_1(x) = \frac{c(x,\overline{w},\overline{r})}{\overline{w}l + \overline{r}k}. \tag{10.3}$$

Here $c(x,\overline{w},\overline{r})$ is the minimized cost of producing x net of materials costs m, given the prices $\overline{w}$ and $\overline{r}$. The measure $S_1(x)$ has the value one if the industry is on the production function and the inputs are selected properly given the input prices w and r.

Let $A(w,r) = \min_x \left[\frac{c(x,\overline{w},\overline{r})}{x}\right]$ be the minimum average cost with respect to x. The scale aspects of technical efficiency can be measured by the ratio

$$S_2(x) = \frac{A(\overline{w},\overline{r})}{c(x,\overline{w},\overline{r})/x}, \tag{10.4}$$

the ratio of minimum average costs to average costs at the actual level of output. The latter are minimal with respect to inputs, given x and the input prices w and r. The product of the two measures,

$$S(x) = S_1(x)S_2(x) = \frac{A(\overline{w},\overline{r})x}{\overline{w}l + \overline{r}k}, \tag{10.5}$$

is an overall measure of technical efficiency at the input prices w and r.

The principal problem of implementing this measure is that output in physical units is not available. Minimum average costs may be estimated using the U.S. industry as a standard. Similarly, appropriate shadow prices for labor and capital can be estimated, and the capital intensity of an industry can be measured with available data. But the output measures that we have are in value terms and therefore contain monopoly rents; they therefore tend to inflate the output measure.

To measure technical efficiency we begin with industry value added. Value added is related to technical efficiency in the following way. If labor and capital actually earn their shadow prices $\overline{w}$ and $\overline{r}$, then value added is

$$VA = \overline{w}l + \overline{r}k. \tag{10.6}$$

If p is the output price and m the unit materials cost, then value added is also equal to

$$VA = (p - m)x. \tag{10.7}$$

It follows that

$$x = \frac{VA}{(p - m)}. \tag{10.8}$$

From the definition of technical efficiency we have

$$S(x) = \frac{Ax}{\overline{w}l + \overline{r}k} = \frac{A(VA)}{(\overline{w}l + \overline{r}k)(p - m)}. \tag{10.9}$$

Let $Q = \dfrac{k}{l}$ be the capital-labor ratio. We divide the numerator and denominator of 10.9 by the amount of labor l, then take logs. The result is

$$\log (S(x)) = \log (v) + \log A - \log (p - m) - \log (\overline{w} + \overline{r}Q),$$

where $v = \dfrac{VA}{l}$, the value added per worker. The term that is difficult to measure is $\log (p - m)$, because the inability to measure output directly implies an inability to estimate price levels directly from value data or from shipments and inputs.

Our strategy has been to attempt to measure technical efficiency in a Canadian industry relative to its U.S. counterpart by making assumptions about the relative price levels of the industry's output in the two countries. At this point variables are subscripted, c for Canada and u for the United States. We assume that $S_u = 1$, so that A becomes the average costs in the U.S. counterpart industry, the standard of comparison. With that assumption, we have

$$\log (S_c) = \log \left(\frac{v_c}{v_u}\right) + \log \left(\frac{\overline{w}_u + \overline{r}_u Q_u}{\overline{w}_c + \overline{r}_c Q_c}\right) + \log \left(\frac{p_u - m_u}{p_c - m_c}\right). \tag{10.10}$$

If we knew the relation between prices for output and materials in the two countries, we could develop a measure of technical efficiency.

Canadian industries are on average more highly concentrated than their U.S. counterparts (see chapter 3). Moreover, they are protected by tariffs. We have therefore assumed that the tariffs are the principal constraint on prices in the Canadian industry, and that the high concentration permits the Canadian industry to elevate prices to the levels allowed by the tariff. When we estimate the determinants of technical efficiency, this strong assumption is relaxed. But accepting it for the moment, and letting n be the Canadian nominal tariff on output and t the Canadian nominal tariff on materials (assumed to be tradable), the relation between Canadian and U.S. prices is

$$p_c = p_u(1 + n),$$
$$m_c = m_u(1 + t). \tag{10.11}$$

The effective rate of protection is defined to be

$$E = \frac{p_u(1 + n) - m_u(1 + t)}{p_u - m_u} - 1 = \frac{p_c - m_c}{p_u - m_u} - 1, \tag{10.12}$$

using equations 10.11. Thus, under our assumptions, the ratio $\dfrac{(p_c - m_c)}{(p_u - m_u)}$ is equal to one plus the effective rate of protection. Substituting in 10.10, we have

$$\log S_c = \log \frac{v_c}{v_u} + \log \frac{w_u + r_u Q_u}{\overline{w}_c + \overline{r}_c Q_c} - \log (1 + E), \tag{10.13}$$

where E is the effective rate of protection for the Canadian industry.

The data permit one to measure the value added per worker in the two countries. Similarly, the capital-labor ratio can be approximated. The effective rate of protection in Canada has been estimated for most of the industries in the sample. For the rates of return on capital, we have used the average in manufacturing industries in each of the countries. This may be higher than the opportunity cost of capital for a variety of reasons, including the structure of corporate and personal taxes, but it is the best estimate available to us. For the wages we have used the actual average earnings per employee in the industry. The error involved in including in wages any monopoly rents that may be appropriated by labor is not expected to be large, on the evidence of chapter 9. That is, wage rates are closer to the shadow price of labor than the measured rate of return is to the cost of capital, at least in some very profitable industries.

The left-hand side of 10.13 is a measure of the relative technical efficiency of the Canadian industry, with the U.S. industry as the standard of comparison. The variables on the right-hand side are observable. This measure is premised on the strong assumption that Canadian prices are equal to U.S. prices times one plus the relevant Canadian ad valorem tariff. It is unlikely that the output price would exceed this limit. When the Canadian output price is below $p_u(1 + n)$, then our measure *understates* real relative Canadian efficiency. It does so by attributing too much of the value added to noncompetitive rents and too little to physical output.

Henceforth the measure of technical efficiency is referred to as TE. It is defined by equation 10.13, so that $TE = S_c$ or S_c/S_u, with S_u assumed to be equal to one. Equate 10.13 gives the value of log (TE).

For our sample of 84 matched Canadian and U.S. industries, the measure of relative technical efficiency was computed for each industry. Table 10.1 reports the means, standard deviations, and simple correlations for the four variables TE, v_c/v_u, E, and $(\overline{w}_u + \overline{r}_u Q_u)/(\overline{w}_c + \overline{r}_c Q_c)$. It can be seen that TE is most highly correlated with the ratio of value added per worker in the two countries. The latter is negatively correlated with R, the measure of relative factor costs.[2] The mean of TE is 0.743, which means that by this measure, Canadian manufacturing on average produces roughly 75 percent of the U.S. output per U.S. dollar of input. The mean of v_c/v_u is 79.6 percent, higher than our measure. If v_c/v_u were adjusted for factor prices (R) but not for output prices (e), average technical efficiency would be 92.5 percent. Note also that the ratio of the two value-added-per-worker figures is positively correlated with the effective rate of protection, a fact that would be counterintuitive if v_c/v_u were a strict measure of efficiency.

10.3   The Determinants of Technical Efficiency

The determinates of technical efficiency (as measured here) fall into two classes. The first group includes factors that directly affect techni-

Table 10.1   Means, standard deviations, and simple correlations of the Measure of relative technical efficiency and its components.

Variable	Mean	Standard deviation	Correlation coefficients		
			v_c/v_u	E	R
TE	0.743	0.193	0.716	−0.453	−0.152
v_c/v_u	0.796	0.169	—	0.144	−0.552
E	0.267	0.196	—	—	0.062
R	1.162	0.113	—	—	—

Note: Here, $R = (w_u + \overline{r}_u Q_u)/(w_c + \overline{r}_c Q_c)$ is the ratio of input costs adjusted for factor intensities.

2. The reason for this negative correlation is that the variance in efficiencies is greater than the variance in factor prices.

cal efficiency. The second group consists of those industry characteristics that determine the extent to which Canadian prices will in fact
rise to the levels permitted•by the tariffs. This second group is to be
regarded as an attempt to control for mismeasurement of technical
efficiency in the formulas in section 10.2. Mismeasurement results in
mistaking to some degree allocative *efficiency* for technical *inefficiency*.
That is, if the Canadian industry fails to get the prices up to the levels
permitted by tariffs, then its measured efficiency is lowered because
value added per worker is lower. Hence greater allocative efficiency is
mistaken for technical inefficiency.

If the second group of variables were uncorrelated with the first, the
inclusion of the second group would not be necessary if our objective
were simply to estimate the impact of direct determinants. But the required lack of correlation is unlikely. Factors such as economies of
scale that affect technical efficiency are correlated with entry barriers
and hence with allocative performance as well.

Direct Determinants

We follow the practice of previous chapters of measuring minimum
efficient scale (MES) using the figure drawn from the U.S. data (*MESU*).
The variable for either Canada (*MESC*) or the United States (*MESU*)
is measured by the shipments of the minimum-efficient-scale plant divided by industry shipments. The minimum-efficient-scale plant is
the mean-sized plant among the largest establishments accounting for
one-half of industry employment. A high MES combined with the
limited Canadian market is expected to reduce the measured technical
efficiency of the Canadian industry.

The cost disadvantage ratio (CDR) also affects the expected efficiency of the Canadian industry. The cost disadvantage is the ratio of
value added per worker in plants below MES divided by the same
ratio for plants above MES. But here we meet a form of the truncation effect described in chapter 1. For differentiated-product industries, the small-market-share products made by the U.S. industry are
likely to be missing from the Canadian industry's output, since it is
cheaper to import them than to manufacture them domestically. A low
value of the U.S. cost disadvantage ratio implies that small establishments have a cost disadvantage. That combined with the smaller scale
of the Canadian market indicates that the technical efficiency of the
Canadian industry is low. Now, when the Canadian cost disadvantage
ratio is high relative to the U.S. ratio, the reason is likely to be that
the scale economies are sufficient to cause the elimination of the small-

market-share segment of the industry in Canada. That is, when scale economies are significant, and the tariff wall is not excessively high, then the Canadian industry has two properties. It is relatively inefficient, and it is a truncated version of the U.S. industry so that Canadian CDR statistics tend to be high. Thus we expect a positive coefficient on $CDRU$, the U.S. cost disadvantage ratio, but the expected coefficient on $CDRC$, the Canadian ratio, is negative.[3]

In the regressions, the cost disadvantage variables are $CDRU$ and $(CDRC - CDRU)$. The latter is intended to capture the truncation effect and its consequences.

The variable REG, which has the value one if the industry is regional and zero otherwise, is included because regional industries are believed to be less disadvantaged in Canada as a result of the smaller national market than would industries that are not regional. The variable REG captures some of the differential transportation effects between the two countries, which apply most to nonregional industries.

Selling, general, and administrative expenses are subject to increasing returns. We expect therefore Canadian costs to be higher in this area. In particular, goods with heavy selling costs should suffer disproportionately the diseconomies of small scale. To capture this effect, we include the convenience-good dummy ($CONO$), since convenience goods generally have higher advertising costs and other selling expenses that are subject to significant scale economies. The variable $CONO$ has the value one if the industry's major products are sold through convenience-good outlets and is zero otherwise. For a fuller description, see Porter (1976b). The sign of the coefficient is expected to be negative.

There is another measure of overhead. It is NPW, the ratio of the number of nonproduction workers to total employees. We use this ratio in the Canadian industry divided by the ratio for the U.S. counterpart as the independent variable. It is expected to have a negative impact.

The influence of foreign ownership is ambiguous. On the one hand, foreign firms may be more efficient because of their ability to transfer skills and technology to the Canadian operation at relatively low cost. On the other, foreign direct investment may occur more in industries for which the tariff barriers are high, causing a negative correlation of foreign ownership and measured technical efficiency. The two-stage least-squares estimates appear to isolate a positive causal influence.

---

3. Similar effects can be found in the analysis of the determinants of the Canadian cost disadvantage ratio in chapter 3.

The variable is *FSE*, the fraction of industry assets in subsidiaries of foreign-owned companies.

Perhaps the most significant single determinant of differences in technical efficiency is the smaller scale of the Canadian market. This factor is implicit in the specification of the regression equation. To the extent that it operates on all industries, it appears as a component of the constant in the regression. Its interaction with other factors is reflected in the coefficients of the latter.

Variables Controlling for Mismeasurement

Because of the strength of the assumption about Canadian prices, it is desirable to include variables that capture the extent to which monopoly rent potential is realized in the Canadian market. These variables are similar to those that appear in the rate-of-return equation (chapter 9), and the expected signs are the same. For example, if concentration is low, then prices may not reach the levels permitted by the tariff, causing the technical efficiency measure to be low.

The variables intended to control for mismeasurement are the following. For the pressure of exposure to foreign trade, imports as a fraction of domestic disappearance, or $IMP/(1 + IMP - EXP)$, is used. The expected signs are positive. Here IMP and EXP are imports and exports as a fraction of industry shipments.

An industry with a substantial export market does not suffer the diseconomies of the smaller Canadian market. Its market is larger. And such industries tend to be those, such as natural resources, in which Canada may have a significant, exogenously determined, cost advantage. For both reasons, exports as a fraction of shipments (*EXP*) is expected to have a positive sign. The export variable in the regression is squared (EXP^2) to capture the idea that exports have a significant effect on efficiency only in those industries where exports are large in relation to total shipments.

Having controlled for exposure to foreign competition and part of the mismeasurement of *TE*, we must still acknowledge that industries are not equally capable of exploiting the potential rents created by a combination of entry barriers and tariff protection. Elsewhere (Spence, 1978) it has been argued that successful collusion is influenced by the interaction of three factors: randomness in demand, seller concentration, and the character of the buying side of the market. The argument in brief suggests that collusion is difficult when there is a combination of high demand variability and relatively high buyer concentration, unless seller concentration is very high. Letting four-firm concentration be *C4* and sales variability be *SSI*, we define and use the following variables (*SSI* is the standard deviation of the regression of the log of sales on time over an 11-year period from 1961 to 1971):

$$DCC = (1 - C4^2) \, SSI, \qquad \text{if a convenience good,}$$
$$= 0 \qquad \qquad \qquad \text{otherwise;}$$
$$DCN = (1 - C4^2) \, SSI, \qquad \text{if a nonconvenience good,}$$
$$= 0 \qquad \qquad \qquad \text{otherwise;}$$
$$DCP = (1 - C4^2) \, SSI, \qquad \text{if a producer good,}$$
$$= 0 \qquad \qquad \qquad \text{otherwise.}$$

These variables should have a *negative* impact on Canadian prices. Viewed as a correction to the measured efficiency, when these variables are high, we should add something to the measure. Thus their impact should be negative. Moreover, the theory suggests a stronger effect for *DCN* and *DCP*, because effective buyer concentration is higher in producer and nonconvenience industries.

Regression Results

Generally, the results reported in table 10.2 confirm the expectations based on our theory. However, the two-stage estimates differ qualitatively from the OLS estimates in several important respects. We therefore concentrate on the two-stage estimates where they differ from the ordinary least-squares results.

The U.S. cost disadvantage ratio appears by itself and in the difference $(CDRC - CDRU)$. Netting out the coefficients, we have a positive sign. The higher CDR, the smaller the measured cost disadvantage of the smaller firms. When the cost disadvantage is small, the Canadian industry tends to be more efficient, relative to the U.S. industry. The coefficient on the Canadian cost disadvantage ratio is negative. We believe this is the result of the truncation effect. When the Canadian ratio is high, the combination of returns to scale and limited tariff barrier cause the smaller tail of the U.S. size distribution of establishments and products to be truncated in the Canadian industry. This occurs when the Canadian industry tends to be inefficient because of returns to scale.

The minimum efficient scale in the United States is negative and significant in the two-stage estimates and in the OLS estimates (B) with the filled-in sample. When the industries with missing data are eliminated (regression A), the coefficient is positive and insignificant. Overall, a large minimum efficient scale is detrimental to the efficiency of the Canadian industry. The difference between regressions A and B

Table 10.2 Determinants of technical efficiency in Canada.

Independent variable	Estimation method		
	A	B	C
FSE	−0.2532	0.1212	0.6304[b]
	(−1.324)	(0.8975)	(1.737)
$\dfrac{IMP}{1 + IMP - EXP}$	−0.1473	0.1580	0.8265
	(−0.4547)	(0.8494)	(1.17)
$(EXP)^2$	0.0198	−0.057	0.15
	(0.0433)	(−0.2081)	(0.269)
DCC	−0.00689	−0.0038[a]	−0.00798[b]
	(−0.4317)	(−2.5)	(−2.139)
DCN	−0.0073	−0.00278[b]	0.0023
	(−1.315)	(−1.732)	(0.4913)
DCP	−0.0046[c]	−0.0022[b]	0.00076
	(−1.508)	(−1.788)	(0.2998)
CDRC − CDRU	−0.5608[c]	−0.3562[b]	−1.208[a]
	(−1.594)	(−2.158)	(−2.596)
MESU	0.7599	−3.898[a]	−7.402[a]
	(0.1886)	(−2.432)	(−2.436)
CDRU	−0.4157	−0.3527[c]	−1.004[b]
	(−0.923)	(−1.63)	(−2.302)
CONO	−0.1355	−0.1293[c]	−0.3746[b]
	(−0.7935)	(−1.387)	(−1.902)
REG	0.1130	0.1309[b]	0.2896[b]
	(1.37)	(1.681)	(2.252)
Constant	0.0719	−0.0603	0.3248
	(0.1915)	(−0.281)	(0.7044)
$\overline{R}^2$	0.5532	0.2252	—
F	2.516	1.902	—
D.f.	20	72	72

Note: Levels of statistical significance (one-tailed test) are a = 1 percent, b = 5 percent, c = 10 percent. The independent variables listed above the horizontal line are endogenous in the model.

is evidence of the potential problems associated with simply throwing away industries for which there are missing data in some variable.

The convenience-good dummy has a negative sign and is significant in the two-stage estimates. This result seems to confirm the view that the increasing returns associated with marketing convenience goods render the Canadian industry relatively more costly and less efficient for these kinds of goods.

The variable measuring degree of foreign ownership is positive and insignificant in the two-stage regressions. In the OLS regression with missing data thrown out, the sign is negative and nearly significant. We are inclined to accept the two-stage estimates as more accurate, in part because they accord better with reasonable hypotheses. There is, however, a counterhypothesis that leads to a negative sign. If foreign investment occurs in industries that have high tariff barriers, and if high tariff barriers protect inefficient industries, then the correlation between foreign investment and efficiency might be negative. But then the cause of the inefficiency is not really foreign investment but rather the high tariffs that caused it. In our model foreign investment is an endogenous variable. The two-stage procedure is designed to eliminate this type of misleading first-order correlation. On balance, then, the impact of foreign ownership seems to be marginally positive.

The regional dummy (which is one if the industry is highly regionalized) has a positive and significant sign, as expected. This holds across all the regressions in table 10.2. The export term (which was included on the hypothesis that industries that export a large fraction of output do not suffer as much from diseconomies of scale and may also be industries in which Canada has a cost advantage) is positive and insignificant in the two-stage estimates, negative and insignificant in other equations. Either this effect is not important or we do not have a sufficient sample to capture it. Again, the sign is reversed in the two-stage estimates compared with the OLS equations. Import exposure is positive in the two-stage estimates and not significant, though its t-statistic is clearly respectable. The sign is the proper one.

The variables that control for the imperfect ability to collude to achieve supernormal rents (DCC, DCN, DCP) are negative as expected. However, the most significant coefficient attaches to DCC, which is the variable associated with convenience goods. This is not what the theory predicts, nor is it in accord with other regressions explaining rates of return. This result might have been expected if the convenience-good dummy had not been included on its own. But it was included, and it is significant. In chapter 9 we also failed to find the relative performance of DCP, DCC, and DCN neatly lined up according to expectations.

In various alternative specifications some of the full set of right-hand-side variables were dropped. Generally, the results in the first regression hold. Both foreign ownership and the convenience-good dummy lose significance when the control variables, DCC, DCN, and DCP are dropped. The regional dummy is reduced in significance, because it is correlated with omitted variables and thus captures some of their influences. For example, regionality is negatively correlated with foreign ownership. Thus when the industry is regional, it is more efficient, and when it is not regional, it is more likely to be foreign owned and hence to be more efficient. The losses of significance result from that sort of canceling effect and are not worrisome.

To summarize briefly, the relative efficiency of the Canadian industry is determined primarily by factors that capture returns to scale in both production and marketing. It is also influenced positively by foreign ownership and weakly by trade exposure. Our ability to control for mismeasurement of efficiency, by including variables designed to capture the determinants of the ability of the Canadian industry to raise prices to the levels permitted by the tariffs, seems limited.[4] Further work is required in this area.

10.4 General and Industry-Specific Differences in Technical Efficiency

In assessing the relative technical efficiency of the two countries, one is interested not only in interindustry differences but also in differences between the countries that are uniform across industries. The variable TE measured the relative efficiency of the Canadian industry. Let T_i be the measured efficiency for industry i and let $\hat{T}_i$ be its predicted value, from a cross-industry regression.

Our interest is in the extent to which the divergence of T_i from one can be explained. The appropriate measure is

$$S^2 = \frac{\Sigma_i (\hat{T}_i - 1)^2}{\Sigma_i (T_i - 1)^2}. \tag{10.14}$$

Let $\overline{T}$ be the sample mean of T_i. We can rewrite 10.14 in the following form:

$$S^2 = \frac{\Sigma_i (\hat{T}_i - T)^2 + N(\overline{T} - 1)^2}{\Sigma_i (T_i - \overline{T})^2 + N(\overline{T} - 1)^2}, \tag{10.15}$$

where N is the number of industries. The unadjusted R^2 from the cross-industry regression is

4. Hazeldine's (1978) analysis of the degree to which Canadian industries price at the level permitted by the tariff suggests only one factor that we have not controlled—differences between Canadian and U.S. material-input prices not associated with tariffs on inputs.

$$R^2 = \frac{\Sigma(\hat{T}_i - \overline{T})^2}{\Sigma(T_i - \overline{T})^2}.$$

Therefore the measure of explained relative efficiency can be written

$$S^2 = R^2 \frac{\sigma_T^2}{\sigma_T^2 + (\overline{T} - 1)^2} + \frac{(\overline{T} - 1)^2}{\sigma_T^2 + (\overline{T} - 1)^2}, \qquad (10.16)$$

where σ_T^2 is the sample variance of T. That is, the explained relative efficiency is a weighted sum of two components: the divergence of T from one consists of the divergence of the mean of T from one and the variance of T about the mean. The second term in 10.16 measures the relative importance of the former. These are the differences that are common to all industries. The fraction of the variance attributable to interindustry differences is

$$\frac{\sigma_{\hat{T}}^2}{\sigma_{\hat{T}}^2 + (\overline{T} - 1)^2}.$$

The R^2 indicates the fraction of these interindustry differences that can be explained by the regression.

For the measure of efficiency employed here, the fraction of the variance that is not industry specific is 0.6374. That is, in our sample $\dfrac{(\overline{T} - 1)^2}{\sigma_{\hat{T}}^2 + (\overline{T} - 1)^2} = 0.6374$. The fraction due to interindustry differences is therefore 0.3626. And the fraction of the latter explained by the regression is roughly 0.25.

To summarize, roughly two-thirds of the difference in measured efficiency between Canada and the United States is due to differences between the countries. These differences may include the scale of the market and managerial capabilities. The remaining one-third is due to industry-specific factors. Of the variance due to industry-specific influences, we are able to explain 25 percent in the cross-industry regressions.

10.5   The Determinants of Actual Plant Sizes Relative to Efficient Scale

Included in the data base is the variable $BIGE$, which measures the fraction of the Canadian industry's value added that comes from plants that are larger than U.S. minimum efficient scale (MES). It can be thought of as a measure of the extent to which Canadian output is produced in plants that are not suboptimally small. This is an interesting variable because it captures one of the sources of inefficiency, wrapped up in overall technical efficiency associated with suboptimal plant scale.

Canadian plants tend to be smaller than U.S. MES especially when U.S. MES is high. That tendency is enhanced by high tariff barriers and reduced by large cost disadvantages of small-scale plants. These three interacting factors are captured by the variable $MESU * EFT * CDRU$. Canadian plants are expected to be larger in certain producer-good industries, such as machine tools, where multiplant operation is less economical. The variable $(1 - CNPR)$ is included to capture this producer-good effect.

Foreign ownership is expected to have a negative effect in non-convenience goods (including producer goods) because foreign direct investment multiplies the number of domestically produced products and fragments the market. In convenience goods, however, the low transport costs per unit value of the products and the returns to scale in marketing combine to reverse this effect. Firms and plants tend to be large. Foreign-owned firms bring cost advantages in the form of reduced product development and marketing costs, enhancing this effect.

Scale of plant is greater where Canada has a comparative advantage and hence access to foreign markets. Comparative advantage is measured by the variable $\dfrac{(EXPC - IMPC)}{(EXPC + IMPC)}$. It is important to be careful about the direction of causation here. A firm with a large plant may have lower costs and hence be more able to compete in foreign markets. Here, however, the notion is that some Canadian industries are relatively less disadvantaged in terms of their cost functions. As a result, they produce at large scales to serve foreign markets and hence are more efficient. Scale is also greater for industries subjected to strong import competition. Import competition is measured by the ratio of imports to domestic disappearance $\dfrac{IMPC}{(1 + IMPC - EXPC)}$.

Regional industries should differ by less than the average from their U.S. counterparts in incentives to build plants of suboptimal scale. Hence the variable REG is expected to have a positive sign.

Primary-good industries where Canada has a comparative and often an absolute advantage should be of relatively large scale and efficient. Therefore the variable RAW, the ratio of primary sector inputs to all purchased inputs for the industry, is included with the expectation of a positive sign.

Finally, overhead costs in the form of nonproduction workers should tend to increase plant size. Therefore a positive sign is expected on the ratio $\dfrac{NPW67}{NPWUS}$.

These hypotheses were tested by running a regression of $BIGE$ on the independent variables just described, and the results are reported in table 10.3.

Table 10.3 Determinants of the fraction of Canadian industry value added in plants larger than minimum efficient scale $(BIGE)$.

Independent variable	Estimation method		
	A	B	C
$\dfrac{IMPC}{1 + IMPC - EXPC}$	0.1371 (0.701)	−0.061 (−0.439)	0.2583 (0.922)
$FSE\,(1 - CONO)$	−0.4137[a] (−2.89)	−0.1213 (−1.1)	−0.3054[b] (−1.96)
FSE	0.2277[c] (1.50)	0.093 (0.8456)	0.0477 (0.309)
$\dfrac{EXPC - IMPC}{EXPC + IMPC}$	0.01266 (0.186)	0.0749[a] (2.645)	0.1571[a] (3.086)
$EFT * MESU * CDRU$	−1.12 (−0.260)	−6.229[a] (−2.947)	−5.088[b] (−2.069)
$\dfrac{NPW67}{NPWUS}$	0.0052 (0.43)	0.0056 (0.046)	0.003 (0.215)
RAW	0.003 (1.27)	0.0013 (0.987)	−0.00045 (−0.285)
$1 - CNPR$	0.2195[a] (3.11)	0.088[b] (1.675)	0.1096[b] (1.74)
REG	0.0633 (0.912)	−0.0223 (−0.398)	−0.024 (−0.359)
Constant	0.2327[b] (2.17)	0.4131[a] (5.795)	0.4755[a] (4.213)
$\bar{R}^2$	0.4188	0.2527	—
F	2.562	2.78	3.903
D.f.	32	74	74

Note: Levels of statistical significance (one-tailed test) are a = 1 percent, b = 5 percent, c = 10 percent. The independent variables listed above the horizontal line are endogenous in our model or contain endogenous components.

There are some striking differences between the OLS and two-stage estimates. For example, the interaction of minimum efficient scale, tariff protection, and cost advantage has a significant negative impact in the two-stage regression (C) and in the OLS regression with the filled-in sample (B), but not in the regression (A) with missing observations deleted.

The significant determinants of *BIGE* in the two-stage estimates are the following: *BIGE* is larger in producer-good industries, confirming our earlier hypothesis. Foreign ownership has the expected negative effect on plant scale in industries other than convenience goods, but not across the whole sample. Comparative advantage has a strong positive impact on plant scale. Exposure to imports is positive in the two-stage least-squares regression (the proper sign) but is not significant. We have found elsewhere that imports frequently behave as if they were differentiated from domestic output and hence have only weak competitive effects. The combination of minimum efficient scale, tariff protection, and cost disadvantage has a significant negative effect on the size of Canadian establishments relative to U.S. establishments.

The raw material variable and the regional dummy were expected to be positive. In the regressions they are insignificant. Similarly, the nonproduction worker measure of overhead costs is insignificant in its effect on plant size.

The variable $FSE(1 - CONO)$ may in part be capturing the effect of the presence of nonproduction establishments of multinationals in Canada. The establishments of multinationals in these industries may be small because they are merely assembly operations or are otherwise not representative of manufacturing establishments in the U.S. industry. For example, multinational plants may import and assemble parts, while domestically owned plants may be more vertically integrated. The measured effect of foreign ownership should not reflect smaller scale in comparable manufacturing units but rather differences in degree of vertical integration backward between foreign-owned and domestic plants.

Generally, these results confirm the earlier results on technical efficiency. Minimum efficient scale, tariff protection, cost disadvantages of small scale, and market fragmentation by the entry of foreign firms reduce the size and efficiency of Canadian operations, particularly in consumer-good industries.

10.6 Summary

Technical efficiency in Canada in our sample of 84 manufacturing industries is 25 percent below that in the United States. Sixty-three percent of the difference is attributable to small scale and other factors that afflict all Canadian industries. The remaining 37 percent is due to industry-specific factors.

In the regressions the statistically significant determinants of measured efficiency include the minimum efficient scale and the cost disadvantage ratio. Regional industries are not afflicted with as serious efficiency problems. We find that measured efficiency is likely to be particularly low in convenience goods. We believe that this fact results from the higher overhead costs associated with marketing convenience goods. The regressions explain 25 percent of the interindustry variation in technical efficiency.

Plant scale in Canadian manufacturing industries relative to their U.S. counterparts is larger in producer goods. It is significantly larger when Canada has a comparative advantage. Foreign ownership in nonconvenience goods and producer goods has a significant negative impact on scale. This "miniature replica" effect occurs when the Canadian industry is protected from imports; that protection is reflected in the amount of foreign direct investment. Finally, tariff protection combined with large minimum efficient scale and limited disadvantages of small scale produces a significant negative impact on plant scale in Canada.

PART THREE

Large Companies in Their Market Context

11 Corporate Size and Its Bases

Although our study of the system of industrial organization in Canada has concentrated on the populations of firms classified to industries, some questions important for the understanding of industrial structure and performance are best addressed by studying individual firms. In this chapter we take up the determinants of the size and output diversity of Canada's largest corporations, in order to confirm and extend the findings of chapter 8. The statistical analysis rests on a population of 125 firms classified as engaged principally in manufacturing and for which income statements and balance sheets are available. The 125 were selected from the public companies covered in the tabulations prepared by the Financial Research Institute by a process of eliminating all companies not engaged primarily in manufacturing and all manufacturing companies so diversified that we could not with confidence assign them to a principal manufacturing industry. This sample is thus biased against "free-form conglomerates" and against multinational enterprises' fully owned subsidiaries for which separate income statements and balance sheets are not available. The sample does, however, contain a significant population of foreign subsidiaries that are public companies in Canada.

These 125 companies were classified to their primary manufacturing industries on the basis of information secured from several public sources (see appendix A). For most of them we also had estimates of the distribution of their manufacturing activities among the 123 Canadian industries in our data base. This concordance permitted us to associate the firms with structural characteristics of their principal industries or with weighted averages of structural traits of all manufacturing industries in which the companies participate (using their own estimated employment in each industry as weights and following the procedure described in section 8.1). These vectors of activities of the sampled companies also allowed us to calculate measures of their diversification.

Our approach to corporate size diverges substantially from the main tradition of economic research. The relations among corporate size, growth, and profitability have been much studied for large companies in the United States and other countries—but largely outside the context of the product markets in which the companies operate. Our concern is with the size and growth of companies in relation to that context. A company can be large because it operates in large markets, operates in many markets, accounts for large shares of activity in its markets, or because of some combination of these. Public policy can hardly confront the problem of corporate bigness intelligently without an understanding of how much of large companies' size is due to these various sources or components.

11.1 Sources of Corporate Size

Large companies account for a substantial fraction of activity in Canada's manufacturing sector. In 1970 the largest 100 manufacturing enterprises accounted for 47 percent of the value of manufacturing shipments, 45 percent of value added, and 37 percent of total employees. The concentration of shipments and value added apparently declined a little between 1965 and 1970, but the concentration of employment may have increased (Statistics Canada, 1973, table A, and 1975, table A). Concentration of the largest companies in Canadian manufacturing exceeds that in the United States, where in 1970 the largest 100 accounted for 33 percent of value added by manufacture and the largest 200 for 43 percent. To place this conclusion in perspective, one should note that the largest 100 corporations account for a much larger fraction of all manufacturing companies in Canada than in the United States, and it appears that the largest x percent (any arbitrary small number) of companies in Canada account for a smaller proportion of manufacturing value added than does the same percentage of the largest U.S. companies.

Regression Analysis of Corporate Size

We seek to explain the variation among our large companies in their total assets (averaged over 1961–1974). This measure of size—chosen arbitrarily over sales and employees—is related by means of formal identities to market size, market share, and output diversity, and similar variables. The variables as actually measured only approximate the theoretical components of a closed identity; therefore we can employ regression analysis to determine the relative contributions of the identity components to explaining intercompany variations in size. Two alternative identities are employed, distinguished principally by whether they concentrate on the company's base industry or on the average characteristics of all industries in which it operates. First, suppose that the size of the company in our sample were, except for its diversification, typical of companies in its base industry. In that case the following relations would hold:

$$DE3 * TOTA \equiv (ECA67/NENT)KLC,$$
$$TOTA \equiv \frac{(ECA67/NENT)KLC}{DE3}.$$

$TOTA$ is total assets of the company, $ECA67$ total employment in its base industry in 1967, $NENT$ is total number of enterprises in that industry, KLC assets per employee in that industry ($1/LAB2C$ in our data base), and $DE3$ is the fraction of the company's employment in its base industry. Apart from the fact that the large company in our sample is surely not typical of companies in its industry, the relation does not hold empirically as an identity because of inconsistencies in the measurement of the variables. We take logarithms of our data and estimate equation 1 of table 11.1. Equations in the table contain regression coefficients computed from standardized variables rather than from natural units, and so they directly indicate the independent variables' explanatory power. The average (employment) size of company in the firm's base industry makes a substantial contribution to explaining the variance of total assets, but the capital intensity of the base industry is also important. Within our sample of large companies, variation in the proportion of activity in the base industry does not explain much of the variation in size. Equation 2 modifies equation 1 by defining the independent variables as weighted-average observations of all industries in which the company is active. Variables prefixed by W are weighted averages of the industry variables, the weights being the company's own employment allocated to the industry. NS is the number of industries (four-digit, in the U.S. standard industrial classification) in which the company is active. Thus equation 2 relates a company's size to the number of industries in which it is active, the

Table 11.1 Relation between total assets and components of company size, large manufacturing companies.

Regression equation	$\bar{R}^2$	Degrees of freedom
1. $LTOTA = 0.423 \log (ECA67/NENT) + 0.249 \log KLC - 0.111 \log DE3$ (4.37) (2.59) (−1.49)	0.387	108
2. $LTOTA = 0.302 \log (WECA67/WNENT) + 0.330 \log WKLC + 0.440 \log NS$ (3.60) (3.92) (6.36)	0.484	108
3. $LTOTA = 0.413 \log ECA67 + 0.364 \log C468 + 0.396 \log KLC - 0.121 \log DE3$ (5.02) (3.99) (4.85) (−1.65)	0.427	107
4. $LTOTA = 0.311 \log WECA67 + 0.287 \log WC468 + 0.415 \log WKLC + 0.396 \log NS$ (4.00) (3.27) (5.19) (5.67)	0.505	107

Note: Beta coefficients are shown instead of conventional regression coefficients; t-statistics appear in parentheses beneath them. Constant terms are omitted.

weighted average of their mean sizes of firms and their weighted-average capital intensity. When equation 2 is compared with equation 1, we find that size of industry recedes somewhat in importance while capital intensity increases, consistent with the conclusion of chapter 8 that companies tend to diversify into industries with smaller company sizes than their principal businesses. The large coefficient of *WKLC* suggests a complementarity between capital-intensive production processes and diversification. Finally, the beta coefficients of *NS* in equation 2 is considerably larger (in absolute size) than that of *DE3* in equation 1: size variations among large firms are associated more with differences in the number of industries where they are active than in the proportion of their activities outside their base industries.[1]

Equation 3 explores a different set of relations. Suppose that our sampled companies were typical in size (employees) of the largest four firms in their base industries and were similarly capital intensive. Then the following identity would hold:

$$TOTA \equiv \frac{ECA67 * C468 * KLC}{DE3},$$

where *C468* is the four-firm concentration ratio and the other variables are as defined before. The relation is estimated in logarithms in equation 3. The R^2 value, higher than in equation 1, confirms that the size of the typical large company resembles the top four more than the average of all sellers in its base industry.[2] Equation 4 resembles equation 2 in transforming this identity into weighted-average variables. The results differ from equation 3 in the same way that 2 differs from 1. Weighted-average industry size is less important and capital intensity more important than their base-industry counterparts. High seller concentration contributes less to company size outside the base industry than within it, suggesting that the largest companies have no tendency to diversify into the most concentrated industries.

We omitted multiplant operation from the preceding analysis, although it can be included in an identity relating corporate size to its

1. Gort (1962, chap. 4) reports a similar result: beyond a certain size, companies' diversity continues to increase when measured by the number of activities in which they engage, but it stays constant in terms of the proportion of activity carried on outside their principal businesses.

2. To pursue this question further, we added to these equations the coefficients of variation of the sizes of the largest eight companies (*CVC* in our data base), to see whether our leading companies' sizes are attributable to the unevenness of sizes among the leading firms in its base industry. This variable contributes nothing to explaining the variation of asset size of large companies.

components. The segregation was imposed in part by traits of our data base,[3] but it stemmed more positively from our desire to compare multiplant development in Canada with that in the United States. Evidence cited in chapter 8 indicates that Canadian plants of a given scale are more diversified than plants of similar size in the United States. The explanation for this result leads to the corollary that Canadian companies should possess fewer plants whose primary outputs differ from the parent company's: a smaller national market induces them to cram diversifying products into plants engaged mainly in their principal activity rather than to build separate specialized plants.[4] Therefore we expect U.S. companies to possess more plants with principal products that are diversified from the company's primary output.

For each of 64 industries in Canada (1968) and the United States (1967) we developed data on the number of single-industry companies (single- or multiplant) and the plants belonging to them, as well as the number of multi-industry companies and plants belonging to them (both within and outside the primary industry). The information is summarized in table 11.2.[5] A surprising conclusion of Rosenbluth's (1957) study of industrial organization was that in 1948 companies in Canadian industries on the average differed little from companies in their U.S. counterpart industries in either absolute size or the inequality of sizes between an industry's large and small companies. The higher level of seller concentration in Canadian industries, he found, was due to the smaller number of companies that could be accommodated in the smaller economy.[6] Our data for 20 years later lead to similar conclusions about multiplant operation. There is no significant difference between the mean numbers of plants per single-industry company in the two countries (table 11.2, line 3), although the number of companies and plants in the average Canadian industry

3. Information on plants belonging to companies in our sample comes from Dun and Bradstreet records. These exclude plants employing less than 50 workers or those engaged primarily in nonmanufacturing activities, and their completeness for other plants (though thought to be high) could not be verified.

4. The geography of the two countries' internal markets is relevant to the prediction. However, both Canada and the United States are large countries and have spatially dispersed markets, so that it does not seem worth controlling for differences in market density.

5. One noncomparability between the Canadian and U.S. numbers is that the former include administrative establishments while the latter do not. Administrative establishments could be included for the United States only along with various other types of auxiliary establishments, and it seemed better to omit them all.

6. Rosenbluth (1957, pp. 80–85).

Table 11.2 Statistics on multiplant operation, 64 Canadian and U.S. industries, 1967–1968.

Variable	Mean value		Correlation
	Canada	United States	
1. Single-industry companies (*SIE*)	399.0	3130.0	0.855
2. Primary plants of single-industry companies (*SIP*)	412.2	3254.6	0.862
3. Primary plants of single-industry companies, per single-industry company	1.03	1.04	0.769
4. Multi-industry companies (*MIE*)	16.3	105.2	0.349
5. Multi-industry companies, proportion of single-industry companies	0.041	0.034	0.927
6. Primary plants of multi-industry companies (*MPP*)	36.0	306.6	0.496
7. Primary plants of multi-industry companies, per multi-industry company	2.95	2.91	0.362
8. Diversified plants of multi-industry companies (*MDP*)	50.9	933.3	0.318
9. Diversified plants of multi-industry companies, proportion of total plants of multi-industry companies	0.522	0.701	0.288
10. Total number of plants belonging to companies classified to industry	448.2	3561.2	0.861
11. Total number of companies classified to industry	415.4	3235.3	0.856

Note: Data sources for lines 1, 2, 4, 6, and 8 are given in appendix A under the symbol shown in each entry. Figures shown in lines 3, 5, 7, and 9 are ratios of means (not means of ratios), computed from unrounded data, and correlations computed across ratios for individual industries.

is much smaller. There is also no difference between the mean number of primary plants (plants classified to the same industry as the primary activity of the parent company) of multi-industry companies that also operate plants in other industries. The Canadian ratio of these means, shown in line 7, is actually a bit higher than the U.S. ratio. Also, multi-industry companies are slightly more numerous relative to single-industry companies in Canada than in the United States (line 5). The only marked difference in the summary statistics for the two nations' industries comes in the proportion of multi-industry companies' plants that are classified to other industries; the proportion for the United States (70 percent) is significantly higher than the Canadian proportion (52 percent) at the 1 percent confidence level, as we predicted. Thus insofar as U.S. companies exceed the size of Canadian companies through multiplant development, it is because the U.S. companies possess more plants classified to other industries. Given the evidence of part II that other dimensions of Canada's industrial structure are affected by the smallness of the national market, one wonders at the similarity between the multiplant development of primary-industry plants in Canada and in the United States (line 7 of table 11.2). Canadian plants are typically more diversified than U.S. plants of similar size (although the plants of Canadian multiplant companies could still be less diversified than the plants of U.S. multiplant companies). In chapter 8 we found that Canadian companies' diversity increases with their number of plants, even after controlling for company size. Is there some force that impels Canadian multiplant companies to build (or acquire) primary plants that are too numerous and too diversified? Is this a result of the country's low population density? Without a data base that permits full comparative treatment of Canadian and U.S. companies, we can only raise the question.

Table 11.2 also contains the correlations between measures for the individual industries. All are significant at the 5 percent confidence level. The lowest correlation is between the proportions of diversified plants in multi-industry companies (line 9). That is, Canadian and U.S. multiplant development within the base industry is more similar than multiplant operation outside the base industry. This finding suggests that the characteristics of the base industry control the diversification of multi-industry companies less closely than they control multi-plant development within the industry,[7] leaving room for diversification to respond to forces not tied to the base industry.

7. The correlation shown in line 9 differs significantly from the one shown in line 3 at the 1 percent confidence level, but it differs from that shown in line 6 at only the 13 percent confidence level.

11.2 Growth of Companies' Sales

The results of section 11.1 can be supplemented by an analysis of what determines large companies' rates of growth and levels of output diversity. We focus not on the ultimate sources of corporate growth—whatever they may be—but on facilitating environmental factors that are significant for industrial organization. For instance, have larger firms been growing faster than smaller ones, thereby increasing their share of Canadian manufacturing assets? Has corporate growth been associated with increasing seller concentration in the fast-growing firm's base industry? How closely are companies' growth rates correlated with increases in their diversification?

We seek to explain the growth rates of the 125 companies in our sample, calculated in the following way:

GRS   Annual growth rate of sales computed by regressing the logarithm of sales on time over the years 1961–1974 (or as much of this period as data are available).

We wish to control for differences among firms in the growth opportunities present in their base industry, and so we include among the independent variables the growth rate of shipments in each firm's principal industry over 1961–1971 (GSI) and alternatively the weighted-average growth rate of manufacturing industries in which it operates, with the industries weighted by their importance in the firm's own activities (WGSI). How closely a firm is tied to its base industry depends on several factors. If an industry were monopolized and the monopolist's output diversity did not change, the rate of growth of the company and the industry would be the same. On the other hand, a firm holding a small market share can grow at a rate diverging greatly from that of sales in its principal industry. The difference might, of course, run in either direction. Therefore we allow the coefficient of the industry growth rate (GSI or WGSI) to take a different slope (and statistical significance) in settings where seller concentration in the company's base industry is below the mean for all industries in our sample (four-firm concentration ratio in 1968—C468—of 54.8). The variable LGSI or LWGSI is the industry-growth variable for companies with base industries of lower-than-average concentration. In the regression explaining GRS the standard error of this term is expected to exceed that for HGSI or HWGSI, the industry growth rate for firms found in concentrated industries.

Firms also differ in their opportunities to diversify or in the inclination of their managers to seek growth through diversification. The re-

COMPETITION IN THE OPEN ECONOMY

lations that we could test between growth and diversification are limited by the fact that we observed diversification only at the end of the period for which growth is measured. We could inquire whether growth was obtained through diversification but not whether initial diversification influenced growth. For this purpose we needed to observe the firm's diversification relative to the average for firms in its base industry, as a control for its opportunities to diversify, so we simply took the difference between them as our independent variable. This control for the industry's diversification stacks the deck somewhat against the hypothesis, if all firms in an industry have been growing through diversification but our sampled firm no faster than the others. The diversification measures we used are

DDH   Herfindahl measure of output diversity for the company minus
        the Herfindahl measure of diversity for the employment-weighted
        average of all firms in its base industry.
DDC   Concentric measure of output diversity for the company minus
        the concentric measure of diversity for the employment-weighted
        average of all firms in its base industry.

These measures of output diversity were explained in chapter 8.

The next relation to be explored is between companies' growth rates and their average size, important for the trend in overall corporate concentration. To measure a company's size we use

LTOTA   Logarithm of the total size (assets) of the company averaged
          over the years 1961-1974.

Because $LTOTA$ is averaged over the same period for which the dependent variable (GRS) is calculated, the two variables should not be spuriously correlated (our confidence would be greater, however, if GRS were a geometric rather than an arithmetic average). We expect a negative relation because the maximum feasible growth rate appears to diminish with the company's absolute size, and previous studies of corporate growth and survival covering a wide size range of U.S. companies have generally found that small companies that survive grow faster than surviving large companies.[8] If our sampled companies are representative of large enterprises in Canada, a positive coefficient of $LTOTA$ would suggest that concentration of corporate assets in the hands of the largest companies is rising. The predicted negative sign,

8. This hypothesis need not imply declining corporate concentration; it is consistent with a stable overall size distribution of companies because the mortality rate for small companies is higher. See Mansfield (1962) and Sherman (1968).

however, could be consistent with a decreasing, stable, or even increasing concentration in the whole population of companies.[9]

The independent variables so far included amount to much less than a full model of determinants of firms' growth rates. There may be substantial differences among large companies in firm-specific assets that are intangible or at least hard to measure—technological knowledge, marketing skills, heterogeneous natural resources, pure managerial and organizational effectiveness. These may account for much of the variance in large firms' growth rates. We can only observe these assets partially and indirectly through their effect on the gap between the firm's accounting rate of profit and the weighted average of profit rates of the industries in which it operates:

$$DPRF = PEQR - WROI,$$

where $PEQR$ and $WROI$ are company and industry profit rates defined in our data base. This specification does not work, of course, if fast-growing firms are growth maximizers or at least sacrifice short-run profits.

Table 11.3 contains regression equations relating these independent variables to GRS. One-tailed tests of significance are displayed for consistency with other tables in this volume, but the lack of theoretical predictions about the signs of most variables makes two-tailed tests appropriate. The explanatory power of the equations is very low, as expected. The coefficient of asset size is negative and significant at 5 percent in a two-tailed test, tending to confirm the negative size-growth relation among surviving firms that has been reported in other studies. The coefficient of industry growth in concentrated industries is surprisingly insignificant though always positive, and its coefficient exceeds its standard error. For companies in the less concentrated industries there is no relation between company and industry growth, and indeed the regression coefficient is usually negative. If a company's growth is unrelated to growth in the industries it occupies, we surely expect to find its growth positively related to the output diversification that it had attained at the end of the period. Indeed, DDC and DDH are both positive, although at best marginally significant in an appropriate, one-tailed test. Given that our growth variable spans the conglomerate movement of the 1960s it is hardly surprising that the

9. Our companies have been among the largest in Canada for the whole period under study. Company concentration could be stable or rising, even if size and growth were inversely related for this group, if companies that were initially smaller than those sampled grew faster during the period (Prais, 1958).

Table 11.3 Determinants of growth rates of sales, large Canadian manufacturing companies, 1961–1974 (GRS).

Equation	Constant	Independent variables				$\bar{R}^2$	Degrees of freedom
		Industry growth	Diversification	LTOTA	DPRF		
1.	0.181	+0.096 HGSI (0.276) −0.115 LGSI (−0.302)	+0.077 DDH[c] (1.596)	−0.014[b] (−2.080)	—	0.030	72
2.	0.187	+0.091 HGSI (0.261) −0.164 LGSI (−0.428)	+0.026 DDC[c] (1.417)	−0.014[b] (−2.115)	+0.211[b] (1.692)	0.040	76
3.	0.165	+0.459 HWGSI (1.213) +0.018 LWGSI (0.045)	+0.082 DDH[b] (1.750)	−0.014[b] (−2.205)	—	0.067	78
4.	0.171	+0.462 HWGSI (1.232) −0.043 LWGSI (−0.105)	+0.028 DDC[c] (1.572)	−0.015[b] (−2.265)	+0.233[b] (1.906)	0.084	76

Note: Levels of statistical significance (one-tailed test) are a = 1 percent, b = 5 percent, c = 10 percent. Note that two-tailed tests are appropriate for some hypotheses tested in this analysis.

faster-growing firms wound up more diversified.[10] The variable representing the firm's profit-rate differential is positive and significant at 5 percent in the appropriate one-tailed test. This fact plus the low explanatory power of the equation confirms our expectation that firms' growth rates cannot be explained without information on the specific assets that they possess.

In the first section of this chapter we found companies' size to be associated with all the contributing factors identified by our identity relations. The equations of table 11.3 present first-difference versions of those relations. The models of levels and charges are not the same, and the variables could not be measured to make them fully equivalent. Therefore any comparison between the two sets of results must be undertaken with caution. Nonetheless, it may be significant that diversification survives in the first-difference relations whereas the variable indicating the relations between the firm's size and its industry's size does not. This pattern suggests that resort to diversification by the modern industrial corporation has to a large degree liberated the growth rate of the company from the growth rate of its base industry, except insofar as that base industry determines the firm's specific assets usable for achieving growth.

Several other questions about company growth can be answered by correlation coefficients among variables in our data base. The absence of a relation between company and industry growth raises the possibility that the growth rates of large companies might be associated with changes in seller concentration in their industries. If shipments grew at the same rate in all industries and the diversified proportion of companies' activities went unchanged, divergences between large companies' growth and their industries' growth would have to be associated with changing seller concentration. Data are not available to observe changes in concentration over the period for which we observe company growth. The variable GRS covers the years 1961–1974, but we have concentration data only for 1965, 1968, and 1970. Despite the resulting misspecification, we examined the correlations between GRS and changes in four-firm and eight-firm concentration over the period 1965–1970 for both the base industries of our firms and the weighted average of industries in which they operate. The correlation coefficients are all positive but very low, around 0.05, and insignificant. Apparently the variance among companies' growth rates has little systematic connection to changes in seller concentration.

10. Compare Berry (1975, chap. 4); he found fast growth to be associated with close-to-home diversification but not with free-form conglomeration.

We can also note the relation between companies' growth and certain features of their financial flows and financial structures. Growth may be positively associated with the instability of companies' financial flows (sales, profits, dividends). Roughly speaking, one expects rapid growth to involve taking certain chances and experiencing uneven rates of expansion of new ventures. If such an association exists, it has implications for testing hypotheses about the effect of statistically measured risk on the cost of capital. To test this hypothesis, the firm's risk exposure should be measured relative to the norm of industries in which it operates.

$$DSSI = SDS - WSSI,$$

where SDS is the standard deviation of the company's sales around its trend (1961–1974), SSI is the standard deviation of an industry's sales around its trend (1961–1971), and $WSSI$ is the weighted average of industry values of SSI appropriate to the firm.[11] The correlation between $DSSI$ and GRS is a highly significant $+0.58$.[12] How fully does this growth-instability relation extend to reported profits and returns to shareholders? We use the measure of profit instability.

> IBP Average of absolute values of proportional annual changes in net profit after taxes, 1961–1974.

Its correlation with GRS is $+0.29$—lower but still highly significant. Finally, we consider

> VDG Standard deviation of dividends plus capital gains to shareholders around their time trend.

Its correlation with GRS is only $+0.09$, not statistically significant. Apparently expectations of "permanent" earnings levels operate to dampen the influence of earnings fluctuations on fluctuations in the wealth of shareholders. Another financial adaptation to growth oppor-

---

11. It would have been more appropriate to form the weighted aggregation of industry sales figures and then calculate the standard deviation, but the computation costs were prohibitive. One can argue that this comparison should utilize the difference between the company's growth rate and its industry's, analogous to the construction of $DSSI$. The negative results of table 11.3 and the lack of temporal correspondence between the industry and the company figures deterred us from this course.

12. We employed another measure of sales variability analogous to $DSSI$, but we calculated it by taking the mean of absolute values of proportional annual changes. The company-industry differential for this measure is correlated with GRS to the extent of $+0.93$. The two variables have something approaching an identity relation to each other, however.

tunities is observed in the correlation between growth and companies leverage (*LEV*, ratio of long-term debt to equity averaged over 1961–1974), a significant +0.23. Any financial risk associated with growth seems not to deter the employment of high leverage by a company with opportunities for rapid expansion of its sales.

11.3 Diversity of Large Companies' Outputs

Output diversity makes some contribution to explaining the sizes of large companies and a greater contribution to explaining their growth. Hence we analyze factors underlying corporate diversity itself, as an extension of the analysis in section 8.4 of diversity at the industry level. We found there that we could explain very little of diversity's variation among industries and suggested that analysis of individual firms might prove more revealing. The indexes of output diversity described in chapter 8, available for about two-thirds of the 125 manufacturing enterprises in our data base, provide the dependent variables. They can be related to variables describing conditions in the companies' base industries, the weighted average of the industries into which they have diversified, or the weighted average of all industries in which they produce. These variables let us extend and refine some hypotheses that were presented in section 8.4.

We expected diversification to be positively related to seller concentration in the base industry, because concentration can discourage the profitable firm from expanding in its base industry and thereby promote diversification. A composite and interactive concentration variable is included here.

$$C4GR \equiv C648 * CVC \, (1 + ROI)/(1 + GSI).$$

Here *C468* is the four-firm concentration ratio (1968) in the firm's base industry, *CVC* the coefficient of variation of the sizes (shipments of the eight largest firms). Their product provides a measure of concentration that combines the share held by the leading firms and a measure of their size inequality (this variable is discussed in chapter 9). *ROI* is the profit rate in the firm's base industry, *GSI* the growth rate of shipments. Thus *C4GR* expresses the hypothesis that companies diversify out of industries that are slow growing but concentrated and profitable. Since we expect this diversification incentive to be weaker in export industries, we include

$$CGRX \equiv C4GR * EXP,$$

EXP being exports expressed as a fraction of domestic shipments. The sign of *C4GR*'s coefficient should be positive, *CGRX*'s negative.

Two other variables seek to detect the competitive significance of diversification processes. Diversification by large companies out of an industry may occur in response to the competitive threat posed by the diversification of other companies into their base industries. This mechanism of threat and counterthreat implies a positive relation between diversification and

OWN   Fraction of the base industry's value added accounted for by establishments controlled by companies based in other industries.

On the other hand, a positive relation to OWN might mean no more than that technical complementarities promote diversification either into or out of the firm's base industry. The competitive significance of diversifying firms also depends on whether they leap over entry barriers that would stop newborn firms. Do they diversify into industries tenanted by establishments of larger average size than those in their base industry? If so, diversity would be positively related to

$$DVPE \equiv WVPE - VPE,$$

where VPE is value added per establishment in the firm's base industry and $WVPE$ is the weighted-average establishment size in all industries in which it operates. On the other hand, the evidence of table 8.5 (with OWN as a dependent variable) suggested that diversifying firms move toward industries populated by smaller establishments. This would be confirmed by a negative sign for $DVPE$.

Certain assets possessed by the firm and others in its base industry may dispose it toward diversification. Diversification was found in chapter 8 to be strongly related to research and development, consistent with research based in an industry leading to commercial discoveries that often overspill its boundaries.

We test this hypothesis again by means of the variable

RDIU   Research and development outlays as a fraction of sales in the U.S. counterpart of the firm's base industry.

U.S. data seemed appropriate because Canadian companies frequently depend on imported technology, though the effects of imported technology on their diversification decisions should be similar to the effects of homegrown technology. Contrary to the hypothesis embodied in $RDIU$, it is suggested that firms diversify to gain access to research capabilities and proprietary technology. That behavior implies a positive relation between diversity and differential rates of R&D outlay between the base industry and the industries entered.

$$DRD \equiv WRDIC - RDIC$$

where $RDIC$ is research and development outlays as a fraction of sales in the company's base industry and $WRDIC$ is its weighted-average counterpart. Because $RDIC$ and $RDIU$ are very highly correlated, $RDIU$ and DRD cannot be entered meaningfully into the same equation.

Another tentative finding of chapter 8 was that advertising is hostile to diversification, at least when the latter is measured as coarsely as in this study. Again we include ADI, advertising outlays as a fraction of sales in the firm's base industry. Another base-industry attribute that may affect a firm's diversity is its capital intensity, because capital-intensive processes tend to require a higher level of administrative capability in the firm, and this administrative cadre may develop excess capacity usable for diversification. Diversity would then be positively related to

KLC Assets per employee in the company's base industry.

KLC is the inverse of $LAB2C$ in our data base.

In chapter 8 we found diversity to increase with companies' size. Hence we control for the association between size and diversity by including

$TOTA$ Average total assets of the firm.

We regressed each of the firm-specific diversity measures defined in chapter 8 on these variables and compared the results to see whether they were sensitive to the measure chosen. They were not. Therefore table 11.4 contains only DH, the Herfindahl measure, and $VDE4$, the fraction of manufacturing employment outside the firm's principal four-digit industry. Results for the other diversity measures were quite similar to one or the other of these.

The result emerging most strongly from table 11.4 is that research and development is a significant promoter of diversification. $RDIU$ is significant at the 1 percent level. Furthermore, the uncertain sign predicted for differential R&D (between the firm's entered industries and base industries) turns out to be a significant negative coefficient. Apparently the typical large firm diversifies to use proprietary knowledge, not to acquire it. The hypothesis that the intangible assets secured through advertising do not conduce to diversification is confirmed. Another significant variable is the measure of differential plant size, $DVPE$, which supports the hypothesis that firms diversify into industries characterized by smaller-size plants than their base industry.

Table 11.4 Regression analysis of determinants of diversification, company data.

Independent variables	Dependent variable			
	(1) *DH*	(2) *DH*	(3) *VDE4*	(4) *VDE4*
C4GR[1]	−0.650	−0.850	−0.690	−0.820
	(−0.792)	(−1.043)	(−0.975)	(−1.176)
CGRX[1]	−6.180[a]	−5.650[a]	−0.443[a]	−0.407[b]
	(−3.198)	(−2.790)	(−2.684)	(−2.350)
OWN	0.224[c]	0.180	0.250[b]	0.213[c]
	(1.382)	(1.072)	(1.807)	(1.483)
DVPE[1]	−0.030[b]	−0.020[b]	−0.020[b]	−0.020[c]
	(−1.856)	(−1.673)	(−1.709)	(−1.515)
RDIU	0.023[a]	—	0.025[a]	—
	(2.933)		(3.651)	
DRD	—	−0.050[b]	—	−0.056[a]
		(−2.128)		(−2.789)
ADI	−3.085[a]	−4.160[a]	−3.160[b]	−3.394[b]
	(−2.386)	(−2.377)	(−2.214)	(−2.266)
KLC	−0.531	−0.521	−0.383	−0.389
	(−1.204)	(−1.110)	(−1.015)	(−0.967)
TOTA[1]	0.130[c]	0.140[c]	0.070	0.090
	(1.384)	(1.428)	(0.923)	(1.007)
$\bar{R}^2$	0.263	0.191	0.279	0.200
F	5.65	4.25	6.03	4.43
D.f.	96	102	96	102

Note: Levels of significance (one-tailed tests) are a = 1 percent, b = 5 percent, c = 10 percent. Constant terms were calculated but are omitted.

1. We have divided these variables by 1,000 in order to scale their coefficients conveniently.

Although the finding suggests that going firms do not typically leap over entry barriers into large-scale industries, we must recognize that there is some arithmetical necessity behind the negative sign of *DVPE*: if all plants in any given industry were the same size but plant size differed between industries, and if no firms were multiplant within an industry, a firm's base industry would be defined as the one having the largest establishments, even if it had entered from a smaller-scale industry.

If the base industry's research intensity is a strong predictor of diversification, its capital intensity (KLC) is not. Indeed, $KLC's$ sign is regularly negative.

The size of the diversifying firm is a weakly significant predictor of diversification as measured by the Herfindahl coefficient (DH), but among a group of large firms the proportion of activity outside the chief four-digit industry $(VDE4)$ does not increase with the size of firm. Evidence supporting the same finding was presented in chapter 8.

In chapter 8, where industrywide diversity was our dependent variable, $C4GR$ was correctly signed and close to being significant. In table 11.4, however, it consistently takes an incorrect negative sign. We have no explanation for the poorer performance of this hypothesis for this sample of large firms than for the larger group of firms represented by the industry data. The negative influence of the correction for export orientation $(CGRX)$, however, is highly significant.[13] Our measure of inbound diversification to an industry (OWN) does have its predicted positive effect on outbound diversification at a weak level of significance. Again, recall that this variable could reveal either a pattern of competitive behavior or simply the existence of complementarities causing diversification in either direction.

11.4 Summary

We analyze the sizes of large companies in Canada by relating them to the markets in which they participate—the number and sizes of those markets and the shares that the companies hold in them. All these variables contribute something to explaining size differences among large companies, but diversification is relatively unimportant: large companies differ little in the proportions of their activities outside their base industries, although they do differ in the number of activities they carry on. Industry size and seller concentration contribute less to explaining variations in companies' sizes outside their primary industry than in that industry.

When multiplant operations are compared in matched Canadian and U.S. industries, differences in average company size and multi-

---

13. The relation between diversification and exports is complex. The negative sign of $CGRX$ was expected because a concentrated industry selling on worldwide markets should not present its member firms with an incentive to diversify in order to avoid expanding and "spoiling" a small domestic market. On the other hand, if export industries are especially risky, we would expect the industries into which firms diversify to be less export oriented than those in which they are based, and this hypothesis was confirmed in our earlier study (Caves et al., 1977, table 5.2).

plant development within the primary industry are found to be small. American companies differ from Canadian ones mainly in having more plants whose primary activities are not the same as those of their parent companies. This finding is consistent with the conclusions of chapter 8 about the greater output diversity of Canadian plants than plants of similar size in the United States.

Our questions about the correlates of companies' sizes can be translated into propositions about the correlates of their growth. We found the growth of large companies tied only weakly to their industries' growth rates where seller concentration is high and quite independent where concentration is low. Companies' growth rates over the period 1961–1974 were, however, significantly related to the level of output diversity that they had attained by the end of the periods. We also found fast growth to be positively related to firms' profits and the instability of their shipments (both relative to their competitors). Among our sample of large companies, growth is negatively related to average size, suggesting the absence of any trend toward increased corporate concentration (at least among these large firms).

We analyzed the output diversity of our sampled companies in order to test at the corporate level some hypotheses tested at the industry level in chapter 8. We confirmed that research and development promotes diversification (large companies on balance diversify into industries that are less research intensive than their base) and high levels of advertising discourage it. Large companies tend to diversify away from base industries that also attract substantial diversification inbound from other industries, and they expand into sectors with smaller establishment sizes than their base industry. We retested the hypothesis that firms diversify away from industries that are concentrated and profitable but growing slowly; this was not confirmed for our large companies, although we did confirm its corollary that the effect should be less evident in concentrated industries selling on export markets.

12 Corporate Strategy, Market Structure, and Performance

Economists studying the causes and effects of corporate diversification have treated it as an essentially continuous phenomenon to be described by statistical measures such as those used in chapters 8 and 11. Researchers in business administration, however, have portrayed diversification as a discontinuous process characterized by a variety of distinct strategies for achieving what economists would measure as the same level of diversification. Furthermore, business researchers have emphasized that diversification is or should be accompanied by qualitative changes in the firm's internal organization. The two camps derive rather different conclusions about how diversification affects corporate performance.

Students of business have sometimes regarded the firm's decision to undertake a strategy of diversification as dependent on the assets owned by the firm or its state of evolutionary development and not closely controlled by its market environment. By contrast, the economist is prone to look to the market environment for structural causes of diversification that can be identified theoretically and tested empirically. We test our ability to explain the "strategic choices" involving diversification made by a sample of large Canadian manufacturing enterprises, consider the effect of the firm's diversification strategy on its market performance, and draw out some other determinants of performance in order to supplement the results of chapter 9.

12.1 Market Structure and Corporate Strategy

The "business policy" view of the diversification process (Andrews, 1971) turns on the concept of the company's strategy: its long-run plan for maximum attainment of its corporate objectives through the use of those resources and capabilities attached semipermanently to the firm. It possesses a "basic business"—a collection of activities unified through the employment of its special strengths or capabilities. From this base it may become diversified, with the added activities linked directly to the basic business by use of the firm's core strengths, linked to it indirectly through other diversified activies, or even starting and remaining unrelated to the basic business.

Chandler (1962) first employed this view of diversification to explain the organizational development of large American companies. Wrigley (1970) showed that the strategic choices of large companies (the *Fortune* 500) could be classified into four groups—single product, dominant product, related product, and unrelated product. The classification scheme was devised inductively; Wrigley observed a bimodal distribution of his firms according to the percentage of sales accounted for by their basic business—many 80 percent or more, many others 60 percent or less, but few in between. Two of Wrigley's strategies fall on each side of his gap—single- and dominant-product firms with more than 80 percent accounted for by their basic businesses, related- and unrelated-product firms with 60 percent or less. Dominant-product firms were distinguished from single-product companies at the more arbitrary line of 95 percent, but dominant-product firms also tended to differ in being large and vertically integrated. Related-product and unrelated-product companies, with the basic business accounting for less than 70 percent of sales, were distinguished by the presence or absence of a relation between the avenues of diversification and the firm's basic business.

Why the gap in extent of diversification between the dominant-product or related- and unrelated-product firms? A possible explanation lies in the fact that movement to a more diversified strategy is often accompanied or followed by a qualitative shift from a functional to a multidivisional form of organization (Chandler, 1962; Williamson, 1970). The latter is evidently much more effective for maximizing the value of a strategy involving diversification, and its adoption may feed back to increase the diversification that the firm undertakes.

What forces impel the firm to choose a strategy of diversification? Chandler, especially in his recent work (1977), emphasized the influence of opportunities embedded in market structures and technology as well as the inducement due to shriveled opportunities for growth in the firm's basic business. Scott (1973) was somewhat disposed to treat the successful firm's move toward a more diversified strategy as an ineluctable evolutionary process, thus presumably not depending closely on market structure. This neglect of environmental forces is somewhat hazardous if the objective is to determine which strategy is superior for the firm (and, presumptively, is the best use of society's resources as well). Consider, for example, Rumelt's finding (1974, chap. 3) that companies diversifying into unrelated activities are less profitable than those whose diversification employs and builds on the business's strengths in its basic activities. If the firm's basic strengths are extensible, they should be used. But the superiority of related diversification cannot be demonstrated from a cross section of firms, unless we control for differences in the base industries from which the sampled companies departed on their routes to diversification. The unrelated diversifiers may have been stuck in industries that provided them with no strengths (that is, intangible or other transferable assets) that could be profitably moved to other sectors. For them diversification might represent nothing but a way to arbitrage capital from low-return uses to those yielding a better profit. Related diversifiers, on the other hand, might owe their success to having initially prospered in a sector where they could accumulate intangibles usable for related diversification.[1] This problem of inference explains our concern with explaining the strategic choices made by businesses and testing the implications for economic performance. In fact, we shall argue that one cannot do the latter properly without doing the former.

The multidivisional company, as Chandler (1962) argued, was an organizational innovation of great importance, allowing companies to coordinate diverse and heterogeneous activities efficiently. Like any innovation, it diffused over time from the large U.S. companies that discovered it (around World War I) to other American firms. Several investigators have found that strategies of diversification, depending on this organizational form, have also diffused to other industrial countries. Wrigley (1977) classified the diversification strategies of the 86 largest industrial companies in Canada in 1961 and 1972 and compared their distribution to the distributions of the diversification strategies of the 100 largest in the United Kingdom and the 500 largest in the United States in (roughly) the same years. The results, shown in table 12.1, suggest that Canadian companies are changing over time at a pace similar to that of their foreign peers and that the process

1. Rumelt (1977) subsequently reexamined the profitability of his sample of companies, controlling for their opportunities by comparing each company's profits to the average of competing companies in its principal industry. On this test the single-product businesses emerged as the star performers, and the related diversifiers barely outperformed their base-industry companions. Unrelated-product companies, however, still turned in inferior performance.

COMPETITION IN THE OPEN ECONOMY

Table 12.1 Use of diversified strategies by large industrial corporations, United States, United Kingdom, Canada.

Country	Year	Number of companies	Strategic classification (%)[1]			
			Single	Dominant	Related	Unrelated
United States	1959	207	16	37	40	7
	1969	183	6	29	45	19
United Kingdom	1960	96	20	35	41	4
	1970	100	6	34	54	6
Canada	1961	86	27	25	31	3
	1972	86	10	33	38	5

Source: Rumelt (1974, p. 51), Channon (1973, p. 67), Wrigley (1977, p. 21).
1. Percentages may not add to 100 because of rounding.

may be a bit retarded in Canada. However, the lag may be due to the mix of industries found in Canada or to other structural traits of the economy. In any case, we shall not be directly concerned with its causes.

Of the 125 Canadian companies in our data base, the strategies of 56 of them could be identified from a tabulation made available by Wrigley. Wrigley indicated their strategic choices in 1961 and in 1974, as well as in the years in which any intervening changes took place. We made our own classification for as many as possible of the remaining firms, winding up with only 10 unclassified in 1974 (12 in 1961).[2] From our data base we could then calculate for firms using any given strategy the average values of many variables describing the structure and performance of the firm and its base industry. Statistical tests of the differences among these means then allowed us to test our characterization of the four strategies.

Economic Theory and Strategic Choice

The economic theory of diversification can provide a priori predictions about the structural bases for strategic choice, if we use a few key traits that previous investigators have found to characterize each strategic type. That the spread of diversification strategies involves the

2. We followed Wrigley in classifying firms to only one of four principal strategies rather than to the strategic subcategories developed by Rumelt. This may be unfortunate, because Rumelt found that the subcategories more than doubled his model's power to predict corporate performance. On the other hand, the room for differences of opinion on the classifications surely widens when the subcategories are used, and the degrees of freedom are seriously reduced.

dissemination of innovations in corporate organization, however, poses a problem for the theoretical exercise. Do we deduce the structural environment that would cause a firm to choose a given strategy in long-run equilibrium? Or do we try to explain who in the short run would first adopt the innovation? Do we assume that our firms are typically in long-run equilibrium or in short-run transit toward equilibrium? Theory proves most helpful if we opt for the former course and assume long-run equilibrium, because theory then supplies us with rich predictions about the traits of the firm and its base industry that should be associated with each strategy. When we turn to the data, though, we must watch for evidence that some firms may be laggard in adopting an optimal strategy or may simply be at an early stage of corporate development that should lead them to different strategies in time.

The theory of diversification (chapter 8) addresses both the opportunities for the firm to improve profits by diversifying and the threats posed by failing to reduce its commitment of resources to its base industry. The distinction between opportunities and threats proves useful in the following analysis.

It is easiest to start our discussion of the determinants of strategic choice with the dominant-product enterprise, because of the strong hints about it found in the corporate-strategy literature. Why should a firm have diversified only a little? The answer suggested by Wrigley (1970), Rumelt (1974), and Channon (1973) is that its diversified activities are proportionately small because its base-industry operation is so large—affected by scale economies, capital intensive, and often vertically integrated. If we assume that there are ultimate limits to the absolute size (assets) of the firm, it follows that a massive commitment of resources to its base industry should curb its diversification. The size (assets) of dominant-product firms should be larger than that of firms in other categories. Resource-extractive industries, among others, often have these weighty asset bases, and so the dominant-product firms should make heavy purchases of raw-material inputs and should (given Canada's comparative advantage) be heavy exporters. Also, the base industries of dominant-product firms should not provide such a rich stock of assets and skills for diversification that it carries them past the barrier of a heavy commitment to the base industry.

Related-product firms can be identified with a base-industry activity that gives access to some opportunity to diversify by exploiting a common technology, common distribution channels or input sources, common production skills, complementary or jointly supplied products, or the products of a joint research facility. The related-product firm thus closely fits one model of the diversified firm used in chapter 8, which emphasized that certain fixed assets held by the firm are likely to display excess capacity, because they are either lumpy or intangible. Such assets lower the firm's cost of any activity requiring them below the competitive shadow price of an undiversified firm. Not all these assets show up clearly in our data base, but we expect related-product firms to make large outlays on research and development, to have large proportions of nonproduction workers, and to employ highly skilled labor in both production and nonproduction capacities. Whether they should run heavily to the production of consumer goods is not clear. Distribution networks tend to have excess capacity and hence provide a base for diversification; on the other hand, as we found in chapter 8, heavy advertising does not seem to promote diversification.

Unrelated-product firms have found some reason to move capital out of their base industry, despite the lack of any assets that supply the specific advantages of related diversifiers. Growth maximization is one possibility, not testable directly. More generally, they may have experienced threats in their base industry because it is unprofitable, risky, or both. A large firm based in a purely competitive industry can hope for something better than normal profits elsewhere by entering industries with modest entry barriers to new firms, especially where capital-cost barriers are present.[3] More subtly, the base industry could be highly concentrated and profitable but slow growing, making cash available for reinvestment but giving no incentive to plow it back in the base industry. The base industry could be risky because of extensive exposure to international trade, an absence of cushioning product differentiation, and so forth. Of course, unrelated-product firms' base industries should be low on the opportunities for exploiting assets or skills characteristic of related-product firms.

Finally, the single-product firms that have chosen not to diversify must be short on opportunities but also free of threats. In contrast to the unrelated-product firms, their base industries should be free from elements of high risk and afford at least minimal insulation from competitive pressures (high concentration and entry barriers). One protection is product differentiation; we expect them on average to be heavy advertisers. Unlike the dominant-product firms, they should not be highly capital intensive or large scale. Indeed, they could be relatively small firms, especially if they are young and growing rapidly

3. The better-than-normal profits cannot be expected, though, if the diversifying firm buys an established enterprise in the competitive market for corporate control.

relative to their base industry. In that case single-product status may be temporary, and our assumption of long-run equilibrium does not hold.

Empirical Evidence on Strategic Differences

To test these conjectures and to search inductively for other analytically interesting differences, we followed the simple procedure of testing the significance of difference between mean values of characteristics of the firms classified to different strategic categories. We grouped our firms by strategic category, calculated for each category the mean values of many variables describing the firm and its base industry, and tested for statistically significant differences between the means for each variable in each pair of strategic categories. The 125 firms were assigned to strategic classifications in 1961 and 1974 as follows:

Category	1961	1974
Single product	61	43
Dominant-product	22	33
Related-product	23	30
Unrelated-product	7	9
Not classified	12	10
Total	125	125

The trend toward more diversified strategies, evident here, echoes the findings of Wrigley (1977) and investigators who have studied corporate strategies in other countries.[4] Strategic classifications are available for any year from 1961 to 1974 and are shown in appendix A. The variables in our data base are all averages or single-year observations taken within this period, but for diverse years. Thus it was not feasible to match the timing of the strategic classification to the period covered by every descriptive variable. Although the choice of a year for the classification affected the relations among means for a few variables, the same general patterns emerged whatever year was employed. In table 12.2 we report the significance of differences between

4. The relative paucity of unrelated-product firms may result from nothing more than our procedure for selecting the 125 firms, for we passed over some highly diversified companies having substantial proportions of their activities outside the manufacturing sector. We tabulated the strategic transitions for 25 firms whose strategies changed and could be determined in both 1961 and 1974. Of these, 17 moved from single to dominant, 2 from single to related, 5 from dominant to related, and 1 from dominant to unrelated. One reverted from unrelated to dominant, another from dominant to single.

Table 12.2 Mean values of variables describing companies classified by corporate strategy and their base industries, with tests of significant of differences among means.

	Mean value				Tests of statistical significance (t)					
Variable	Single product	Dominant product	Related product	Unrelated product	SP − DP	SP − RP	SP − UP	DP − RP	DP − UP	RP − UP
A. Company variables										
ADCG	0.172	0.103	0.116	0.084	2.07b	1.62c	1.66c	−	+	+
BETAR	−0.008	0.000	−0.000	0.001	−2.44a	−2.35b	−1.52c	+	−	−
GRS	0.123	0.109	0.097	0.146	+	+	−	+	+1.15	−1.50c
IBP	3.04	0.458	1.67	0.793	1.58c	+	+	−	−	+
LEV	0.518	0.306	0.367	0.326	1.70b	1.17	+	−	−	+
NP	3.93	6.85	11.1	10.3	−1.79b	−4.25a	−2.46a	−2.41b	−1.31c	+
PAS	0.094	0.090	0.087	0.088	+	+	+	+	+	−
PEQR	0.087	0.102	0.096	0.100	−	−	−	+	+	+
SDS	0.021	0.026	0.017	0.084	−	+	−2.72a	+	−2.45a	−2.79a
TOTA	54.6	321.3	180.6	111.5	−3.99a	−1.82b	−	1.94b	1.93b	+
B. Base-industry variables										
ADI	0.016	0.012	0.008	0.010	1.13	2.19b	1.07	1.04	+	−
BIGE	0.401	0.410	0.447	0.244	−	−	2.03b	−	2.11b	2.54a
C468	52.8	64.6	50.7	44.6	−2.18b	+	+	2.36b	2.27b	+
CDRC	0.985	0.907	0.955	0.990	1.90b	+	−1.05	−1.08	−1.24	−
CDRU	0.895	0.998	0.921	0.951	−3.08a	−	−	2.12b	+	−
CONO	0.415	0.406	0.067	0.000	+	3.27a	2.54a	3.04a	2.43b	+
CONS	0.417	0.293	0.131	0.143	1.74b	3.86a	2.41b	1.69c	1.29	−
CVC	0.684	0.898	0.744	0.574	−2.67a	−	+	1.77b	2.49a	1.29
EFT	0.252	0.192	0.210	0.309	1.53c	1.03	−	−	−1.83b	−1.53c
EXP	0.144	0.153	0.241	0.176	−	−1.67c	−	−1.45c	−	+
FRP	0.831	0.845	0.918	0.788	−	−2.03b	+	−1.62c	+	1.91b
FRS	0.505	0.995	0.539	0.419	−2.66a	−	+	2.28b	1.93b	+

FSE	0.372	0.420	0.473	0.705	—	-1.59c	-3.40a	—	-2.85a	-2.29b
GSI	0.073	0.073	0.078	0.072	0	—	+	-1.13	-1.51c	+
IMP	0.149	0.217	0.303	0.389	—	-2.12b	-2.15b	2.24b	1.19	—
LAB167	11.4	11.9	10.7	10.9	—	1.39c	+	—	+	+
LAB2C	58.9	43.9	47.4	39.1	1.73b	1.28	1.43c	—	+	—
MESC	0.052	0.067	0.048	0.063	-1.54c	+	—	1.79b	+	+
MESU	0.020	0.033	0.021	0.018	-2.54a	—	+	2.16b	1.80b	+
OWN	0.181	0.113	0.150	0.215	1.99b	+	—	-1.00	-1.84b	-1.15
PRB	0.223	0.163	0.128	0.139	1.13	1.72b	+	+	+	—
PROT	7.99	9.60	11.6	15.2	-1.13	-2.45a	-3.17a	-1.30c	-2.41b	-1.53c
RAW	10.7	21.4	8.43	4.03	-2.53a	+	+	2.82a	2.52a	+
RDIC	0.752	0.507	2.16	2.59	+	-3.10a	-2.63a	-3.47a	-2.92a	—
RDIU	1.00	1.01	3.26	2.69	—	-3.49a	-1.69c	-3.31a	-1.65c	—
REG	0.293	0.344	0.233	0.000	—	+	1.79b	1.00	2.06b	1.38c
ROI	0.108	0.101	0.077	0.066	+	2.33b	2.06b	1.72b	1.68c	+
RPR67	0.768	0.779	0.814	0.788	—	-1.45c	—	-1.05	—	—
SSI	0.006	0.006	0.007	0.005	0	—	+	—	+	1.43c
VPE	2.84	6.04	3.47	2.60	-2.75a	—	+	2.04b	1.86b	+
WNP	6.85	7.33	7.25	7.28	-2.28b	+1.82b	-1.28	+	+	+
WPW	2.63	2.91	2.95	2.70	-2.18b	-2.42b	—	—	1.01	1.15

Note: Full definitions of variables appear in appendix A, and short definitions are given in the text where they are discussed. Tests of significance of difference among means are made on the assumption that variance of the whole sample of firms is an estimate of the variance of the population and that the variances for the different strategic classifications are equal to each other. Levels of significance of the t-ratios are a = 1 percent, b = 5 percent, c = 10 percent. In the column headings for the tests, SP = single-product, DP = dominant-product, RP = related-product, and UP = unrelated-product firms. SP − DP thus indicates the mean for the single-product firms minus the mean for the dominant-product firms. The t-ratios are not shown when their absolute values are less than one; only their signs then appear.

COMPETITION IN THE OPEN ECONOMY

mean values for 1974. This year seems a priori the best choice to report, because it allows us to observe firms utilizing strategies that might have been signaled to them by their market-structure context in the preceding years.[5] Because so many descriptive variables could be examined, it is too cumbersome to report the results variable by variable. Hence we shall address the strategic categories one at a time, indicating the results of the hypotheses and adducing other properties that were not predicted but emerge from the data. Symbols are given in the text for the variables, and these appear in alphabetical order in table 12.2.

Single-Product Firms

In a sample reaching across all size classes of firms, single-product firms would necessarily be smaller than diversified ones if any scale economies exist in individual product lines. Our sample consists only of relatively large firms, but nonetheless the single-product companies hold average total assets ($TOTA$) less than half of those of any other group, and all differences are significant. They also operate less than half as many plants (NP), although their plant sizes (VPE) are significantly exceeded only by the dominant-product group. They operate in industries where small establishments do not suffer serious productivity disadvantages in Canada ($CDRC$). Their work forces, both production (WPW) and nonproduction (WNP) workers, appear to be low skilled on the basis of their compensation levels, and their base industries are relatively labor intensive ($LAB2C$) as predicted. Research and development outlays in their industries in both Canada and the United States ($RDIC$, $RDIU$) are lower than in the highly diversified groups. However, advertising (ADI) is higher (though not significantly), and the single-product firms sell a significantly larger share of their output destined for final demand to the household sector ($CONS$). Although these companies do not dwell in particularly concentrated industries, their base industries are notably insulated from external competition. They are low on both imports (IMP) and

5. Some definite evidence on this point appears in the study by Armour and Teece (1978) of business organization and profitability in large petroleum companies. For the period 1955–1968 it appeared that the more successful firms had moved or were moving toward multidivisional organization, appropriate to a large firm diversified in geographic or product space. For 1969–1973, however, the difference disappeared, as if all firms that could profitably go this route had already done so.

exports (*EXP*), face relatively little competition from multinational companies (*FSE*), and are more fragmented regionally (*REG*) than those of the highly diversified firms. (The base industry has a weak tendency to low productivity relative to that of the United States (*RPR*), consistent with its sheltered character.) All these findings agree nicely with our conjecture that single-product firms are free from threats in their base industries but also low on opportunities to diversify.

Relative to their base industries, single-product firms could be either more profitable (enjoying some firm-specific asset that offsets threats to their continued profitability) or less profitable (laggards in picking up the option of diversified operations). Their base industries are in fact more profitable than those of any other group (*ROI*), but the single-product firms' own profits (*PEQR*) are lower relative to their industry than those of any other group.[6] Yet the single-product firms have been growing faster (*GRS*) than any group except unrelated-product; they are highly leveraged (*LEV*) and do somewhat better on profits on total assets (*PAS*), and they exhibit low beta coefficients (*BETAR*) that should favorably affect their cost of equity capital. These traits together suggest that the single-product group contains young firms that are doing fairly well in environments that are not competitively threatening; they either have little incentive to diversify or have not reached that stage in their development. This characterization is not strongly at odds with Rumelt's (1977) finding that single-product firms in the United States do better relative to their base industries than any other group.[7]

Dominant-Product Firms

Dominant-product firms in Canada strongly confirm our predictions, which were derived in part from observations on their counterparts in other countries. These companies are much larger (in assets) than

6. Unfortunately, the measure of profits on equity contained in our data base for firms covers years different from the years covered for industries—1961–1974 versus 1968–1971. The same holds for growth rates of sales (1961–1974 and 1961–1971). Therefore we can give no interpretation for any one group of the absolute value of its mean firm-to-industry ratio. But we can compare values of these ratios between groups.

7. In the previous version of this study (Caves et al., 1977, pp. 192–197), our smaller sample of single-product companies showed high profits relative to their base industries, but the result did not survive enlargement of the group from 9 to 61 firms.

firms in any other group (*TOTA*) and operate the largest establishments (*VPE*). Their base industries are capital intensive both relative
to other Canadian industries (inverse of *LAB2C*) and relative to their
U.S. counterparts (*LAB167*). Minimum efficient scale is large in both
Canada and the United States (*MESC, MESU*), and small plants are
at a large cost disadvantage in Canada (*CDRC*). They make extensive
use of raw-material inputs (*RAW*). Their work forces are highly
skilled (or at least highly paid, *WPW* and *WNP*). We agree with U.S.
investigators (Chandler, 1962, chap. 7; Rumelt, 1974, chap. 4) that the
dominant-product firms are no more diversified because their base industries are on so large a scale and probably tax their top manage-
ments with the problems of coordinating production in that sector.[8]

Given these traits and knowledge of Canada's comparative advantage, one would expect the dominant-product companies to be heavy exporters (*EXP*). But that is not so. Examination of the list of dominant-
product firms shows that the group includes both raw material
fabricators and some large consumer-good firms that serve mainly
the domestic market, both categories sharing the technological characteristics just described. Dominant-product firms are much more active in consumer goods (*CONS*), especially convenience goods (*CONO*),
than are more diversified firms, and they do somewhat more advertising (*ADI*) although little R&D (*RDIC*). The observed high seller
concentration (*C468*) in the companies' industries is implied by their
size, and there is also considerable size inequality among the leading
firms (*CVC*), perhaps due to the consumer-good members of the group.
Trade exposure is only moderate (*EXP, IMP*), although tariffs (*EFT*)
are low; there is not much foreign investment (*FSE*), and the sizes
of domestic-controlled establishments are large relative to foreign-
controlled ones (*FRS*).

Dominant-product firms' profits (*PEQR*) are insignificantly higher
than those of other groups, but profits in their base industries (*ROI*)
are also good, and so there is nothing unusual about their relative performance. Exactly the same statement applies to the growth of the
dominant-product firms (*GRS*) and of their base industries (*GSI*).
Dominant-product firms are typically protected from competitive

8. The large, durable, specific investments in their base industries may also
induce dominant-product firms to maintain a larger proportion of their assets
that are potentially usable for diversification in liquid form and available to
defend the base. This would be rational behavior under uncertainty, for the cash
flow that could be lost for want of defensive investment is larger for these firms
than for other strategic categories.

threats by high concentration and entry barriers and face limited multinational rivalry, and this absence of threat may contribute to explaining why they have not diversified more extensively.

Related-Product Firms

Our predictions about related-product companies center on the modes of relatedness, such as skills, research, distribution channels. Some of these indeed appear in the traits of these firms' base industries—more highly skilled production workers (WPW), more professional and technical employees than in less diversified groups ($PROT$), and a moderately high level of R&D in Canada ($RDIC$) but a higher one still in the United States ($RDIU$)—suggesting that these firms operate in an environment of copious international flows of technology. Somewhat unexpected is the strong orientation of these firms to producer-good markets (low $CONS$ and $CONO$) and correspondingly low advertising (ADI).

The base industries of the related-product companies are quite international, with high exports (EXP), fairly high imports (IMP), and relatively low tariffs (EFT). This sort of industry is predictably prone to high levels of intraindustry trade, and its markets may be correspondingly segmented. Concentration is moderate ($C468$); company ($TOTA$) and plant (VPE) sizes are moderately large, and there is little room for small companies with working proprietors (PRB). But neither capital intensity (inverse of $LAB2C$) nor minimum efficient scale ($MESC$) is particularly high. The incidence of foreign investment (FSE) is fairly high, but domestic-controlled companies do well in both plant size (FRS) and productivity (FRP) relative to foreign subsidiaries. Compared with the less diversified groups, the related-product firms appear to face more competitive threats in their base industries, and this contributes to the incentive for diversification found in their specific opportunities for related businesses.

Compared with less diversified groups, the related-product companies are more profitable ($PEQR$) relative to their base industries (ROI). Their own profits are no higher than less diversified groups, but their base industries' profits are lower—confirming an element of threat. These firms are not fast growing (GRS) relative to their base industries (GSI); as we would expect, related diversification does not appear to be a route to explosive corporate growth. The international status of their base industries leads us to expect that productivity is high in Canada relative to that in the United States (RPR); the data confirm this, although the difference is not significant. Canadian establishment sizes relative to minimum efficient scale in the United States ($BIGE$) are significantly larger than for other groups, as befits an international industry.

Unrelated-Product Firms

Our data base yields few statistically significant differences in means for the unrelated-product firms because the sample is small, but the data tend to confirm the prediction that they have fled from unappetizing base industries. Concentration ($C468$) is low, the leading firms are evenly matched in size (low CVC), and diversification into the industry (OWN) is high. Although the industries are capital intensive (inverse of $LAB2C$), the cost disadvantage of small plants is low, as are establishment sizes (absolute sizes, VPE, and sizes relative to U.S. minimum efficient scale, $BIGE$). The industries are strongly oriented toward producer goods (low $CONS$) and do little advertising (ADI). Trade exposure is high, especially import competition (IMP) despite high tariffs (EFT), and intraindustry trade must be extensive as with the related-product firms. All these factors suggest that the base industries of unrelated-product firms offer little shelter from competitive threats and hence supply the risk-averse firm with an incentive to diversify.

Somewhat surprising, given the facts noted so far, is that the unrelated-product firms appear to be based in highly research intensive industries ($RDIC$), which attract a high level of foreign direct investment (FSE). The high foreign investment itself can be explained by the research intensity and tariffs, but the research intensity seems more attuned to related-product diversification. We would be tempted to put the result down as a fluke but for Rumelt's (1974, chap. 4) similar finding for the United States. Perhaps the standard procedure for detecting relatedness neglects the role of a fungible basic competence in "scientific" areas of production.[9]

Unrelated diversification allows the firm to liberate its growth rate from that of its base industry, and our unrelated-product firms have indeed grown much faster than their unappealing base industries (the ratio of GRS to GSI is one-third higher than for any other group). But their profits have also been higher ($PEQR$) relative to their base industry (ROI) than for any other group. This conclusion diverges from Rumelt's (1977) finding for the United States, and the difference may

9. Canada has had rather few free-form conglomerates that are little more than holding companies, and none is included in our data base.

reflect the absence of free-form conglomerates from our sample and the prominence of foreign investment in this Canadian group. The unrelated-product firms' sales were more unstable than other groups (SDS), although their reported net income (IBP) was not. Their shareholders did less well (dividends plus capital gains on market value of equity, ADCG) than did those of the fast-growing, single-product companies.

12.2 Strategic Choice and Companies' Performance

Does the firm's choice of strategy affect the allocation of resources in the economy? Let us, for the sake of argument, put aside the possibility that market power is augmented through diversification. Then any variation in firms' profits due to diversification should be positively correlated with welfare changes.[10] Data on company profits seem to promise a simple test for the performance of diversifying companies. Reflection on the results of section 12.1, however, warns us that the test poses a subtle problem of research design. We concluded that the firm's opportunity set, as represented by the structural traits of its base industry, has a great deal of power to explain its strategic choice. We reached that conclusion on the basis of theoretical reasoning that associated structural traits of the firm's base industry with opportunities for the firm to diversify profitably. The effect of the strategic choice per se therefore cannot be tested simply by comparing the profits attained by firms making different strategic choices. It cannot be tested ideally even by comparing the profits of firms in a given strategic category to the profits of other firms in their respective base industries. Competitors of the firms that we sampled may have made the same strategic choice as the sampled firms themselves and for the same reasons. Alternatively, because of firm-specific differences in their opportunity sets, its competitors may have rationally followed a course different from that of a firm in our sample.

What we require is a research design that assesses the probability that each firm has made the best strategic choice, given the opportunities open to it, and then tests the hypothesis that a firm's profit increases with the probability that it has made the best strategic choice. In this section we seek to develop that test.[11] In outline, the test involves regressing companies' long-run average profit rates on a set of

10. This statement is consistent with an overall bias toward excessive diversification due to the tax system's preference for retention of corporate profits.

11. This form of test has various antecedents in research on organizational behavior. See Woodward (1965) and Armour and Teece (1978).

market-structure variables indicating their profit opportunity sets and on the probabilities of correct strategic choice. There is a question about which controls to impose for financial and other characteristics of the firm itself. This test, required to complete our analysis of strategic choice, provides us with a stone that can be lofted at two other birds. We can test at the level of the large firm the hypotheses about market power set forth in chapter 9, and we can investigate certain questions about the financial structures of large firms that pave the way for the investigation of chapter 13.

Calculating the Probability of Correct Strategic Choice

We shall first explain our method for attaching to each firm a probability that it belongs to each of the strategic groups, including the one to which it in fact belongs. The calculation of these probabilities is based on the following assumptions and reasoning.

Each firm i is characterized by a vector of attributes x_i and by the strategic group to which it belongs, $j = 1, \ldots, 4$. We assume that the vector x is distributed normally conditional on the strategic group. For strategic group j, the mean of x is denoted $\bar{x}_j$ and the variance-covariance matrix V_j.

The fraction of firms in strategic group j is α_j. Let the set of firms in strategic group j be $\Gamma_j, j = 1, \ldots, 4$.

We begin by estimating $\bar{x}_j$ and V_j as follows:

$$\hat{x}_j = \sum_{i \varepsilon \Gamma_j} x_i/n_j,$$

where n_j is the number of firms of type j, and

$$V = \frac{1}{n} \sum_{i \varepsilon \Gamma_j} (x_i - \hat{x}_j)(x_i - \hat{x}_j)^T.$$

Next we calculate the conditional probability that a firm is of type j, given that it has the vector of attributes x. Let $N(x;m, V)$ be the normal density with mean m and variance-covariance V.[12] The required conditional probability is

$$P_j(x) = \frac{\alpha_j N(x;m_j, V_j)}{\sum_{k=1}^{4} \alpha_k N(x;m_k, V_k)}.$$

12. That is $N(x;m, V) = \dfrac{1}{(2\pi)^{1/2}|V|^{1/2}} \exp\left[\frac{1}{2}(x - m)^T V^{-1}(x - m)\right].$

Finally, for each firm i, we calculate the conditional probabilities that it would be in each strategic group j, given that it has the vector of attributes x_i. The four probabilities are $P_j(x_i)$, $j = 1, \ldots, 4$. We are especially interested in the probability that it has the strategy we observe. That probability is $P_{ji}(x_i)$. The probability $P_{ji}(x_i)$ is a measure of the extent to which the firm's choice of diversification strategy conforms to those of other firms with similar characteristics.

The elements x_i, on the analysis of the preceding section, should be the characteristics of the base industry with which the firm has been identified. The characteristics of the base industry's market structure were ranked subjectively, on the basis of their theoretical and empirical power to discriminate among strategic categories, and a ranked list of these market-structure elements was the key input into the calculation of the $P_{ji}(x_i)$. The list had to be ranked because the number of potentially relevant structural characteristics turned out to exceed substantially the number of effectively usable observations in our least populous strategic category—the unrelated-product firms. We were limited not just by the total number of firms in the subsample but also (and for every strategic category) by the lack of observations on some industry variables in the company data base.[13] In the end, we were forced to abandon the unrelated-product category, because its retention would have let us use only a few base-industry characteristics in the strategic classification model. Confining the calculation of probabilities to firms classified to the other three strategies, we were able to use ten industry characteristics: overall exposure to international trade (exports plus imports as a proportion of production, *TRAD*), seller concentration *(C468)*, proportion of output going to consumption *(CONS)*, foreign subsidiaries' share of industry sales *(FSE)*, proportion of purchased inputs coming from primary sector *(RAW)*, labor intensity *(LAB2C)*; industry profit rate *(ROI)*, average size (value added) of establishments in the industry *(VPE)*, wages per production worker *(WPW)*, and proportion of total employees in technical and professional categories *(PROT)*. The estimated probability that each firm is correctly a member of the strategic group to which it actually belongs is designated

    PRSP   Conditional probability of belonging to single-product group, for firms actually in the single-product group.

    PRDP   Conditional probability of belonging to dominant-product group, for firms actually in the dominant-product group.

13. The industry variables in our company data base were not subjected to the filling-in process used to generate the B and C equations in our industry model (part II).

PRRP Conditional probability of belonging to the related-product group, for firms actually in the related-product group.

We must set forth with some care exactly what conclusions can be drawn when we test for a significant positive relation of these variables to companies' profits. Our procedure for deriving the probabilities assumes that large firms *tend* to adopt strategies appropriate to the opportunities inherent in the market structures of their base industries; if that were not true, the model would have no power to predict a firm's profit-maximizing strategic choice. On the other hand, it must also be true that not every firm is observed in a fully optimized long-run adjustment of its strategy to its opportunities, or the correct probabilities would all be unity (by definition), and our calculated probabilities would be random noise resulting from the omission of variables from our model.[14] Thus *rejection* of the null hypothesis implies that differences among firms in the correct adaptation of strategy to opportunities are significant for the efficient allocation of resources, but *acceptance* of the null hypothesis could mean that either nobody or everybody makes the correct choice, and that correct choice either does or does not matter significantly for resource allocation.

Determinants of Companies' Profits

The probabilities just described served as one group of independent variables into a regression analysis with the dependent variable

PEQR Net income as reported by the company divided by the sum of common equity (book value) and preferred stock capital, averaged over all years available (maximum 1961–1974).

The other independent variables used in the analysis served three broad purposes.

1. We sought to determine the extent to which the profits of large firms are determined by the same variables used in chapter 9 to explain the whole industry's profits. Two divergent lines of analysis have been invoked to associate the profits of large firms with variables reflecting seller concentration and entry barriers. On the one hand, strategic-group differences within industries may reflect the success of some firms in undertaking bundles of activities that are difficult for

14. The distribution of our estimated probabilities of optimal strategy is fairly even in the (0, 1) interval but with a slight tendency to cluster near zero and a rather large cluster near one.

others to replicate, so that entry barriers take on a significance within an industry as well as surrounding it overall. Hence different factors might influence the profits of large and of medium-sized competitors (Porter, 1979) or those of foreign subsidiaries and domestically controlled firms. On the other hand, differences among competing firms in luck, skill, or the attainment of scale economies could in principle account for an association between concentration and the profits of industries' largest firms. We are not at present concerned with discriminating between these two positions (Caves, Gale, and Porter 1977).

2. Our data base contains not only variables describing each firm's base industry but also variables that are weighted-average characteristics (the firm's own distribution of activities supplying the weights) of all Canadian manufacturing industries in which it is active. On the one hand, we can view the firm's overall profit rate as a weighted average of rates earned in the markets in which it participates, so that the weighted-average independent variables should have more explanatory power than base-industry structural traits. On the other hand, profits in a firm's diversified businesses may depend partly on the diversification process itself, so that the components of its profits contributed by a large firm's diversifying businesses may show a weaker relation to their ambient market structures than do the profits reaped in its base activity (or by specialized independent firms).[15] And, of course, our measurement of the distribution of the firm's activities may be subject to large errors.

3. A company's profit rate on equity reflects both the profit opportunities offered by its surrounding market structure and the supply price of equity capital. That supply price in turn depends on the risk characteristics of the firm's profit stream and perhaps on its choice of financial structure. Therefore we include company financial variables in the analysis.

The industry-related variables used to explain *PEQR* are identical to those employed in chapter 9, so we provide only a summary listing here.

CONM1   Seller concentration adjusted for import competition.
   BARR   A consolidated measure of the height of entry barriers.
 BARAD   The product-differentiation component of entry barriers.

15. We also note the conclusions of section 8.5, which showed that diversifying firms usually slide into industries with structural traits closer to atomistic competition than their base activity.

CBARR   Product of *CONM1* and *BARR*.

DCP   A measure of the uncertainty of collusive agreements in producer-good industries; its counterpart in consumer convenience-
good industries is *DCC,* in other consumer-good industries is
DCN.

RDIC   Research and development outlays as a proportion of sales.

EXP   Exports as a proportion of shipments.

ADEX   Product of *EXP* and the advertising-to-sales ratio.

REG   Dummy variable indicating regional industry.

GSI   Compound growth rate of shipments, 1961–1971.

In chapter 9 we also employed *ATS*, the industry's ratio of assets to
sales, to test the hypothesis that heavy fixed costs complicate the
maintenance of collusive understandings when demand is slack and
thus reduce long-run average profits. Here we replace *ATS* with a
more appropriate variable measured from the balance sheets of our
sampled firms:

FFS   Ratio of total noncurrent assets to sales, averaged over 1961–
1974.

FFS should be negatively related to profits.

Several other variables specific to the company were employed—not
(like *FFS*) to proxy industry conditions but rather to reveal attributes
of the firm itself. Unless all assumptions of the Modigliani-Miller
model are satisfied, the structure of the firm's financial liabilities influences its supply price of equity capital. The key variable is

LEV   Ratio of debt to equity, averaged over 1961–1974.

LEV is a policy variable that the firm (in equilibrium) determines in
recognition of supply conditions in the capital market; although *LEV*
and profits on equity (*PEQR*) are jointly determined (Hurdle, 1974),
a positive relation should exist between them because higher leverage
increases the variance of returns to equity capital and hence its supply
price. On the other hand, this positive relation between the two variables is not a reduced form, and indeed it could be displaced empirically by a negative relation if *LEV* serves as a good proxy for the
riskiness of the firm's business. If a high level of risk prompts the firm
to choose low leverage, it may still have to pay a penalty price for
equity capital, and *PEQR* would appear negatively related to *LEV*
(Gale, 1972). If we assume that some firms are observed out of equilibrium, however, we get a different prediction that implies a quadratic relation between *PEQR* and leverage. Some companies reporting
extremely high leverage may have suffered adversities that leave them

with a low profit rate on equity and deeply in debt. Some firms utilizing extremely low leverage may be exercising a managerial aversion to uncertainty, earning lower profits on equity than they could because they fail to take advantage of access to tax-deductible debt. Because the optimal leverage is an interior solution, firms with nonoptimal leverage ratios are more likely to be at the ends of the spectrum. This hypothesis about firms observed out of long-run profit-maximizing equilibrium leads us to include both *LEV* and its square, *LEV2*. A positive sign for the former and a negative sign for the latter would support this disequilibrium hypothesis. On the other hand, a linear relation (with either sign) could confirm the hypotheses that assume that all firms are observed only randomly displaced from equilibrium.

Because of the joint determination of financial variables, any ordinary least-squares analysis is subject to simultaneous-equation bias and must be billed as exploratory. To proceed further with an analysis of the firm's financial structure and cost of capital would require too elaborate an excursion into the modern theory of capital markets and its implications for the characteristics of large corporate borrowers. Chapter 13 presents our attempt to make some progress in this relatively unplowed field.

Another firm-specific variable that we shall employ is addressed to a problem noted in chapter 11, where we discovered the apparent absence of a relation between the growth rate of the firm and that of the industries in which it operates. The firm's own growth rate, relative to those of its competitors, should reflect the quality of any unobserved specific advantages or disadvantages that it possesses. Although some economists have urged that all relations among profits, growth, and size (market share) at the level of the firm should be associated with such elements of "luck" or "skill,"[16] we believe that they are simply one additive component of the variation of profits across an interindustry sample of firms. To assess the consequences of including (or omitting) such a control, we utilize

DGRO   Compound annual growth rate of the firm's sales, 1961–1974, minus the compound annual growth rate of its base industry's shipments, 1961–1971 (*GRS* − *GSI*, in our data base).

It should be positively related to the firm's profit rate.

One variable specific to the sampled firms was used in the following regression analysis, although not in the main model—size of firm, measured by

16. Demsetz (1973), Mancke (1974). Compare Caves, Gale, and Porter (1977).

COMPETITION IN THE OPEN ECONOMY

$TOTA$ Total assets, averaged over 1961–1974.

The hypothesis that overall corporate size conveys either advantages or disadvantages that systematically reveal themselves across the industrial population is in our view too short on theoretical foundation to command much interest. Nonetheless, in view of the correlation between seller concentration and firm size (chapter 11), we felt the need to make sure that any apparent relation between the profits of large firms and the seller concentration in their industries was not just a proxy for a profit-size relation. The circumstances of the Canadian economy do suggest one specification that might sort out some of the diverse hypotheses that have been offered about the profit-size relation. Baumol (1959) proposed an unqualified positive relation because the large firm can do anything that the small one can, but not vice versa. On the other hand, "deep pocket" hypotheses about the threat capability of the large firm make the positive relation turn on some proportionality between the firm's size and that of the markets in which it operates (and its rivals therein). Because market size evidently differs greatly between firms selling mainly in the Canadian market and those significantly involved with exports, we allow the slope of $TOTA$ to differ for firms classified to industries exporting a substantial proportion of their output. Specifically, we use the variable

$TOTHX$ Total assets for firms classified to base industries in which exports exceed 15 percent of production.

A negative coefficient for $TOTHX$ coupled with a positive one for $TOTA$ would incline us toward the hypothesis that absolute size matters relative to the typical size of ambient markets and of large firms encountered within them.

Statistical Results

In table 12.3 we present regression results for the usable subset of 67 of the 125 firms in our data base.[17] Equations 1–3 employ variables pertaining to the firm's base industry, equations 4 and 5 to weighted-

17. This considerable attrition has several causes. Unrelated-product firms were dropped because there were too few to calculate their probabilities of correct strategic choice. Industry variables were totally lacking for firms whose base industries were not included in our data base (although we employed the 123-industry data base developed for Caves et al., 1977, appendix A, rather than the reduced 84-industry base used in part II of this study). Finally, some variables in the industry data base have observations missing, and we did not employ the filling-in procedure used to secure the B and C equations in part II.

Table 12.3 Regression analysis of determinants of profit rates on equity capital (*PEQR*), sample of large Canadian companies.

Independent variable	Base-industry variables			Weighted-average variables	
	(1)	(2)	(3)	(4)	(5)
CONMI[1]	0.182 (0.48)	–	–	–	–
BARAD	0.009 (0.98)	–	0.005 (0.05)	–	–
CBARR[1]	–	0.034 (1.22)	–	0.067 (1.14)	0.053c (1.67)
DCP	–	–	−15.3b (−2.25)	–	–
DCC	–	–	−15.7c (−1.58)	–	–
DCN	–	–	−28.6a (−2.78)	–	–
RDIC	−0.020a (−3.31)	−0.017a (−4.39)	−0.022a (−3.06)	−0.022a (−2.90)	−0.018a (−4.43)
EXP	−0.079c (−1.56)	−0.025 (−0.86)	−0.111b (−2.28)	−0.066 (−1.14)	−0.014 (−0.44)
ADEX	5.83 (0.40)	−7.17 (−0.80)	16.6 (1.02)	−8.56 (−0.59)	−13.3c (−1.65)
REG	−0.087a (−4.11)	−0.049a (−3.77)	−0.074a (−3.42)	−0.066a (−2.52)	−0.057a (−4.01)
FFS	−0.067a (−2.57)	−0.055a (−3.14)	−0.081a (−3.01)	−0.063b (−2.39)	−0.052a (−3.10)
GSI	0.114 (0.36)	–	0.394 (1.22)	–	–
DGRO	–	0.180a (2.74)	–	0.022 (0.18)	0.155a (2.40)
LEV	–	0.076a (2.70)	–	–	0.96a (3.57)
LEV2	–	−0.029a (−5.58)	–	–	−0.328a (−6.87)
PRSP	–	−0.003 (−0.14)	0.030 (1.15)	0.027 (0.88)	0.000 (0.02)
PRDP	–	0.032b (1.83)	0.043c (1.58)	0.060b (1.92)	0.035b (1.98)

Table 12.3 *(cont.)*

Independent variable	Base-industry variables			Weighted-average variables	
	(1)	(2)	(3)	(4)	(5)
PRRP	—	0.007	0.050c	0.043c	0.010
		(0.41)	(1.69)	(1.37)	(0.56)
Constant	0.170a	0.136	0.202a	0.159a	0.132a
	(4.51)	(6.33)	(4.09)	(4.41)	(6.56)
$\overline{R}^2$	0.259	0.749	0.357	0.175	0.762
F	3.89	17.4	3.81	2.40	18.6
D.f.	58	54	53	56	54

Note: Levels of statistical significance (one-tailed test) are a = 1 percent, b = 5 percent, c = 10 percent.
1. We have divided this variable by 1,000 in order to scale it conveniently.

average industry variables. Equation 1 reproduces the principal specification used to explain industries' profits in chapter 9. It differs in several striking ways from its counterpart in table 9.1. Concentration (adjusted for imports) is not by itself a significant determinant of large companies' profits, nor is the advertising component of entry barriers. On the other hand, participation in regional markets (unrelated to industries' profits) displays a highly significant negative relation to companies' profits; rather than flourishing in the shelter of concentrated regional markets, large companies seem to be penalized by regional operations. Indicators of market power display a significant relation to companies' profits only when the specification is changed. In chapter 9 we found the empirical evidence mixed on the hypothesis that concentration and entry barriers should be jointly necessary to sustain significant departures from competitive conditions. For large companies, however, the amalgamated variable *CBARR* is always more significant than either *CONM1* of *BARAD* separately.[18] Nonetheless, as in equation 2, it is generally not significant at 10 percent when the base-industry variables are used. As equations 4 and 5 show, it becomes significant (though only at 10 percent) with the weighted-average industry variables in use and some control imposed for corporate financial structure. The other industry vari-

18. The scale-economies component of entry barriers, *BARSC*, is always as insignificant a determinant of companies' profits as it was of industries' profits.

ables behave more or less as they did in determining industries' profits (chapter 9).[19]

Let us next consider the probabilities of correct strategic choice (*PRSP*, *PRDP*, and *PRRP*), which motivated this analysis. Their signs are always positive, except that *PRSP* becomes negative when some combinations of company-specific variables are employed. With only base-industry variables in use (equation 3), all three are positive with *t*-values exceeding unity, and *PRDP* and *PRRP* are significant at 10 percent (sometimes 5 percent for *PRDP*). Thus there is appreciable (if not strong) evidence that correct strategic choice contributes to companies' profits. If our strategic probabilities are likely to fail for any strategic classification, it would be the single-product firms (*PRSP*). As we concluded in section 12.1, this group probably includes a significant number that are evolving toward a more diversified strategy.[20]

We now consider the variables measured from company data. Although industry growth is never a significant determinant of companies' profits (either base-industry or weighted-average), the company's growth differential (*DGRO*) is significant at the 1 percent level in some specifications. Its substitution for *GSI* (industry growth) does not appreciably affect the significance of any of the other variables measured from industry data. The inclusion of leverage in a quadratic form results in a highly significant (two-tailed test) positive coefficient for *LEV* and an even more significant negative one for *LEV2*, whereas *LEV* by itself is insignificant. The quadratic form greatly increases the proportion of *PEQR*'s variance that can be explained. It appears that firms with nonoptimal leverage earn subnormal profits on equity, although a final judgment would require careful attention to simultaneous-equation bias. We note that the presence of *DGRO*, *LEV*, and *LEV2* eliminates the weak positive coefficient of *PRSP*. It may well be

19. One exception is *ADEX*, introduced to test the hypothesis that heavy imports could raise profits if the domestic market can be segregated from the international one and price discrimination employed. *ADEX* performs variably here, tending to be negative and significant in the weighted-average equations. Before we adopted the formulation of product-differentiation entry barriers embodied in *BARAD* (advertising in convenience-good industries only), we found that companies' profits are positively related to the simple advertising-to-sales ratio, but that there is an offsetting significant negative relation in export-exposed sectors (where advertising to build entry barriers should be infeasible). The negative performance of *ADEX* for companies' profits may reflect this relation.

20. One might fear that our probabilities of correct strategic choice simply proxy omitted variables that make the level of profits vary systematically from one strategic group to the next. When we replaced the variables *PRSP*, *PRDP*, and *PRRP* with dummy variables, the dummies proved completely insignificant.

that single-product strategic classification interacts with a disequilibrium state in the firm's financial structure.[21]

Table 12.3 does not present equations containing the variable total assets, $TOTA$. We found that size is not very closely correlated with $CBARR$ and that adding $TOTA$ and $TOTHX$ (size of firms in high-export industries) leaves the significance of $CBARR$ unchanged (or increases it a bit, in the weighted-average equations). $TOTA$ takes a positive sign but with a t-statistic only slightly exceeding one. $TOTHX$ takes a negative coefficient with almost the same magnitude and t-statistic, just offsetting the effect of $TOTA$. There is thus the weakest evidence that absolute size contributes to profitability for firms operating largely in the Canadian domestic market, but it clearly does not affect the profits of firms that deal substantially in the larger world market.

12.3 Summary

This chapter has approached the large and diversified firm in terms of its choice of a corporate strategy and the causes and consequences of that choice. The best-known classification of strategic choices, due to Chandler (1962) and Wrigley (1970), emphasizes the extent and character of the firm's diversification. We have shown that strategic choices can be associated with economic models of the opportunities to diversify inherent in the structure of a firm's base activity and with inducements to diversify that result from an insecure or unpromising base-industry environment. Specifically, we found the following:

1. Single-product firms enjoy market environments relatively secure from domestic and international competition, although they also lack resources specifically productive for diversification.

2. Dominant-product firms have diversified only slightly because their base industry demands large-scale and capital-intensive production and coordinated vertical integration, so that limits to the absolute size of the firm (and perhaps considerations of defensive investment) discourage extensive diversification.

3. Related-product firms possess a variety of assets (skills, technology) that are intangible or otherwise subject to excess capacity and thus tend to lower their cost of entering diversified activity. The firms that require these assets also face relatively competitive environments in their base industries.

21. There is, however, also some adverse effect on the significance of $PRRP$.

4. Unrelated-product firms dwell in base industries that are poorly protected from domestic and international competition and low on assets usable for related diversification. However, they are also research intensive in Canada, and their diversification may rest partly on a basic scientific competence.

Testing the consequences of a firm's strategic choice poses a delicate problem of research design, because one must hold constant the opportunities inherent in the firm's environmental market structure. We developed a model that estimates (on the basis of a vector of characteristics of the firm's base industry) the probability that it should choose any one of the available strategic categories. We then tested the hypothesis that a firm's profits are greater when the probability that it chose the correct strategy is greater. We controlled for the determinants of its profit opportunities that have been identified by the theory of markets and confirmed in previous empirical research in industrial organization. We found at least weakly significant evidence that correct choice of dominant-product and related-product strategies increases the firm's profits (unrelated-product firms were too few in number and had to be dropped). The probability of correct choice by single-product firms was not significant; perhaps many are evolving toward a maturity in which they will shift to a different strategy.

Our design for determining the effect of strategic choice also allowed us to test numerous hypotheses about the determinants of the profits of large companies. The effects of the principal theoretical sources of market power are not strong, although we find a weak confirmation that a large company's profits are increased when the industries in which it operates on the average exhibit high concentration, high entry barriers, and low import competition. We also found that operating in regional industries has a strong negative effect. Otherwise, the effect of industry-structure variables on large companies' profits is about the same as the influence of these variables on the profits of all companies in the industry.

Additional tests were made of the association between companies' profits and various of their economic and financial traits. The differential between the company's growth rate and that in its industries is a positive, significant influence on profits and helps to control for unobserved firm-specific elements of luck or skill. There is a powerful quadratic relation between profits and financial leverage. This result was deduced from the hypothesis that firms observed with extreme values of leverage are likely to be out of profit-maximizing equilibrium. Finally, the relation between the company's profits and the sources of market power in its industries (weak though that relation is) does not simply proxy a relation between company profits and company size. Our data suggest only the weakest relation between profits and size, and that relation only for large firms operating principally in the domestic market (not export markets).

13 Corporate Finance and Market Structure

This chapter uses insights from the field of industrial organization to expand two central concepts in corporate finance, namely a firm's riskiness and its appropriate financial policy. By means of these concepts we address the question whether large, diversified firms with market power enjoy advantages in capital markets, both in lower long-run average costs of capital and in favored access to funds when the Bank of Canada tightens monetary policy. If a firm's market power and its other characteristics affect its ability to exchange long-term assets for funds, the market for corporate funds has an important power to shape the evolution of enterprise structure in a modern mixed economy. Theoretical analysis and empirical evidence on these questions are presented for economists and policymakers concerned with concentration of sellers within industries and the superconcentration associated with large conglomerate enterprises. After presenting the relevant theory, we use our sample of large corporations to test the hypothesis that firms with smaller size, less diversity, and less market power pay more for long-term funds. We develop a theoretical relationship between (1) a firm's market power and the maturity structure of its assets and (2) its optimal use of long-term relative to short-term liabilities, and we then present evidence on that theory and the relevance of a firm's financial structure. We contrast the theoretical and empirical approach used in this chapter with that used by other researchers studying the relationship between industrial organization and corporate finance.

13.1 Firms' Characteristics and Their Ability to Attract Funds

We shall first explore the theoretical relationships between the required rate of return that a firm must offer on its long-term securities and such structural characteristics as its market power and the riskiness of its environment. The analysis combines analytical tools and insights from the fields of corporate finance and industrial organization. From the former we draw on the capital asset pricing model, but a major purpose of this section is to relax two of its assumptions and derive the implications of their abandonment for the behavior of capital markets. The assumptions to be relaxed are that transactions costs are either infinite or zero (Jensen, 1972, pp. 381–382) and that investors' subjective probability distributions of returns on long-term assets are symmetrical or, if not, that investors care only about the first two moments of those distributions.

The oldest and simplest view of markets for funds proposes that there is a price of capital determined by supply and demand in a perfect market. If the capital market is competitive, all borrowers pay the same price whether or not they are monopolists in their product markets. There is no room for an influence of market power. The capital asset pricing model (CAPM) provides a more sophisticated view, beginning with the idea that diversification can reduce risk for the lender. Under strict assumptions the equilibrium rate of return, and hence price, for a capital asset can be derived. That price depends on a certain form of risk. We first identify that risk and show that its importance is lessened once transactions costs are incorporated into the model. The distinction between systematic and own-risk is drawn; the latter, deprecated by the CAPM, regains importance once transactions costs are recognized. Ultimately, of the many possibly relevant dimensions of a firm's market environment, diversification and market power emerge as theoretically and empirically relevant determinants of a firm's cost of capital. Both characteristics may influence a firm's own-risk by altering both the variance and the skewness of the distribution of the firm's rate of return.

The Traditional Capital Asset Pricing Model

We shall begin with insights from the theory of capital asset pricing and, by relaxing its assumptions, reach hypotheses about the relationships between firms' characteristics and their costs of funds. We assume that all investors have the same subjective perception of the longer-term assets that firms offer to investors in return for funds. Investors perceive the rates of return on those assets to be random variables distributed with mean μ_i and variance σ_i^2. By storing their wealth in various combinations of these risky assets, investors can expect to realize various combinations of return (μ_p) and risk (σ_p) on their portfolio. Diversification is assumed to be costless. That is, there are no transactions costs. The segment AB is the relevant part of the opportunity set depicted in figure 13.1a. Assume that one asset is risk free, having a rate of return of μ_0 and risk of $\sigma_0 = 0$, and can be borrowed in unlimited amounts at the rate μ_0. Investors can vary the proportions of their wealth in the risk-free asset and in "the" efficient portfolio of risky assets (Z) having expected rate of return μ_m and risk σ_m, and they can obtain any combination of risk and expected return on the line segment through μ_0 and Z. Z denotes "the" market portfolio of risky assets, because in equilibrium all assets must be included in "the" market portfolio. Figure 13.1b depicts the case of several efficient portfolios of risky assets. Note that all efficient portfolios of risky assets are perfectly correlated. If they were not, combinations of the portfolios would provide risk-return possibilities dominating those obtained by any of the portfolios individually. Those individual portfolios could therefore not have been efficient.

If we assume that the investors maximize expected utility and that utility depends only on percentage changes in wealth, then utility is a function of the net rate of return on the portfolio. Given the additional and rather arbitrary assumption that either the utility function is quadratic in the rate of return on the portfolio or the rates of return on all assets are joint normally distributed, expected utility depends only on μ_p and σ_p^2 (Yellen, 1973; Tobin, 1958). Then the investor's indifference curves and equilibrium portfolio can be depicted as in figure 13.1c. E is the equilibrium for the investor with the indifference curves pictured. At E, the investor has chosen the point on the efficient frontier such that the rate at which he is willing to exchange risk for return equals the rate at which he can exchange them in the market for funds.

The model determines a market price of a unit of expected returns in terms of risk. By altering the proportions of the market portfolio and the risk-free asset in his personal portfolio, the investor can purchase any combination of risk and expected return along the line through μ_0 and Z. Each additional unit of expected return above the risk-free rate costs the investor $\sigma_m/(\mu_m - \mu_0)$ units of risk.

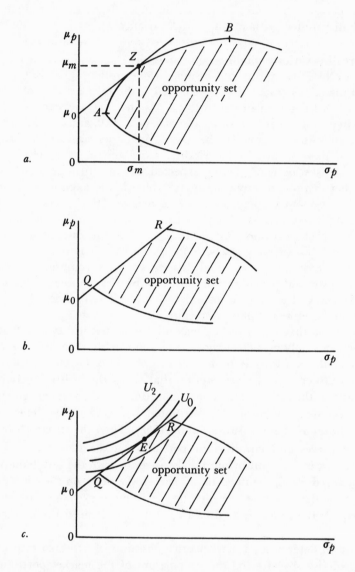

Figure 13.1 The traditional model. (*a*) Opportunity set with one dominant market portfolio. (*b*) Opportunity set with multiple efficient portfolios. (*c*) Opportunity set with multiple efficient portfolios and investor's preferences. (Sharpe, 1972.)

What does this model imply about the required rate of return that firms must offer on their long-term securities and thereby about the cost of funds for differently situated firms? The required rate of return on any long-term asset is the risk-free rate plus $(\mu_m - \mu_0)\sigma_m$ units of expected return for every unit of risk that the asset imposes on its buyers. If a higher or lower coupon rate were offered, assuming that capital markets worked well, the price of the asset would rise or fall respectively until each unit of relevant risk that the asset imposed did in fact cost the firm that required rate.[1]

What is that relevant risk of a risky asset? The capital asset pricing model identifies that relevant risk as the addition to the investor's total risk exposure—risk on the investor's efficient portfolio of the riskless asset and "the" market portfolio of risky assets—resulting from his incremental investment in the particular asset. If h_i is the fraction of the investor's portfolio invested in equilibrium in the ith asset, the return on which is a random variable $\tilde{r}_i$ with expected return μ_i, and if the investor's efficient portfolio has return $\tilde{r}_p$ with expected return μ_p and standard deviation $\sigma(r_p) = \sigma_p$, defined as risk, and if "the" efficient market portfolio has return $\tilde{r}_m$ and risk $\sigma(\tilde{r}_m) = \sigma_m$, then as Jensen (1972, p. 362) has shown, the relevant risk of the ith asset is

$$\frac{\partial \sigma_p}{\partial h_i} = \frac{\text{cov}(\tilde{r}_i, \tilde{r}_m)}{\sigma_m}.$$

Similarly, we can conceptualize the relevant risk of the ith asset as its marginal contribution to the total risk inherent in the market portfolio. If x_i is the weight received by asset i in the market portfolio, then (Jensen, 1972, p. 363)

$$\frac{\partial \sigma_m}{\partial x_i} = \frac{\text{cov}(\tilde{r}_i, \tilde{r}_m)}{\sigma_m}.$$

Thus the required rate of return μ_i for the ith risky asset equals the risk-free rate plus $(\mu_m - \mu_0)/\sigma_m$ units of expected return for every unit of *relevant* risk that the asset imposes on its buyers or on society.[2] Algebraically,

1. The model therefore fixes quantities and assumes perfectly flexible prices. See Hirshleifer (1965, pp. 522–523) for pertinent, insightful comments.

2. Although our development of the CAPM's result is heuristic, it is easily seen to be rigorously correct. Equilibrium implies that adjustment in h_i by switching into more of the risky asset at the expense of one's investment in the riskless asset while holding constant the fractions of one's portfolio invested in any other risky asset will not increase (expected) utility. At the maximum, the rate of change in

$$\mu_i = \mu_0 + \left[\frac{\mu_m - \mu_0}{\sigma_m}\right]\left[\frac{\operatorname{cov}(\tilde{r}_i,\tilde{r}_m)}{\sigma_m}\right]$$

$$= \mu_0 + (\mu_m - \mu_0)\,\frac{\operatorname{cov}(\tilde{r}_i,\tilde{r}_m)}{\sigma_m^2}$$

$$= \mu_0 + (\mu_m - \mu_0)\,\rho_{im}\,(\sigma_i/\sigma_m) = \mu_0 + (\mu_m - \mu_0)\beta,$$

where investors' perceptions of β—the systematic risk, explained by the covariance with the market—have often been estimated by the regression coefficient from a regression of the ith asset's "excess" returns on the excess returns of the market portfolio, that is, by the covariance of the historical series of the asset's and the market portfolio's excess returns divided by the variance in the historical series of the excess returns on the market portfolio.[3] An asset's required rate of return is greater the

---

(expected) utility with respect to h_i is zero. This implies that at the maximum the slope of the investor's indifference curve equals

$$(\partial\mu_p/\partial h_i)/(\partial\sigma_p/\partial h_i) = (\mu_i - \mu_0)/(\operatorname{cov}(\tilde{r}_i, \tilde{r}_m)/\sigma_m).$$

But at the maximum that slope also equals the slope of the opportunity set. Then

$$(\mu_i - \mu_0)\sigma_m/\operatorname{cov}(\tilde{r}_i, \tilde{r}_m) = (\mu_m - \mu_0)/\sigma_m,$$

which when rearranged gives the fundamental equation for CAPM. Thus in equilibrium the rate at which the investor is willing to exchange risk for return (the slope of the indifference curve, which equals the ratio of the marginal disutility of risk to the marginal utility of expected return) must equal the rate at which the investor is able to exchange risk for return in the market. We have examined two conceptual experiments that give the latter rate. In one the investor can decrease his investment in the riskless asset and increase investment in the market portfolio of risky assets. In the other the investor can rearrange investment in the riskless and a specified risky asset. In equilibrium these two rates at which the investor can exchange risk for return must be equal.

3. The logic of estimating β in this way is that in theory equilibrium requires that in investors' minds $\mu_i = \mu_0 + \beta_i(\mu_m - \mu_0)$, implying $\tilde{r}_i - \mu_0 = \beta_i(\tilde{r}_m - \mu_0) + \varepsilon_i$, where $E(\varepsilon_i) = 0$. This should be true in every time period t; hence $\tilde{r}_{it} - \mu_{0t} = \beta_{it}$ $(\tilde{r}_{mt} - \mu_{0t}) + \varepsilon_{it}$ for all t. If we assume $\beta_{it} = \beta_{is} = \beta_i$ for all t and s (that is, β_i is the same in all time periods), then if ε_{it} is uncorrelated with the measure (in practice an index) of $\tilde{r}_{mt}$, if $E(\varepsilon_{it}) = 0$, if $\operatorname{var}(\varepsilon_{it}) = \sigma_i^2$, if $E(\varepsilon_{it}, \varepsilon_{is}) = 0$ for $t \neq s$, then the ordinary least-squares estimate of $\beta_i, \hat{\beta}_i$, from the regression of the excess returns for the ith risky asset on a column of ones and the excess returns for the market portfolio, has desirable properties. (By excess returns we mean the difference between the rate of return on the risky asset and the riskless asset. Then $\hat{\beta}_i$ is, by the algebra of least squares, the sample covariance of the excess rate of return on the ith asset, with the excess rate of return on the market portfolio divided by the sample variance of the excess return on the market portfolio.) The intercept is "expected" to be zero. The assumptions necessary for $\hat{\beta}_i$ computed in this way to have the desirable properties are questionable. Further, the historical β_i may have nothing to do with β_i for the forward-looking investor, and the theoretical equation

higher the correlation of its returns with the return on the market portfolio and the larger the ratio of the standard deviation of its returns to the standard deviation of the return on the market portfolio. If the expected return on the ith risky asset is greater than μ_i, there will be excess demand for the asset. If the expected return is less than μ_i, there will be excess supply. In equilibrium, the relationship

$$\mu_i = \mu_0 + \text{(market price of risk) (relevant risk of } i\text{th asset)}$$

holds.

Given the temptation and the observed propensity to estimate β in this manner, it is worth noting that the covariances calculated from historical time-series data may correspond poorly to the subjective covariances that affect investors.[4] Suppose that an investor's portfolio consists of stock in a tin-can company and that the investor is thinking of diversifying into glass jars. If the short-run returns to the two industries are governed by fluctuations in demand for containers, the covariance will be positive and high. Yet the "real" risk could be shifts in relative input costs (glass or tin plate), and the investor's subjective covariance associated with long-run *internal* rates of return could well be negative. Once we admit transactions costs, this argument is most cogent, because such costs may lock in the investor and make his decisions to buy or sell irreversible in the short run.

Asset Pricing with Finite Transactions Costs

By transactions costs we mean all the costs, tangible (such as explicit costs of searching for information or brokerage fees) and intangible (psychological and physical, such as the bother of information search). Finite transactions costs imply that investors actually face an opportunity set over means and standard deviations that is different from the opportunity set of the traditional capital asset pricing model. The model traditionally assumes that there are no costs associated with constructing a well-diversified portfolio when in fact such costs clearly exist. Once we admit transactions costs, owning the stock of two or

---

with which we began must hold in investors' minds. Nothing says that the actual stochastic process generating $\tilde{r}_t$ will look like that, but the logic of the estimating procedure assumes that the subjective evaluation is the actual process. Finally, the point of this chapter is that it is far too simple to assume that the CAPM result has any bearing on the subjective assessments that actually drive the market.

4. See footnote 3 for further technical discussion.

three well-diversified companies may be preferable to diversifying one's portfolio into all stocks offered, if the companies themselves can diversify at proportionally lower transactions costs than the investor.[5] Just as clearly, if efficient portfolios of just a few stocks are the rule rather than the exception, then we expect the own-variance (nonsystematic risk) of the individual risky asset to be important for determining its price, because the variance of each asset accounts for a larger percentage of the variance of the efficient portfolio.

For expository purposes, a very simple model shows how transactions costs affect the traditional capital asset pricing model. Assume that an investor has \$100 to invest in a portfolio and that all the assumptions of the traditional model (Jensen, 1972, pp. 358–359) hold, with the exception that transactions costs of one dollar are associated with the purchase of each risky asset. Figure 13.2a shows the mapping that transforms the traditional opportunity set depicted in figure 13.1a into the actual opportunity set faced by the investor. We assume that transactions costs are not stochastic and then σ_p remains the same for each portfolio since σ_p consists of terms

$$X - E(X) = X - t - E(X - t),$$

where E is the expected-value operator, X represents an asset's rate of return which is a random variable, and t is the nonstochastic transactions cost associated with the asset. We let z equal the number of assets in the market portfolio Z, and the portfolio denoted by C includes $z/10$ assets.

Because of the transactions costs, the market portfolio is no longer efficient for the investors with the opportunity set pictured. The effective capital-market line showing the rate at which these investors can exchange risk for return is depicted in figure 13.2b under the assumption that there is no transactions cost for holding the riskless asset. In the traditional CAPM, all efficient portfolios had to be perfectly correlated, because otherwise they would be dominated by combinations of themselves and hence could not be efficient. But with transactions costs the bulge in the traditional opportunity set (a bulge resulting from efficient combinations of different portfolios) above the effective capital-market line is no longer relevant, having been erased by the transactions costs of putting portfolios together. With transactions

---

5. Are mutual funds a better alternative for the individual investor? For many investors there is a great deal of misinformation or lack of information about such funds. Investors often end up paying a lot in commissions. And how does one know that the fund will be managed properly? One might rather invest in a few well-diversified companies that one has learned a lot about.

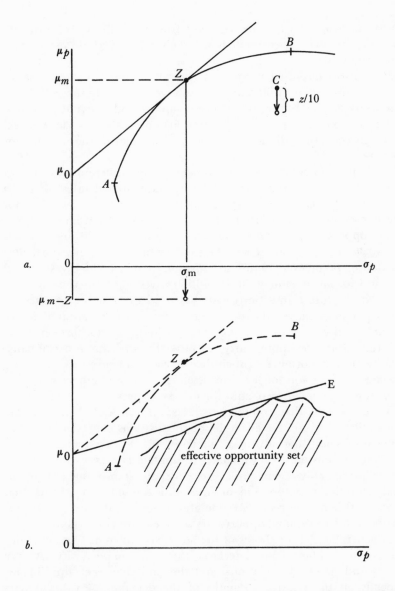

Figure 13.2 The opportunity set with transactions costs. (*a*) The mapping transforming the traditional opportunity set into the actual opportunity set faced by the investor under assumptions in text. (*b*) The effective capital-market line ($\mu_0 E$) for investors with the particular effective opportunity set pictured. (The effective opportunity set lies within the traditional one.)

costly, investors may be able to choose from several efficient portfolios that are not perfectly correlated, and the market portfolio may not be a relevant option.

With this conceptual framework, we can explore different types of transactions costs for different types of investors, verify the validity of assertions at the beginning of the chapter, and provide a formal statement explaining why finite transactions costs provide a direct link between firms' characteristics and advantages in the markets for corporate funds.

We expect different classes of investors to face different opportunity sets because transactions costs affect their anticipated rates of return differently. For example, if we posit a fixed transactions cost of $1 for every asset in an investor's portfolio, the distortion from the traditional opportunity set, which for an investor with $100 invested was t ($\mu_{\text{effective}} = \mu - t$ where t was the number of assets in any particular portfolio), becomes $t/10$ for an investor with $1,000 invested and $t/10,000$ for an investor with $1 million invested. Thus the existence of fixed absolute transactions costs based on the number of assets in one's portfolio makes the opportunity set faced by an individual, albeit wealthy, investor dealing through his local stockbroker quite different from the opportunity set faced by an insurance company. The relative importance of such diverse classes of investors in the aggregate demand for longer-term assets is then an important determinant of the final array of equilibrium asset prices.

To the extent that transactions costs vary with the value of the transaction (because, for example, of commissions expressed as a percentage of sales), the advantage of large-volume investors who must pay commissions on stock purchases is blunted. However, the large investor presumably incurs overhead costs of establishing a team of analysts and transactors and of informing himself about individual assets; and hence he realizes economies of scale and incurs some distortion of the traditional opportunity set due to transactions costs.

In general, different classes of investors face different types of transactions costs. Those costs determine the actual opportunity set over means and standard deviations, and the capital market equilibrium depends on the relative strengths of the demands of the different classes of investors. Clearly there can be both fixed and variable costs of changing portfolios, and the level of either class of cost and the mix of types of cost could vary with investors. As long as investors face some of either kind of cost, the basic modification of the capital asset pricing model is important. If all the costs are fixed costs of informing or transacting, then the transactions costs converge to zero as the size of the investor grows. If all the costs are variable, the transactions costs do not converge to zero but rather to the variable cost.

Fixed transactions costs create opportunities for intermediation, and the relative importance of fixed and variable costs for an economy should determine the type of intermediation. If transactions costs were mostly fixed and all investors of the same size, we would observe investors pooling their funds until there was only one huge mutual fund in the economy. For one transaction—buying into the fund—the investor reaps the benefit of spreading the fixed costs of investing in the market portfolio over all the investable funds in the economy. If transaction costs were mostly fixed and investors differed in size, large investors might not be willing to accommodate the small ones; managers of funds would note that attracting a large investor benefited the fund's members more than attracting a small one, and differential fixed charges for entering the fund would emerge. If transactions costs were mostly variable, regardless of the uniformity of investors' sizes, there would be little advantage in pooling funds before selecting stocks. Only if transactions costs were mostly fixed and all investors of the same size would we expect transactions costs to converge to zero and the traditional opportunity set of the capital asset pricing model to be relevant. That we do not observe one huge fund in our economy suggests diversity in investors' sizes and a significant amount of variable costs in the investment process. This observation might be construed as rendering the unmodified capital asset pricing model empirically empty, although that is not necessarily so if the relevant smaller portfolios have rates of return that are highly correlated with that of the market portfolio.[6]

Note that in the traditional CAPM with no transactions costs, there is no incentive for firms that issue securities to diversify if the diversification entails no "real" effects in the sense that it could have been accomplished with financial transactions by investors themselves. Yet if the company faces no transactions costs for diversification into certain types of assets while investors in general face costs if they diversify, we expect to find that diversification itself affects the required rate of return. It would be more efficient for company 1 to buy company 2 than for the investors in company 1 to buy stock in company 2. The appropriate diversification of firms can be efficient even if it entails no higher real return on their combined resources. In general, transactions costs imply that the assets of diversified firms command a premium in the markets for funds because, by diversifying,

6. With regard to the desirability of such smaller portfolios in the form of mutual funds, see footnote 5.

COMPETITION IN THE OPEN ECONOMY

the firm has provided a service that would have been costly for the investor to accomplish. It seems empirically reasonable that diversification might have been more costly for the investor than for the firm knowledgeable of optimal paths of diversification, given the nature of its business.

To make the point that an asset's own-variance regains importance in a model with transactions costs, we operate under the assumptions that transactions costs are (a) nonstochastic, (b) a function only of the number of risky assets in the investor's portfolio, and (c) nonexistent for the riskless asset. Then note from figure 13.2's new effective capital-market line for the class of investors with the particular effective opportunity set pictured that the market price of risk is $(\mu_{ei} - \mu_0)/\sigma_{ei}$, where μ_{ei} and σ_{ei} are the subjectively evaluated expected *effective* return and standard deviation of the ith efficient portfolio of risky assets. For the class of investors depicted, this market price of risk is equal for all i. Within any efficient portfolio (combining the riskless asset with one of the efficient portfolios of risky assets), the same economic logic applies that determined the equilibrium prices for capital assets in the traditional CAPM. The required rate of return on an individual asset is in equilibrium

$$\mu_j = \mu_0 + \frac{\mu_{ei} - \mu_0}{\sigma_{ei}} \cdot \frac{\mathrm{cov}(\tilde{r}_j, \tilde{r}_{ei})}{\sigma_{ei}},$$

where ei refers to the ith particular efficient portfolio of which the jth asset is a part. Suppose for simplicity that there is only one efficient portfolio for each class of investors and denote the ith class with the subscript i. Then for all i, that is, for all efficient portfolios of which the jth asset is a part, the equation must hold. It follows immediately that the effect of the variance of each individual asset on its own required rate of return is no longer on the order of $1/n$, where n is the number of risky assets in the market, but rather on the order of a weighted average of one divided by the number of risky assets for each of the efficient portfolios in which it appears, with the $(1/n_i)$'s being weighted by the dollar volume of the investments in the jth asset by investors in each particular portfolio. It also follows that the traditional beta coefficient is in general not the sole or even the most important determinant[7] of the equilibrium price of a risky asset *if investors for whom transactions costs are important bulk large enough in aggregate*

7. Note that even if only one class of transactors holds the market portfolio, then the CAPM result holds simultaneously with the equations that imply the importance of own-variance.

to have an appreciable impact on the equilibrium outcome. Indeed the empirical work of Lintner and Douglas[8] supports the theoretically derived expectation that beta coefficients should be less important than own-variance as a determinant of the required rate of return on capital assets, although their work can be interpreted in other ways. The empirical research in this chapter also supports the hypothesis that transactions costs bulk large enough to imply that nonsystematic risk is an important determinant of the prices of capital assets.

This modification of the traditional CAPM is taken from Scott (1977, pp. 212–13). Levy (1978) presents a discussion that is substantively similar but differs in an important respect; namely, Levy's model neglects the formal inclusion of transactions costs. Once those costs are included, sufficient conditions for his discussion to require only a trivial modification are our assumptions a, b, and c. A formal discussion is provided in Scott (1978).

Asset Pricing and Investors' Subjective Evaluations

Analysts have traditionally, and reasonably, assumed that investors care about characteristics of assets other than subjectively evaluated means and variances of returns. The restriction of investors' expected-utility maximization problem to a choice over just two parameters of subjectively evaluated probability distributions of returns is arbitrary. For example, the skewness of investors' subjectively evaluated distribution of returns should be important (Van Horne, 1971, p. 26). For a highly leveraged firm, for example, investors in the firm's equity might reasonably attach greater probability to very low returns, other things equal, because the probability of bankruptcy is greater; and therefore, because bankruptcy is not costless, there is a greater probability that equity holders will suffer loss. Or perhaps smaller firms will not be able to absorb as easily various unpredictable shocks—say a squabble among managers at plant B—and hence, investors' subjectively evaluated distribution of the returns on a firm's assets may again be skewed. Or perhaps undiversified firms, with "all their eggs in one basket" may be considered more likely to exit; hence we again expect skewness.

Monopoly Power and the Market for Corporate Funds

This study asks whether firms enjoy an advantage in the market for corporate funds due not only to their size and diversity but also to

8. See Jensen (1972, p. 364).

their monopoly power. What are our expectations about the effect of monopoly power on the required rate of return, both in steady-state conditions free of monetary disturbances and in the short run with variable conditions in the markets for funds? Our discussion of the relationship between market power and risk is a very general one and in that sense markedly different from the discussion of Thomadakis (1976). The conclusion to this chapter contrasts the two approaches and contrasts our empirical approach with that taken by Bothwell and Keeler (1976) and Sullivan (1978).

That a firm earns monopoly profits on its real assets itself implies nothing about the return on the market value of its equity shares. Nonetheless, we might reasonably expect the required rate of return on long-term assets offered for funds to be less for firms with monopoly power than for firms in perfectly competitive industries, things other than monopoly power being equal. The expected rate of return on investment for firms with monopoly power, other things equal, would be greater; and hence, the coefficient of variation σ/μ would be less for any given σ. Traditionally, investors have been assumed to be concerned with the relative dispersion of the net operating income of the firm, and the coefficient of variation reflects that relative dispersion (Van Horne, 1971, p. 22).[9]

Further, a reduction in market demand or increase in costs that would not cause a monopolist to exit would imply a finite probability of exit for one firm in a competitive industry. And an increase in demand or decrease in costs that would imply additional long-run profits for a monopoly (assuming entry barriers) may imply only short-run profits for firms in a competitive industry. Because firms exit from competitive industries following profit-reducing shocks and enter them after profit-increasing shocks, we expect investors' subjective evaluations of the probability distributions of returns for firms in competitive industries to be relatively skewed, with more of the probability over very low returns.

These arguments are valid even with uniform credit market conditions, where by uniform we mean an unchanging equilibrium in the markets for funds with constant rates and flows. With credit-market conditions variable, all the profit-shock considerations become more important, because monetary phenomena can create changes in demand and cost conditions of various markets. Furthermore, once

9. Of course there is the possibility that relatively oligopolistic markets experience higher returns but greater variance in returns because unstable tacit agreements occasionally break down (Caves and Yamey, 1971). Such instability could outweigh attempts by the oligopolists to lead the quiet life.

we realistically assume periodic easing and tightening of credit markets, we expect small, undiversified firms without market power to be the prime candidates for the fringe of unsatisfied borrowers that grows during a tightening of credit markets. Since the marginal costs of a bank's lending of a dollar to a firm in the fringe include the present discounted value of earnings lost with the steady (large, diversified firm with market power) customer who went elsewhere when denied the dollar, those marginal costs become quite high when funds are scarce. We might expect small, undiversified firms without market power to be among the first to be priced out of the markets for funds during a credit crunch.[10] The very fact that a firm is having trouble borrowing from a bank implies that other sources of funds will be more wary of purchasing the firm's offerings.

13.2 The Data, Empirical Specifications, and Results

We now present empirical evidence lending good support to the hypothesis that diversified firms with market power possess an advantage in the markets for corporate funds. The regressions presented control for own-variance (which may be influenced by market power and diversification) and then include market power, diversification, and size to capture the skewness effects.

Profits on physical assets should vary directly with barriers to the mobility of new firms into the firm's industry or strategic industry subgroup (Caves and Porter, 1977). Yet reasonably well functioning capital markets would imply that equity owners' earnings relative to the market value of their equity would be equalized across firms even when monopoly power implies greater expected streams of earnings, other things such as risk (monopoly power can affect that too) being equal. The streams of quasi rents resulting from any monopoly power are capitalized in the market value of the firm, and those not fortunate enough to be original owners and realize the capitalization of the quasi rents simply earn a normal rate of return. But the presence of monopoly power may lower the required rate of return on equity because it alters perceptions of risk. Similarly, our analysis suggests that the rate of return that the firm must offer to secure longer-term funds will vary directly with nonsystematic risk and financial risk yet vary

10. This is not the traditional idea of rationing in a competitive market but rather the notion of different classes of borrowers for whom the lenders face different marginal cost curves. Observers might think they see rationing since those priced out of the market will surely protest that at the rates at which funds are being loaned, they would borrow if the funds were offered.

inversely with size and diversification—even apart from any effect of size and diversification on perceptions of risk. Size and diversification should be associated with lower own-variance unless oligopolistic interdependence itself is a significant source of disturbances. But apart from the effect on perceptions of own-variance, these variables may influence perceptions of the skewness of the firm's distribution of returns. Thus even with own-variance controlled we expect size, diversification, and market power to vary inversely with the required rate of return on long-term assets.

The following variables are for the sample of 125 Canadian firms described in appendix A. Because some firms did not report some variables, the number of observations used in the regressions varies.

Dependent Variables

To measure the rate of return that the firm must pay to secure longer-term funds, we used the following two variables.

$ADCG$ Average from 1962 to 1974 of the actual yearly return to common-equity holders of the firm. $ADCG$ is the average of the yearly observations: (dividends plus capital gains on common equity) / (market value of common equity) $= DCG$.

$APCR$ Similar to $ADCG$ but uses net income available for common-equity holders rather than dividends.[11] Perhaps available net income rather than dividends provides a better estimate of optimistic equity holders' evaluation of returns from the firm. (Net income available for common-equity holders is net income minus taxes currently payable minus preferred dividend requirements.) $APCR$ is the average of the yearly observations: (net income available for common-equity holders plus capital gains on common equity) / (market value of common equity) $= PCR$.

Purists will prefer $ADCG$. They may look at every other table. Unfortunately, the correspondence between empirical measures constructed after the fact and the ideal theoretical ones is not sufficiently certain to allow a single, best measure.

11. We want a measure of what people expect to get as a return on their investment. Why should that expectation be the historical return? It may well be something greater because equity holders are by and large an optimistic group (relative to those choosing fixed-income securities). Imagine a world with no capital gains for a given stock but a price throughout the period that reflects the expectation in perpetuity of dividends equal to the net income available to stockholders (not dividends). And, of course, there can be movement in market value through time without changing the fact that it is movement around "too high" a level.

Independent Variables

To test the importance of the characteristics of firms for their required rates of return, we used the following variables to measure characteristics hypothesized to be important for investors' subjectively evaluated distributions of returns.

Nonsystematic risk   To measure each firm's nonsystematic risk, we use both the historical variance in returns and the historical variance of returns around the trend in industrial production, as well as measures of the firm's traits such as size, diversification, market power, and financial risk that may also affect investors' evaluations of the firm's longer-term assets.

VDCG   Variance of the yearly observations used to construct the variable *ADCG*.

VPCR   Variance of the yearly observations used to construct the variable *APCR*.

DRESG   Variance of the residuals from the ordinary least-squares regression $DGG_t = a + b\,INDP_t$ where $t = 1962, 1963, \ldots , 1974$ and *INDP* is the index of industrial production described in appendix A.

PRESR   Variance of the residuals from the ordinary least-squares regression $PCR_t = a + b\,INDP_t$ where $t = 1962, 1963, \ldots , 1974$.

Market power   To measure market power, we use the conventional concentration ratios.

C468   Four-firm concentration ratio for the firm's primary industry in 1968.

C868   Eight-firm concentration ratio for the firm's primary industry in 1968.

Size   To measure each firm's size, we employ both total assets and the number of manufacturing plants.

TOTA   Total assets of the firm, averaged over 1961–1974.

NP   Number of plants engaged in manufacturing controlled by the firm.

Diversification   To measure each firm's diversification, we used three measures, *DW, DH,* and *DC* (defined in chapter 8).

Financial risk   To measure each firm's financial risk, we used the ratio of debt to equity.

LEV   Average ratio of debt to equity, 1961–1974 (leverage).

Systematic risk   To measure each firm's systematic risk, we employed the covariance of the firm's rate of return with the index of industrial production for Canada divided by the variance of that index. The measure is thus analogous (and only analogous—it is obviously not the same thing) to the beta coefficient of the capital asset pricing model. However, since the index of industrial production increased continuously from 1962 to 1974, a high beta in this case might be considered a desirable characteristic which lowers the required rate of return.

BETAG   Ordinary least-squares estimate of b from the regression used to derive *DRESG*.

BETAR   Ordinary least-squares estimate of b from the regression used to derive *PRESR*.

Tables 13.1 and 13.2 use ordinary least squares (OLS) to present an analysis of the determinants of the return on the market value of equity, and table 13.3 contains the simple correlation coefficients for the variables used. The hypothesized relationships between a firm's characteristics and its required rate of return on long-term assets evidently hold for this sample. The signs of the coefficients of the variables in the tables remain the same, and their t-statistics about the same, when *TOTA* or *NP* is added to each specification as a measure of size. Although *TOTA* and *NP* always have the hypothesized negative sign, the t-statistics for their coefficients are always less than one.

The estimated impact of seller concentration in the primary industry is fairly substantial, and significant when measured by *C868* in the equations explaining *APCR*. Concentration is measured in percentage form (that is, on a scale from 0 to 100), while the dependent variables are measured as fractional rates of return (for example, 0.06 is a return of 6 percent). An increase in concentration of 10 points (for example from 40 to 50) results in an estimated decrease in the required rate of return of between 0.004 and 0.01 or between 0.4 percent and 1 percent.

We have proceeded under the assumption that investors use certain characteristics of a firm to form subjective evaluations of its stream of returns. The result is a market price for the firm's stock and, in the context of actual dividend policy, an observed measure of the required rate of return that the firm must pay to obtain equity capital. Clearly, in a larger system of equations, this historical cost of equity capital influences the firm's choice of leverage, its ability to grow and its choice of investments, and hence observed size, diversification, and ultimately market characteristics such as seller concentration. Thus tables 13.4 and 13.5 use two-stage least squares (TSLS) to reestimate the equations presented in tables 13.1 and 13.2. The instruments used for the two-stage estimation procedure are those used for estimation method C, explained in chapter 2. These instruments constitute the set of variables assumed to be exogenous to the industry and to the firms therein. The TSLS results are qualitatively similar to the OLS results, the exception being that *LEV* no longer appears significant.

Table 13.1 Regression analysis of determinants of return on market value of equity (dividends plus capital gains, $ADCG$).

Equation	Constant	$VDCG$	$DRESG$	$C468$	$C868$	DW	DH	DC	LEV	$BETAG$	Corrected R^2	Degrees of freedom
1	.14[a] (4.6)	—	.11[a] (7.3)	−.00040 (−.94)	—	−.045[c] (−1.6)	—	—	.039[b] (2.2)	−4.6[a] (−6.1)	.45	108
2	.15[a] (4.3)	—	.11[a] (7.4)	—	−.00054[c] (−1.3)	−0.46[b] (−1.7)	—	—	.039[b] (2.2)	−4.5[a] (−6.1)	.46	108
3	.14[a] (4.4)	.11[a] (7.6)	—	−.00046 (−1.0)	—	−.043[c] (−1.4)	—	—	.050[a] (2.7)	—	.38	109
4	.16[a] (4.2)	.11[a] (7.7)	—	—	−.00059[c] (−1.3)	−.044[c] (−1.5)	—	—	.051[a] (2.7)	—	.38	109
5	.15a (4.1)	—	.11[a] (7.5)	−.00043 (−1.0)	—	—	−.054[c] (−1.3)	—	.036[b] (2.0)	−4.5[a] (−6.0)	.45	108
6	.16[a] (4.0)	—	.11[a] (7.6)	—	−.00057[c] (−1.3)	—	−.058[c] (−1.4)	—	.036[b] (2.0)	−4.5[a] (−6.0)	.45	108
7	.16[a] (4.3)	.11[a] (7.9)	—	−.00051 (−1.1)	—	—	−.070[c] (−1.6)	—	.047[a] (2.5)	—	.38	109
8	.18[a] (4.2)	.11[a] (7.9)	—	—	−.00066[c] (−1.4)	—	−.073[b] (−1.7)	—	.047[a] (2.5)	—	.39	109
9	.14[a] (4.2)	—	.11[a] (7.4)	−.00041 (−.96)	—	—	—	−.022[c] (−1.4)	.037[b] (2.1)	−4.5[a] (−6.0)	.45	108
10	.16[a] (4.1)	—	.11[a] (7.4)	—	−.00055[c] (−1.3)	—	—	−.023[c] (−1.5)	.037[b] (2.1)	−4.5[a] (−6.0)	.45	108
11	.15[a] (4.2)	.11[a] (7.7)	—	−.00048 (−1.0)	—	—	—	−.023[c] (−1.4)	.049[a] (2.6)	—	.38	109
12	.17[a] (4.1)	.11[a] (7.7)	—	—	−.00061[c] (−1.3)	—	—	−.024[c] (−1.5)	.049[a] (2.6)	—	.38	109

Note: Levels of statistical significance (one-tailed test) are a = 1 percent, b = 5 percent, and c = 10 percent; t-statistics in parentheses below the coefficients.

Table 13.2 Regression analysis of determinants of return on market value of equity capital (earnings plus capital gains, APCR).

Equation	Constant	VPCR	PRESR	C468	C868	DW	DH	DC	LEV	BETAR	Corrected R^2	Degrees of freedom
1	.21[a] (5.7)	—	.087[a] (6.7)	-.0068[c] (-1.3)	—	-.031 (-.91)	—	—	.025 (1.1)	-4.9[a] (-5.9)	.41	108
2	.24[a] (5.5)	—	.087[a] (6.7)	—	-.00093[b] (-1.8)	-.034 (-.99)	—	—	.025 (1.2)	-4.9[a] (-5.9)	.41	108
3	.22[a] (5.4)	.089[a] (6.8)	—	-.00075[c] (-1.3)	—	-.034 (-.92)	—	—	.040[b] (1.7)	—	.32	109
4	.25[a] (5.3)	.090[a] (6.9)	—	—	-.00099[b] (-1.8)	-.037 (-1.0)	—	—	.040[b] (1.7)	—	.33	109
5	.21[a] (4.8)	—	.088[a] (6.8)	-.00069[c] (-1.3)	—	—	-.030 (-.61)	—	.023 (1.0)	-4.9[a] (-5.8)	.40	108
6	.24[a] (4.8)	—	.089[a] (6.9)	—	-.00095[b] (-1.8)	—	-.037 (-.74)	—	.023 (1.0)	-4.9[a] (-5.8)	.41	108
7	.23[a] (4.9)	.091[a] (7.0)	—	-.00079[c] (-1.4)	—	—	-.055 (-1.0)	—	.037[c] (1.6)	—	.32	109
8	.27[a] (4.9)	.091[a] (7.1)	—	—	-.0010[b] (-1.8)	—	-.062 (-1.2)	—	.037[c] (1.6)	—	.33	109
9	.21[a] (5.1)	—	.087[a] (6.7)	-.00068[c] (-1.3)	—	—	—	-.014 (-.71)	.024 (1.1)	-4.9[a] (-5.8)	.40	108
10	.24[a] (5.1)	—	.088[a] (6.8)	—	-.00094[b] (-1.8)	—	—	-.016 (-.81)	.024 (1.1)	-4.9[a] (-5.8)	.41	108
11	.23[a] (5.0)	.090[a] (6.9)	—	-.00076[c] (-1.3)	—	—	—	-.018 (-.89)	.038[c] (1.6)	—	.32	109
12	.26[a] (5.0)	.090[a] (6.9)	—	—	-.0010[b] (-1.8)	—	—	-.020 (-.99)	.039[b] (1.7)	—	.33	109

Note: Levels of statistical significance (one-tailed test) are a = 1 percent, b = 5 percent, and c = 10 percent; t-statistics in parentheses below the coefficients.

Table 13.3 Simple correlations for variables used in tables 13.1 and 13.2.

	APCR	ADCG	VPCR	VDCG	PRESR	DRESG	C468	C868	DW	DH	DC	LEV	BETAR	BETAG
APCR	1.0													
ADCG	.97	1.0												
VPCR	.56	.58	1.0											
VDCG	.57	.59	.99	1.0										
PRESR	.46	.48	.98	.98	1.0									
DRESG	.47	.49	.98	.98	.99	1.0								
C468	−.13	−.11	−.060	−.061	−.026	−.026	1.0							
C868	−.15	−.11	−.036	−.038	.0042	.0028	.96	1.0						
DW	−.11	−.15	−.12	−.11	−.12	−.12	−.11	−.12	1.0					
DH	−.08	−.12	−.024	−.018	−.023	−.020	−.16	−.19	.79	1.0				
DC	−.11	−.14	−.099	−.093	−.10	−.10	−.13	−.15	.95	.93	1.0			
LEV	.15	.20	.039	.020	.028	.014	−.048	−.031	.091	−.034	.027	1.0		
BETAR	−.40	−.42	−.069	−.079	.10	.10	.069	.071	.0070	.087	.039	−.13	1.0	
BETAG	−.39	−.40	−.061	−.073	.10	.10	.078	.080	−.020	.062	.0099	.12	.99	1.0

Table 13.4 TSLS analysis of determinants of return on market value of equity (dividends plus capital gains, ADCG).

Equation	Constant	VDCG	DRESG	C468	C868	DW	DH	DC	LEV	BETAG	Degrees of freedom
1	.23a (3.2)	—	.11a (3.4)	−.00098c (−1.3)	—	−.11c (−1.5)	—	—	−.00066 (−.016)	−2.5c (−1.5)	62
2	.27a (3.4)	—	.11a (3.6)	—	−.0013b (−1.7)	−.11c (−1.6)	—	—	−.0028 (−.067)	−2.5c (−1.6)	62
3	.24a (3.4)	.10a (3.5)	—	−.00097c (−1.3)	—	−.12c (−1.6)	—	—	.0014 (.032)	—	63
4	.27a (3.5)	.10a (3.7)	—	—	−.0012c (−1.6)	−.13b (−1.8)	—	—	−.00022 (−.0053)	—	63
5	.25a (3.0)	—	.12a (3.9)	−.00095 (−1.2)	—	—	−.14c (−1.4)	—	−.0057 (−.13)	−2.5c (−1.5)	62
6	.30a (3.1)	—	.13a (4.0)	—	−.0013b (−1.7)	—	−.16c (−1.6)	—	−.0093 (−.22)	−2.4c (−1.4)	62
7	.26a (3.3)	.12a (4.1)	—	−.00091 (−1.2)	—	—	−.17b (−1.7)	—	−.0022 (−.050)	—	63
8	.31a (3.4)	.12a (4.2)	—	—	−.0013c (−1.6)	—	−.19b (−1.9)	—	−.0054 (−.12)	—	63
9	.24a (3.0)	—	.11a (3.6)	−.00092 (−1.2)	—	—	—	−.056c (−1.4)	−.0030 (−.069)	−2.5c (−1.5)	62
10	.29a (3.2)	—	.11a (3.8)	—	−.0012c (−1.6)	—	—	−.062c (−1.5)	−.0058 (−.14)	−2.4c (−1.5)	62
11	.25a (3.3)	.11a (3.8)	—	−.00090 (−1.2)	—	—	—	−.066b (−1.7)	−.000067 (−.0015)	—	63
12	.29a (3.4)	.11a (3.9)	—	—	−.0012c (−1.5)	—	—	−.071b (−1.8)	−.0025 (−.057)	—	63

Note: Levels of statistical significance (one-tailed test) are a = 1 percent, b = 5 percent, and c = 10 percent; *t*-statistics in parentheses below the coefficients.

Table 13.5 TSLS analysis of determinants of return on market value of equity capital (earnings plus capital gains, *APCR*).

Equation	Constant	VPCR	PRESR	C468	C868	DW	DH	DC	LEV	BETAR	Degrees of freedom
1	.32[a] (3.8)	—	.086[a] (3.2)	−.0013[c] (−1.4)	—	−.12[c] (−1.4)	—	—	−.021 (−.41)	−3.1[b] (−1.8)	62
2	.38[a] (3.9)	—	.088[a] (3.3)	—	−.0017[b] (−1.8)	−.14[c] (−1.6)	—	—	−.024 (−.48)	−3.1[b] (−1.8)	62
3	.35[a] (4.0)	.082[a] (3.0)	—	−.0014[c] (−1.4)	—	−.15[b] (−1.7)	—	—	−.021 (−.38)	—	63
4	.40[a] (4.0)	.083[a] (3.2)	—	—	−.0017[b] (−1.8)	−.16[b] (−1.8)	—	—	−.023 (−.43)	—	63
5	.35[a] (3.4)	—	.10[a] (3.6)	−.0012[c] (−1.3)	—	—	−.17[c] (−1.4)	—	−.027 (−.52)	−3.1[b] (−1.7)	62
6	.42[a] (3.6)	—	.10[a] (3.8)	—	−.0018[b] (−1.8)	—	−.20[c] (−1.6)	—	−.032 (−.62)	−3.0[c] (−1.6)	62
7	.38[a] (3.9)	.099[a] (3.6)	—	−.0013[c] (−1.4)	—	—	−.23[b] (−1.8)	—	−.027 (−.48)	—	63
8	.45[a] (3.9)	.10[a] (3.7)	—	—	−.0018[b] (−1.8)	—	−.25[b] (−2.0)	—	−.031 (−.55)	—	63
9	.34[a] (3.5)	—	.092[a] (3.4)	−.0012[c] (−1.3)	—	—	—	−.069[c] (−1.4)	−.024 (−.46)	−3.1[b] (−1.7)	62
10	.40[a] (3.7)	—	.094[a] (3.5)	—	−.0016[b] (−1.8)	—	—	−.077[c] (−1.6)	−.027 (−.54)	−3.0[b] (−1.7)	62
11	.37[a] (3.9)	.088[a] (3.3)	—	−.0013[c] (−1.3)	—	—	—	−.088[b] (−1.8)	−.023 (−.41)	—	63
12	.43[a] (4.0)	.090[a] (3.4)	—	—	−.0017[b] (−1.7)	—	—	−.095[b] (−1.9)	−.026 (−.47)	—	63

Note: Levels of statistical significance (one-tailed test) are a = 1 percent, b = 5 percent, and c = 10 percent; *t*-statistics in parentheses below the coefficients.

We also used alternative measures of market power in OLS equations otherwise identical to the preceding ones. These alternative measures were

> WC468 Weighted-average four-firm concentration ratio for the industries in which the firm operates.
>
> WC868 Weighted-average eight-firm concentration ratio for the industries in which the firm operates.

Although the sign on these alternative measures remained negative as hypothesized, the result was not significant in the OLS equations, perhaps because the estimated coefficients were smaller. Additionally, the simple correlations between the weighted concentration measures and the diversification measures were twice those between the primary-industry concentration measures and the diversification measures. For example, the simple correlation between DW and $C468$ was -0.11 while for DW and $WC468$ it was -0.20. Hence multicollinearity may have been a factor. The signs and significance of the remaining variables were similar, except that diversification (DW) appeared more significant. When TSLS was used to evaluate the equations using the alternative measures of market power, the weighted concentration measures had the (weakly) significant negative sign as hypothesized.

13.3 The Relevance of a Firm's Financial Policy

A firm's search for profits takes place in a risky world, and decisions must be based not only on expected return but on risk as well. One measure of risk is the probability that the firm will fail. If the firm's management evidences a concern with that probability, then the relevance of financial policy, in a world with certain types of transactions costs, is quite clear, even if the arbitrage process that underlies the Modigliani-Miller (1958) proposition about the irrelevance of such policy is freely obtained. Our discussion begins with an assets-liabilities or balance-sheet model of the firm that shows precisely why a concern about risk-return combinations implies the relevance of a firm's financial policy. A distinction between efficient risk-return combinations and value maximization is used to reinterpret the relevance of the Modigliani-Miller proposition. Incomplete information (Ross, 1977) about the actions of the firm, tax distortions, and the pertinence of the arbitrage process have been the focus of discussions of the realism of this proposition.[12] Assume for the sake of argument that we have

12. See Van Horne (1977, pp. 239–253).

full information, no tax distortions, and an unencumbered arbitrage process. Then our discussion focuses on a central reason why an attempt to explain the irrelevancy propositions to a corporate treasurer is such a sobering experience and why it is simply cute, and nothing more, to suggest that if the necessary assumptions are realistic, then the irrelevancy propositions rob financial managers of their stock in trade.[13]

In particular, the Modigliani-Miller proof (1958) implicitly assumes that within the universe of a firm's characteristics, the set of characteristics that can affect the stream of returns available for distribution to stockholders and bondholders (the set of returns in each period for each state of nature) is disjunct from the set of possible financial policies. Then the stream of returns is invariant to financial policy, and as Modigliani and Miller explain (1958, p. 279), their proof then relies "merely on the fact that a given commodity cannot consistently sell at more than one price in the market; or more precisely that the price of a commodity representing a bundle of two other commodities cannot be consistently different from the weighted average of the prices of the two components (the weights being equal to the proportion of the two commodities in the bundle)."

Our discussion begins by explaining why the two sets are not disjunct.[14] That is, financial policy has an impact on the stream of returns available to the firm, and if that impact is reversible, then the choice of an inefficient risk-return combination for the firm can be undone by throwing out the incompetent managers. Indeed, a freely working arbitrage process in corporate control would insure that the market valuation of the firm represented the discounted present values of efficient streams of returns. Perfect arbitrage in corporate control requires acceptance of a greater dose of frictionless economics than a freely working arbitrage process in securities markets. The failure of studies of frictionless cases in economics to address the hierarchy

13. Pertinent discussion can be found in Ross (1977, p. 24) and Stiglitz (1974, p. 851).

14. We choose to emphasize "obvious" reasons rather than exotic ones relying on divergent expectations or playing on the question whether there are as many securities as states of nature (Stiglitz, 1969, pp. 790–791). In particular, one could use the arbitrage proof to show that two firms with the same stream of earnings but different degrees of leverage have the same value, yet that does not necessarily imply that capital structure is irrelevant. Irrelevance requires that if one began with two unlevered firms with the same stream of operating earnings and then levered one of them, the subjective assessments of the stream of operating earnings for the levered firm would not change. We point up why this is not so.

COMPETITION IN THE OPEN ECONOMY

of extant frictions excludes many real-world phenomena from their implications.[15] We shall show that the two sets are not disjunct; thus if we assume a hierarchy of frictions that assigns greater friction to arbitrage in corporate control than in securities markets, then the "operation of a financial intermediary"[16] to purchase a fraction of the bonds and shares of a firm and then to reissue bonds and shares in the optimal ratio need not remedy the situation where those exercising corporate control have set the wrong financial policy. In any case, with perfect arbitrage in corporate control, market valuation would be invariant to the most boneheaded reversible financial policy. But such policy would be relevant to the managers of the firm if they valued their jobs. The essence of the distinction drawn is that the Modigliani-Miller proposition ensures that the equilibrium is invariant to financial policy without saying anything about the dynamics of the problem.[17] At least one dynamic path results in the managers' being thrown out.

Balance-Sheet Model and Efficient Risk-Return Combinations

This section uses a balance-sheet model of the firm to show that the probability of bankruptcy is intimately related to financial policy. Under the assumption that the tenure of a firm's managers depends, among other things, on the choice of policies with efficient risk-return characteristics,[18] financial policy is then clearly relevant to the firm's managers and hence to its operation. This relevance holds even in a world where the arbitrage process underlying the Modigliani-Miller proposition works perfectly.

To show the relationship between financial policy and the efficiency of risk-return combinations, we use the following symbols. Let tildes denote random variables; D_0 is the initial value of the firm's nonequity liabilities; Z is the average contracted $(t - 0)$ period rate of interest on those liabilities; $\tilde{D}_t$ is the uncertain value of the firm's initial nonequity liabilities at time $t > 0$; $A_0 = (D_0 + N_0)$ is the initial value of the firm's assets, where N_0 is the initial value of equity liabilities; and

15. See Stiglitz (1974, p. 866) for a discussion of the value of research on frictionless cases.

16. See Stiglitz (1974, fn. 18, p. 864; figure 3, p. 865).

17. I thank Geoffrey Woglom for this comment.

18. A policy with efficient risk-return characteristics is one for which no alternative policy has both a higher rate of return and an equivalent or lesser amount of risk or both a lesser amount of risk and an equivalent rate of return.

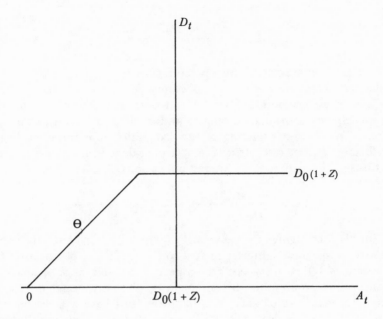

Figure 13.3 The function θ.

$\bar{A}_t = (D_0 + N_0)\Sigma_i(1 + \bar{r}_i)h_i$ is the uncertain value of the firm's initial assets at time t, where r_i is the uncertain $(t - 0)$ period rate of return on the ith asset and incorporates the uncertain costs of liquidating the asset at time t, and h_i is the fraction of $(D_0 + N_0)$ invested in the ith asset.

Then define the function $\Theta(A_t) = D_t$, the value of initial nonequity liabilities at time t. D_t is $D_0(1 + Z)$ if $A_t > D_0(1 + Z)$. The function Θ has the shape depicted in figure 13.3 and reflects the fact that as A_t, the liquidation value of assets at time t, falls below $D_0(1 + Z)$, borrowing quickly ceases to be an option. The firm's probability of failure is then a function of the distribution of $\bar{D}_t$. The distribution of $\bar{D}_t$ is in fact determined by the distribution of $\bar{A}_t$. $\bar{D}_t$ can take on values from zero to $D_0(1 + Z)$.

Simply for the sake of developing a tractable and well-defined argument, and with no loss of generality with respect to our central point that there is a relationship between financial policy and the efficiency of the risk-return combinations available to the firm, assume that $\bar{A}_t$ is distributed normally. Then the probability that $A_t < D_0(1 + Z)$—and hence, the probability that $D_t < D_0(1 + Z)$ and the firm fails, is inversely related to

COMPETITION IN THE OPEN ECONOMY

$$\psi = \frac{E(\tilde{A}_t) - D_0(1 + Z)}{\sigma(\tilde{A}_t)}$$

where E is the expected-value operator. Further, let $\tilde{r} = \Sigma_i \, \tilde{r}_i \, h_i$ be the uncertain weighted-average rate of return on assets, and let $E(\tilde{r}) = \bar{r}$.

With these symbols defined, we can now show the conceptual relationship between financial policy and efficient risk-return combinations. To aid understanding of the economics, it is useful to begin with the simplest case. Assume first a pure-debt firm ($N_0 = 0$; excess returns are burned) with no interest obligations ($Z = 0$). Then

$$\psi = \frac{D_0(1 + \bar{r}) - D_0}{\{E[D_0(1 + \tilde{r}) - D_0(1 + \bar{r})]^2\}^{\frac{1}{2}}} = \frac{\bar{r}}{\sigma(r)}.$$

In this simplifying case the probability of failure is simply the probability of loss and is directly related to the coefficient of variation for the rate of return on assets. One aspect of the relevance of financial policy is clear even in this simple case. Namely, some degree of maturity matching of assets and liabilities will have a favorable impact on the risk-return combination associated with a given collection of assets. The efficient degree of maturity matching depends on the costs and returns to the effort.

Since the uncertain ($t - 0$) period rate of return on an asset incorporated the uncertain cost of liquidating the asset at time t, the general effect of maturity matching is clear. Perfect matching of the maturities of liabilities to assets would render nil the impact of uncertain liquidation costs on assets' rates of return. Liquidation costs would be known with certainty to be zero. Thus, all other things equal, maturity matching would increase $\bar{r}$ and decrease $\sigma(\tilde{r})$. Offsetting these benefits would be costs of arranging the "perfect" liability structure, transactions costs incurred in the matching effort and the differences in costs of different types of liabilities. Of course, an asset's life is itself imperfectly known, and consequently the notion of arranging a perfect liability structure is a theoretical archetype only.

Assume now that $N_0 > 0$ but that $Z = 0$; then

$$\psi = \frac{\bar{r}}{\sigma(\tilde{r})} + \frac{N_0}{(N_0 + D_0)\sigma(\tilde{r})},$$

and financial policy in the form of the debt-to-equity ratio clearly has an impact on one aspect of the firm's riskiness—the probability that it will fail. In this second and more complete case, financial policy is relevant both for the reason discussed in the first case and because leverage itself has an impact on the probability of bankruptcy. The point of general significance in both cases is that financial policy has an impact on the risk-return combinations available to the firm as a whole, if we assume that there are liquidation costs. Note the implication of the second case for the behavioral significance of the arithmetic of the arguments for the invariance of the firm's weighted-average cost of capital to changes in its leverage (Van Horne, 1977, pp. 233–235). The risk to both shareholders and bondholders increases with the firm's leverage because the probability of bankruptcy—which is not costless—increases. Thus eventually further leverage increases the weighted-average cost of capital. We must of course assume that the partial effect of changes in leverage on the probability of failure is not completely offset by changes in the distribution of $\tilde{r}$ given h, which is in fact a characterization of the business of the firm in question. As leverage becomes large, that seems a most reasonable assumption. Finally, the case in which both Z and N_0 are greater than zero simply adds another layer of importance to financial policy because the commitment of interest obligations on debt has an impact on the probability of bankruptcy.

We turn now to a hypothesized relationship between market structure and financial structure. This hypothesis, along with the preceding discussion, provides the basis for our empirical exploration of the relevance of financial policy. In particular, we examine the possibility of a systematic bias against the use of equity or long-term debt as the competitiveness of a firm's environment increases.

The testable implication of such a bias is that firms with market power will use relatively more long-term financing than those without such power.[19] Imagine two industries facing identical aggregate industry demand and identical cost conditions. Suppose the first to be perfectly competitive and the second to be a monopolized version of the same industry (all the firms merged into one). An investor could invest in the competitive industry or in the monopoly. There is a

19. A further testable implication (not tested in this work) is that, other things equal, there will be higher seller concentration in industries with a long payout period for significant amounts of fixed capital. Higher concentration is expected because it is especially likely that there are financial economies to be accrued by the firm or firms that successfully dominate the industry. For such an industry, it is possible that production-related (as contrasted with financing-related) economies of scale are insufficient in themselves, relative to market demand, to result in a natural oligopoly or monopoly. In that case, the benefits of greater competition could be realized if there were a way to circumvent the costs to investors of diversifying their portfolios into the maximum number, given market demand, of firms exhausting production-related economies.

transactions cost for dividing the investment among the firms in the competitive industry. Hence the investor decides whether investment in a single competitive firm or the monopoly is preferable.

One can imagine a decrease in demand or increase in costs (equivalent in each industry) that would result in the failure and exit of one or more firms in the competitive industry and yet leave the monopoly profitable. Thus the probability of losing one's investment because of unpredictable demand or cost shocks is greater if the investment is made in the competitive firm rather than in the monopoly. In general, market power, diversification, and size should to some extent insulate a firm from such demand and cost shocks and should thus serve to decrease the probability that an investor in the firm would lose.

A corollary of that proposition is that such advantaged firms have an incentive to use relatively more long-term financing than less-advantaged firms. Conversely, small, undiversified firms without market power find it advantageous to use relatively more short-term financing. Imagine a seasonal business for which demand and cost conditions for the season determine success or failure. Suppose that at the outset of any particular season the probability of succeeding in that season is x for the firm in the competitive industry and y for the monopoly regardless of the number of seasons for which the firm has been in business; we know that $x < y$. We assume that the cost of funds varies directly with the probability that the investors will lose those funds, and that probability in turn varies directly with the probability that the firm will fail.

Consequently, the one-season cost of funds c_1 for the competitive firm is greater than that cost m_1 for the monopoly. The competitive firm's relative seasonal cost of funds (c_1/m_1) increases as its relative probability of success (x/y) decreases. Further, the probability that a given competitive firm survives for the next n seasons is x^n. For the monopoly, that probability is y^n. Since $(x/y)^n$ is less than x/y for $0 < x < y < 1$,[20] the relative probability (x^n/y^n) that the competitive firm will survive n seasons[21] is less than the relative probability (x/y) of its survival for one year. Then with the competitive firm's cost of long-term n-season funds denoted by c_n and the monopolist's cost as m_n, it is plausible that c_n/m_n is greater than c_1/m_1. In general, the rela-

20. Since $(x/y)^{n-1} < 1$.
21. This is the relevant probability for the long-term investor if we assume that the probability of losing one's principal is directly related to the probability that the firm will fail during the period of investment.

tive disadvantage of the competitive firm increases with the term to maturity of the financial instruments employed. Further, the bias is greater when we recognize that at the outset of any season the monopolist's probability of success in that season probably increases with the number of previous seasons of operation, since successful investment in goodwill can insulate against shifts in factor prices and in the relative price of substitute products and can elevate barriers to entry by new firms.

Thus the competitive firm finds long-term financing relatively expensive and uses relatively less of it than the monopolist under the following conditions. The profit-maximizing firm combines factors of production in such a way that the ratio of the marginal productivity of one factor to that of another equals the ratio of their marginal factor costs. Assume that the marginal productivity of each factor is greater than zero and that over the relevant range marginal productivity decreases as use of a factor increases; then for a given level of output the ratio of the amount of one factor employed to the amount of another varies inversely with the ratio of their marginal factor costs.

The expectation that economies of large-scale (relative to market size) long-term financing are especially important in industries with significant amounts of long-term capital follows from the fact that long-term assets are most safely financed with long-term liabilities. Financing long-term assets with short-term liabilities exposes the firm to the risk of an unpredicted upturn in short-term rates and the consequent plight of paying more for financing than is earned from the assets. Thus in industries where fixed assets are relatively important in the production process and are quite durable, long-term funding is more efficient. In such industries the general expectation of financing economies for firms that dominate the market is reinforced by an expectation of the importance of larger economies for long-term as contrasted with short-term financing. Thus we expect that a few "large" firms may come to dominate the industry.

13.4   Tests of the Relevance of Corporate Financial Structure

Our theory leads directly to the expectation that a firm's financial structure, its choice of sources of funds as reflected in its liabilities, should in the long-run equilibrium be determined by the nature of its business as reflected in the maturity structure of its assets; characteristics, such as market power, size, and diversification, which influence the probability that the firm will survive; and other things, such as tax incentives, which are assumed constant across the firms in our sample.

The empirical evidence for the sample of 125 Canadian firms described in appendix A, except those that did not report all the information used in the regressions, supports the maturity-matching hypothesis and the importance of market power and size for an optimal financial policy. Diversification, however, does not appear to be an important determinant of financial structure in this sample.

Dependent Variable

To measure the long-run equilibrium financial or liabilities structure of the firm, this study uses the ratio of short-term to long-term liabilities.

SLL   The average ratio of short-term to long-term liabilities over the years 1961–1974.

In particular,

$$SLL = \frac{1}{m} \sum_{i=1}^{m} \left(\frac{x - y}{z - x + y} \right)_i$$

where $i = 1, \ldots, m$ denotes the first to the mth year for which data were reported for the company in question, $x =$ current liabilities including the current portion of long-term debt, $y =$ current portion of long-term debt which is included in current liabilities, and $z =$ total liabilities and shareholders' equity.

Independent Variables

To test the theory of an optimal financial structure, we used the following variables to measure the maturity structure of assets and the probability of survival.

Asset structure Corresponding to the degree of disaggregation in the dependent variable, the maturity structure of assets is measured by the ratio of noncurrent assets to current assets.

LSA   The average ratio of long-term to short-term assets over the years 1961–1974. Maturity matching implies that SLL decreases as LSA increases, other things equal.

Survival probability The firm's ability to survive should be positively correlated with its market power, size, and diversification. Hence, as these three variables increase, the theory of section 13.3 predicts that *SLL* will decrease, all else equal. To measure market power, size, and diversification, we use the measures described in section 13.2 plus the Herfindahl index of seller concentration for 1968, *HFL68*.

Table 13.6 presents the results of ordinary least-squares regressions which support the importance for financial structure of maturity matching and characteristics influencing the firm's probability of survival. An independent test of the importance of financial stucture is provided in Scott (1977) in which an examination of the determinants of the profitability of the firms in our sample found a nonlinear relationship between profits and leverage. Profitability increased with leverage up to a point, other things being equal, but beyond that, additional leverage reduced profits. Temporary disequilibria characterized by nonoptimal amounts of leverage evidently exist.

13.5 Summary

Our methodology differs considerably from that used in other recent studies of market power and risk. Empirically, the appropriate measure of risk is not assumed to be a simple notion of a beta coefficient but rather a complex, subjectively evaluated characteristic that is jointly determined by numerous other characteristics of the firms that we study. Thus our study differs from those of Bothwell and Keeler (1976) and Sullivan (1978). Theoretically this discussion of market power, risk, and valuation is a general one that posits a general hypothesis. It then differs from the theoretical work of Thomadakis (1976) which, even when corrected and properly stated,[22] imposes unrealistic assumptions in order to reach a mathematically tractable model of market power. In particular, Thomadakis ignores all the game-theoretic possibilities that are the crux of the problem of market power in the context of the conjectural interdependence of sellers.

To summarize, this chapter has explored the relation between market structure and the cost of capital. The theoretical discussion is more general than that allowed by the capital asset pricing model, a model that restricts the investor's expected utility-maximization problem to a choice over only two parameters of subjectively evaluated probability distributions of returns and then juxtaposes the resulting pref-

22. Thomadakis (1976, p. 152) does not introduce his parameter μ at the stage of his demand function for the firm. Then, illogically, a firm in a competitive market is not a price taker in terms of the demand curve it faces, yet its marginal revenue equals its price.

Table 13.6 Regression analysis of determinants of liability structure (*SLL*).

Equation	Constant	LSA	Concentration	Diversity	Size	$\overline{R}^2$	Degrees of freedom
1	.66[a] (12)	−.16(LSA)[a] (−8.2)	−.0013(C468)[c] (−1.6)	—	—	.36	114
2	.63[a] (16)	−.16(LSA)[a] (−8.2)	−.36(HFL68)[b] (−1.8)	—	—	.37	114
3	.68[a] (12)	−.16(LSA)[a] (−8.4)	−.0017(WC468)[b] (−1.9)	—	—	.37	118
4	.65[a] (16)	−.16(LSA)[a] (−8.4)	−.48(WHFL68)[b] (−2.2)	—	—	.38	118
5	.67[a] (10)	−.16(LSA)[a] (−7.9)	−.0012(C468)[c] (−1.4)	.11(DW) (.19)	−.0040(NP)[c] (−1.4)	.36	112
6	.65[a] (9.1)	−.16(LSA)[a] (−7.8)	−.0011(C468)[c] (−1.3)	.019(DC) (.59)	−.0044(NP)[c] (−1.6)	.37	112
7	.62[a] (11)	−.15(LSA)[a] (−7.7)	−.23(HFL68) (−1.1)	.0034(DC) (.11)	−.00012(TOTA)[b] (−1.7)	.37	112
8	.63[a] (11)	−.16(LSA)[a] (−7.8)	−.30(HFL68)[c] (−1.5)	.016(DC) (.50)	−.0041(NP)[c] (−1.4)	.37	112
9	.67[a] (10)	−.16(LSA)[a] (−7.8)	−.0013(WC468)[c] (−1.3)	−.013(DW) (−.25)	−.00011(TOTA)[c] (−1.6)	.37	112
10	.70[a] (10)	−.16(LSA)[a] (−7.9)	−.0017(WC468)[b] (−1.8)	.0043(DW) (.076)	−.0039(NP)[c] (−1.4)	.37	112
11	.65[a] (12)	−.16(LSA)[a] (−7.8)	−.36(WHFL68)[c] (−1.5)	−.017(DW) (−.31)	−.00010(TOTA)[c] (−1.5)	.38	112
12	.66[a] (12)	−.16(LSA)[a] (−8.0)	−.46(WHFL68)[b] (−2.0)	−.00038(DW) (−.0067)	−.0036(NP)[c] (−1.3)	.37	112

Note: The *t*-statistics are in parentheses below the coefficients. The signs and significance of the coefficients for variables other than diversification remain the same no matter which of our three measures of diversification, *DW*, *DC*, or *DH*, is used. Diversification is never significant. Levels of statistical significance (one-tailed test) are a = 1 percent, b = 5 percent, and c = 10 percent.

erences with the opportunity set that results with costless diversification. Relaxing the latter assumption implies that the own-variance of an asset's rate of return regains importance in the determination of equilibrium expected rates of return and, hence, equilibrium prices of capital assets. Further, if investors care about skewness, costly diversification implies a theoretical role (in the determination of assets' prices) for market power and diversification—even apart from their impact on own-variance. The empirical study supports the theoretically derived arguments that a firm's cost of equity capital increases as its own-variance and financial risk increase but decreases as its market power (measured by seller concentration in its primary market) and diversification increase.

Additional empirical work expands our understanding of the relation between market structure and corporate finance. In a world where the Modigliani-Miller theorem is not relevant, the maturity structure of a firm's assets implies an optimal use of long-term relative to short-term liabilities. After developing that hypothesis, we showed that optimal capital structure is related to the degree of market power possessed by the firm. If market power increases a firm's probability of survival, then longer-term funds are relatively inexpensive for the firm and their use is encouraged. The empirical investigation supports these propositions that were developed as a priori theory.

Perhaps our most important conclusion is that the cost of capital changes with market structure because the pattern of returns across the states of nature is not invariant to structural changes. The lack of such invariance is expected because sellers' recognition of their mutual interdependence as markets become more concentrated implies something other than competitive pricing in some states of nature. Our evidence suggests that investors may look favorably on oligopolistic patterns of returns. If so, we face a policy quandary, as explained in chapter 14.

PART FOUR

Conclusions for Policy

14 Industrial Policy in a Small, Open Economy

Our study has presented a model of the system of industrial organization in a small, open economy, using Canada as its clinical subject. This model, like the economic theory of markets on which it rests, is built to attain a normative goal. That goal is to identify the behavioral and structural determinants of the key aspects of market performance: efficient allocation of resources between sectors (allocative efficiency), a minimum-cost production of any given output (technical efficiency), and the optimal allocation of resources to the production and acquisition of industrial knowledge ("progressiveness"). Although this normative goal is one that our research shares with the work of many previous investigators, we have pursued it in a nontraditional way. What we have estimated is not a series of single equations to explain the interindustry variance of these performance variables but rather a system of equations in which the performance variables are the ultimate determinates. The development of this systemic approach and its applications to a small and open economy have been our chief objectives.

In this chapter we draw out the implications of the model for industrial policy.[1] A summary of the formal model is provided in table 14.1, which presents a list of the dependent and independent variables contained in each of the principal equations of our model. The table does not attempt to indicate which hypotheses were confirmed and

---

1. We appropriate the vague term *industrial policy* to describe the instruments of microeconomic policy applicable to securing better performance in allocative efficiency, technical efficiency, and progressiveness. This set of instruments may be somewhat broader than those we usually associate with antitrust or competition policy.

Table 14.1 Qualitative summary of statistical model of Canadian industrial organization.

Table	Dependent variable	Expected sign[1]	Independent variables
3.1	Seller concentration	+	Scale economies at plant level (inferred from U.S. data)
		+	Product-differentiation entry barriers[2]
		−	Market size (domestic and export components distinguished)[2]
		−	Labor intensity of U.S.-counterpart industry
		−	Regional fragmentation of industry
		+	Capital-cost entry barriers
3.4	Cost disadvantage of small plants (measured inversely)	−	Capital intensity of U.S.-counterpart industry
		−	Importance of nonproduction workers (overhead-cost component)
		−	Scale economies at plant level (inferred from U.S. data)
		+	Advertising-to-sales ratio[2]
		+	Regional fragmentation of industry
		+	Effective rate of tariff protection
3.5	Minimum efficient scale as percentage of output	+	Capital intensity in U.S.-counterpart industry
		−	Regional fragmentation of Canadian market
		?	Effective rate of tariff protection
		−	Product differentiation (in trade-sheltered conditions)[2]
		−	Market size
		+	Market share of foreign subsidiaries[2]
4.1	Imports as percentage of domestic disappearance	+	R&D-to-sales ratio, U.S.-counterpart industry
		−	Advertising-to-sales ratio[2]
		+	Scale economies at plant level (inferred from U.S. data)
		+	Seller concentration (adjusted for market size)[2]
		−	Natural-resource intensity of industry's inputs
		?	Capital intensity of U.S.-counterpart industry
		?	Skill level of labor force

		—	Effective rate of tariff protection
		—	Transport costs (proxied by regional fragmentation)
4.2	Proportion of output exported	+	Natural-resource intensity of industry's inputs
		?	Capital intensity of U.S.-counterpart industry
		?	Skill level of labor force
		+	Scale economies at plant level (inferred from U.S. data)
		—	Transport costs (proxied by regional fragmentation)
		—	Proportion of output going to final consumption
		+	Establishment size (interacted with market share of foreign subsidiaries)[2]
4.4	Market share of foreign subsidiaries	+	Advertising-to-sales ratio[2]
		+	Proportion of output exported[2]
		+	R&D-to-sales ratio, U.S.-counterpart industry
		+	Effective rate of tariff protection
		+	Skill level of labor force
		—	Unit cost of production, Canada relative to United States[2]
		—	Transportation cost per unit value
		+	Multiplant operation, U.S.-counterpart industry
6.1	Advertising-to-sales ratio	+	Consumer-good status of industry
		+	Convenience-good status of industry
		n	Seller concentration[2]
		+	Effective rate of tariff protection
		—	Imports as percentage of production[2]
		—	Exports as percentage of production[2]
		+	Price-cost margin (less advertising, R&D outlays)[2]
		+	Growth rate of shipments (higher for convenience goods)
		+	R&D-to-sales ratio (higher for convenience goods)[2]
		+	Market share of foreign subsidiaries[2]
7.1	R&D-to-sales ratio	+	Technological opportunity (R&D-to-sales ratio, U.S. counterpart industry)
		n	Seller concentration[2]
		—	Regional fragmentation of market

Table 14.1 (cont.)

Table	Dependent variable	Expected sign[1]	Independent variables
		?	Imports as percentage of production[2]
		?	Exports as percentage of production[2]
		+	Effective rate of tariff protection
		+	Profit rate[2]
		+	Growth rate of shipments
		+	Advertising-to-sales ratio[2]
		+	Diversification[2]
		+	Market share of foreign subsidiaries[2]
		+	Government-financed share of R&D
8.4	Diversification (outbound from industry)	+	Company size
		−	Base-industry profit prospects[2]
		+	Risk exposure in export markets[2]
		+	R&D-to-sales ratio, U.S.-counterpart industry
		−	Advertising-to-sales ratio[2]
		+	Instability of output, base industry
		−	Regional fragmentation of market
8.5	Diversification (inbound to industry)	+	Potential for inbound vertical integration
		n	Seller concentration[2]
		−	Capital-cost entry barriers
		−	Advertising-based entry barriers[2]
		+	R&D-to-sales ratio[2]
		−	Imports as percentage of production[2]
9.1	Profit rate	+	Seller concentration (interacted negatively with imports and positively with entry barriers)[2]

9.2	Exports as percentage of production[2]	−
	Ability to discriminate between domestic, export markets[2]	+
	R&D-to-sales ratio (less negative where foreign subsidiaries important)[2]	−
	Growth rate of shipments	+
	Capital intensity (assets-to-sales ratio)	?
	Proportion of employees under collective-bargaining agreements[2]	−
	Market conditions deterring collusion	−
9.4	Proportion of employees covered by collective-bargaining agreements	
	Barriers to entry into the industry[2]	+
	Seller concentration (interacted with foreign-subsidiaries' share)[2]	+
	Average size of establishments (employees)	+
	Regional fragmentation of market	−
	Female proportion of industry's workforce	−
9.5	Average wages, production workers	
	Excess profits per unit of labor input[2]	+
	Seller concentration[2]	?
	Proportion of employees covered by collective-bargaining agreements[2]	+
	Importance of finished-good inventories	−
	Growth rate of number of establishments	+
	Skill level of work force	+
	Geographic differences in living costs	+
	Variability of employment	+
	Female proportion of workforce	−
10.2	Overall technical efficiency	
	Scale economies at plant level (inferred from U.S. data)	−
	Cost disadvantage of suboptimal-scale plants, Canada relative to United States[2]	+
	Scale economies in selling expenses	−
	Importance of nonproduction workers (overhead-cost component)	−
	Market share of foreign subsidiaries[2]	?
	Regional fragmentation of market	+

Table 14.1 (*cont.*)

Table	Dependent variable	Expected sign[1]	Independent variables
		−	Market conditions deterring collusion
		+	Imports as percentage of domestic disappearance[2]
		+	Exports as percentage of production
10.3	Proportion of capacity in plants larger than minimum efficient scale	−	Importance of scale economies (inferred from U.S. data), interacted with effective rate of tariff protection
		+	Producer-good status of industry
		−	Market share of foreign subsidiaries (except in convenience goods)[2]
		+	Net exports divided by total trade
		+	Regional fragmentation of market
		+	Natural-resource intensity of industry's inputs
		+	Importance of nonproduction workers (overhead-cost component)

1. Hypothesized signs do not always agree with actual results. A question mark indicates that theoretical predictions raise opposite-signed possibilities. The letter *n* indicates that a nonlinear relation is predicted with mixed signs.

2. Variable is endogenous in the model or contains an endogenous component.

which were rejected. Too many nuances of interpretation would be lost if we mechanically reduced our findings to tests of significance.[2] The policy implications in this chapter are grouped around three areas: market power and the conventional instruments of competition policy; linkages to the international economy and policy instruments that strengthen or weaken them; and the large, multimarket corporation and policies addressed to it.

The system of regression equations estimated in this volume can be used in various ways to generate conclusions for industrial policy. Macroeconomic model builders customarily solve their systems in order to determine how normatively important endogenous variables respond to changes in initial conditions or in variables exogenous in the system, then simulate to determine the effects of shifts in the economy's underlying structure. Or they compute policy multipliers to show how much a normatively significant variable responds to a given pull on a lever of policy. These procedures are feasible with our model, but several considerations suggest that they are not sensible for strict application to the determinants of optimal industrial policy. For instance, few cross-sectional analyses (ours included) rest on theoretical models so tight or statistical estimates so confidence inspiring that one would freely convert the estimated coefficients into policies intended for mechanical application throughout the economy. One wants to know (for example) not how much a given reduction in seller concentration should lower allocative inefficiency but rather that lower concentration has a significant effect in that direction. If so, we know that a deconcentration policy is a potentially useful instrument; the magnitude of its effect becomes an urgent concern only when we set about applying the policy to a particular sector. Therefore what we distill from the hypotheses that were confirmed and rejected is guidance as to which general instruments of industrial policy should be kept at hand and which ones may go into storage.

14.1 Allocative Efficiency, Technical Efficiency and the Conventional Tools of Competition Policy

In this section we draw together our model's conclusions about the traditional instruments of competition policy. What forces permit allocative efficiency to be impaired in a small, open economy such as

2. A short account of our substantive findings can be found in the summaries of the preceding chapters, which can be read independently of the chapters themselves.

Canada's? What instruments are potentially effective for cutting these losses? Does any action taken to increase allocative efficiency threaten an offsetting drain in technical efficiency?[3]

Our theoretical model of the determinants of allocative efficiency in an open economy establishes three necessary conditions for the exercise of market power—high seller concentration, high entry barriers, and an absence of tight linkages to the international economy. The hypothesis of their joint necessity is largely confirmed, except that entry barriers seem to wield an additive influence on two of our three measures of allocative efficiency and to enter multiplicatively into the determination only of the remaining one. Exposure to international trade is important but not overwhelming in its effect on allocative efficiency and leaves room for the domestic determinants of market power. Competing imports act like a fringe of small domestic rivals rather than a force locking Canadian prices to those in the world market, and the procompetitive effect of participating in export markets is curbed where Canadian sellers can practice price discrimination against domestic buyers. Thus a small, open economy such as Canada's still finds scope for competition policy, and measures to reduce seller concentration, entry barriers, or firms' opportunities to collude still hold promise for securing more efficient allocations of resources.

Seller Concentration

Seller concentration is a variable that brings the dilemma of industrial policy in Canada to its sharpest focus. Would the country be better off, in general, with higher concentration to permit more efficient scales of activity, or lower concentration for better allocative efficiency? Actual concentration is certainly high enough in many Canadian manufacturing industries for its level to allow some market power to be realized and thus to make the trade-off between competition and minimizing costs a vexing one (Williamson, 1968). In the sample of matched industries used in part II of this volume, we found the largest four firms to hold a market share 47 percent higher in Canada than in the United States. Hence many Canadian industries exhibit concentration high enough for the joint exercise of market power to be a

3. We shall not be concerned here with the details of competition policy in Canada or of the important changes in policy that have recently been under consideration. For papers dealing with these matters see Prichard, Stanbury, and Wilson (1979).

real possibility. The countervailing power of the retailing sector is less than in the United States (chapter 5).

Our study also contains some evidence on how tightly actual levels of concentration conform to the dictates of minimum efficient scale. Concentration, if it were entirely dictated by scale economies in production, should not be significantly influenced by sources of entry barriers other than those related to scale economies. In chapter 3, however, we did find a significant relation between concentration and advertising, after we controlled for minimum efficient scale and market size. The statistical result may imply either that advantages of large-scale sales promotion allow some firms to expand to sizes larger than warranted by scale economies or that they allow some firms to wrest market shares just large enough to exploit scale economies in production. These alternative outcomes hold very different implications for policy toward sales-promotion outlays. Whichever outcome prevails, our findings show that advertising promotes concentration only in industries selling convenience goods to consumers. Outside this sector, our findings suggest, advertising merely reflects the existence of product differentiation, which makes viable firms that are too small to attain minimum efficient scale in production and thus reduces concentration.

If seller concentration in Canada is not completely constrained to its present level by production scale economies, it follows that concentration may be more a proximate than a primary determinant of technical efficiency. Our model of the determinants of technical efficiency therefore includes not concentration but indicators of scale economies (minimum efficient scale and the disadvantage of suboptimal-scale units) measured directly. In chapter 10 we found that the productivity of Canadian industries (relative to their U.S. counterparts) was lower where scale economies are more important. As a question of policy, whether higher concentration would promote technical efficiency therefore depends on whether raising concentration would cause the realization of greater economies of scale in plant size or in the size of the average production lot—an important question that could not be investigated with the data available for this project. Such gains depend on the particular reorganization contemplated and cannot be determined from cross-sectional evidence.

Two conclusions about scale economies and concentration, reached in chapter 3, further illustrate how complex and indirect is the relation among concentration, allocative efficiency, and technical efficiency in Canada. Where scale economies are extensive enough to make a high level of seller concentration necessary for technical efficiency, they also tend to make the industry's firms similar in size. Looking at the same influence the other way around, we found that enlargement of the market (given scale economies) typically promotes larger-size leading companies and more multiplant operations, even though it increases the total number of companies enough that seller concentration declines. Greater equality in the sizes of the leading firms, we found in chapter 9, reduces the degree of monopolistic distortion associated with a given level of seller concentration. Thus the tendency of large scale economies (or small market size) to equalize the sizes of companies makes the allocative-efficiency cost of a technically efficient industry less than if technical efficiency demanded a few dominant firms.

This analysis of concentration and its causes and effects indicates the following conclusions for policy: (1) High concentration does reduce allocative efficiency in some industries despite the openness of the Canadian economy. (2) The present levels of concentration are necessary for efficient-scale production in some Canadian industries but probably not all. (3) Where scale economies do mandate high concentration, the lossess in allocative efficiency would be greater but for the procompetitive effect of the reduced variance of firm sizes— also imposed by scale economies that are large relative to the market. (4) Our findings do not give much support to the hypothesis that higher levels of concentration by themselves would increase the efficiency of Canadian industry. Without beating the drum for divorcement and divestiture as instruments of competition policy for Canada, one can nonetheless support policies that resist increased concentration unless international competition is tightly constraining or there is compelling and specific evidence that efficiencies in scale will result in the particular industry.

"Contrived" Entry Barriers

Both the goal of technical efficiency and the intrinsic limitations of the instruments of competition policy militate against direct action to lower seller concentration. Hence there is a strong case for lowering barriers to entry instead, or for keeping firms from acting to raise them. Legislation recently proposed to amend competition policy in Canada has included provisions to authorize action against the undue enhancement of entry barriers. Many ways to enhance them have been discovered, and unfortunately only a few of the relevant patterns of behavior are captured by our model. Here we concentrate on advertising, a leading suspect among business policies that might raise entry barriers.[4] We found that in convenience-good industries advertising increases concentration (chapter 3). There is only weak evidence, however, that entry barriers due to advertising directly increase profits (chapter 9). Our study contains a good deal of evidence on advertising and retail distribution in Canada that is relevant to setting public policy toward advertising outlays.

Advertising outlays as a percentage of industry sales are on the average lower in Canada than in the United States. Also, advertising outlays are less concentrated on television and nationwide magazines and more on local media. Hence the average advertising dollar probably buys more useful information and exerts less pure persuasion power than in the United States. When we investigated how advertising in Canada is related to the concentration of Canadian manufacturing industries (chapter 6), we discovered that the positive influence of concentration on advertising levels is apparent in the moderately concentrated industries. This pattern is consistent with the hypothesis that incomplete oligopolistic understandings tend to bias rivalry toward nonprice forms. If the heaviest advertising were found in the most concentrated industries, one would suspect more strongly that it was intended to deter entry. Nonetheless, elevation of entry barriers may be the substantial if incidental result of heavy advertising in some concentrated industries. Our analysis of what determines advertising-to-sales ratios in Canadian industries relative to their U.S. counterparts yielded a conclusion that is disquieting in this regard. This Canadian-U.S. difference not only increases with the excess of seller concentration in Canada over its level in the U.S. counterpart industry but increases more than proportionally. This result could arise because the nationwide sales-promotion media used by heavy advertisers are less efficient in Canada than in the United States (due to Canada's small, far-flung, and linguistically divided population) or because highly concentrated Canadian industries do more building of advertising-based entry barriers than their counterparts in highly

4. This is no place to replay the prolonged debate over the economic efficiency of advertising, but we shall state our position briefly. A problem of market failure may arise because advertisers can exploit "impacted information" and transactions costs faced by consumers seeking information on the qualities of competing brands (Porter, 1976a). Although advertising can be a second-best signal of quality, even in this context, it need not be an efficient one (Schmalensee, 1978). The impacted-information failure is compounded into an entry barrier if scale effects in the "efficient" use of advertising media sufficiently inflate the initial investment cost of an entrant who would establish his goodwill against the goodwill assets already cultivated by established sellers.

concentrated U.S. industries. Taking together all our evidence on the causes and effects of advertising, we find that we cannot rule out the possibility that the advertising policies of leading firms serve as a significant entry barrier in some Canadian industries; these barriers could promote the attainment of scale economies but need not do so.

Optimal Competition Policy in an Open Economy

These empirical conclusions about the instruments of competition policy in Canada can be translated into actual policy choices only with reference to the theory of competition policy in an open economy. Although the evidence we uncovered on the empirical extent of Canada's openness has not yet been summarized, for the present we need only assume that many industries face substantial important competition or enjoy substantial export opportunities or both. The following points are not new, but they have gained little familiarity against the weighty closed-economy tradition of competition policy.

To deal first with the obvious, the dilemma of optimizing between low-cost production and competitive market structures may be resolved when the industry is exposed either to import competition or to opportunities in the export market. That is, any gains in technical efficiency from shrinking the number of competitors or making other anticompetitive changes in market structure incur no offsetting cost in allocative efficiency so long as they do not lower the intensity of the industry's exposure to trade. Unfortunately, these conditions are difficult to check in actual markets, because one must know where the competitive shadow price lies relative to the delivered price of imports and the world-market f.o.b. price of exportables. Competition policy in the open economy is like tariff policy—what is optimal for a single nation need not be optimal for the world as a whole.[5] Consider a concentrated export industry that sells part of its output on the home market. Assume that the industry cannot price-discriminate between domestic and foreign markets and that the demand it faces in export markets is less than perfectly elastic. The nation's welfare is not maximized by making this industry function in purely competitive fashion; some amount of monopoly is in the national interest. This is because the exporting nation is enriched by monopoly profits captured from foreign markets and does not suffer the deadweight loss that occurs when foreigners curtail their consumption. This gain should be optimally traded off, however, against the deadweight loss that this

5. This problem is discussed in Auquier and Caves (1979).

same monopolistic behavior causes in the domestic market. In general, pure competition does not maximize national welfare under the conditions stated. If the country could impose a tax on its exports while making the industry behave competitively, it would achieve a first-best outcome.

The theoretical problem considered here is of course the same as that addressed by the theory of optimal tariffs, which shows that the tariff that maximizes national welfare may be positive while the one that maximizes global welfare is (under familiar assumptions) zero. The analysis can be extended symmetrically to industries in their capacity as buyers, indicating the desirability from a national point of view of some monopsony power if an import tariff for some reason cannot be used to maximize gains from trade. It also has extensive implications—most of them pessimistic—about the possibility of reaching international agreement on the coordination of competition policy across national boundaries. In short, it is one thing to establish the policies that can promote effective competition in a small, open economy; it is another to show that such competition maximizes national welfare.

14.2 International Influences and Market Performance

Our model gives extensive attention to international influences on the structure and performance of Canadian industries—international trade, the multinational company, and the international flow of proprietary knowledge. All these are subject to influence by industrial policy. An effect of tariffs often recognized in Canada is to allow protected domestic producers to elevate prices. But many other national policies can or do promote or discourage international trade, attract or repel the multinational company, and foster or discourage the acquisition abroad of productive knowledge—all with effects on market performance. Here we collect our conclusions about the effects of international linkages on performance and draw their implications for policy.

Import Competition and Export Exposure

Import competition mitigates market power. Tariffs reduce imports and thus may increase market power, depending on the industry's cost conditions (see the theoretical analysis of chapter 1). In principle, tariffs can affect competition and allocative efficiency in at least three ways. An elevated tariff, besides simply lowering the level of competing imports, may curb competition directly by supplying a higher focal point on which oligopolistic domestic sellers can collude. But a higher tariff can also have a third, procompetitive effect of inducing foreign producers to enter the Canadian market by means of subsidiaries rather than export shipments. These theoretical possibilities are complex, and our statistical findings are correspondingly intricate.

Import competition, we found, improves the allocative efficiency of Canadian industries in the same way that an enlarged fringe of domestic competitors would.[6] After we control for their shrinkage of imports, tariffs seem to have no additional effect on allocative efficiency, despite Hazeldine's (1978) finding that concentrated industries price up to the tariff more fully than do competitive industries. This may be because tariffs were found in our model to wield a pervasive and malign influence on technical efficiency, so that much of the potential monopoly rents they create are probably squandered in excessive input costs.[7] In chapter 3 we concluded that tariffs increase the prevalence of small plants, especially in consumer-good industries and improve the viability of units smaller than minimum efficient scale. In chapter 10 we confirmed that these tariff-sustained fringes lower the proportion of Canadian output that emanates from plants that are large enough to attain minimum efficient scale as estimated in the U.S. market. The lower the efficient-scale proportion, the larger the minimum efficient scale in the United States. Thus tariffs make Canadian sellers less concentrated than they would otherwise be, but they induce no competitive reduction in prices to consumers and they have a large cost in technical efficiency (because more suboptimal-scale units can prosper, although perhaps in other ways as well).

Because in general equilibrium import restrictions reduce the economy's exports as well as its imports, and because public policies are occasionally used to restrict exports of particular goods, it is worth noting that exports wield various favorable effects on industrial performance. Exposure to export markets increases the allocative efficiency of Canadian markets except where sellers are able to segregate the domestic market and charge a higher price there (chapter 9). We did not find a significant effect of export exposure on our overall

6. Theoretically, the causation can also run from domestic competition to imports, because prices elevated by oligopolistic sellers are likely to induce more imports. We did not find any statistical effect of seller concentration on imports, however, after allowing for the fact that imports, by shrinking the market available to domestic sellers, tend to raise the concentration of domestic sellers.

7. As Bloch (1974) concluded from a simpler analysis.

measure of technical efficiency, but we detected a favorable effect on the scales of Canadian plants relative to minimum efficient scale in the United States.

The Multinational Company

The structure and performance of Canadian industries is pervasively influenced by multinational companies, yet discussions of competition policy in Canada have been notable for their lack of clear thinking about the effect of the multinational presence on market performance. Our analysis of the determinants of seller concentration (chapter 3) showed that multinationals are a significant source of market entrants, because concentration in Canadian industries is lower relative to their U.S. counterparts in those industries where foreign subsidiaries claim a larger share of the market. Concentration levels in industries with large populations of foreign subsidiaries are also more similar to concentration levels in their U.S. counterparts, which supports the miniature-replica hypothesis the multinationals are able to claim market shares in Canada similar to those that they attain in the larger U.S. market.

These effects of multinationals on concentration do not by themselves necessarily indicate the effects of multinationals on overall market performance, because foreign investment may modify allocative and technical efficiency in diverse ways. The measured profits of foreign subsidiaries appear to contain large random components that make any conclusion about their relation to allocative efficiency uncertain. With this qualification noted, we can report that we do not find foreign subsidiaries' profits significantly related to seller concentration in Canadian markets, although they are related to the market's rate of growth and to advertising-based entry barriers (which may result in significant part from the multinationals' marketing skills). We conclude that foreign subsidiaries may raise entry barriers to Canadian markets. We find some evidence of another anticompetitive effect often blamed on multinationals in Canada—that they sometimes transplant to the Canadian market collusive arrangements and patterns of oligopolistic behavior devised in other countries. We found (chapter 4) the share that foreign subsidiaries hold in the Canadian market to be more closely related to seller concentration in the United States than in Canada. The relation is a quadratic one, supporting Knickerbocker's (1973) hypothesis that foreign investment may function as one form of imitative nonprice rivalry in partially collusive oligopolies. Whether the subsidiaries thus transplanted make Canadian markets more or less competitive than otherwise cannot be deduced, but it certainly follows that the character of competition in Canada may be altered.

The effects of foreign subsidiaries on technical efficiency are rather complex, if only because the multinational's presence itself is explained by a number of structural and policy variables (chapter 4). In chapter 10 we reached two seemingly contradictory conclusions about the effect of multinational companies on technical efficiency: our overall measure of technical efficiency shows a significant positive relation to the proportion of sales accounted for by foreign-controlled companies, but the proportion of output coming from efficient-scale plants in Canada is negatively related to the multinational presence[8] (except in consumers' convenience-good industries[9]). These findings can be shown to be consistent when we recognize that overall technical efficiency includes not only the attainment of efficient scale but other dimensions as well. One point of reconciliation is that multinational companies transfer proprietary intangible assets via their subsidiaries, whose value added hence includes rents to these assets. This flow of rents is indicated by our finding (chapter 4) that Canadian-controlled companies achieve lower levels of productivity relative to their multinational competitors in industries that are research intensive in the United States. A second consideration is that multinationals may secure some inputs, notably capital, more cheaply than domestic companies. We found in exploratory research that the operating scales of domestic companies are smaller relative to the foreign subsidiaries in industries where capital-cost entry barriers are important. A third consideration is that multinationals may possess transferable advantages in managerial techniques and capabilities that in some industries simply allow them to squeeze more market value out of a given bundle of inputs than can their average domestic competitor; this advantage is suggested by some traits of industries in which multinationals do not flourish—regional industries and those in which small-scale production units are efficient.

8. In chapter 4 we found a strong positive relation between foreign-controlled companies' market share and the average size of the larger establishments in Canada, but this relation disappears when U.S. plant sizes are taken into account. This pattern probably implies no more than that multinationals tend to be found in industries with larger-than-average plant sizes.

9. In these industries the multinationals are particularly favored by the opportunity to exploit their abilities at large-scale sales promotion (see chapter 6), and this achievement raises their scales of production just as it builds product-differentiation barriers to entry.

We now attempt to bring these findings on multinational companies to bear on the problem of setting industrial policy for Canada. We do not detect any case in this evidence for a general restriction of their Canadian activities. The small-scale subsidiary operations induced by tariffs cause losses in technical efficiency, but the problem lies more in the tariff than in the multinationals' response to it. To put it another way, for Canada to approach this problem by attempting to "rational-ize" the structure of foreign subsidiaries would be a second-best solu-tion. Likewise, there is no omnibus case for adopting differential statutory standards of competition policy so as to apply a tougher standard to subsidiaries. True, they tend to populate industries with high seller concentration and have opportunities to contrive entry barriers. The authorities who enforce competition policy aiming to increase allocative efficiency will often clash with these firms. But a bias in the incidence of enforcement is not the same thing as a dual standard of performance.

The dual-standard issue cannot be put aside casually, however. Suppose that only limited resources are available to enforce competi-tion policy in Canada, so that not every putative market failure can be repaired. Under some conditions a given market failure (measured by the conventional tools of partial-equilibrium welfare analysis) will be more costly if the culprits are foreign subsidiaries. Monopolization by a domestically controlled enterprise costs Canadians a triangle of deadweight loss while redistributing income from consumers to the Canadian recipients of the monopoly's rents. The foreign-subsidiary monopolist, however, snatches away from Canadian hands that part of the rents not intercepted by the Canadian government in the form of corporate income tax payments. The use of scarce resources to avert allocative-efficiency losses thus has higher national priority when the losses are caused by multinationals than when they are due to domestic enterprises. That presumption is reversed, however, when the trans-gression brings a loss of technical efficiency. When a domestic firm is responsible, the whole of the welfare loss comes out of Canadian pockets; when a foreign subsidiary is responsible for the technical in-efficiency, part of the loss is borne by foreign shareholders (but with their loss shared by the Canadian government, which thereby collects less corporate income tax from the inefficient firm or firms).[10]

10. The choice between enforcing competition policy against foreign and domestic companies proves artificial whenever market power is shared by a group of tight-knit oligopolists containing members of both groups. The market power is a collective private good (and public bad) for the group, and it is not generally possible to deprive some members but not others.

Technology Transfer and Research Policy

Data are lacking on technology imports to Canada, and so we could not include this variable in our model. Nonetheless, it belongs among the important international influences on industrial organization and performance. Overall, a small country efficiently acquires most of its technology abroad, concentrating its own R&D resources on adaptation of imported technology to local conditions and perhaps creating a few technologies that it is unusually well suited to market worldwide. In individual industries access to foreign technologies should reduce the fixed costs of carrying on technology-intensive activities and should depress barriers to entry.[11] There is no case for public policy to interfere with this influx of technology from abroad, and there may be some reasons for public action to offset imperfections in the international market for proprietary technology.[12] The multinational company is a significant agent for transferring technology to Canada, although exploiting the rents on proprietary technology does not seem to be one of the strongest inducements to foreign investment in Canada (chapter 4). This fact in itself supplies no clear implications for Canadian policy. The multinational company probably transfers technology more cheaply than it can be moved through arm's-length transactions, and a portion of the resulting rents should accrue to Canadians.[13] On the other hand, the multinational is also probably more efficient at extracting the rents from the technology in its possession, so that Canadians may be relieved of a larger proportion of the net consumers' surplus due to an imported technology than if it is bought at arm's length and utilized by a Canadian company.

Commercial research undertaken in Canada is usually a socially productive activity. However, product-oriented R&D can take on a purely defensive role of supporting nonprice competition in the inter-

11. Orr (1974) found the rate of domestic R&D spending to be a barrier to entry into Canadian manufacturing industries.

12. We assume that arm's-length transfers of technology to Canada take place in a largely competitive international market for proprietary technology, or at least that Canada has no significant monopsony power in that market. Neither assumption necessarily holds, and there is some evidence that the Japanese government has acted successfully to beat down the price of technology imports (Peck, 1976).

13. Canadians gain if royalties or profits due to the technology transfer are intercepted by the Canadian tax collector. In addition, theoretical research shows that they may gain from price reductions that follow from cost savings due to the transferred technology (depending on the structure of the market and the size of the cost reduction).

national market. A significant proportion of such outlays in Canada may play this purely defensive role, according to our finding that Canadian R&D spending rates have a negative influence on the profits of Canadian industries (chapter 9). This conclusion supports the implication of the preceding paragraph—hard though it may be for Canadians to swallow—that nearly the only sort of R&D efficiently carried on in Canada is that aimed at adapting foreign technology to Canadian uses. Subsidy programs designed to stimulate original innovation have a poor chance of success. Yet there is substantial indication, as Daly and Globerman (1976) show, that national science policy in Canada has emphasized new innovation and originality in R&D.[14]

Other conclusions that we reach about the determinants of R&D spending in Canada support at least tentative suggestions for areas in which public support of R&D is likely to have the greatest value. Our statistical evidence (chapter 7) strongly supports the hypothesis that more R&D is undertaken by the more diversified industries.[15] One virtue of diversification (it may have severe drawbacks, as well) lies in minimizing the information costs and risks associated with steering an innovation into the markets where it will have value. The productivity of incremental R&D outlays may be greater if placed in the hands of diversified firms. Although foreign subsidiaries do more research than domestic-controlled companies (Safarian, 1969, p. 52), we found that rates of R&D spending in Canadian industries relative to their U.S. counterparts are negatively related to foreign investment in Canada (chapter 7). This evidence confirms that the foreign subsidiary is an accomplished practitioner of R&D, but primarily for the adaptation of technology imported from abroad.

We also investigated some familiar hypotheses about the effect on R&D spending of the sizes of firms and markets and levels of seller concentration. We did find a positive relation between seller concentration and Canadian R&D spending (after controlling for tech-

14. In Canada as elsewhere, the case for public support of scientific research and industrial development often makes the implicit assumption that it is desirable as a cultural achievement and thus as a collective consumption good rather than a calculated investment for economic gain. As Johnson (1972) pointed out, there is nothing intrinsically wrong with this form of consumption, but its claim on society's resources must be weighed against those of other consumption activities (public and private).

15. This finding is supported by our analysis of corporate strategies (chapter 12). Even companies employing an unrelated-product strategy seem typically to be based in science-related industries.

nological opportunity), and this relation persisted weakly when the test was performed on the ratio of Canadian to U.S. values of both variables. We found market size to have a positive but diminishing influence on Canada's rate of R&D spending, but firm size seems to have no influence. We are loath to draw policy conclusions from the relation between concentration and R&D because of the defensive and adaptive nature of much research that is done in Canada.

14.3 Industrial Policy and the Large Corporation

We left to the final section of this chapter the conclusions that we draw about large corporations as actors in Canadian markets. A strong current of criticism of large companies' behavior has been flowing in the stream of Canadian public policy, and it led to the creation of the Royal Commission on Corporate Concentration. In its report (1978), however, the commission's view of large corporations achieved millpond tranquility. The commission found, among other things, that overall concentration among Canada's largest companies has not been increasing, and our evidence for recent years supports this view (chapter 11). The commissioners even leaned against pending measures to strengthen competition policy that would seem desirable on the basis of this study's evidence. But the critical current continues to flow in Canada—often confusing problems of corporate size per se with problems of seller concentration, multinational enterprise, and so forth. (Canadians, of course, have no monopoly on this confusion.) In this section we consider our evidence on those aspects of industrial policy distinctively related to corporate size. These are chiefly the causes and effects to diversification, and the effect of size on the borrower's treatment by the capital markets.

Diversification

Among those ideologically attracted to competition policy, no hypothesis carries more emotive appeal than the one that the large diversified corporation can dig into its "deep pocket" or "long purse" to support temporary losses in particular markets and can thereby intimidate or drive out competitors and discourage entrants. Tests of the effect of the overall size and diversification of a market's leading firms on its performance are notoriously tricky to formulate. This is because an industry's or a company's profits can be either the cause or the effect of its diversification, and even if we convince ourselves that diversification has a positive causal influence on profits, we remain unsure whether diversification increases market power or improves the utilization of resources.

Conscious of these pitfalls, we directed our research effort more toward the causes of diversification than its consequences, in the hope that a convincing account of companies' reasons for diversifying would go some distance toward answering the ultimate normative question of diversification effects on performance. Our conclusions are doomed to incompleteness, however; even if one found that companies diversify only for the most praiseworthy reasons, one could not rule out the possibility that they also find themselves the surprised but pleased holders of an asset generating market power.

Our investigations in chapters 8 and 11 started by addressing the simple question, How closely is diversification related to the size of companies in the Canadian economy?[16] Within a given industry, the proportion of a company's activity that is diversified increases with its size up to a point but then becomes independent of size. However, if we measure diversification by the number of activities that the company carries on, it increases throughout the observed range of companies' sizes. The sizes of large Canadian companies were decomposed into components due to their shares of the markets in which they compete, the sizes of those markets, and the extent of their diversification (chapter 11). Each dimension contributes something to explaining differences in the sizes of the largest companies. However, the contribution of diversification is rather small. It is difficult from this evidence to see diversification as the predominant basis for corporate bigness in Canada.[17]

A popular view holds that the Canadian economy suffers from excessive diversification, especially in the form of short production runs, and that this problem of diversification compounds the costs of smallness. As we noted in chapter 8, the hypothesis as stated is theoretically defective, because it neglects the fact that diversification is a way of mitigating the tendency of small scales in individual outputs to impose diseconomies of small overall scale on the plants in which they are

16. The measures of diversification available to us do not permit vertical integration to be distinguished, so the following empirical conclusions all pertain to both vertical integration and true diversification.

17. Economic theory leads us to expect that foreign subsidiaries will be more diversified than domestic competitors of similar size. This relation does appear for Canadian companies overall (Caves, 1975), but we found only modest support for this hypothesis when comparisons were made within industrial groups (rather than across the whole manufacturing sector).

produced and the firms that produce them. Some of our empirical evidence mirrors the working of this process of trading small size against diversification. For instance, leading Canadian companies do not on the average exhibit much less multiplant development within their principal industries than do U.S. companies, but they have many fewer plants engaged in diversified activities—partly because more of the diversified activities are loaded onto plants chiefly turning out their principal products (chapter 8). The problem for economic policy is whether this adjustment is entirely a natural response to the economy's small size or whether market imperfections and inappropriate policies push companies into overly diversified patterns of activity.

We found evidence to support a number of hypotheses about the determinants of diversification (chapters 8, 12). Research activity tends to promote diversification. Heavy advertising apparently does not; the goodwill assets created by sales promotion are not readily grafted to remote branches of the standard industrial classification tree. Chapter 8 yielded only weak support for the hypothesis that diversification is promoted by seller concentration interacting with slow growth—a combination that should induce firms to expand elsewhere rather than reinvest heavily and fight for market share in their base activity. In our analysis of the diversification strategies of large companies (chapter 12), we found that undiversified firms tend strongly to be found in secure market environments—high concentration, product differentiation, freedom from international competition. Risks in the base industry encourage diversification, but concentration may reduce risk, and so the relation between concentration and diversification is not a strong one unless risk is controlled. There is considerable evidence to support Chandler's (1962) view that firms diversify if and when they have consolidated their position in their base industry and hold assets that are underutilized of intangible and thus usable in other sectors at low opportunity cost. Firms do not diversify just because they are large absolutely and engaged in capital-intensive activities—a finding significant for our analysis of capital markets.

All in all, these conclusions suggest that much diversification takes place for reasons that are probably consistent with a resulting improvement in resource utilization. We found that diversification increases the profitability of companies when their market-structure environment signals that resources can be used more productively this way and that firms that have chosen the right amount of diversification (as indicated by the structures of their base industries) are more profitable than those that have diversified either too much or too little. Yet we found no positive and significant influence of diversification on profits measured at the industry level,[18] which suggests that diversification makes no systematic contribution to market power. We also confirmed (chapter 8) one favorable effect of the diversifying company on market performance. The amount of diversification inbound to an industry shows a strong nonlinear relation to its level of seller concentration, rising linearly up to fairly high values of concentration and then plunging abruptly. This result indicates to us that going firms diversify into other industries that have moderate entry barriers; low-barrier industries are unattractive because anyone can enter and high-barrier industries are inaccessible. The amount of entry into industries with medium entry barriers is thus greater when going firms can diversify than if they are prohibited.

These generally sanguine conclusions about the diversifying corporation need not be applied mechanically to all diversifying companies or to those that diversify through acquisition rather than by starting new subsidiaries. If the buyer substantially changes the policies and assets of the acquired company, the effect on resource allocation in the long run need be no different from those of starting the new venture from scratch. However, in the short run new ventures should have more procompetitive effects than acquisitions. And diversification seems more likely to yield gains in cost reduction when a new subsidiary is started than when a company is bought and retained as an independent division. If the public should impose a preference for an economy containing smaller business units, our evidence marks as the first candidates for disassembly the diversified conglomerates that were built by buying up going concerns. However, even their disassembly is costless only if the conglomerate's services of spreading risks and reallocating capital between industries can be performed equally well by other agents.

Capital Markets

An underexplored question in industrial organization is the relation between the supply price of capital to the firm and its organizational structure and the traits of its product market. The capital asset pricing model, which has guided most recent research into capital-market equilibrium, asserts that no characteristics of the borrower matter ex-

18. This result was not reported in chapter 9 because we did not believe that diversification theoretically belongs in an equation seeking to explain industries' allocative efficiency. If diversification measures are added to the regression equations shown in tables 9.1 and 9.2, their regression coefficients are always insignificant and usually negative.

cept the mean expected return on its real investment and the covariance of its expected returns with the general movement of the economy. The model thus provides no explicit role for characteristics of the company or its industry. We show theoretically (chapter 13) that injecting the simple assumption of transactions costs for holders of financial portfolios allows us to deduce connections between borrowers' structural characteristics and their cost of capital. The variance of the firm's own profit stream is theoretically elevated in importance relative to its covariance as a determinant of capital costs, and we found statistically that a firm's diversification does lower its supply price of equity capital. The same shift of assumptions implies that seller concentration becomes valuable to investors (it truncates the downhill side of the distribution of expected returns), and our regression analysis reveals a weakly significant negative relation of concentration to the supply price of equity capital. Similar reasoning led us to predict that the capital markets would force the firm toward reliance on more costly short-term debt if it operates in a risky environment. The firm that is larger in total size and operates in a less competitive environment, we found, uses significantly more long-term debt (after controlling for the longevity of its assets). Smaller firms in more competitive markets make do with short-term debt. With controls imposed for the firm's size and for concentration in its markets, its diversification has no additional effect on its liability structure.[19]

These findings all suggest to us the unhappy conclusion that a conflict exists between the goals of minimizing the price paid for bearing the economy's risks, on the one hand, and promoting competitive markets and satisfying a social preference for limiting the size of firms, on the other. Our inquiry has covered the Canadian manufacturing sector and not its financial sector, so we cannot rule out the possibility that these relations might somehow result, not from the behavior of a competitive but risk-averse capital market, but from noncompetitive structures or institutional imperfections in the capital market. We cannot rule out the possible case for public action to create financial-market instruments that pool the default risks of small companies.

19. We can mention one independent conclusion reached about companies' financial structures and market performance. There is a strong quadratic relation between profit rates on equity capital and financial leverage (chapter 12). This pattern supports the conclusion of several U.S. studies that firms with market power often forego profits for the quiet life by underutilizing the profit-increasing possibilities of higher leverage (Sullivan, 1974).

APPENDIXES

REFERENCES

INDEX

Data Base: Definitions and Sources

Most of the statistical analyses undertaken in this project utilize data included in a single consolidated data base containing observations on aspects of the structure, conduct, and performance of 123 Canadian manufacturing industries and on 125 large companies operating principally in the manufacturing sector. The variables in the company data base include income-statement and balance-sheet data for the firms themselves and also observations on the industries in which they operate. We classified these companies to their principal industries and recorded for each enterprise all data for its principal industry. We also secured information on the distribution of each enterprise's output among manufacturing industries and used this information to construct weighted-average observations on the characteristics of industries in which the firms operate. The data base was prepared for Canada's Royal Commission on Corporate Concentration. It is available to other users in machine-readable form.[1] In this appendix we describe the principal features of the data base and provide definitions and sources for those variables contained in it that were used in this study.

Selection of Samples

As is often the case with research in industrial organization, the underlying populations and the data available on them precluded any random sampling. Our populations are thus the result of eliminating unsatisfactory entities from the observable population rather than of sampling from the satisfactory ones.

1. Copies of the tape (plus an accompanying technical paper) are available for purchase by writing to Data Base-RCCC, Supply and Services Canada, Printing and Publishing, Hull, Quebec K1A OS9, Canada.

Sample of Industries

The classification of industries used in our analysis is the Canadian standard industrial classification (SIC) prior to its revision in 1970. It is unfortunate that data were available under the new classification for too brief a period to permit its use, because it makes a number of desirable rearrangements and disaggregations of categories from the previous classification, and it is easier to match to the U.S. SIC. The pre-1970 classification was in use between 1960 and 1970 with few changes. We selected 123 of its 140 three-digit categories, deleting only those covering residual groups of products not included elsewhere.

A subsample of these industries was matched to industries in the U.S. standard industrial classification (the version that preceded the revision of 1972). Our matching process closely followed that undertaken by the Department of Industry, Trade, and Commerce in connection with their series of volumes *Comparative Tables of Principal Statistics and Ratios for Selected Manufacturing Industries, Canada and United States.* We excluded a few industries matched by the department through the aggregation of industries in both the U.S. and Canadian classifications, because the resulting aggregate seemed too heterogeneous. For some of the matched industries a single category in the Canadian SIC corresponded to a four-digit industry in the U.S. SIC. More often it was necessary to aggregate data for two or more U.S. four-digit industries to match the Canadian industry. Of our 123 Canadian industries, a maximum of 84 are matched to U.S. data.

The Canadian and U.S. classifications also had to be matched for another purpose—to permit aggregation to the industry level of data on the output diversity of Canadian companies secured from Dun and Bradstreet records. The Dun and Bradstreet data employ the current (post-1972) U.S. SIC; it was matched to the pre-1960 Canadian SIC using information provided by the Department of Industry, Trade, and Commerce in connection with the 1972 edition of *Comparative Tables* and also the Canadian standard industrial classification manuals. Because of difficulties in matching classifications and also because of gaps in the underlying data on diversity, a maximum of 80 Canadian industries could be matched. In addition, for five pairs of Canadian industries these data had to be aggregated to an amalgam of two Canadian SIC categories and the common value of each variable assigned to both.

Table A.1 lists the 123 industries included in our data base and presents some of the data on matching and aggregation.

Table A.1 Industries included in data base, with correspondence to counterpart industries in United States and to aggregated data on companies' output diversity.

Standard industrial classification number	Industry	Matched to U.S. counterpart industry?	Matched to source of data on diversification?
101	Slaughtering and meat processors	yes	no
103	Poultry processors	yes	yes
105	Dairy factories	yes	yes
111	Fish products industry	yes	yes
112	Fruit and vegetable canners and preservers	no	no
123	Feed manufacturers	yes	yes
124	Flour mills	no	no
125	Breakfast cereal manufacturers	no	no
128	Biscuit manufacturers	yes	yes
129	Bakeries	yes	yes
131	Confectionery manufacturers	yes	yes
133	Sugar refineries	yes	yes
135	Vegetable oil mills	yes	yes
141	Soft drink manufacturers	yes	yes
143	Distilleries	yes	yes
145	Breweries	yes	yes
147	Wineries	yes	yes
151	Leaf tobacco processing	yes	no
153	Tobacco products manufacturers	yes	yes
161	Rubber footwear manufacturers	yes	yes
163	Rubber tire and tube manufacturers	yes	yes
172	Leather tanneries	yes	yes
174	Shoe factories	no	no
175	Leather glove factories	yes	yes
183	Cotton yarn and cloth mills	no	no
193	Wool yarn mills	yes	yes
197	Wool cloth mills	yes	yes
201	Synthetic textile mills	no	no
211	Fiber preparing mills	no	no
212	Thread mills	yes	yes
213	Cordage and twine industry	no	no
214	Narrow fabric mills	yes	yes
215	Pressed and punched felt mills	no	yes
216	Carpet, mat, and rug industry	yes	yes
218	Textile dyeing and finishing plants	yes	yes
219	Linoleum and coated fabrics industry	no	no
221	Canvas products industry	yes	yes
223	Cotton and jute bag industry	yes	no
231	Hosiery mills	yes	yes

Table A.1 *(cont.)*

Standard industrial classification number	Industry	Matched to U.S. counterpart industry?	Matched to source of data on diversification?
243	Men's clothing industry	no	no
244	Women's clothing factories and contractors	no	no
245	Children's clothing factories	yes	yes
246	Fur goods industry	yes	no
247	Hat and cap industry	yes	yes
248	Foundation garment industry	yes	yes
251	Shingle mills, saw mills, and planing mills	yes	yes
252	Veneer and plywood mills	yes	yes
254	Hardwood flooring; sash, door and other millwork plants	no	no
256	Wooden box factories	no	no
258	Coffin and casket industry	yes	yes
261	Household furniture industry	yes	no
264	Office furniture industry	yes	yes
266	Miscellaneous furniture industries	no	no
268	Electric lamp and shade industry	no	no
271	Pulp and paper mills	yes	yes
272	Asphalt roofing manufacturers	no	no
273	Manufacturers of carbons, boxes, paper, and plastic bags	no	no
274	Miscellaneous paper converters	no	no
286	Commercial printing	no	no
287	Plate making, typesetting, and trade bindery plants	no	no
288	Publishing only	yes	yes
289	Publishing and printing	yes	yes
291	Iron and steel mills	yes	yes
292	Steel pipe and tube mills	yes	yes
294	Iron foundries	yes	yes
295	Smelting and refining	yes	yes
296	Aluminium rolling, casting, and extruding	yes	yes
297	Copper and alloy rolling, casting, and extruding	yes	yes
298	Metal rolling, casting, and extruding, not elsewhere classified	no	no
301	Boiler and plate works	yes	yes
302	Fabricated structural metal industry	yes	yes
303	Ornamental and architectural metal industry	yes	yes

Table A.1 *(cont.)*

Standard industrial classification number	Industry	Matched to U.S. counterpart industry?	Matched to source of data on diversification?
304	Metal stamping, pressing, and coating industry	no	no
305	Wire and wire products manufacturers	yes	yes
306	Hardware, tool, and cutlery manufacturers	yes	yes
307	Heating equipment manufacturers	no	no
308	Machine shops	no	no
311	Agricultural implements industry	yes	yes
315	Miscellaneous machinery and equipment manufacturers	no	no
316	Commercial refrigeration and air conditioning equipment manufacturers	no	no
318	Office and store machinery manufacturers	yes	yes
321	Aircraft and parts manufacturers	no	no
323	Motor vehicle manufacturers	yes	yes
324	Truck body and trailer manufacturers	yes	yes
325	Motor vehicle parts and accessories manufacturers	yes	yes
326	Railroad rolling stock industry	yes	yes
327	Shipbuilding and repair	yes	yes
328	Boat building and repair	yes	yes
331	Manufacturers of small electrical appliances	yes	yes
332	Manufacturers of major electrical appliances	yes	yes
334	Manufacturers of household radio and television receivers	yes	yes
335	Communications equipment manufacturers	no	no
336	Manufacturers of electrical industrial equipment	yes	yes
337	Battery manufacturers	yes	yes
338	Electric wire and cable	no	yes
341	Cement manufacturers	yes	yes
343	Lime manufacturers	yes	no
345	Gypsum products manufacturers	yes	yes
347	Concrete products manufacturers	yes	yes
348	Ready-mix concrete manufacturers	yes	yes
351	Clay products manufacturers	no	no
352	Refractories manufacturers	yes	yes

Table A.1 *(cont.)*

Standard industrial classification number	Industry	Matched to U.S. counter- part industry?	Matched to source of data on diversification?
353	Stone products manufacturers	yes	yes
354	Mineral wool manufacturers	no	no
355	Asbestos products manufacturers	no	no
356	Glass and glass products manufacturers	no	no
357	Abrasives manufacturers	yes	yes
365	Petroleum refineries	yes	yes
371	Explosives and ammunition manufacturers	no	no
372	Manufacturers of mixed fertilizers	no	no
373	Manufacturers of plastics and synthetic resins	yes	yes
374	Manufacturers of pharmaceuticals and medicines	yes	yes
375	Paint and varnish manufacturers	yes	yes
376	Manufacturers of soap and cleaning compounds	no	no
377	Manufacturers of toilet preparations	yes	yes
378	Manufacturers of industrial chemicals	no	no
381	Scientific and professional equipment manufacturers	yes	yes
382	Jewelry and silverware manufacturers	yes	yes
383	Broom, brush, and mop industry	yes	yes
384	Venetian blind manufacturers	no	no
393	Sporting goods and toy industry	yes	yes
395	Fur dressing and dyeing industry	no	no
397	Signs and display industry	yes	yes

Sample of Companies

Our principal source of data on large companies was a tape provided by the Financial Research Institute (FRI) containing annual income-statement and balance-sheet data on 337 comapnies for the years 1961–1974 (in some cases, a shorter period). The FRI tape includes many companies not based in manufacturing industries or not engaged primarily in manufacturing. Several sources of information were available for determining which companies were engaged primarily in manufacturing and to which primary manufacturing industry they should be classified. We secured the industrial classifications assigned to these companies by Statistics Canada and by Dun and Bradstreet.

These often agree, though not always, and their classification of firms as holding companies provides no useful information about their primary industries. We therefore utilized a third source as well—a tape secured from Dun and Bradstreet showing the activities of the manufacturing establishments of these and other companies. The D&B tape and the assumptions required to process data from it are described in Caves et al. (1977, chap. 4). The assignment of a primary industry when these sources disagree required the exercise of judgment. Because our determination of the distribution of a firm's outputs from the D&B tape is only approximate and because Statistics Canada uses presumably accurate raw data, we tended to believe Statistics Canada when a conflict had to be resolved.

From the 337 FRI companies we selected 125 that we felt could be safely classified as engaged primarily in manufacturing and for which a primary industry could be selected with some confidence. The latter constraint was not very influential, because in any case we planned to represent each company by a weighted average of the industries in which it participates. Those weighted-average variables were calculated from a vector of the proportions of each company's manufacturing employment assigned to each U.S. four-digit industry in which it participates. Each U.S. four-digit industry was then assigned to the Canadian three-digit industry that contains primarily the same economic activity, and the industry variables from our industry data base were weighted to represent the industries in which the firm participates. Not every Canadian industry is included in our data base, and observations are missing on some variables for the industries that are included. Observations missing for either of these reasons were dropped when weighted-average industry variables were calculated for our companies, so that the companies are sometimes represented by less than the full range of industries in which they participate.

The FRI sample of companies has certain peculiarities. Not every company is an ultimate parent enterprise; some are subsidiaries of other domestic companies. Some multinational companies' Canadian subsidiaries are included, though the FRI population of companies is in effect biased against multinational subsidiaries because it includes only public companies that publish separate income statements and balance sheets. Our sample includes at least 26 that are subsidiaries of foreign enterprises. We maintained a dummy variable in the data base to distinguish them, but we did not distinguish large companies that are subsidiaries of Canadian-owned enterprises. These unconsolidated companies were retained in the data base because we did not want to exclude all foreign subsidiaries and because the included subsidiaries of Canadian firms are large companies that developed independently and retained their dependence until recently, so that their acquired subsidiary status should have minimal effects on their behavior.

Table A.2 lists enterprises from the FRI tape included in our sample of manufacturing industries and shows their assigned primary industry. In a few cases the assigned primary industry was not one of our 123, so that the company becomes a missing observation for nearly all the analyses in this volume. Table A.2 also includes our strategic classification of these companies.

Table A.2 Companies contained in data base, with base industries, and strategic classifications.

Company name	Base industry	1961 strategy	Year of change	1974 strategy
Abitibi Paper	271	RP		RP
Alcan Aluminum	295	DP		DP
Algoma Steel	291	DP		DP
Andres Wines	147	SP		SP
Anglo-Canadian Pulp & Paper	271	RP		RP
Atco Industries	254	SP	1971	RP
B.C. Forest Products	251	RP		RP
B.C. Sugar Refinery	133	SP	1970	DP
Bomac Batten	287	n.a.		n.a.
Bombardier	329	SP	1973	DP
Bowes	139	SP		SP
Bridge and Tank	302	SP	1964	RP
Bright, T.G., and Co.	147	SP		SP
Bruck Mills	201	SP		SP
Burns Foods	101	DP		DP
CAE Industries	335	RP		RP
Canada Cement Lefarge	341	SP		SP
Canada Malting	139	SP	1970	DP
Canada Packers	101	RP		RP
Canadian Canners	112	DP		DP
Canadian Cellulose	271	SP	1970	n.a.
Canadian Corporate Mgt.	309	UP		UP
Canadian Food Products	129	SP		SP
Canadian General Electric	336	RP		RP
Canadian Industries (C.I.L.)	371	RP		RP
Canadian Marconi	335	RP		RP
Canron	294	RP		RP
Carling O'Keefe	145	SP		SP
Celanese Canada	201	UP		UP

Table A.2 *(cont.)*

Company name	Base industry	1961 strategy	Year of change	1974 strategy
Chateau-Gai Wines	147	SP		SP
Columbia Brewing	145	SP		SP
Combined Engineering Prod.	315	n.a.		n.a.
Consolidated Bathurst	271	DP	1966	RP
Consolidated Textile Mill	201	SP		n.a.
Consumers Glass	356	SP	1967	DP
Corby Distillery	143	SP		SP
Corporate Foods	129	SP		SP
Crain (R.L.)	286	SP		SP
Crestbrook Forest Industries	251	SP		SP
Crow's Nest Industries	251	UP	1968	DP
Crown Cork & Seal	304	n.a.		n.a.
Crown Zellerbach	271	RP		RP
Dofasco	291	SP	1962	DP
Domco Industries	219	SP		SP
Dominion Bridge	302	RP		RP
Dominion Dairies	105	SP		SP
Dominion Glass	356	SP	1962	DP
Dominion Textile	183	SP	1966	DP
Domtar	271	UP		UP
Donahue	271	SP		SP
Dupont of Canada	378	UP		UP
Eddy Match	379	n.a.		n.a.
Electrohome	334	DP	1972	UP
Enheat	307	UP		UP
Exquisite Form Brassiere	248	SP		SP
Federal Pioneer	336	SP		SP
Fittings	294	SP		SP
Fleetwood	334	SP		SP
Ford Motor	323	DP		DP
Fraser Companies	271	DP		DP
Fruehauf Trailer	324	SP		SP
General Bakeries	129	SP		SP
Goodyear Tire & Rubber	163	DP	1965	RP
Greatwest Steel Ind.	302	n.a.		n.a.
Greb Industries	174	SP		SP
Grissol Foods	129	SP		SP
GSW Ltd.	332	RP		RP
Gulf Oil Canada	365	DP		DP
Hand Chemicals Ind.	371	n.a.		n.a.
Harding Carpets	216	SP		SP
Hawker Siddeley Canada	321	RP		RP

Table A.2 *(cont.)*

Company name	Base industry	1961 strategy	Year of change	1974 strategy
Hayes-Dana	325	RP		RP
Hiram Walker–Goodherham & Worts	143	SP		SP
Imasco Ltd.	153	SP	1965	DP
Imperial Oil	365	SP	1961	DP
Inglis (John) Co. Ltd.	332	RP		RP
Interprov. Steel & Pipe	291	SP		SP
Keep-Rite Products	316	RP		RP
Kelsey-Hayes Canada	325	DP		DP
Labatt, John	145	DP	1969	RP
Lake Ontario Cement	241	SP		SP
Laura Secord Candy	131	SP		SP
Leigh Instruments	381	n.a.		UP
Livingston Industries	256	n.a.		DP
Maclean Hunter	289	DP	1969	RP
Macmillan Bloedel	271	RP		RP
Maple Leaf Mills	124	DP		DP
Massey-Ferguson	311	RP		RP
Melchers Distilleries	143	SP		SP
Miron Company	341	DP		DP
Mitchell, Robert	304	UP		UP
MLW Worthington	326	SP		SP
More Corp.	286	DP		DP
National Sea Products	111	SP		SP
Niagara Wire	305	SP		SP
Petrofina Canada	365	DP		DP
Phillips Cables	338	DP	1964	SP
Price Company	271	RP		RP
Readers Digest Assn Canada	288	n.a.		DP
Redpath Industries	133	SP	1967	DP
Reichhold Chemicals	373	n.a.		UP
Rio Algom Mines	291	SP	1963	DP
Rolland Paper	271	SP		SP
Ronalds-Federated	286	SP		SP
Rothmans of Pallmall	153	SP	1970	DP
Schneider, J. M.	101	SP		SP
Scott Paper	271	SP		SP
Seagram Co.	143	SP	1964	DP
Shaw Pipe	339	n.a.		n.a.
Shell Canada	365	DP		DP
Silverwood Industries	105	SP	1969	DP
Sklar Furniture Ltd.	261	SP		SP

Table A.2   (*cont.*)

Company name	Base industry	1961 strategy	Year of change	1974 strategy
Southam Press	289	RP		RP
St. Lawrence Cement	341	DP	1966	RP
Stafford Foods	112	DP		DP
Steel Co. of Canada	291	DP		DP
Texaco Canada	365	SP		SP
Thomson Newspapers	289	SP		SP
Toronto Star Ltd.	289	SP		SP
Union Carbide Canada	378	RP		RP
Vulcan Industries	304	SP	1964	DP
WCI Canada	332	n.a.		n.a.
Weldwood of Canada	232	SP		SP
Westeel-Rusco	304	RP		RP
Westinghouse Canada	336	RP		RP

Definitions of Variables and Sources of Data

We now proceed to define the variables contained in the data base and indicate their sources. Four of those sources are tapes.

1. *Financial Research Institute* tape includes observations on a maximum of 92 income-statement and balance-sheet variables for each of 337 companies over the period, at the maximum, 1961–1974.

2. *Statistics Canada* tape contains the Census of Manufactures Principal Statistics for the years 1961–1971, data by industry and year on 33 variables.

3. *The Dun and Bradstreet* tape contains all of Dun and Bradstreet's records for establishments in Canada (excluding branches of enterprises located in foreign countries) that are engaged primarily in manufacturing and employ 50 or more. Usable data on these records are confined to the activities carried on in each establishment, described by four-digit categories of the U.S. SIC (maximum of six of these, ranked in order of importance), number of employees at the location, and an identification number that allows the ownership of the establishment to be traced to the next higher level of the company's organization. By using these numbers we assembled the D&B establishment records into 2,167 companies.

4. *The Elliott Research* tape contains data on advertising expenditures in Canada for 1,324 companies operating in the country in 1972. The data are broken down by media (radio, network television, spot television, magazines, and other print media—largely newspapers)

and include only media costs and not the preparation cost of the advertisements. These data were aggregated to the Canadian industries in our sample by matching them manually to company names of the Dun and Bradstreet tape and using the determination of each company's primary industry from that source.

The operational concept of the four-part classification of firms as single-product, dominant-product, related-product, and unrelated-product originates with Wrigley (1970). Wrigley had classified a number of Canadian companies by their strategy, including 58 of our 125. We sought to classify as many as possible of the rest of the 125, using annual reports, various manuals and published tabulations, and correspondence with the companies themselves. Following Wrigley, we identified each company's classification in 1961 and 1974 and also dated any intervening changes. Table A.2 shows the 1961 and 1974 classification and the date of any intervening change.[2] A total of 113 firms were classified for 1961, 115 for 1974.

There follows a two-part alphabetical listing of the variables in the research data base that were actually used in this study. Data pertaining to industries come first, then data pertaining to companies. For each variable we provide an exact definition and source plus comments on any special problems with its construction.

Industry Variables

ADI Ratio of reported total advertising costs (both internal and external to the firm) to the value of industry shipments, 1965. The source follows the SIC classification of industries but includes only selected industries. Although the text does not state this explicitly, it is clear that the omitted industries do very little advertising at the manufacturer level. For these industries a value of 0.1 percent was recorded, rather than show them as missing observations. *Source:* Dominion Bureau of Statistics, Merchandising and Services Division, *Advertising Expenditures in Canada, 1965,* Catalogue No. 63-216 (Ottawa: Information Canada, 1968), table 19.

ATPS Profits on sales before interest but after direct taxes, averaged for 1968–1971. *Source:* Statistics Canada, *Corporation Financial Statistics, 1969,* Catalogue No. 61-207 (Ottawa: Information

2. In a few cases more than one change took place, but the transition from the initial to the terminal class seldom took more than two years. The year of change shown for these companies in table A.2 is the midpoint of the transition period, and only the initial and terminal classifications are given.

Canada, 1972), table 2; idem, *1971,* Catalogue No. 61-207 (Ottawa: Information Canada, 1974), tables 2A, 2B. Some industries are grouped together; the common average value is then assigned to each component industry in our data base. Of 123 industries, 62 are so grouped.

ATS   Total assets divided by total income (sales, rental, investment), 1969. *Source:* Statistics Canada, *Corporation Financial Statistics, 1969,* Catalogue No. 61-207 (Ottawa: Information Canada, 1972), table 2. Some industries are grouped together; the common average value is then assigned to each component industry in our data base. Of 123 industries, 62 are so grouped.

BIGE   Proportion of industry value added in establishments larger than the establishment that accounts for the 50th percentile of employment in the U.S. counterpart industry. This median-size U.S. plant was determined by deleting plants employing 1–10, counting down the employment size classes from the largest to isolate the one containing the 50th percentile of employment and assuming a rectangular distribution of plants by employment in that size class. In the Canadian industry, value added per worker was assumed to be the same for all establishments in the size class that contains the estimated size of the U.S. establishment accounting for the 50th percentile of employment. Total value added in the Canadian industry is determined after deleting plants employing 1–5, or plants employing 1–15 whenever averaging plant size in the class is less than 7 workers. *Source:* U.S. Bureau of the Census, *Census of Manufactures, 1967* (Washington, D.C.: U.S. Government Printing Office, 1972), vol. 1, table 3; Statistics Canada, *Manufacturing Industries of Canada: Type of Organization and Size of Establishments, 1969,* Catalogue No. 31-210 (Ottawa: Information Canada, 1973), table 9. The same year could not be used for both countries because the U.S. figures are available only for census years, the Canadian ones not before 1969.

C468   Percentage of shipments accounted for by the largest four enterprises, 1968. For a few industries disclosure rules precluded the publication of a figure by Statistics Canada, but one can be closely approximated. For a few others the concentration ratio for the three-digit industry is approximated by a shipments-weighted average of some or all of its four-digit components. *Source:* Statistics Canada, *Industrial Organization and Concentration in the Manufacturing, Mining, and Logging Industries, 1970* Catalogue No. 31-402 (Ottawa: Information Canada, 1975), table 2.

C868   Percentage of shipments accounted for by the largest eight enterprises, 1968. For method of construction and source see *C468.* An approximate figure was entered for six industries where disclosure rules prohibited publication of the true figure by Statistics Canada, but a close approximation was possible.

CDRC   Cost disadvantage ratio: value added per worker in the smallest establishments accounting for (approximately) half of employment in the industry divided by value added per worker in the largest establishments accounting for the other half, 1969. The smallest size class of establishments (1–15 employees) was dropped whenever its average size was less than 7. An observation was not recorded when either the large or small establishment groups accounted for less than 20 percent of industry employment. *Source:* Statistics Canada, *Manufacturing Industries of Canada: Type of Organization and Size of Establishments,* Catalogue No. 31-210 (Ottawa: Information Canada, 1973), table 9.

CDRU   Cost disadvantage ratio in the U.S. counterpart industry. *CDRU* was constructed like *CDRC,* except that the smallest size class dropped before undertaking the calculation was 1–10 employees. *Source:* U.S. Bureau of the Census, *1967 Census of Manufactures* (Washington, D.C.: U.S. Government Printing Office, 1971), vol. 1, chap. 2, table 3.

CNPR   Dummy variable, equals one if the industry is judged to manufacture primarily consumer goods, zero if it manufactures primarily producer goods. *CNPR* is constructed with reference to the input-output table (see *CONS*) but takes account of the primary orientation of the industry's marketing strategy (for example, rubber tires and tubes are classified as a consumer-good industry although a large fraction of shipments are made to producers).

CONO   Dummy variable, equals one if the consumer-good industry is judged to sell a convenience good, zero otherwise. The variable is constructed judgmentally on principles discussed by Michael E. Porter, *Interbrand Choice, Strategy, and Bilateral Market Power* (Cambridge, Mass.: Harvard University Press, 1976).

CONS   Consumers' expenditures on products classified to the industry (including imported products) divided by total domestic shipments (including exports) plus imports, 1966. *Source:* Statistics Canada, *The Input-Output Structure of the Canadian Economy 1961–66,* Catalogue No. 15-501E (Ottawa: Information Canada, 1976), tables 36, 42. The medium-level aggregation is the finest shown in this document, so that individual SIC industries were often assigned average values for larger input-output sectors.

CVC Coefficient of variation of shares of the eight largest enterprises, 1968. For ten industries, the coefficient for the three-digit industry is approximated by a shipments-weighted average of some or all of its four-digit components. *Source:* Statistics Canada, *Industrial Organization and Concentration in the Manufacturing, Mining, and Logging Industries, 1968,* Catalogue No. 31-514 (Ottawa: Information Canada, 1973), table 5.

DCI Concentric measure of diversification, weighted average of all enterprises classified to the industry. For source and details of construction see R. E. Caves et al., *Studies in Canadian Industrial Organization* (Ottawa: Department of Supply and Services, 1977), chap. 4, sec. 4.2.

DE31 Fraction of employees in manufacturing establishments engaged in activities classified to the enterprise's principal three-digit industry (U.S. standard industrial classification), weighted average of all enterprises classified to the industry. For sources and details of construction see *DCI.*

DE41 Fraction of employees in manufacturing establishments engaged in activities classified to the enterprise's principal four-digit industry (U.S. standard industrial classification), weighted average of all enterprises classified to the industry. For sources and details of construction see *DCI.*

DHI Herfindahl measure of diversification, weighted average of all enterprises classified to the industry. For source and details of construction see *DCI.*

DWI Weighted measure of diversification, weighted average of all enterprises classified to the industry. For source and details of construction see *DCI.*

ECA67 Number of employees, 1967. *Source:* Canada, Department of Industry, Trade, and Commerce, *Comparative Tables of Principal Statistics and Ratios for Selected Manufacturing Industries, Canada and United States, 1967, 1963 and 1958* (Ottawa, 1971).

EFT Effective rate of protection, 1963, constructed on the assumption that unspecified inputs carry average nominal tariffs of 5 percent. Most industries in the source directly match the three-digit industries in our data base, though for one (381) a shipments-weighted average was taken of four-digit products. Because the auto pact was in effect during the years to which most of our data pertain, the tariff rate for this industry was set equal to zero. *Source:* James R. Melvin and Bruce W. Wilkinson, *Effective Protection in the Canadian Economy,* Special Study No. 9 (Ottawa: Economic Council of Canada, 1968), table 1.

EUS67 Number of employees in manufacturing establishments classified to the U.S. counterpart industry, 1967. For source see *ECA67.*

EXP Net exports (net of reexports) divided by value of shipments, 1961. *Source:* Dominion Bureau of Statistics, Input-Output Research and Development Staff, *The Input-Output Structure of the Canadian Economy, 1961,* Catalogue No. 15-501 (Ottawa: Information Canada, 1969), vol. 2, table 13. Figures for the motor-vehicles industry (323) and the motor-vehicle parts and accessories industry for the years 1966–1968 were taken from Carl E. Beigie, *The Canada-U.S. Automotive Agreement: An Evaluation* (Montreal and Washington: Canadian-American Committee, 1970), various tables. Most industries in the finest disaggregation of the input-output table match three-digit SIC categories, but in a few cases it was necessary either to aggregate finer subcategories or to assume that figures for subcategories are the same as for the broader category into which they are aggregated.

FSE Value of shipments and other revenue, establishments classified as belonging to enterprises 50 percent or more foreign controlled, 1969, divided by value of shipments by all establishments in the industry. *Source:* Statistics Canada, *Domestic and Foreign Control of Manufacturing Establishments in Canada, 1969 and 1970,* Catalogue No. 31-401 (Ottawa: Information Canada, 1976), table 10.

GEOG Index of the effect on production-worker wages of the geographic distribution of the Canadian industry among provinces. It was calculated by multiplying the proportion of the industry's employment in each province (1969) by the average hourly wage in all manufacturing in that province. Where employees are not shown for a province because of disclosure rules, employment was assumed to be distributed among the affected provinces in proportion to the number of establishments. *Source:* Statistics Canada, *General Review of the Manufacturing Industries of Canada,* vol. 1, *Industry by Province, 1969,* Catalogue No. 31-203 (Ottawa: Information Canada, 1972), table 8; *Canada Year Book, 1972,* pp. 844–845.

GNE Slope coefficient from regression of logarithm of total number of establishments on time ($1961 = 1$, $1962 = 2$, . . . , $1971 = 11$). *Source:* Statistics Canada tape.

GOUT Value of shipments of goods of own manufacture reflecting change in the relevant inventories, averaged over 1961–1971. *Source:* Statistics Canada tape.

GRDC Government-financed research and development expressed as a percentage of all internal and external R&D outlays, 1969. *Source:* Dominion Bureau of Statistics, *Industrial Research and Development in Canada, 1969,* Catalogue No. 13-203 (Ottawa: Information Canada, 1971), tables 3, 7, 10.

DATA BASE: DEFINITIONS AND SOURCES

GRDU   Federal government-financed research and development expressed as a percentage of total funds for R&D performance, United States, 1969. *Source:* National Science Foundation, *Research and Development in Industry, 1970,* NSF 72-309 (Washington, D.C.: U.S. Government Printing Office, 1971), tables 3, 7.

GSI   Slope coefficient from regression of logarithm of total value of shipments and other revenue on time (1961 = 1, 1962 = 2, . . . , 1971 = 11). *Source:* Statistics Canada tape.

HFL   Herfindahl measure of seller concentration, 1968. For source see *C468.*

IMP   Imports divided by value of shipments, 1961. For source and method of construction see *EXP.*

KTS   Ratio of debt capital (equity plus noncurrent debt plus bank loans) to sales, 1969. The denominator is sales of goods only (small sales of services are also shown for most industries) except for printing and publishing. For source and other notes on construction see *ATPS.*

LAB1   Ratio of payroll to value added, Canadian industry, divided by ratio of payroll to value added in the counterpart U.S. industry, 1967. For source see *ECA67.*

LAB2C   Total number of employees divided by total assets, 1967. Some industries were omitted because of the aggregation of industries beyond the three-digit level in the published corporate financial statistics. *Source:* Numerator, see *ECA67;* denominator, Statistics Canada, *Corporate Financial Statistics, 1967,* Catalogue No. 61-207 (Ottawa: Information Canada, 1970), table 2. Data on the companies classified to an industry include their assets in the form of plants classified to other industries and omit assets in the form of primary establishments belonging to companies in other industries.

LAB2U   Total number of employees in the U.S. counterpart industry divided by its total assets, 1967. *Source:* Numerator, U.S. Bureau of the Census, *Census of Manufactures,* vol. 1: *Summary Statistics* (Washington, D.C.: U.S. Government Printing Office, 1971), table 3; denominator, U.S. Bureau of the Census, *Enterprise Statistics, 1967* (Washington, D.C.: U.S. Government Printing Office, 1971), vol. 3.

MABC   Average shipments per establishment, largest establishments accounting for (approximately) 50 percent of the industry's employment, 1969. *MABC* is the numerator of *MESC;* see *CDRC* and *MESC* for further information.

MABU   Average shipments per establishment, largest establishments accounting for (approximately) 50 percent of employment in the U.S. counterpart industry, 1967. *MABU* is the numerator of *MESU*. For method of construction and source see *CDRU*.

MDPC   Number of manufacturing establishments owned by multi-industry enterprises classified to the industry but themselves classified to other industries, 1968. For source see *MIEC*.

MDPU   Number of manufacturing establishments owned by multi-industry enterprises classified to the industry but themselves classified to other industries, U.S. counterpart industry, 1967. For source see *MIEU*.

MESC   Shipments by the estimated minimum-efficient-scale establishment divided by industry shipments, 1969. The minimum-efficient-scale establishment is estimated as the mean size of the largest establishments accounting for (approximately) half of the industry's employment; the procedure for determining this half was the same as that used for *CDRC*. For source see *CDRC*.

MESU   Shipments by the estimated minimum-efficient-scale establishment divided by industry shipments, U.S. counterpart industry, 1967. For method of construction and source see *MESC* and *CDRU*.

MIEC   Number of multi-industry enterprises (owning plants classified to more than one industry), 1968. *Source:* Statistics Canada, *Industrial Organization and Concentration in the Manufacturing, Mining, and Logging Industries, 1968,* Catalogue No. 31-514 (Ottawa: Information Canada, 1973), table 7.

MIEU   Number of multi-industry enterprises (owning plants classified to more than one industry), U.S. counterpart industry, 1967. *Source:* U.S. Bureau of the Census, *Enterprise Statistics, 1967* (Washington, D.C.: U.S. Government Printing Office, 1972), chap. 2, table 1.

MPLNT   Shipments by establishments classified to the U.S. counterpart industry and belonging to enterprises that are multiplant within that industry, divided by all shipments by establishments classified to the U.S. industry, 1967. *Source:* U.S. Bureau of the Census, *Enterprise Statistics, 1967* (Washington, D.C.: U.S. Government Printing Office, 1971), vol. I, tables 1–1, 2–1, 4–1. The Enterprise Statistics industrial classification is somewhat more aggregated than ours, so it was sometimes necessary to assume that the observation for one of our industries is that of a larger aggregate. Some observations are missing because the two classification systems disagree.

MPPC Number of manufacturing establishments classified as primary to the industry and owned by multi-industry enterprises classified to the industry, 1968. For source see *MIEC*.

MPPU Number of manufacturing establishments classified as primary to the industry and owned by multi-industry enterprises classified to the industry, U.S. counterpart industry, 1967. For source see *MIEU*.

NCA Number of establishments classified to the industry, 1967. For source see *ECA67*.

NENT Number of companies classified to the industry, 1968. *Source:* Statistics Canada, *Industrial Organization and Concentration in the Manufacturing, Mining, and Logging Industries, 1968,* Catalogue No. 31-514 (Ottawa: Information Canada, 1973), table 1.

NOT Nominal rate of tariff protection, 1963. For source and methods of construction see *EFT*.

NPC Employment-weighted average number of manufacturing establishments belonging to enterprises classified to the industry. *Source:* Dun and Bradstreet tape [for details see R. E. Caves et al., *Studies in Canadian Industrial Organization* (Ottawa: Department of Supply and Services, 1977), chap. 4, sec. 4.2].

NPU Number of manufacturing establishments owned by enterprises classified to the industry divided by number of enterprises classified to the industry, U.S. counterpart industry, 1967. *Source:* U.S. Bureau of the Census, *1967 Enterprise Statistics* (Washington, D.C.: U.S. Government Printing Office, 1972), part 1, table 2–1.

NPW Nonproduction workers divided by total employees, all manufacturing establishments, averaged over 1961–1971. *Source:* Statistics Canada tape.

NPWUS Number of nonproduction workers divided by total number of employees, manufacturing establishments classified to the U.S. counterpart industry, 1967. For source see *ECA67*.

NSI Unduplicated number of industries (four-digit classes in the U.S. standard industrial classification) in which each enterprise is active, weighted average of all enterprises classified to the industry. For source and details of construction see R. E. Caves et al., *Studies in Canadian Industrial Organization* (Ottawa: Department of Supply and Services, 1977), chap. 4, sec 4.2.

OWN One minus ownership specialization ratio (defined as the ratio of value added of the primary establishments of the enterprises classified to the industry to the value added of all establishments classified to the industry). Not infrequently the source gives a range of values rather than a specific number (because of disclosure rules); the value assigned to these industries was the midpoint of the range. No figure is given for some industries in which only a tiny fraction of establishments belong to enterprises classified to other industries. In these cases it was assumed that the fraction of value added accounted for by owning enterprises outside the industry is the same as the fraction of the number of establishments so owned (in most cases this rounds to 0.0). Source: Statistics Canada, *Industrial Organization and Concentration in the Manufacturing, Mining, and Logging Industries, 1968,* Catalogue No. 31-514 (Ottawa: Information Canada, 1973), table 8.

OWNU   The variable's construction is identical to that of *OWN,* but it pertains to the U.S. counterpart industry for 1967. *Source:* U.S. Bureau of the Census, *1967 Enterprise Statistics* (Washington, D.C.: U.S. Government Printing Office, 1972), part 1, table 1-2.

PLCN   Number of establishments per enterprise for the largest four enterprises in the industry, divided by number of establishments per enterprise for all enterprises in the industry, 1968. For source see *NENT.*

PLSZ   Value of shipments per establishment for establishments belonging to the largest four enterprises, divided by shipments per establishment for all establishments classified to the industry, 1968. For source see *NENT.*

PRB   Working owners and partners divided by number of establishments classified to the industry, averaged over 1961–1971. *Source:* Statistics Canada tape.

PRMG   Percentage of advertising outlays spent on magazine advertising, 1972. *Source:* Elliott Research tape, Dun and Bradstreet tape. Companies listed by Elliot Research were matched to the companies constructed from establishment records on the Dun and Bradstreet tape and assigned to the base industry deduced for them from the activities of their establishments recorded by Dun and Bradstreet. Companies were then assigned to the Canadian industries in our data base by means of a concordance with the U.S. standard industrial classification; outlays on magazine advertising were then summed and divided by all recorded advertising outlays of companies assigned to the industry.

PRNT   Percentage of advertising outlays spent on network television advertising, 1972. For sources and methods of construction see *PRMG.*

PRNW   Percentage of advertising outlays spent on newspaper and other printed media (excluding magazines), 1972. For sources and methods of construction see *PRMG*.

PROT   Personnel in managerial, scientific, religious, teaching, medical, and artistic occupations expressed as a percentage of total personnel classified to the industry, 1971. For further notes and sources see *CLRK*.

PRRD   Percentage of advertising outlays spent on radio, 1972. For sources and methods of construction see *PRMG*.

PRSP   Percentage of advertising outlays spent on local television and television spot announcements, 1972. For sources and methods of construction see *PRMG*.

PWFM   Proportion of production workers who are female, 1969. *Source:* Statistics Canada, *Domestic and Foreign Control of Manufacturing Establishments in Canada, 1969 and 1970,* Catalogue No. 31-401 (Ottawa: Information Canada, 1976), table 10.

PWUN   Percentage of production workers covered by collective-bargaining agreements, 1969. In a few cases the data source aggregates three-digit industries; the common value was assigned to each of the component industries. *Source:* Department of Labour, *Working Conditions in Canadian Industry, 1969,* Catalogue No. L2-15/1969 (Ottawa: Information Canada, 1970), part 1, table 6.

RAW   Expenditure on primary commodities out of $100 spent by the industry on all inputs, 1961. Sum of input coefficients for rows 1–23 of table 14 in source. *Source:* Dominion Bureau of Statistics, *The Input-Output Structure of the Canadian Economy, 1961,* Catalogue No. 15-501 (Ottawa: Queen's Printer, 1969), vol. 2, table 14.

RDIC   Sum of internal and external research and development expenditures divided by total sales of firms performing R&D. *Source:* Dominion Bureau of Statistics, *Industrial Research and Development in Canada, 1969,* Catalogue No. 13-203 (Ottawa: Information Canada, 1971), tables 3, 10, and 38.

RDIU   Funds for R&D performance expressed as a percentage of net sales by companies performing R&D, United States, 1969. *Source:* National Science Foundation, *Research and Development in Industry, 1970,* NSF 72-309 (Washington, D.C.: U.S. Government Printing Office, 1971), table 40.

REG   Dummy variable equals one where the industry is judged subject to significant regional fragmentation, zero otherwise. Thirty industries were so classified. *Source:* Department of Consumer and Corporate Affairs, *Concentration in the Manufacturing In-*

dustries of Canada (Ottawa: Information Canada, 1971), table A-5.

ROI   Net profit (loss) after taxes divided by total equity (common shares, preferred shares, retained earnings, other surplus), averaged over 1968–1971. *Source:* Statistics Canada, *Corporation Financial Statistics, 1969*, Catalogue No. 61-207 (Ottawa: Information Canada, 1972), table 2; idem, *1971*, Catalogue No. 61-207 (Ottawa: Information Canada, 1974), tables 2A, 2B. Some industries are grouped together; the common average value is then assigned to each component industry in our data base. Of 123 industries, 62 are so grouped.

RPAL   Value added per worker in Canadian manufacturing establishments larger than the establishment that accounts for the 50th percentile of employment in the U.S. counterpart industry, divided by value added per worker in U.S. establishments larger than this 50th percentile establishment. The minimum-size plant for inclusion was determined by deleting from the U.S. industry plants employing 1–10, counting down the employment size classes to isolate the one containing the 50th percentile of employment and assuming a rectangular distribution of plants by employment in that size class. In the Canadian industry value added per worker was assumed to be the same for all establishments in the size class that contains the estimated size of the U.S. establishment accounting for the 50th percentile of employment. *Source:* U.S. Bureau of the Census, *Census of Manufactures, 1967* (Washington, D.C.: U.S. Government Printing Office, 1971), vol. 1, chap. 2, table 3; Statistics Canada, *Manufacturing Industries of Canada: Type of Organization and Size of Establishments, 1969*, Catalogue No. 31-210 (Ottawa: Information Canada, 1973), table 9. The same year could not be used for both countries because the U.S. figures are available only for census years, the Canadian ones not before 1969.

RPAS   Value added per worker in Canadian manufacturing establishments smaller than the establishment that accounts for the 50th percentile of employment in the U.S. counterpart industry, divided by value added per worker in U.S. establishments, smaller than this 50th percentile establishment. For source and method of construction see *RPAL*. Note that the smallest size class is excluded from the calculation for both countries: 1–10 workers in the United States; 1–5 in Canada, but 1–15 when that is the smallest class shown and its average establishment employs fewer than 7 workers.

RPR   Value added divided by total number of employees in the Canadian industry; expressed as a ratio to value added divided by total number of employees in the U.S. counterpart industry, 1967. No exchange-rate correction was made; that is, parity of the U.S. and Canadian dollars was assumed. *Source:* Department of Industry, Trade, and Commerce, *Comparative Tables of Principal Statistics and Ratios for Selected Manufacturing Industries, Canada and United States, 1967* (Ottawa: Department of Industry, Trade, and Commerce, 1971).

RPRL Value added per employee in large establishments, Canada, 1969, divided by value added per employees in large establishments, United States, 1967. "Large" establishments were defined by dropping the smallest establishments in terms of employment (fewer than 15 in Canada, fewer than 10 in the United States) and splitting the remaining size classes of establishments as nearly as possible into the larger and smaller establishments, each accounting for half of the balance of the industry's employment. Divergent years were utilized because the data are not published for Canada before 1969 and are available for the U.S. only in census years. Industries were dropped when less than 20 percent or more than 80 percent of employment was unavoidably assigned to "large" establishments (because of the limited number of employment size classes published). *Source:* Statistics Canada, *Manufacturing Industries of Canada: Type of Organization and Size of Establishments, 1969*, Catalogue No. 31-210 (Ottawa: Information Canada, 1973), table 9; U.S. Bureau of the Census, *1967 Census of Manufactures* (Washington, D.C.: U.S. Government Printing Office, 1971), vol. 1, chap. 2, table 3.

RPRS Value added per employee in small establishments, Canada, 1969, divided by value added per employee in small establishments, United States, 1967. For source and method of construction see *RPRL*. "Small" establishments are those neither deleted at the bottom end of the size distribution nor included among "large" establishments in calculating *RPRL*.

SACI Mean of absolute values of proportional annual changes in total value of shipments and other revenue, 1961–1971. *Source:* Statistics Canada tape.

SIEC Number of single-industry enterprises, 1968, including both single-plant and multiplant enterprises. *Source:* Statistics Canada, *Industrial Organization and Concentration in the Manufacturing, Mining, and Logging Industries, 1968*, Catalogue No. 31-514 (Ottawa: Information Canada, 1973), table 7.

SIEU Number of single-industry enterprises, 1967, U.S. counterpart industry, including both single-plant and multiplant enterprises. *Source:* U.S. Bureau of the Census, *Enterprise Statistics, 1967*

(Washington, D.C.: U.S. Government Printing Office, 1972), chap. 2, table 1.

SIIC Number of single-plant companies, 1968. For source see *SIEC*.

SIPC Number of manufacturing establishments belonging to single-industry enterprises, 1968. For source see *SIEC*.

SIPU Number of manufacturing establishments belonging to single-industry enterprises, U.S. counterpart industry, 1967. For source see *SIEU*.

SKIL Index of the effect on production-worker wages of the mix of production-worker skills observed in the U.S. counterpart industry, 1969. The U.S. Census of Population breaks down blue-collar workers into craftsmen and foremen, operatives, and laborers. The average wage for each class in all U.S. manufacturing was multiplied by the proportion of each group in the U.S. counterpart industry's labor force, to derive the index. The industries are broken down in the source only to the two-digit level, so that it was necessary to assign each Canadian industry the value of the U.S. two-digit industry in which it is included. *Source:* U.S. Bureau of the Census, *Census of Population 1970, Occupation by Industry, Final Report,* PC(2)-7C (Washington, D.C.: U.S. Government Printing Office, 1972), tables 1, 4.

SMCI Mean proportional annual change in total value of shipments and other revenue, 1961–1971. *Source:* Statistics Canada tape.

SPL One *minus* enterprise industry specialization ratio (defined as value added by establishments classified to the industry divided by value added by all establishments belonging to enterprises classified to the industry). Not infrequently the source gives a range of values for the enterprise industry specialization ratio rather than a specific number; in these cases the midpoint of the range was taken as an estimate of *SPL*. *Source:* Statistics Canada, *Industrial Organization and Concentration in the Manufacturing, Mining, and Logging Industries, 1968,* Catalogue No. 31-514 (Ottawa: Information Canada, 1973), table 7.

SSI Standard deviation of total value of shipments and other revenue around its logarithmic regression on time. For source and method of construction see *GSI*.

TRN Weighted average of rail and truck shipping costs per dollar's worth of product between Cleveland and Chicago. *Source:* F. M. Scherer et al., *The Economics of Multi-Plant Operation: An International Comparisons Study* (Cambridge, Mass.: Harvard University Press, 1975), appendix table 5.1. Scherer's procedure involved finding a measure of the wholesale value of each U.S. four-digit industry's products per pound of shipping weight, obtaining truck and rail commodity rates for (usually) a standard haul between Cleveland and Chicago, calculating these two rates as a fraction of wholesale value per pound, then combining them into an index using as weights the amounts of the industry's output actually moving by truck and rail. Value added in the U.S. industry (1967) was used when necessary to construct weighted averages from Scherer's U.S. four-digit industries; sometimes some of the U.S. four-digit industries matched to a Canadian industry are unavailable, in which case the available ones are used.

US467 Proportion of shipments by the U.S. counterpart industry accounted for by the largest four enterprises classified to that industry, 1967. *Source:* U.S. Bureau of the Census, *Census of Manufactures, 1967* (Washington, D.C.: U.S. Government Printing Office, 1971), vol. 1, chap. 9, table 5.

US867 Proportion of shipments by the U.S. counterpart industry accounted for by the largest eight enterprises classified to that industry, 1967. For source see *US467.*

VPE Value added minus entreprenurial withdrawals divided by total number of establishments classified to the industry, averaged over 1961–1971. *Source:* Statistics Canada tape.

VPW Value added minus entrepreneurial withdrawals divided by total number of employees, all manufacturing establishments, averaged over 1961–1971. *Source:* Statistics Canada tape.

VRTD Dummy variable, equals one (otherwise zero) if the industry is characterized by small-scale establishments and either buys most of its purchased inputs or sells most of its output to another industry characterized by at least moderately high seller concentration and large establishments. *VRTD* was constructed judgmentally from the information contained in variables *VPE* and *C868* with some reference to the input-output table. Values of unity were assigned to industries numbered 135, 151, 252, 272, 273, 274, 294, 296, 297, 298, 305, 325, 343, 345, 351, 355, and 372.

WPW Average wages paid per hour to manufacturing production and related workers, all manufacturing establishments, averaged over 1961–1971. *Source:* Statistics Canada tape.

WPWUS Wages paid to production workers divided by man-hours worked, manufacturing establishments classified to the U.S. counterpart industry, 1967. For source see *ECA67.*

XPROF Excess profits per production-worker hour. The numerator of this variable is total pretax profits (averaged for 1968–1971) minus the opportunity cost of capital. The opportunity cost of capital is the average level of interest-bearing debt (equity, debt, and bank loans) over 1968–1971 multiplied by 6 percent (as a rough and conservative estimate of the opportunity cost of capital). The denominator is total number of production hours worked in 1969. *Source:* Numerator, same as *ATPS;* denominator, Statistics Canada, *General Review of the Manufacturing Industries of Canada, 1969* (Ottawa: Information Canada, 1972).

Company Variables

ADCG   Average rate of return on the market value of the firm's common equity, measured by the average of yearly observations for the firm of common dividends in year t plus capital gains in year t on common equity divided by the market value of common equity in year $t - 1$. *Source:* FRI tape.

APCR   Average rate of return on the market value of the firm's common equity as measured by the average of yearly observations of net income in year t (as reported) available for common equity plus capital gains in year t divided by the market value of common equity in year $t - 1$. Net income available for common equity represents that part of income that the company reports it has available for distribution to common shareholders, and it depends on the method of reporting taxes. In general, it is net income minus taxes currently payable minus preferred dividend requirements. *Source:* FRI tape.

BETAG   Slope coefficient from the regression $DCG_t = a + b(INDP)_t$ where DCG_t is the observation for the firm of common dividends in year t plus capital gains in year t on common equity divided by the market value of common equity in year $t - 1$. *Source:* FRI tape.

BETAR   Slope coefficient from the regression $PCR_t = a + b(INDP)_t$ where PCR_t is the observation for the firm of net income in year t (as reported) available for common equity plus capital gains in year t, divided by the market value of common equity in year $t - 1$. See *APCR* and *INDP. Source:* FRI tape.

DC   Concentric measure of diversification. For method of construction see R. E. Caves et al., *Studies in Canadian Industrial Organization* (Ottawa: Department of Supply and Services, 1977), chap. 4, sec. 4.2.

DE3   Proportion of employees allocated to the company's principal three-digit industry (U.S. standard industrial classification). For method of construction see *DC*.

DATA BASE: DEFINITIONS AND SOURCES

DE4 Proportion of employees allocated to the company's principal four-digit industry (U.S. standard industrial classification). For method of construction see *DC*.

DH Herfindahl measure of diversification. For method of construction see *DC*.

DW Weighted measure of diversification. For method of construction see *DC*.

FD Dummy variable, equals one if the company's ultimate parent is a U.S. enterprise, zero otherwise. (Subsidiaries of non-U.S. multinational companies could not be identified from the information at hand.) *Source:* Dun and Bradstreet tape.

FFS Ratio of total noncurrent assets to sales, 1961–1974. *Source:* FRI tape.

GRS Growth rate of sales: slope coefficient in regression of logarithm of sales on time (first year reported plus 1).

IBP An index of the instability of net income (numerator of *PEQR*) calculated by dividing the absolute value of the difference between each pair of adjacent years' values of net income by the sum of the two years' figures, and summing over all adjacent-year pairs available (maximum 1961–1974). *Source:* FRI tape.

INDP A yearly index of industrial production. Since the base year changed during the period covered, and the series using the different bases overlapped, all figures were converted to base $1963 = 100$. *Source: International Financial Statistics,* International Monetary Fund, Washington, D.C. "Industrial Production." vol. 21, no. 12 (Dec. 1968), p. 68; vol. 22, no. 12 (Dec. 1969), p. 66; vol. 23, no. 12 (Dec. 70), p. 70; vol. 24, no. 12 (Dec. 71), p. 74; vol. 25, no. 12 (Dec. 72), p. 74; vol. 26, no. 12 (Dec. 73), p. 76; vol. 27, no. 12 (Dec. 74), p. 78; vol. 29, no. 3 (Mar. 1976), p. 92.

LEV Ratio of debt to equity: long-term debt plus preferred redemption premiums and preferred dividends in arrears to sum of common equity (book value), preferred stock capital, and equity of minority shareholders in consolidated subsidiaries, 1961–1974. *Source:* FRI tape.

LSA Ratio of long-term assets to short-term assets, averaged over years available within the period 1961–1974. *Source:* FRI tape.

NGA Ratio of net value of property, plant, and equipment to gross value of property, plant, and equipment, 1961–1974. *Source:* FRI tape.

NP   Number of plants engaged principally in manufacturing activities, as recorded in Dun and Bradstreet files. *Source:* Dun and Bradstreet tape.

NS   Unduplicated number of activities (four-digit level of the U.S. standard industrial classification) carried out by manufacturing establishments belonging to the company. *Source:* Dun and Bradstreet tape.

PEQD   Net income (pretax income less current and deferred income taxes and minority interest) dividend by sum of common equity (book value) and preferred stock capital, averaged over all years available (maximum 1961–1974). *Source:* FRI tape.

PEQF   Net income (pretax income less current income taxes and minority interest) divided by sum of common equity (book value) and preferred stock capital, averaged over all years available (maximum 1961–1974). *Source:* FRI tape.

PEQR   Net income as reported by the company divided by sum of common equity (book value) and preferred stock capital, averaged over all years available (maximum 1961–1974). *PEQR* is identical to either *PEQD* or *PEQF*.

PRESG   Variance of the residuals from the regression $DCG_t = a + b(INDP)_t$ where DCG_t is the observation for the firm of common dividends in year t plus capital gains in year t on common equity divided by the market value of common equity in year $t - 1$. *Source:* FRI tape.

PRESR   The variance of the residuals from the regression $PCR_t = a + b(INDP)_t$ where PCR_t is the observation for the firm income in year t as reported—available for common equity plus capital gains in year t divided by the market value of common equity in year $t - 1$. See *APCR* and *BETAR*. *Source:* FRI tape.

PS3   Principal three-digit industry (in U.S. standard industrial classification) that accounts for more of the company's allocated employment than any other. *Source:* Dun and Bradstreet tape.

PS4   Principal four-digit industry that accounts for more of the company's allocated employment than any other. *Source:* Dun and Bradstreet tape.

SDP   Standard deviation of net income (numerator of *PEQR*) from trend, calculated by regressing net income on time (first year reported = 1). Logs were not taken because some profit figures are negative. *Source:* FRI tape.

SDS   Standard deviation of net sales around trend line (from the regression used to compute *GRS*). *Source:* FRI tape.

> *SLL* Short-term liabilities divided by long-term liabilities, the ratio averaged over years available within the period 1961–1974. *Source:* FRI tape.
>
> *SMC* Mean proportional annual change in net sales, 1961–1974. *Source:* FRI tape.
>
> *TOTA* Total assets (in millions of dollars), average of 1961–1974. *Source:* FRI tape.
>
> *VDCG* Variance of the yearly observations for the firm of common dividends in year t plus capital gains in year t on common equity divided by the market value of common equity in year $t - 1$. *Source:* FRI tape.
>
> *VPCR* Variance of the yearly observations for the firm of net income in year t (as reported) available for common equity plus capital gains in year t divided by the market value of common equity in year $t - 1$. See *APCR*. *Source:* FRI tape.

Besides these variables pertaining specifically to the companies, the company data base also includes for each company's base industry all the industry variables listed in the industry data base. The notation is the same as for the industry data base. It also includes a weighted-average value of each industry variable for all industries in which the company is active (the company's own-employment serving as weights). This weighting procedure made use of the Dun and Bradstreet tape. Weighted-average industry variables for each company are identified by adding the prefix *W* to the symbol for each industry variable.

Advertising: Canadian and Comparative U.S. Data

Data on advertising in Canada and on comparative advertising in the U.S. were derived from three basic sources.

1. Dominion Bureau of Statistics, *Advertising Expenditures in Canada, 1965,* October 1968. This source contains a variety of data on advertising in Canada by industry. The primary data taken from this source were advertising-to-sales ratios in a wide sample of Canadian four-digit manufacturing industries (table 15, Advertising Ratios in Manufacturing for Selected Industries, 1965). These advertising-to-sales ratios were averages of all firms in the industry and included media costs, advertising agency commissions, and the preparation costs of the advertisements. Marketing research and sales promotion with samples and premiums were not included, nor were advertising outlays outside Canada. Based on aggregate figures for manufacturing industries presented in the report, advertising outside Canada by firms operating in Canada amounted to only 1.6 percent of total advertising by manufacturing industries.

2. Elliott Research. This source contains data on Canadian advertising expenditures by advertising medium for 1,324 firms operating in Canada in 1972. Included media are radio, network television, spot television, magazines, and other print media (largely newspapers). Advertising outlays in the Elliott data included media cost only, and not advertising agency fees and the preparation cost of the advertisements. However, nonmedia costs were estimated at only approximately 10 percent of advertising cost for Canadian manufacturers (Dominion Bureau of Statistics, *Advertising Expenditures in Canada, 1965*). Point-of-sale advertising and trade-publication advertising were

not included. These data were unavailable for years other than 1972.

3. U.S. Internal Revenue Service, *Sourcebooks of the Statistics of Income, 1965*. This source contains income and balance sheet data for approximately three-digit "IRS Minor" U.S. industries, constructed by summing data for the individual firms classified to their primary industries. Total advertising expenditures of the firms in the industry could be related to total industry shipments. These advertising expenditures include all media and preparation costs and are thus consistent with the Canadian data in source 1. However, they also include any advertising expenditures made outside the United States by the firm and to this extent are not consistent with the Canadian data. Since total sales are similarly all-inclusive, the bias introduced by this difference is likely to be minor.

These three basic sources were utilized to perform the following three broad classes of analysis.

Effect of Advertising Rates on Firm Performance

One segment of our research was the investigation of firm strategy classifications, diversification, and other aspects of firm behavior. The basic research design and sources of data for this study are described in the text and in appendix A. Advertising expenditures of the firms in the sample were not included in the FRI data, and the Elliott Research data were used to construct advertising data for some of the firms in the FRI sample. Of the firms in our FRI sample, 54 could be identified in the Elliott Research data. For these firms, their total advertising on the media given in the Elliott data and the percentage of their total advertising represented by expenditures on each medium were added to the FRI data base.

Media Mix and Industry Performance

The 1,324 Elliott firms were classified to their primary Canadian industry where possible. The firms were then grouped by industry, and the average media mix for the firms in each industry was computed for each of the 28 Canadian consumer-good industries that contained at least 5 Elliott firms. The average media mix for the group of firms classified in the industry was computed as follows. For each advertising medium outlays of all the industry's firms on it were summed. These were in turn summed to yield the total outlays on all media of the firms in the industry. This procedure yielded a weighted-average

media mix for the industry, weighted by the size of advertising outlays of individual firms. The media mix variable was included in the
Canadian industry sample described in appendix A.

Comparative Canadian and U.S. Industry Advertising Rates

In order to compute comparable advertising rates for Canada and the
U.S. industries, it was necessary to match industries across the two
countries at the IRS Minor Industry level of aggregation, which were
somewhat more aggregated than the industries used in other industry
regressions in the study. IRS Minors are at approximately the three-
digit level of aggregation, and in many cases were broader than the
corresponding Canadian industries. Using concordance tables, however, it was possible to aggregate the Canadian SIC industries to their
IRS Minor counterparts in many cases. In the few cases where the
Canadian SIC was broader than the IRS Minor classification, IRS
Minors were aggregated to be consistent to the Canadian industry.

For a total of 46 industries, 31 of which were consumer-good industries, a satisfactory match was possible. These are listed in table B.1,
which gives the Canadian industries that make up the IRS Minor
industry. For these matched industries the following data were
tabulated.

Advertising-to-sales ratio
(A/S)

Canadian ratios were taken from source 1
and U.S. ratios were taken from source 3.
Where necessary, Canadian-industry observations were weighted by 1965 industry shipments to yield the weighted average A/S at
the matched level of aggregation.

U.S. four-firm and eight-firm
concentration ratios, 1963

Concentration ratios were obtained from
*Concentration Ratios in Manufacturing In-
dustry*, 1963 for four-digit U.S. industries.
These were weighted using 1963 value of
shipments to yield the weighted average concentration ratios for IRS Minor industries.

Canadian four-firm and
eight-firm concentration
ratios, 1965

The source of this data is described in appendix A. Where necessary, observations for
Canadian industries were weighted by 1965
industry shipments to yield the weighted-
average Canadian concentration ratios at the
matched level of aggregation.

Table B.1 Comparative advertising-to-sales ratios in matched Canadian and U.S. industries, 1965.

Canadian industry	Canadian SIC	Advertising to sales (%)	U.S. industry	U.S. IRS minor	Advertising to sales (%)
1. Meat and poultry slaughtering, packing	1011, 1013, 103	0.36	Meat products	2010	0.57
2. Dairy and cheese	105, 107	0.65	Dairy products	2020	1.78
3. Fish products; fruit and vegetable canners	111, 112	1.96	Canned and frozen foods	2030	2.84
4. Grain, mill products	123, 124, 125	1.85	Grain mill products	2040	3.24
5. Bakery products	128, 129	1.28	Bakery products	2050	2.50
6. Confectionary	131	4.78	Confectionary and related products	2070	3.21
7. Sugar refineries	133	0.19	Sugar	2060	0.31
8. Soft drink manufacturer	141	8.20	Bottled soft drinks and flavoring	2086	5.99
9. Distilleries	143	2.74	Distilled, rectified, and blended liquors	2085	2.62
10. Breweries	145	6.56	Malt liquors and malt	2082	6.82
11. Wineries	147	3.99	Wines, brandy, and brandy spirits	2084	4.47
12. Tobacco products	151, 153	6.13	Tobacco manufacturers	2100	5.78
13. Tire and tube manufacturers	163	1.40	Tires and inner tubes	3010	2.23
14. Luggage, handbag, and other leather goods	172, 175, 179	0.90	Leather tanning and finishing	3198	0.81
15. Shoe factories	174	1.15	Footwear, except rubber	3140	1.51
16. Wool cloth mills	197	0.11	Broadwoven fabric mills and finishing, wool	2220	0.29
17. Carpet, rug, and mat	216	1.11	Carpets and rugs: woven, tufted, and braided	2270	0.92

Table B.1 (*cont.*)

Canadian industry	Canadian SIC	Advertising to sales (%)	U.S. industry	U.S. IRS minor	Advertising to sales (%)
18. Hosiery and knitting mills	231, 239	1.09	Knitting mills	2250	1.07
19. Men's clothing	243	1.31	Men's and boy's clothing	2310	1.30
20. Women, children's clothing, foundation garments	244, 245, 248	0.87	Women's children's, and infants clothing	2330	0.85
21. Veneer and plywood; doors; hardwood flooring	252, 2541, 2542	0.38	Millwork, veneers, plywood and prefabricated structural products	2430	0.54
22. Household furniture	261	1.11	Household furniture	2510	1.11
23. Office and other furniture	264, 266	1.12	Furniture, fixtures, except household furniture	2590	0.93
24. Paper box, bag, and other converted paper	273, 274	0.58	Converted paper, and paperboard products	2640, 2650	0.51
25. Commercial printing	286	0.43	Printing: books and business forms	2720	0.52
26. Iron and steel mills, pipe tube, foundries	291, 292, 294	0.16	Blast furnaces, steel works, foundries, and forgings	3310	0.25
27. Nonferrous smelting, refining, fabrications	295, 296, 297, 298, 338	0.18	Smelting, refining, rolling, alloying of nonferrous metals	3330	0.49
28. Hardware, tool, and cutlery	306	3.41	Cutlery, hand tools, general hardware	3420	3.32
29. Agricultural implements	311	0.98	Farm machinery and equipment	3520	0.95
30. Office and store machinery	318	0.82	Office, computing, and accounting machines	3570	**0.90**

No.						
31.	Motor vehicles, parts; trucks and trailers	323, 234, 235	1.08	Motor vehicles, parts, accessories	3711, 3714	1.05
32.	Electrical appliance, small, major	331, 332	2.26	Household appliances	3630	2.76
33.	Household radio and TV	334	3.00	Radio and TV receiving sets, except communication	3650	1.68
34.	Communications equipment	335	0.47	Communication equipment and electronic communication	3661, 3612	0.76
35.	Electrical industrial equipment	336	0.62	Electrical transmission equipment, electrical industrial equipment	3611, 3612	1.38
36.	Cement manufacturers	341	0.85	Cement, hydraulic	3240	0.34
37.	Lime, gypsum, and concrete	343, 345, 347, 348	0.62	Concrete, gypsum, and plastic products	3270	0.48
38.	Clay products	351	1.01	Pottery and structural clay products	3250, 3260	0.87
39.	Pharmaceuticals and medicines	374	8.65	Drugs	2830	9.09
40.	Paint and varnish	375	3.32	Paints and allied products	2350	1.54
41.	Soap and cleaning compounds	376	10.85	Soap and related products	2841	10.90
42.	Toilet preparations	377	15.22	Perfumes, cosmetics, and toiletries	2842	12.70
43.	Instruments, orthopedic surgical, and ophthalmic goods	3811, 3813, 3814	1.92	Scientific instruments; medical, optical, ophthalmic, and photographic goods	3810, 3830, 3860	1.99
44.	Watches, clocks	3812	6.70	Watches and clocks	3870	5.13
45.	Jewelry and silverware	382	0.65	Jewelry and silverware	3910	1.70
46.	Sporting goods, toys, and games	3931, 3932	3.68	Toys and sporting goods	3920	4.07

U.S. industry growth in shipments, 1958–1965	Growth was computed by dividing 1965 business receipts by 1958 business receipts for each IRS Minor industry, as taken from the Internal Revenue Service, *Sourcebook of Statistics of Income* 1965 (line 34) and 1958 (line 37).
Canadian industry growth in shipments, 1958–1965	The source of this data is described in appendix A.
Effective rate of tariff protection for the matched Canadian industry	The source of this data is described in appendix A. Where necessary, observations for component Canadian industries were weighted by 1965 shipments to yield weighted-average effective tariff protection for the matched level of aggregation.
Imports for the matched Canadian industry	The source of this data is described in appendix A. Where necessary, observations for component Canadian industries were weighted by 1965 shipments to yield weighted-average imports for the matched level of aggregation.
Foreign ownership share for the matched Canadian industry	The source of this data is described in appendix A. Where necessary, observations for component Canadian industries were weighted by 1965 shipments to yield weighted-average foreign ownership share for the matched level of aggregation.

Where no data were available on *FSE* for an industry or any member of the group of four-digit industries in the three-digit industry, FSE was assumed to be zero.

Canadian SIC	Group	Assumed Value
172	172, 175, 179	0
175	172, 175, 179	0
179	172, 175, 179	0
239	231, 239	0
245	244, 245, 248	0

In other industries for which *FSE* was available for some four-digit industries in the three-digit industry, it was assumed that FSE equaled the weighted average of the other industries in its group.

107	105, 107	0.290
264	264, 266	0.181
338	295, 296, 297, 298, 338	0.644
343	343, 345, 347, 348	0.235

Total sales of the U.S. industry, 1965

1965 business receipts, from Internal Revenue Service *Sourcebook of Statistics of Income*, 1965, Line 34.

Total sales of the Canadian industry, 1965

1965 Shipments of Goods of Own Manufacture, from Dominion Bureau of Statistics, *Census of Manufactures*, 1965, vol. 1, table 7. Where necessary, the sales of component Canadian industries were summed to yield total sales of the industry at the matched level of aggregation.

References

Alemson, M. A. 1970. "Advertising and the Nature of Competition in Oligopoly over Time: A Case Study." *Economic Journal* 80 (June): 282–306.

Andrews, K. R. 1971. *The Concept of Corporate Strategy*. Homewood, Ill.: Dow Jones–Richard D. Irwin.

Armour, H. O., and D. J. Teece. 1978. "Organizational Structure and Economic Performance: A Test of the Multidivisional Hypothesis." *Bell Journal of Economics* 9 (Spring): 106–122.

Arrow, K. J. 1962. "Economic Welfare and the Allocation of Resources for Invention." In *The Rate and Direction of Inventive Activity*, ed. R. Nelson. New York: National Bureau of Economic Research.

Arrow, K. J., and M. Nerlove. 1962. "Optimal Advertising Policy under Dynamic Conditions." *Economica* 29 (May): 129–142.

Ashenfelter, O., and G. E. Johnson. 1972. "Unionism, Relative Wages, and Labor Quality in U.S. Manufacturing Industries." *International Economic Review* 13 (October): 488–508.

Auquier, A. 1977. "Industrial Organization in an Opening Economy: French Industry and the Formation of the European Common Market." Ph.D. dissertation, Harvard University.

Auquier, A. A., and R. E. Caves. 1979. "Monopolistic Export Industries, Trade Taxes, and Optimal Competition Policy." *Economic Journal* 89 (September): 559–581.

Bain, J. S. 1956. *Barriers to New Competition*. Cambridge, Mass.: Harvard University Press.

—— 1966. *International Differences in Industrial Structure: Eight Nations in the 1950s*, Studies in Comparative Economics, No. 6. New Haven, Conn.: Yale University Press.

—— 1968. *Industrial Organization*, 2d ed. New York: John Wiley.

—— 1972. *Essays on Price Theory and Industrial Organization*. Boston: Little, Brown.

Baker, R. W. 1965. "Marketing in Nigeria." *Journal of Marketing* 29 (July): 40–48.

Balassa, B. 1966. "Tariff Reduction and Trade in Manufactures among the Industrial Countries." *American Economic Review* 56 (June): 466–473.

Baumann, H. G. 1975. "Merger Theory, Property Rights, and Pattern of U.S. Direct Investment in Canada." *Weltwirtschaftliches Archiv* 111, no. 4: 676–698.

———— 1976. "Structural Characteristics of Canada's Pattern of Trade." *Canadian Journal of Economics* 9 (August): 408–424.

Baumol, W. J. 1959. *Business Behavior, Value, and Growth*. New York: Macmillan.

Berry, C. H. 1975. *Corporate Growth and Diversification*. Princeton, N.J.: Princeton University Press.

Bloch, H. 1974. "Prices, Costs, and Profits in Canadian Manufacturing: The Influence of Tariffs and Concentration." *Canadian Journal of Economics* 7 (November): 594–610.

Boddewyn, J., and S. C. Hollander, eds. 1972. *Public Policy towards Retailing*. Lexington, Mass.: D. C. Heath and Company.

Bond, R. S. 1974. "A Note on Diversification and Risk." *Southern Economic Journal* 41 (October): 288–289.

Borden, N. 1942. *The Economic Effects of Advertising*. Chicago: Richard D. Irwin.

Bothwell, J. L., and T. E. Keeler. 1976. "Profits, Market Structure, and Portfolio Risk." In *Essays on Industrial Organization in Honor of Joe S. Bain*, ed. Robert T. Masson and P. David Qualls. Cambridge, Mass.: Ballinger.

Buzzell, R. D., and P. W. Farris. 1977. "Marketing Costs in Consumer Goods Industries." In *Strategy + Structure = Performance*, ed. H. B. Thorelli. Bloomington, IN: Indiana University Press.

Cable, J. 1972. "Market Structure, Advertising Policy, and Intermarket Differences in Advertising Intensity." In *Market Structure and Corporate Behavior*, ed. Keith Cowling. London: Gray-Mills.

Canada, Department of Consumer and Corporate Affairs. 1971. *Concentration in the Manufacturing Industries of Canada*. Ottawa: Information Canada.

Canada, Dominion Bureau of Statistics. 1968. *Advertising Expenditures in Canada, 1965*. Catalogue No. 63-126. Ottawa: Information Canada.

Carlsson, B., and L. Ohlsson. 1976. "Structural Determinants of Swedish Foreign Trade: A Test of the Conventional Wisdom." *European Economic Review* 7 (February): 165–174.

Cateora, P. A., and J. M. Hess. 1975. *International Marketing*. Homewood, Ill.: Richard D. Irwin.

Caves, R. E. 1971. "International Corporations: The Industrial Economics of Foreign Investment." *Economica* 38 (February): 1–27.

———— 1974. "Causes of Direct Investment: Foreign Firms' Shares in Canadian and United Kingdom Manufacturing Industries." *Review of Economics and Statistics* 56 (August): 279–293.

―――― 1975. *Diversification, Foreign Investment, and Scale in North American Manufacturing Industries.* Ottawa: Economic Council of Canada.

―――― 1976. "Economic Models of Political Choice." *Canadian Journal of Economics* 9 (May): 278–300.

Caves, R. E., B. T. Gale, and M. E. Porter. 1977. "Interfirm Profitability Differences: Comment." *Quarterly Journal of Economics* 91 (November): 667–675.

Caves, R. E., and J. Khalilzadeh-Shirazi. 1977. "International Trade and Industrial Organization: Some Statistical Evidence." In *Welfare Aspects of Industrial Markets,* ed. A. P. Jacquemin and F. W. de Jong. Leiden: Martinus Nijhoff.

Caves, R. E., and J. Khalilzadeh-Shirazi, and M. E. Porter. 1975. "Scale Economies in Statistical Analyses of Market Power." *Review of Economics and Statistics* 57 (May): 133–140.

Caves, R. E., et al. 1977. *Studies in Canadian Industrial Organization,* Royal Commission on Corporate Concentration, Study No. 26. Ottawa: Minister of Supply and Services.

Caves, R. E., and M. E. Porter. 1977. "From Entry Barriers to Mobility Barriers: Conjectural Decisions and Contrived Deterrence to New Competition." *Quarterly Journal of Economics* 91 (May): 241–261.

―――― 1978. "Market Structure, Oligopoly, and the Stability of Market Shares." *Journal of Industrial Economics* 26 (June): 289–313.

Caves, R. E., and B. S. Yamey. 1971. "Risk and Corporate Rates of Return: Comment." *Quarterly Journal of Economics* 85 (August): 513–517.

Chamberlin, E. H. 1962. *The Theory of Monopolistic Competition,* 8th ed. Cambridge, Mass.: Harvard University Press.

Chandler, A. D., Jr. 1962. *Strategy and Structure: Chapters in the History of the Industrial Enterprise.* Cambridge, Mass.: MIT Press.

―――― 1977. *The Visible Hand: The Managerial Revolution in American Business.* Cambridge, Mass.: Harvard University Press.

Channon, D. F. 1973. *The Strategy and Structure of British Enterprise.* Boston: Division of Research, Graduate School of Business Administration, Harvard University.

Comanor, W. S. 1967. "Market Structure, Product Differentiation, and Industrial Research." *Quarterly Journal of Economics* 81 (November): 639–657.

Comanor, W. S., and T. A. Wilson, 1967. "Advertising, Market Structure, and Performance." *Review of Economics and Statistics* 49 (November): 423–440.

―――― 1974. *Advertising and Market Power.* Cambridge, Mass.: Harvard University Press.

Conklin, M. R., and H. T. Goldstein. 1955. "Census Principles of Industry and Product Classification, Manufacturing Industries." In *Business Con-*

centration and Price Policy, ed. Universities-National Bureau Committee for Economic Research. National Bureau of Economic Research, Special Conference Series No. 5. Princeton, N.J.: Princeton University Press.

Cowling, K., and M. Waterson. 1976. "Price-Cost Margins and Market Structure." *Economica* 43 (August): 267–274.

Daly, D. J., and S. Globerman. 1976. *Tariff and Science Policies: Applications of a Model of Nationalism.* Toronto: University of Toronto Press for Ontario Economic Council.

Daly, D. J., B. A. Keys, and E. J. Spence. 1968. *Scale and Specialization in Canadian Manufacturing.* Economic Council of Canada Staff Study No. 21. Ottawa: Queen's Printer.

Demsetz, H. 1973. "Industry Structure, Market Rivalry, and Public Policy." *Journal of Law and Economics* 16 (April): 1–10.

Donsimoni, M. P. J. 1978. "An Analysis of Trade Union Power: Structure and Conduct of the American Labor Movement." Ph.D. dissertation, Harvard University.

Dorfman, R., and P. O. Steiner. 1954. "Optimal Advertising and Optimal Quality." *American Economic Review* 44 (December): 826–836.

Doyle, P. 1968. "Advertising Expenditure and Consumer Demand." *Oxford Economic Papers* 20 (November): 394–416.

Dreze, J. 1960. "Quelques reflexions sereines sur l'adaptation de l'industrie belge au Marche Commun." *Comptes Rendus de Travaux de la Société d'Economie Politique de Belgique,* No. 275 (December).

Dunning, J. H. 1958. *American Investment in British Manufacturing Industry.* London: George Allen & Unwin.

Eastman, H. C., and S. Stykolt. 1960. "A Model for the Study of Protected Oligopolies." *Economic Journal* 70 (June): 336–347.

——— 1967. *The Tariff and Competition in Canada.* Toronto: Macmillan.

Economic Council of Canada. 1967. *Fourth Annual Review: The Canadian Economy from the 1960 to the 1970s.* Ottawa: Queen's Printer.

——— 1971. *Report on Intellectual and Industrial Property.* Ottawa: Information Canada.

English, H. E. 1964. *Industrial Structure in Canada's International Competitive Position.* Montreal: Canadian Trade Committee.

Else, P. K. 1966. "The Incidence of Advertising in Manufacturing Industries." *Oxford Economic Papers* 18 (March): 88–110.

Esposito, L., and F. F. Esposito. 1971. "Foreign Competition and Domestic Industry Profitability." *Review of Economics and Statistics* 53 (November): 343–353.

Farrell, M. J. 1957. "The Measurement of Productive Efficiency." *Journal of the Royal Statistical Society,* Series A, 120, no. 3: 253–282.

Fellner, W. 1949. *Competition among the Few.* New York: Knopf.

Ferguson, J. M. 1974. *Advertising and Competition: Theory, Measurement, Fact.* Cambridge, Mass.: Ballinger.

Fisher, Malcolm R. 1961. "Towards a Theory of Diversification." *Oxford Economic Papers* 13 (October): 293–311.

Frenkel, J. A. 1971. "On Domestic Demand and Ability to Export." *Journal of Political Economy* 79 (May/June): 668–672.

Fullerton, D. H., and H. A. Hampson. 1957. *Canadian Secondary Industry.* Ottawa: Queen's Printer.

Gale, B. T. 1972. "Market Share and Rate of Return." *Review of Economics and Statistics* 54 (November): 412–423.

Gaskins, D. W., Jr. 1971. "Dynamic Limit Pricing: Optimal Pricing under Threat of Entry." *Journal of Economic Theory* 3 (September): 306–322.

Gilbert, D. 1971. "Mergers, Diversification, and the Theories of the Firm." Ph.D. dissertation, Harvard University.

Gorecki, P. K. 1976a. "The Determinants of Entry by Domestic and Foreign Enterprises in Canadian Manufacturing Industries: Some Comments and Empirical Results." *Review of Economics and Statistics* 58 (November): 485–488.

—— 1976b. *Economies of Scale and Efficient Plant Size in Canadian Manufacturing Industries.* Bureau of Competition Policy, Research Branch, Research Monograph No. 1. Ottawa: Department of Consumer and Corporate Affairs.

Gort, M. 1962. *Diversification and Integration in American Industry.* National Bureau of Economic Research, General Series, No. 77. Princeton, N.J.: Princeton University Press.

Gort, Michael, Swarnjit Arora, and Robert McGuckin. 1972. "Firms' Data and Industry Aggregates in the Analysis of Diversification and Integration." *Annals of Economic and Social Measurement* 1 (January): 37–41.

Grabowski, H. G. 1968. "The Determinants of Industrial Research and Development: A Study of Chemical, Drug, and Petroleum Industries." *Journal of Political Economy* 76 (March/April): 293–306.

Gray, H. P. 1976. *A Generalized Theory of International Trade.* London: Macmillan.

Greer, D. F. 1971. "Advertising and Market Concentration." *Southern Economic Journal* 38 (July): 19–32.

Grubel, H. G. 1967. "Intra-Industry Specialization and the Pattern of Trade." *Canadian Journal of Economics and Political Science* 33 (August): 374–388.

Grubel, H. G., and P. J. Lloyd. 1975. *Intra-Industry Trade.* London: Macmillan.

Gruber, W., D. Mehta, and R. Vernon. 1967. "The R&D Factor in International Trade and International Investment of United States Industries." *Journal of Political Economy* 75 (February): 20–37.

Gupta, Vinod V. 1977. "Structure, Conduct, and Performance in Canadian Manufacturing Industries: A Simultaneous Equations Approach." Ph.D. dissertation, University of Toronto.

Haldi, J., and D. Whitcomb. 1967. "Economies of Scale in Industrial Plants." *Journal of Political Economy* 75 (August): 373–385.

Harberger, A. C. 1954. "Monopoly and Resource Allocation." *American Economic Review* 44 (May): 77–87.

Hassid, J. 1975. "Recent Evidence on Conglomerate Diversification in U.K. Manufacturing Industry." *Manchester School of Economic and Social Studies* 43 (December): 372–395.

Hausman, Jerry A., and A. Michael Spence. 1977. "Non-Random Missing Data." Working Paper No. 200, Massachusetts Institute of Technology.

Hazeldine, T. 1978. "Protection and Prices, Profits and Productivity in Thirty-Three Canadian Manufacturing Industries." Economic Council of Canada, Discussion Paper No. 110. Ottawa: Minister of Supply and Services.

Hirshleifer, J. 1965. "Investment Decision under Uncertainty: Choice-Theoretic Approaches." *Quarterly Journal of Economics* 79 (November): 509–536.

Holton, R. H. 1962. "The Role of Competition and Monopoly in Distribution: The Experience in the United States." In *Competition, Cartels and Their Regulation*, ed. J. P. Miller, pp. 263–307. Amsterdam: North Holland.

Hood, W., and R. D. Rees. 1974. "Inter-Industry Wage Levels in United Kingdom Manufacturing." *Manchester School of Economic and Social Studies* 42 (June): 171–185.

Horst, T. 1972a. "The Industrial Composition of U.S. Exports and Subsidiary Sales to the Canadian Market." *American Economic Review* 62 (March): 37–45.

—— 1972b. "Firms and Industry Determinants of the Decision to Invest Abroad: An Empirical Study." *Review of Economics and Statistics* 54 (August): 258–266.

—— 1975. "The Industrial Composition of U.S. Exports and Subsidiary Sales to the Canadian Market: Reply." *American Economic Review* 65 (March): 235.

Howe, J. D., and D. G. McFetridge. 1976. "The Determinants of R&D Expenditures." *Canadian Journal of Economics* 9 (February): 57–71.

Hufbauer, G. C. 1970. "The Impact of National Characteristics and Technology on the Commodity Composition of Trade in Manufactured Goods." In *The Technology Factor in International Trade*, ed. R. Vernon, pp. 145–231. Universities-National Bureau Conference Series No. 22. New York: National Bureau of Economic Research.

Hurdle, G. J. 1974. "Leverage, Risk, Market Share and Profitability." *Review of Economics and Statistics* 56 (November): 478–485.

Jenny, F. Y. 1975. "Industrial Structure and Economic Performance in France." Ph.D. dissertation, Harvard University.

Jensen, M. C. 1972. "Capital Markets: Theory and Evidence." *Bell Journal of Economics and Management Science* 3 (Autumn): 357–398.

Johns, B. C. 1978. "The Production and Transfer of Technology." In *Growth, Trade and Structural Change in an Open Australian Economy*, ed. W. Kasper and T. G. Parry, pp. 239–253. Kensington, Australia: Center for Applied Economic Research, University of New South Wales.

Johnson, H. G. 1972. "Some Economic Aspects of Science Policy." *Minerva* 10 (January): 10–18.

Jones, J. C. H., L. Laudadio, and M. Percy. 1973. "Market Structure and Profitability in Canadian Manufacturing Industry: Some Cross-Section Results." *Canadian Journal of Economics* 6 (August): 356–368.

——— 1977. "Profitability and Market Structure: A Cross-Section Comparison of Canadian and American Manufacturing Industry." *Journal of Industrial Economics* 25 (March): 195–211.

Kaldor, N., and R. Silverman. 1948. *A Statistical Analysis of Advertising Expenditures and the Revenue of the Press.* Cambridge: Cambridge University Press.

Kamien, M., and N. Schwartz. 1975. "Market Structure and Innovation: A Survey." *Journal of Economic Literature* 13 (March): 1–37.

Khalilzadeh-Shirazi, J. 1974. "Market Structure and Price-Cost Margins in U.K. Manufacturing Industry." *Review of Economics and Statistics* 56 (February): 67–76.

——— 1976. "Market Structure and Price-Cost Margins: A Comparative Analysis of U.K. and U.S. Manufacturing Industries." *Economic Inquiry* 14 (March): 116–128.

Khemani, F. S. 1978. "Concentration in Canadian Manufacturing Industries, 1948–1972: A Sample Study." Ph.D. dissertation, London School of Economics.

Knickerbocker, F. T. 1973. *Oligopolistic Reaction and Multinational Enterprise.* Boston: Division of Research, Harvard Business School.

Kochan, T. A., and R. N. Block. 1977. "An Interindustry Analysis of Bargaining Outcomes: Preliminary Evidence from Two-Digit Industries." *Quarterly Journal of Economics* 91 (August): 431–452.

Kumar, P. 1975. *Relative Wage Differentials in Canadian Industries.* Research and Current Issues Series, No. 25. Kingston: Industrial Relations Centre, Queen's University.

Lapp, J. S. 1976. "Market Structure and Advertising in the Savings and Loan Industry." *Review of Economics and Statistics* 58 (May): 202–208.

Leibenstein, H. 1966. "Allocative Efficiency vs. 'X-Efficiency.'" *American Economic Review* 56 (June): 392–415.

Lemelin, A. 1978. "Patterns of Inter-Industry Diversification by Canadian Manufacturing Industries." Ph.D. dissertation, Harvard University.

Levitt, T. 1965. "Exploit the Product Life Cycle." *Harvard Business Review,* November/December, pp. 81–94.

Levy, H. 1978. "Equilibrium in an Imperfect Market: A Constraint on the Number of Securities in the Portfolio." *American Economic Review* 68 (September): 643–658.

Mallen, B. 1971. "Just How Different are U.S. and Canadian Retailing and Their Markets." *Business Quarterly,* Winter, pp. 52–59.

Mancke, R. B. 1974. "Interfirm Profitability Differences." *Quarterly Journal of Economics* 88 (May): 181–193.

Mann, H. M., J. A. Henning, and J. W. Meehan, Jr. 1973. "Advertising and

Market Concentration: Comment." *Southern Economic Journal* 39 (January): 448–451.

Mansfield, E. S. 1962. "Entry, Gibrat's Law, Innovation, and the Growth of Firms." *American Economic Review* 52 (December): 1032–51.

———— 1968. *Industrial Research and Technological Innovation: An Econometric Analysis.* New York: Norton.

———— 1969. "Industrial Research and Developments: Characteristics, Costs and Diffusion of Results." *American Economic Review* 59 (May): 65–71.

Mansfield, E. S., A. Romeo, and S. Wagner, 1979. "Foreign Trade and U.S. Research and Development." *Review of Economics and Statistics* 61 (February): 49–57.

Marshall, H., F. A. Southard, and K. Taylor. 1936. *Canadian-American Industry: A Study in International Investment.* New Haven, Conn.: Yale University Press.

Masters, S. H. 1969. "An Interindustry Analysis of Wages and Plant Size." *Review of Economics and Statistics* 51 (August): 341–345.

McFetridge, D. G. 1973. "Market Structure and Price-Cost Margins: An Analysis of the Canadian Manufacturing Sector." *Canadian Journal of Economics* 6 (August): 344–355.

———— 1977. *Government Support of Scientific Research and Development: An Economic Analysis.* Toronto: University of Toronto Press for Ontario Economic Council.

Modigliani, F. 1958. "New Developments on the Oligopoly Front." *Journal of Political Economy* 66 (June): 215–232.

Modigliani, F., and M. H. Miller. 1958. "The Cost of Capital, Corporation Finance, and the Theory of Investment." *American Economic Review* 48 (June): 261–297.

Mueller, Dennis C., and John E. Tilton. 1969. "Research and Development Costs as a Barrier to Entry." *Canadian Journal of Economics* 2 (November): 570–579.

Mulvey, C. 1976. "Collective Agreements and Relative Earnings in UK Manufacturing in 1973." *Economica* 43 (November): 419–428.

Munn, H. L. 1966. "Retailing in Nigeria." *Journal of Retailing,* Fall, pp. 26–40.

Nelson, R. R. 1969. "The Simple Economics of Basic Scientific Research." *Journal of Political Economy* 61 (June): 297–306.

Newman, H. H. 1978. "Strategic Groups and the Structure-Performance Relationship." *Review of Economics and Statistics* 60 (August): 417–427.

Oksanen, Ernest H., and James R. Williams. 1978. "International Cost Differences: A Comparison of Canadian and United States Manufacturing Industries." *Review of Economics and Statistics* 60 (February): 96–101.

Ornstein, S. I., et al. 1973. "Determinants of Market Structure." *Southern Economic Journal* 39 (April): 612–625.

Orr, D. 1974. "The Determinants of Entry: A Study of the Canadian Manufacturing Industries." *Review of Economics and Statistics* 56 (February): 58–66.

———— 1975. "The Industrial Composition of U.S. Exports and Subsidiary Sales to the Canadian Market: Comment." *American Economic Review* 65 (March): 230–234.

Osborne, D. K. 1976. "Cartel Problems." *American Economic Review* 66 (December): 835–844.

Pagoulatos, E., and R. Sorenson. 1976a. "International Trade, International Investment, and Industrial Profitability of U.S. Manufacturing." *Southern Economic Journal* 42 (January): 425–434.

———— 1976b. "Domestic Market Structure and International Trade: An Empirical Analysis." *Quarterly Review of Economics and Business* 16 (Spring): 45–60.

Palamountain, J. C. 1958. *The Politics of Distribution.* Cambridge, Mass.: Harvard University Press.

Pashigian, P. 1969. "The Effect of Market Size on Concentration." *International Economic Review* 10 (October): 291–314.

Peck, M. J. 1968. "Science and Technology." In *Britain's Economic Prospects,* ed. R. E. Caves. Washington, D.C.: Brookings Institution.

Porter, M. E. 1976a. "Interbrand Choice, Media Mix, and Market Performance." *American Economic Review* 66 (May): 398–406.

———— 1976b. *Interbrand Choice, Strategy, and Bilateral Market Power.* Cambridge, Mass.: Harvard University Press.

———— 1978. "Optimal Advertising: An Intra-Industry Approach." In *Issues in Advertising: The Economics of Persuasion,* ed. D. Tuerck. Washington: American Enterprise Institute for Public Policy Research.

———— 1979. "The Structures within Industries and Companies' Performance." *Review of Economics and Statistics* 61 (May): 214–227.

Prais, S. J. 1958. "The Statistical Conditions for a Change in Business Concentration." *Review of Economics and Statistics* 40 (August): 268–272.

Prichard, J. R. S., W. T. Stanbury, and T. A. Wilson, eds. 1979. *Canadian Competition Policy: Essays in Law and Economics.* Toronto: Butterworths.

Pryor, F. L. 1972. "An International Comparison of Concentration Ratios." *Review of Economics and Statistics* 54 (May): 130–140.

Pugel, T. A. 1978. *International Market Linkages and U.S. Manufacturing: Prices, Profits, and Patterns.* Cambridge, Mass.: Ballinger.

———— 1979. "Profitability, Concentration, and the Interindustry Variation of Wages." *Review of Economics and Statistics* (in press).

Qualls, P.D. 1974. "Stability and Persistence of Economic Profit Margins in Highly Concentrated Industries." *Southern Economic Journal* (April): 146–158.

Rao, P., and R. L. Miller. 1971. *Applied Econometrics.* Belcont, CA: Wadsworth Publishing Co.

Rapp, W. V. 1976. "Firm Size and Japan's Export Structure: A Microview of Japan's Changing Export Competitiveness Since Meiji." In *Japanese*

Industrialization and Its Social Consequences, ed. H. Patrick, pp. 201–248. Berkeley and Los Angeles: University of California Press.

Romeo, A. A. 1975. "Interindustry and Interfirm Differences in the Rate of Diffusion of an Innovation." *Review of Economics and Statistics* 57 (August): 311–319.

Rosenberg, J. 1976. "Research and Market Share: A Reappraisal of the Schumpeter Hypothesis." *Journal of Industrial Economics* 25 (December): 101–112.

Rosenbluth, G. 1957. *Concentration in Canadian Manufacturing Industries.* National Bureau of Economic Research, General Series, No. 61. Princeton, N.J.: Princeton University Press.

———— 1970. "The Relation between Foreign Control and Concentration in Canadian Industry." *Canadian Journal of Economics* 3 (February): 14–38.

Ross, S. A. 1977. "The Determination of Financial Structure: The Incentive-Signalling Approach." *Bell Journal of Economics* 8 (Spring): 23–40.

Royal Commission on Corporate Concentration. 1978. *Report of the Royal Commission on Corporate Concentration.* Ottawa: Minister of Supply and Services.

Rubin, Paul H. 1973. "The Expansion of Firms." *Journal of Political Economy* 81 (July/August): 936–949.

Rumelt, R. P. 1974. *Strategy, Structure, and Economic Performance.* Boston: Division of Research, Graduate School of Business Administration, Harvard University.

———— 1977. "Diversity and Profitability." Paper MGL-51, Managerial Studies Center, Graduate School of Management, University of California, Los Angeles.

Safarian, A. E. 1966. *Foreign Ownership of Canadian Industry.* Toronto: McGraw-Hill.

———— 1969. *The Performance of Foreign Owned Firms in Canada.* Montreal: Canadian American Committee.

Saunders, R. S. 1978. "The Determinants of the Productivity of Canadian Manufacturing Industries Relative to That of Counterpart Industries in the United States." Ph.D. dissertation, Harvard University.

Saving, T. R. 1961. "Estimation of Optimum Size of Plant by the Survivor Technique." *Quarterly Journal of Economics* 75 (November): 569–607.

———— 1970. "Concentration Ratios and the Degree of Monopoly." *International Economic Review* 11 (February): 139–146.

Scaperlanda, A. E. 1974. *The Financial Structure of the Foreign Affiliates of U.S. Direct Investors.* Washington, D.C.: U.S. Government Printing Office.

Scherer, F. M. 1965. "Firm Size, Market Structure, Opportunity, and the Output of Patented Inventions." *American Economic Review* 55 (December): 1097–1123.

———— 1967. "Research and Development Resource Allocation under Rivalry." *Quarterly Journal of Economics* 81 (August): 359–394.

—— 1970. *Industrial Market Structure and Economic Performance.* Chicago: Rand McNally.

—— 1973. "The Determinants of Industrial Plant Sizes in Six Nations." *Review of Economics and Statistics* 55 (May): 135–145.

Scherer, F. M., et al. 1975. *The Economics of Multi-Plant Operation: An International Comparisons Study.* Cambridge, Mass.: Harvard University Press.

Schmalensee, R. 1978. "A Model of Advertising and Product Quality." *Journal of Political Economy* 86 (June): 485–504.

Schumpeter, J. 1950. *Capitalism, Socialism, and Democracy.* New York: Harper.

Schwartz, N. L., and M. I. Kamien. 1978. "Self-Financing of R&D Projects." *American Economic Review* 68 (June): 252–261.

Schwartzman, D. 1959. "The Effect of Monopoly on Price." *Journal of Political Economy* 67 (August): 352–362.

Scott, B. R. 1973. "The New Industrial State: Old Myths and New Realities." *Harvard Business Review* 51 (March–April): 133–148.

Scott, J. T. 1977. "Industrial Organization and the Market for Corporate Funds" and "Risk and Financial Structure: Determinants and Relation to Profitability." In *Studies in Canadian Industrial Organization* by Richard E. Caves et al. Ottawa: Canadian Royal Commission on Corporate Concentration.

—— 1978. "Equilibrium in an Imperfect Market: Comment." Dartmouth College (September).

Segal, M. 1964. "The Relation between Union Wage Impact and Market Structure." *Quarterly Journal of Economics* 78 (February): 96–114.

Sharpe, W. F. 1972. "Capital Asset Prices: A Theory of Market Equilibrium under Conditions of Risk." In *Modern Developments in Investment Management,* ed. James Lorie and Richard Brealey. New York: Praeger.

Sherman, R. J. 1968. *Profits in the United States: An Introduction to a Study of Economic Concentration and Business Cycles.* Ithaca, N.Y.: Cornell University Press.

Shrieves, R. E. 1978. "Market Structure and Innovation: A New Prospective." *Journal of Industrial Economics* 26 (June): 329–347.

Skinner, W. 1974. "The Decline, Fall, and Renewal of Manufacturing Plants." *Industrial Engineering* (October): 32–38.

Spence, Michael. 1978. "Tacit Co-ordination and Imperfect Information." *Canadian Journal of Economics* 11 (August): 490–505.

Statistics Canada. 1973. *Industrial Organization and Concentration in the Manufacturing, Mining and Logging Industries, 1968.* Catalogue No. 31-514. Ottawa: Information Canada.

—— 1975. *Industrial Organization and Concentration in the Manufacturing, Mining and Logging Industries, 1970.* Catalogue No. 31-402. Ottawa: Information Canada.

—— 1976. *Domestic and Foreign Control of Manufacturing Establishments in Canada, 1969 and 1970,* Catalogue No. 31-401. Ottawa: Information Canada.

—— 1978. *Structural Aspects of Domestic and Foreign Control in the Manufacturing, Mining and Forest Industries, 1970–1972.* Catalogue No. 31-523. Ottawa: Information Canada.

Stiglitz, J. E. 1969. "A Re-Examination of the Modigliani-Miller Theorem." *American Economic Review* 59 (December): 784–793.

—— 1974. "On the Irrelevance of Corporate Financial Policy." *American Economic Review* 64 (December): 851–866.

Strickland, A. D., and L. W. Weiss. 1976. "Advertising, Concentration, and Price-Cost Margins." *Journal of Political Economy* 84 (October): 1109–22.

Stykolt, S. 1969. *Efficiency in the Open Economy.* Toronto: Oxford University Press.

Sullivan, T. G. 1974. "Market Power, Profitability, and Financial Leverage." *Journal of Finance* 29 (December): 1407–14.

—— 1978. "The Cost of Capital and the Market Power of Firms." *Review of Economics and Statistics* 60 (May): 209–217.

Sutherland, D. 1963. "The U.S. Marketer in Canada." *Sales Management* (June): 35–39.

Teece, D. 1976. *The Multinational Corporation and the Resource Costs of International Technology Transfer.* Cambridge, Mass.: Ballinger.

Telser, L. 1964. "Advertising and Competition." *Journal of Political Economy* 72 (December): 537–572.

Thomadakis, S. B. 1976. "A Model of Market Power, Valuation, and the Firm's Returns." *Bell Journal of Economics* 7 (Spring): 150–162.

Thompson, D. N., and D. S. Leighton. 1973. *Canadian Marketing: Problems and Prospects.* Toronto: Wiley.

Tobin, J. 1958. "Liquidity Preference as Behavior towards Risk." *Review of Economic Studies* 25 (February): 65–86.

Utton, M. A. 1977. "Large Firms' Diversification in British Manufacturing Industry." *Economic Journal* 87 (March): 96–113.

Van Horne, J. C. 1971. *Financial Management and Policy,* 2d ed. Englewood Cliffs, N.J.: Prentice-Hall.

—— 1977. *Financial Management and Policy.* 4th ed. Englewood Cliffs, N.J.: Prentice-Hall.

Weiss, L. W. 1966. "Concentration and Labor Earnings." *American Economic Review* 56 (March): 96–117.

—— 1976. "Optimal Plant Size and the Extent of Suboptimal Capacity." In *Essays on Industrial Organization in Honor of Joe S. Bain,* ed R. T. Masson and P. D. Qualls. Cambridge, Mass.: Ballinger.

Weldon, J. C. 1948. "The Multi-Product Firm." *Canadian Journal of Economics and Political Science* 14 (May): 176–190.

Wells, L. T., Jr., ed. 1972. *The Product Life Cycle and International Trade.* Boston: Division of Research, Graduate School of Business Administration, Harvard University.

West, E. C. 1971. *Canada–United States Price and Productivity Differences in*

Manufacturing Industries, 1963. Economic Council of Canada Staff Study No. 32. Ottawa: Information Canada.

White, L. J. 1974. "Industrial Oragnization and International Trade: Some Theoretical Considerations." *American Economic Review* 64 (December): 1013–20.

Wilkinson, B. W. 1968. *Canada's International Trade: An Analysis of Recent Trends and Patterns.* Montreal: Private Planning Association of Canada.

Williamson, O. E. 1968. "Economies as an Antitrust Defense: The Welfare Tradeoffs." *American Economic Review* 58 (March): 18–36.

———— 1970. *Corporate Control and Business Behavior.* Englewood Cliffs, N.J.: Prentice-Hall.

———— 1971. "The Vertical Integration of Production: Market Failure Considerations." *American Economic Review* 61 (May): 112–123.

———— 1975. *Markets and Hierarchies.* New York: Free Press.

Wonnacott, R. J., and P. Wonnacott. 1967. *Free Trade between the United States and Canada: The Potential Economic Effects.* Cambridge, Mass.: Harvard University Press.

Woodward, J. 1965. *Industrial Organization: Theory and Practice.* London: Oxford University Press.

Wrigley, L. 1970. "Divisional Autonomy and Diversification." D.B.A. thesis, Graduate School of Business Administration, Harvard.

Wrigley, L. G. 1977. "Conglomerate Growth in Canada." Brief prepared for Royal Commission on Corporate Concentration. London, Ontario: Research and Publications Division, School of Business Administration, University of Western Ontario.

Yellen, J. 1973. "Notes on the Theory of Portfolio Choice." Harvard University.

Zeltner, H. 1969. "U.S. Ad and Marketing Problems Will Soon Face Canadians." *Marketing,* March 24, pp. 3–4.

Index

Advertising: as entry barrier, 48, 56, 219–220, 244, 247, 373–374; plant size and scale economies, 59, 60; relation to imports, 69, 73; multinational companies' market share, 84, 85; retail sector, 97; information markets, 125–130, 131, 142–143; interindustry differences, determinants, 130–141; international differences, 147–161; changes over time, 150–151; effect on R&D, 178, 185, 188, 192; effect on diversification, 213–214, 215–217, 293; effect on profits, 231, 235, 236, 243, 320, 321n; corporate strategy, 306, 308, 309, 310. *See also* Advertising media; Spillovers

Advertising media: message costs, 127, 143–146; international differences, 144–45

Allocative efficiency. *See* Competition policy; Profits

Bain, J. S., 3–4

Bankruptcy: risk, 337, 338; costs, 350–355

Barriers to entry: effect on seller concentration, 44–49, 56; multinational companies, 53–54, 82, 83, 85, 88, 241, 243; retailing, 98; established firms, 218–220, 292, 293–294; effect on profits, 227, 230–231, 235, 320, 322; trade-union organization, 244, 247; effect on wages, 248, 253; corporate strategy, 302; competition policy, 372–374, 379

Baumann, H. G., 68, 69, 70, 76n

Baumol, W. J., 318

Berry, C. H., 199

Beta coefficient, 307, 330, 342

Bloch, H., 226

Buyer concentration, *see* Concentration

Capital, cost of: capital asset pricing model, 329; determinants, 340–348; competition policy, 385–386

Capital asset pricing model: explained, 326–331; effect on transaction costs, 331–337

Capital-cost entry barriers: established firms, 219–220; effect on profits, 230; effect on union organization, 244, 247

Capital-intensity: differentiated product varieties, 17; seller concentration, 47, 56; scale economies, 58, 60, 61, 64; comparative advantage, 71, 74, 78; effect on profits, 232, 236, 243; company size, 280–281; diversification, 293, 294; corporate strategy, 302, 306, 308, 309, 310

Chamberlin, E. H., 3–4, 44

Chandler, A. D., Jr., 288

Chain stores: market power, 94–96; market share, 98–115; company size, 103–104, 115–117; establishment size, 119–121; effect on manufacturers' advertising, 160

Collective bargaining, *see* Unions

Comanor, W. S., 23, 129, 133

Company size: Canada relative to United States, 57; exports, 76–76; of retail chains, 103–104; and diversification, 205–210, 212, 215, 293; effect on advertising rates, 152–153, 154, 159; effect on R&D, 166, 185; components, large companies, 278–284; and company growth, 286–289; corporate strategy, 306, 308, 309; corporate profits, 317–318, 322; shareholder returns, 341, 342; maturity of financial liabilities, 355–357; industrial policy, 382–386

Comparative advantage: determinants, 76–80; relation to plant size, 271, 273. *See also* Exports; Imports

Competition, pure: capital cost, 337–339; maturity, financial liabilities, 353–355

Competition policy: seller concentration, 370–372; entry barriers, 372–374; open economy, 374–375; multinational companies, 379

Concentration, buyer: retail chains, 93–98; retail enterprises, 115–119, 128; effect on sellers' collusion, 240–241, 266; technical efficiency, 258

Concentration, largest companies, 278

Concentration, seller: identity relations involving, 42–43, 54–56; relation to company size, 54–56, 278–281; determinants, 44–49; differences from United States, 49–54; imports, 70–71, 73; exports, 76; multinational companies, 84, 87, 377–378; advertising, 131–132, 138–139, 152, 154–159, 373–374; R&D, 165–166, 169–170, 176, 180, 188–189, 192; diversification, 212, 215, 217–218, 220, 291, 295; effect on profits, 227, 228–229, 233, 235, 243, 320; effect on recognition of mutual dependence, 240–241, 266; union organization, 245, 246–247; effect on wages, 249, 252–253; changes in, 289; relation to corporate strategy, 308, 309, 310; effect on shareholders' returns, 341, 342, 348; maturity of financial liabilities, 355–357; competition policy, 370–372

Concentric index of diversification, 199

Consumer goods, *see* Convenience goods; Nonconvenience goods

Convenience goods: entry barriers, 48, 219; advertising, 130–131, 135, 140, 148–150; technical efficiency, 264, 267–268, 271, 273; corporate strategy, 308

Convenience retail outlets: characteristics, 96–97; chain-store penetration, 102–103, 111–113

Cost disadvantage ratio: Canada-U.S. differences, 29, 57–58; seller concentration, 45; determinants, 57–61; technical efficiency, 263, 266, 271, 273; corporate strategy, 306, 308, 310

Credit rationing, 339

Daly, D. J., 185

Department stores, 104, 113

Differentiation, product: company size, 14–17; multinational companies, 18–19, 81; imports, 46, 62, 69, 73, 78–79; entry barriers, 48, 56, 231, 235, 302; scale economies, 59, 62, 63, 64; exports, 74, 78–79; retail sector, 95–98, 118; R&D, 169, 178, 185, 192; technical efficiency, 263. *See also* Advertising

Discrimination, price, 11–12, 67, 75, 127, 232

Diversification: multinational companies, 83–84; retail stores, 103, 113–115; effect on R&D, 166, 169, 178, 187, 381; measurement, 195–202; industry patterns, 202–205; relation to company size, 208, 209–210, 278–281; out of an industry, determinants, 211–217, 291–295; into an industry, determinants, 217–220, 293–294; relation to company growth, 285–286, 287–289; corporate strategy, 300–303; cost of capital, 335, 339, 341; effect on maturity, financial liabilities, 355–357; competition policy, 382–383, 385; technical efficiency, 383–384

Dorfman, R., 125

Dreze, J., 16, 79

Dumping, 11–12, 232

Eastman, H. C., 44

Entry barriers, *see* Barriers to entry

Estimation methods: structural system,

26–29; matched Canada-U.S. industries, 30–31; missing observations, 34–36
Exports: price discrimination, 11–12; plant size and efficiency, 13, 15–16, 17, 62; effective market size, 47, 318, 322; multinational companies, 85; advertising, 132, 135, 159; R&D, 171, 173, 177, 185, 192; diversification, 207, 212–213, 215, 291, 295; effect on profits, 231–232, 321n; corporate strategy, 307, 308, 309; technical efficiency, 265, 268, 374, 376–377; competition policy, 374, 376

Fellner, W., 3–4
Financial policy, see Leverage; Maturity, financial liabilities
Fixed assets, 316, 355
Functional relations, form, 26–27

Globerman, S., 185
Gorecki, P. K., 61
Growth, company sales: determinants, large companies, 285–291; corporate strategy, 307, 308, 309, 310; corporate profits, 317, 321
Growth, industry shipments: relation to advertising, 133, 135, 140, 153; relation to R&D, 178, 186, 192; diversification, 212, 215, 291, 295; industry profits, 232, 236; union membership, 246, 247; wages, 250, 252; relation to company growth, 285, 287
Gupta, V. K., 23

Herfindahl index: diversification, 199; seller concentration, 228
Horst, T., 19n, 82

Imports: and price determination, 9–11, 68; plant scale and efficiency, 13, 15, 16, 62; product differentiation, 46, 229, 235, 273; market share, determinants, 69–74; advertising, 135, 157–159; R&D, 177, 184, 192; diversification, 220; effect on profits, 229–230, 235; union membership, 245; technical efficiency, 265, 268, 273, 374, 376; corporate strategy, 306, 308, 309;

competition policy, 374–376
Information costs: household buyers, 95–99; advertising, 125–126; business buyers, 130–131; R&D activity, 170–171
Instability of sales: multinational companies, 89; diversification, 214, 215; effect on recognition of mutual dependence, 240–241, 265; effect on wages, 250, 252; relation to company growth, 290
Intermediation, 335
International trade, see Comparative advantage; Exports; Imports; Tariffs
Intraindustry trade, 14, 78, 79, 309, 310
Inventories, 249, 252

Johns, B. L., 192
Jones, J. C. H., 225–226

Kaldor, N., 150
Khalilzadeh-Shirazi, J., 7
Khemani, R. S., 43n, 47n
Knickerbocker, F. T., 84, 87

Laudadio, L., 225–226
Leverage: corporate growth, 291; profits, 316–317, 321–322; corporate strategy, 307; capital cost, 337, 341, 342; relation to bankruptcy costs, 350–353
Levy, H., 337
Licensing, technology, see Technology transfer
Life cycle, product: advertising, 133, 140; R&D, 171n, 178, 184–185
Liquidation costs, see Bankruptcy

Mallen, B., 143
Market size: relation to company size, 12–13, 14–17, 278–281; product differentiation, 16, 79; seller concentration, 44, 47; attainment of scale economies, 58, 62, 63–64, 271, 273; private-label goods, 118–119; R&D, 171, 175, 177, 184, 187, 192–193; diversification, 205–206; technical efficiency, 263, 265, 266. See also Minimum efficient scale
Mason, E. S., 25
Maturity, financial liabilities: relation to asset maturity, 353–355; empirical determinants, 355–357

McFetridge, D. G., 225
"Miniature replica" effect, 19, 53–54, 263
Minimum efficient scale: Canada-United States difference, 29; seller concentration, 43, 45–46, 51, 56; cost disadvantage ratio, 58; determinants of estimated Canadian value, 61–64; effect on imports, 70, 72; effect on exports, 74; effect on profits, 230, 231, 235; union organization, 244, 247; technical efficiency, 263, 266, 271, 273; corporate strategy, 308, 309
Missing observations, 31–36
Modigliani, F., 13
Modigliani-Miller theorem, 348–350
Monopoly, pure: international trade, 67, 374–375; capital cost, 337–339; maturity, financial liabilities, 353–355; foreign-owned companies, 379
Multidivisional organization, 288–289
Multinational companies: multiplant operation, 13, 81, 84–85; product differentiation, 18–19, 69, 81, 84, 85–86; scale of plants, 18–19, 63–64, 80, 83, 87–89, 271, 273; seller concentration, 53–54, 84, 86–87, 377–378; international trade, 69, 75–76, 83, 85; market share, determinants, 80–89; entry barriers, 82, 83; technical efficiency, 87–89, 264–265, 268, 271, 273, 378; effect on advertising outlays, 134–135, 153–154, 155, 159; relation to R&D outlays, 171, 172–174, 179–180, 193; diversification, 207–210; technology transfer, 237–240, 378; profits, 241–243; transfer pricing, 242; union membership, 245, 246–247; tariffs, 268; corporate strategy, 307, 308, 309, 310; competition policy, 379; research policy, 380, 381
Multiplant operations: multinational companies, 13, 81, 84–85; seller concentration, 42–43, 54–56; diversification, 205, 208–210, 282–284; company size, 283–284; Canada-U.S. differences, 282–284; corporate strategy, 306. See also Chain stores
Mutual dependence recognized: homogeneous goods, 11, 12, 13; differentiated goods, 17; multinational companies, 83, 87; advertising levels, 128, 138–139, 146; R&D, 169; effect of uncertainty, 240–241, 265, 268

Nonconvenience goods, 188. See also Convenience goods
Nonconvenience retail outlets: characteristics, 96, 97–98; chain-store penetration, 103, 111–114
Nonproduction workers: multinational companies, 89; overhead cost, 58, 60, 61, 264, 272, 273; union membership, 244n, 247n

Oligopoly, see Mutual dependence recognized
Ornstein, S. I., 47
Overhead costs, 264, 267–268, 271, 272, 273

Patent system, 169, 170
Percy, M., 225–226
Plant size: differences within industries, 42–43, 54–56; relation to exports, 75–76; domestic and multinational companies, 82, 87–89; retail chain stores, 95; diversification, 206–207, 217, 293–294; union membership, 245, 246–247; wages, 253; suboptimal scale, determinants, 270–273; corporate strategy, 306, 308, 309, 310
Population density, 106, 107–108, 113, 119, 284
Primary industries: comparative advantage, 71, 75, 76, 78; technical efficiency, 271, 273; corporate strategy, 301, 308
Private-label goods, 118–119
Producer-good industries: advertising, 130–131, 139–140; technical efficiency, 271, 273; corporate strategy, 309, 310
Productivity, see Technical efficiency
Profits: effect on advertising, 132–133, 135; effect on R&D, 168–169, 177, 186, 192; effect on diversification, 212, 215, 291, 295; of industries, determinants, 227–243; measurement, 228; effect on wages, 248; relation to company growth, 287, 289; corporate strategy,

307, 308, 309, 310; of companies, determinants, 314–322
Pryor, F. L., 41
Pugel, T. A., 23, 248

Regional industries: seller concentration, 47, 52, 53, 56; relation to scale economies, 59, 60, 61, 62, 63, 64; multinational companies, 84–85, 89; R&D, 176, 184; diversification, 251; profits, 228, 236, 243, 320; union membership, 245, 247; technical efficiency, 264, 268, 269, 271, 273; corporate strategy, 307
Research and development: commodity imports, 69, 72; comparative advantage, 78; effect on multinational companies, 84, 85; relation to advertising, 134, 135, 139–140; interindustry differences, determinants, 168–189; defensive investment, 170, 232; government finance, 179, 187, 193; Canada-U.S. differences, 189–193; diversification, 213, 215, 219–220, 292–293; as entry barrier, 237–240; effect on profits, 232, 237–240; corporate strategy, 308, 309, 310; technology transfer, 380; research policy, 380–381; competition policy, 381–382
Research policy, 380–382
Risk: buyers' behavior, 126–127; and diversification, 213, 214, 215, 342; corporate growth, 290; corporate strategy, 302, 308–309; profits, 315; investors' behavior, 326–331; leverage, 337; bankruptcy, 337; shareholders' returns, 339–341
Robinson-Patman Act, 107n, 117
Rosenbluth, G., 41, 42, 43, 57, 282
Royal Commission on Corporate Concentration, 382
Rumelt, R. P., 289, 307, 310

Safarian, A. E., 172
Saunders, R. S., 23, 85
Scale economies: and international trade, 10–11, 70, 72, 75, 76; differentiated products, 16–17; multinational companies, 19, 83; and seller concentration, 42–43; in chain stores, 99–103; in advertising, 145; as barrier to entry,

230, 235; technical efficiency, 258, 270–273; and competition policy, 371–372. See also Minimum efficient scale; Cost disadvantage ratio
Scherer, F. M., 180
Schwartzman, D., 226
Shareholder returns: and corporate strategy, 311; determinants of, 340–348. See also Risk
Silverman, R., 150
Size, see Company size; Market size; Plant size
Skills, labor force: and comparative advantage, 71–72, 74, 78; multinational companies, 85; effect on wages, 250; and corporate strategy, 302, 306, 308, 309
Spillovers, advertising, 134–135, 153–154, 155
Standardization: chain retail outlets, 100–103; private-label goods, 118
Steiner, P. O., 125
Strategy, corporate: and advertising, 129; multinational companies, 241; defined, 297–299; effect on profits, 311–312, 321; estimating optimal choice, 312–314
Strickland, A. D., 23
Stykolt, S., 44
Substitution, elasticity of, 52, 89

Tariffs: effect on prices, 9–10, 11, 18; effect on plant size and efficiency, 15, 17, 59, 60–61, 62, 63, 64; seller concentration, 52–53; effect on imports, 72, 78, 79–80; effect on exports, 76; multinational companies, 83, 85, 268, 379; and advertising, 132, 138n, 159; and R&D, 177, 185; and technical efficiency, 260–261, 268, 271, 273, 376, 379; corporate strategy, 308, 309, 310; allocative efficiency, 374–375, 376
Taxes: export, 375; corporation income, 379, 380n
Technical efficiency: types of, 257–258; measurement, 259–262; interindustry differences, determinants, 262–269, 270–273; international differences, 269–270
Technology, international transfer, 78–

79, 167, 170, 171–174, 264; and industrial policy, 380–382

Teece, D. J., 171

Transaction costs: retail buyers, 97–98, 105; chain retail stores, 100–103; union organization, 243, 245–247; investors, 326, 331–337; bankruptcy costs, 350–355

Transportation costs: effect on trade, 11, 72, 74, 76; multinational companies, 84, 85; retailing sector, 100, 106, 109

Unions: effect on profits, 237, 242; intersectoral distribution, 243–247; international, 245; effect on wages, 248, 249, 253; technical efficiency, 258

United States: as statistical control, 30–31, 46; seller concentration, 49–54; foreign investment, 53–54, 80, 83–84, 87, 134, 208–210; company size, 57,

282–284; scale economies, 59–61, 64; chain-store penetration, 107–115, 160; concentration, retail stores, 115–118; size, retail establishments, 119–121; advertising media, 144–145; advertising levels, 147–161; R&D, 175–176, 213; technical efficiency, 269–270; multi-plant operation, 282; corporate strategy, 289

Unobserved variables, 25–26

Vertical integration: retail chains, 99–100; entry by established firms, 217–218; corporate strategy, 301

Wages, determinants of, 247–253

Weighted index (diversification), 199

Weiss, L. W., 23, 45n, 61

White, L. J., 75

Wilson, T. A., 23, 129, 133

Wrigley, L., 288, 289, 303